A KNOWN SCRIBBLER

Frances (Burney) d'Arblay by Edward Francis Burney, *c.* 1784–85.
By courtesy of the National Portrait Gallery, London.

A KNOWN SCRIBBLER: FRANCES BURNEY ON LITERARY LIFE

edited by Justine Crump

broadview literary texts

National Library of Canada Cataloguing in Publication Data

Burney, Fanny, 1752-1840
  A known scribbler: Frances Burney on literary life / Justine Crump, editor.

(Broadview literary texts)
Includes bibliographical references.
ISBN 1-55111-320-1

  1. Burney, Fanny, 1752-1840—Correspondence. 2. Burney, Fanny, 1752-1840—Diaries. 3. Novelists, English—18th century—Correspondence. 4. Novelists, English—18th century—Diaries. I. Crump, Justine, 1968-
II. Title. III. Series.

PR3316.A4Z5 2002   823'.6   C2002-902939-2

Broadview Press Ltd. is an independent, international publishing house, incorporated in 1985. Broadview believes in shared ownership, both with its employees and with the general public; since the year 2000 Broadview shares have traded publicly on the Toronto Venture Exchange under the symbol BDP.

We welcome comments and suggestions regarding any aspect of our publications – please feel free to contact us at the addresses below or at broadview@broadviewpress.com.

North America
Post Office Box 1243, Peterborough, Ontario, Canada K9J 7H5
3576 California Road, Orchard Park, NY, USA 14127
Tel: (705) 743-8990; Fax: (705) 743-8353;
e-mail: customerservice@broadviewpress.com

UK, Ireland, and continental Europe
Thomas Lyster Ltd., Units 3 & 4a, Old Boundary Way,
Burscough Rd, Ormskirk, Lancashire L39 2YW
Tel: (1695) 575112; Fax: (1695) 570120
email: books@tlyster.co.uk

Australia and New Zealand
UNIREPS, University of New South Wales
Sydney, NSW, 2052
Tel: 61 2 9664 0999; Fax: 61 2 9664 5420
email: info.press@unsw.edu.au

www.broadviewpress.com

Broadview Press Ltd. gratefully acknowledges the financial support of the Government of Canada through the Book Publishing Industry Development Program for our publishing activities.

Series Editor: Professor L.W. Conolly
Advisory editor for this volume: Colleen Franklin
Typesetting and assembly: True to Type Inc., Mississauga, Canada.

PRINTED IN CANADA

Contents

Acknowledgements

In preparing this volume I am indebted to the institutions and individuals who made their collections of Burney papers available to me, and provided valuable assistance for my researches. I would especially like to thank the staff of the Berg Collection for their painstaking help in locating manuscripts.

I would like to acknowledge the permissions granted me to reproduce materials by the Berg Collection of English and American Literature of the New York Public Library Astor, Lenox and Tilden Foundations, by the British Library, by the James Marshall and Marie-Louise Osborn Collection of the Beinecke Rare Book and Manuscript Library at Yale University, by the Huntington Library in San Marino, California, by the Bodleian Library in the University of Oxford, by the Pierpont Morgan Library of New York, by the National Portrait Gallery, London, by the Director of Dr. Williams's Library on behalf of the Trustees, and by the Marquis of Lansdowne. I owe a special debt of gratitude to John and Cynthia Comyn, who permitted me to see their private collection of Burney materials, which is now in the possession of the Beinecke Library.

This work was made possible through the generous support of a research fellowship provided by the Mary Ewart Trust Fund of Somerville College in the University of Oxford. I would like to thank my colleagues at Somerville College, particularly Roger Dalrymple, Katherine Duncan-Jones, and Fiona Stafford, for their moral and practical support throughout my fellowship. Special thanks are owed to Joanne Wilkes who has generously provided advice and encouragement from the earliest days of my Burney research at the University of Auckland. I owe a debt also to the years of research undertaken by the McGill University Burney Project, under the leadership of Joyce Hemlow and later of Lars Troide. Their work in identifying, dating, and cataloging the international collections of Burney Papers has smoothed the path for all Burney scholars.

Preface

By the closing years of the eighteenth century Frances Burney had
become one of the most renowned and influential of British novelists, but after her death in 1840 she was for many years known
primarily as a diarist. Her voluminous body of journals and letters,
composed between 1768 and 1839, and first published in the
1840s, reflect some of the most important developments in British
and European culture and history. Revolutions in scholarly taste
within the last thirty years have led to the rediscovery of Burney's
four major works, re-establishing her reputation as a novelist and
recognizing her contribution to the development of the novel as a
genre. This volume aims to combine these two projects in Burney
scholarship by presenting a selection from Burney's journals and
correspondence relating to her literary life and production. Though
Burney's life-writings are a valuable source of information about
historical events and cultural developments, they are also a personal history, containing a unique account of the creative, social, and
commercial ambitions and achievements of an eighteenth-century
woman writer.

Burney's manuscript life-writings number thousands of pages,
and this selection represents only a small proportion of these materials. Burney's literary life formed only one focus of her autobiographical writings, which also document her personal and family
life, and her participation in the social and political preoccupations
of her times. In choosing material to represent Burney's literary
life I have combined extracts from her journals and letters, with
selections from letters written to her by family and friends about
her literary activities, extracts from contemporary critical reviews
of her works, and portions from two of her lesser-known publications, her charity pamphlet *Brief Reflections Relative to the Emigrant
French Clergy* (1793) and her biography of her father, *Memoirs of
Doctor Burney* (1832).

In making these selections I aim to represent two aspects of Burney's literary life, by including materials that describe her professional career in the production of novels and plays, and materials
that refer to the creation of Burney's letters and journals as literary
productions in their own right. The selections cover a variety of
topics, including influences acting upon Burney's artistic development in her youth, accounts of the creation, sale, and reception of
Burney's published works, and her own and others' reflections upon

the forms and functions of her life-writing. From these materials we can derive an account of what it was like to be a writer, and specifically a female writer, in eighteenth-century Britain, both in the public world of the literary marketplace and in the private domestic space represented by journals and letters.

We must remember, however, that Burney's account of her literary life in her autobiographical writings is often selective. Though she gave detailed descriptions of some of the obstacles she faced, other aspects of her creative life received little or no attention. For example, Burney seems always to have doubted the propriety of preserving information about the financial transactions connected with her writing, and many surviving references in the journals and letters have been deliberately obscured. Gaps exist in the account of Burney's literary life that can be reconstructed from her life-writings, but a wealth of information remains to detail her negotiation between her creative impulses and the social, literary, and commercial conventions that shaped her writing.

Abbreviations and Short Titles

Persons

ADA	Alexandre-Jean-Baptiste Piochard d'Arblay
CAB/CBF/ CBFB	Charlotte Burney Francis Broome
CB	Charles Burney (Mus. Doc.)
CBjr	Charles Burney Jr. (D.D.)
CFBt	Charlotte Francis Barrett
EAB	Elizabeth (Allen) Allen Burney
EB/EBB	Esther (Hetty) Burney Burney
FB/FBA	Frances Burney d'Arblay
JB	James Burney
MA/MAR	Maria Allen Rishton
MPW	Mary Ann Port Waddington
SC	Samuel Crisp
SEB/SBP	Susan Burney Phillips
SHB	Sarah Harriet Burney
SJ	Samuel Johnson
HLT/HLTP	Hester Lynch Thrale Piozzi

Works & Collections

Barrett	The Barrett Collection of Burney Papers, British Library. Egerton mss. 3690 - 3708.
Berg	The Berg Collection of English and American Literature; The New York Public Library Astor, Lenox and Tilden Foundations.
Berg, D&L	Frances Burney d'Arblay, Diary and Letters, mss., Berg Collection.
Berg, JJ	Frances Burney d'Arblay, Juvenile Journal, mss., Berg Collection.
Bodleian	The Bodleian Library, University of Oxford.
BL	British Library.
Burford Papers	William Holden Hutton, Burford Papers: Being Letters of Samuel Crisp to his Sister at Burford; and other Studies of a Century (1745-1845) (London: Constable, 1905).
Comyn	The collection of John R. G. Comyn, now held by the Beinecke Library, Yale University, New Haven, Connecticut.

DL	*Diary and Letters of Madame d'Arblay (1778-1840)*, ed. Austin Dobson after Charlotte Barrett, 6 vols. (London: Macmillan, 1904-5).
ED	*The Early Diary of Frances Burney, 1768-1778*, ed. Annie Raine Ellis, 2 vols. (London: Bell, 1907).
EJ	*The Early Journals and Letters of Fanny Burney*, ed. Lars Troide and Stewart Cooke, 3 vols. (Oxford: Clarendon, 1988-1994).
HFB	Joyce Hemlow, *The History of Fanny Burney* (Oxford: Clarendon, 1958).
JL	*The Journals and Letters of Fanny Burney (Madame D'Arblay), 1791-1840*, ed. Joyce Hemlow et al., 12 vols. (Oxford: Clarendon, 1972-1984).
Memoirs	*Memoirs of Doctor Burney, arranged from his own manuscripts, from family papers, and from personal recollections. By his daughter, Madame d'Arblay*, 3 vols. (London: Moxon, 1832).
Osborn	The James Marshall and Marie-Louise Osborn Collection of the Beinecke Rare Book and Manuscript Library, Yale University, New Haven, Connecticut.
PML	The Pierpont Morgan Library, New York.
Thraliana	*Thraliana: The Diary of Mrs. Hester Lynch Thrale*, ed. Katharine Balderston, 2nd ed., 2 vols. (Oxford: Clarendon, 1951).
Thraliana ms.	Thraliana, Manuscript HM12183, Huntington Library, San Marino, California.
Williams	Dr. Williams's Library, 14 Gordon Square, London.

Introduction

Burney and the Literary Marketplace

Frances Burney was the daughter of Charles Burney, a musician who achieved social and professional advancement through his writings on the science and history of music.[1] Though she grew up in a household devoted to the arts and frequented by the leading musicians, artists, and authors of the day, Burney had an inauspicious introduction to literacy, and was unable to read until she was past eight years of age. At the time of her mother's death in 1762, when Burney was ten years old, she made rapid progress in both reading and writing. In her *Memoirs of Doctor Burney*, she recalls a sudden expansion at this time into the composition of "Elegies, Odes, Plays, Songs, Stories, Farces,—nay, Tragedies and Epic Poems" (2:124). Burney was transformed from dunce to author, but she ascribed a life-long ambivalence towards reading and writing to her early difficulties with literacy. In the *Memoirs* she described herself:

> [S]he grew up, probably through the vanity-annihilating circumstances of this conscious intellectual disgrace, with so affrighted a persuasion that what she scribbled, if seen, would but expose her to ridicule, that her pen, though her greatest, was only her clandestine delight. (2:124)

The shame Burney attached to her literary efforts was given a fiery expression on her fifteenth birthday in 1767, when she ceremoniously burnt all of her writings, including her journals and the "novel" of *The History of Caroline Evelyn*, whose story formed the precursor to Burney's first published work, *Evelina*. Unable to repress her compulsion to write, the following year Burney began

---

1   Sources for Burney's life include Joyce Hemlow's *History of Fanny Burney*; Kate Chisholm's *Fanny Burney: Her Life 1752-1840* (Chatto & Windus, 1998); and Claire Harman's *Fanny Burney: A Biography* (Harpercollins, 2000). Accounts of Burney's literary life can be found in Margaret Doody's *Frances Burney: The Life in the Works* (Rutgers UP, 1988) and Janice Farrar Thaddeus's *Frances Burney: A Literary Life* (Macmillan, 2000).

a new journal, which, supplemented by letters, would form a written record of her entire life. Alongside these personal writings, Burney persevered in her literary endeavours, working on the novel that would become *Evelina*.

The eighteenth century had seen a significant expansion in all forms of printed material in Britain.[1] A reduction in government restrictions upon the press coincided with a significant growth in literacy, particularly among groups who had not traditionally been readers, such as women and members of the lower ranks, leading to a boom in book and newspaper production. Such rapid and sustained growth in the production and consumption of books created new opportunities for aspiring authors seeking to make a career out of literary publication.

Burney published her first novel, *Evelina, or, a Young Lady's Entrance into the World*, anonymously in 1778. Burney's epistolary novel drew upon the experience of self-inscription gained from her journalistic and epistolary writing to create a dramatic portrait of a young girl's progress from the rural retirement in which she was raised through the pitfalls and perils of life in the great world. The novel, like Burney's life-writings, records a journey of self-discovery, as the heroine, Evelina Belmont, proceeds through a quest alternately comic and near tragic to obtain acknowledgement from her father, who had disavowed his marriage to Evelina's mother, Caroline Evelyn.

Burney preserved her anonymity by conducting negotiations with the bookseller Thomas Lowndes for the sale of her novel by means of letters. Lowndes addressed his anonymous correspondent as "Sir," providing the young author with a masculine persona through which to conduct business. Burney's anonymity unexpectedly afforded her an agency in her negotiations which she was never again to experience as an acknowledged author, since her

---

1 My account of the book trade in Britain is derived from Richard Altick, *The English Common Reader* (U of Chicago P, 1957); Terry Belanger, "Publishers and Writers in Eighteenth-Century England," *Books and their Readers in Eighteenth-Century England*, ed. Isabel Rivers (Leicester UP, 1982), pp. 5-25; John Feather, *A History of British Publishing* (Routledge, 1988); and Terry Lovell, *Consuming Fiction* (Verso, 1987). Cheryl Turner's *Living by the Pen: Women Writers in Eighteenth-Century London* (Routledge, 1994) and Catherine Gallagher's *Nobody's Story: The Vanishing Acts of Women Writers in the Marketplace, 1670-1820* (Clarendon, 1994) contain useful accounts of Burney's experience in publishing.

later works were disposed of through the intervention of her father or of her brother Charles.[1]

Anonymity had further benefits. In protecting Burney's reputation it perhaps more importantly protected that of her father. Dr. Burney's professional reputation could have been damaged had his daughter been known as the author of a disreputable or inferior work. In her journal for 1777, Burney recorded that her father was prepared to permit the venture without demanding to see her novel, provided she maintained a "total secresy & silence to all the World." Anonymity gave Burney creative freedom in her first novel, and spared her interference from her father, whose anxiety about the family's prestige would become an issue in the production of her later, acknowledged works.

Lowndes offered Burney twenty guineas for the copyright of *Evelina*. Eighteenth-century authors commonly received nothing at all for their works, for the publication of new books was a considerable financial risk on the part of the bookseller, and it was common for authors to be asked to defray part or all of the production costs of their works. To be offered payment for the copyright meant that Burney was already ahead of the game, and the price she was offered, though it seems low, was in fact higher than usual, at a time when the copyright of a novel usually fetched between five and ten guineas. As things turned out, the sum was below the novel's market value. Later, upon the appearance of a third edition of the novel in February 1779, Lowndes gave Burney a further ten pounds. This kind of gratuity, customary in the case of exceptional success, formed an investment on the bookseller's part, to persuade the author to give him first sight of any subsequent manuscripts. Burney does not seem to have regarded the extra payment in this light, and sent an indignant answer to Lowndes's letter of complaint to Dr. Burney that he had not been offered her second novel, *Cecilia*.

For most authors, novels were not a lucrative literary form, for their length entailed much labour for small return. However, novel-

---

1 After Burney married, under British law she was considered a minor, technically disqualified from negotiating contracts on her own behalf, since ownership of her works and the profits thereof automatically devolved upon her husband. In practice d'Arblay assisted but did not direct the negotiations Burney carried out through her brother; who acted as her agent.

writing, in allowing composition in the vernacular upon familiar subjects, was attractive to authors denied participation in elite education and culture, such as women and men from the lower ranks. This accessibility in turn diminished the novel's literary status. Though novels were popular with the reading public, they were not for the most part regarded as high culture, and Mrs. Thrale dismissed Burney's second work, *Cecilia*, as ephemeral because of its author's lack of formal education: "as nothing in the Book is derived from Study, so it can have no Principle of duration" (*Thraliana* 1:535). Burney signified her own family's literary consequence by informing readers in the dedication to her last novel, *The Wanderer*, that the only novel owned by Dr. Burney was Fielding's *Amelia*. Readers of novels may also have been deterred from purchasing them by the relatively high costs of what was usually considered to be an ephemeral work. Cheryl Turner reports that at mid-century, when novels cost between two and three shillings per volume, two shillings and sixpence could purchase a whole pig, or a pair of woman's shoes.[1] Novels like *Evelina*, which was sold for seven shillings and sixpence, were beyond the purchasing power of most of the populace. The public might satisfy its appetite for novels by hiring works at a circulating library.[2]

If novel-writing was not illustrious it could be innocuous, and Burney's cautious dealings over *Evelina* suggest that as a money-making venture, it was comparatively free from risk. Nevertheless, in Burney's retrospective account of the sale of *Evelina* from the *Memoirs of Doctor Burney*, she revised some aspects of the transaction to imply that her project was the idle fancy of a leisured gentle-woman, who wrote merely for her own amusement. In fact, as Doody points out, Burney was constantly engaged as her father's copyist and amanuensis. Though unpaid, Burney was a working woman.[3] In the *Memoirs*, Burney recorded that Lowndes's offer "was accepted with alacrity, and boundless surprise at its magnificence!!" (2:132) A letter composed after 11 November 1777 tells a

---

1 Turner 143–45.

2 For an account of eighteenth-century circulating libraries see Thomas Kelly, *Early Public Libraries: A History of Public Libraries in Great Britain before 1850* (Library Association, 1966); and James Raven et al. eds., *The Practice and Representation of Reading in England* (Cambridge UP, 1996).

3 Doody, *Life* 39.

different story. There, Burney asserted that the monetary value of her work exceeded Lowndes's offer, in terms that did not attempt to conceal her irritation:

> I must acknowledge that, though it was originally written merely for amusement, I should not have taken the pains to Copy & Correct it for the Press, had I imagined that 10 Guineas a Volume would have been more than its worth.

In this letter Burney requested the return of her manuscript, in order to ascertain its real market value by submitting it to the judgment of an independent arbiter, possibly her old friend and literary mentor Samuel Crisp. It is not certain whether Burney ever put her threat to withdraw the manuscript into execution. She eventually accepted Lowndes's offer, but the existence of this letter indicates the seriousness of her professional aspirations for her first novel, aspirations whose propriety she seems later to have doubted. *Evelina* was a popular success, and Burney's authorship was soon discovered. She was rapidly elevated to the status of a literary celebrity, and under the patronage of the Bluestocking Hester Thrale was admitted into London literary society, acquiring other influential patrons and friends, including Samuel Johnson, Richard Brinsley Sheridan, and Arthur Murphy. After the public acknowledgement of *Evelina*, Dr. Burney took over the management of his daughter's career. In 1779 she wrote a promising comedy, *The Witlings*, but after reading a draft of the work, Dr. Burney and Samuel Crisp combined to denounce the play, not criticizing it in terms that invited revision but condemning it as unfit for performance. Dr. Burney wished not only the play but all details of the plot to be suppressed, for fear that the comedy's satire of the intellectual and literary pretensions of the female "witlings" might antagonize the Bluestockings upon whose friendship and patronage both he and his daughter depended. Burney acquiesced in her censors' decree, in two letters written around 13 August 1779, which, superficially obedient, nonetheless express her disappointment.

Dr. Burney regarded fiction as a much safer venture for his daughter, and he urged her to the production of a second novel, *Cecilia, or Memoirs of an Heiress*, in order to capitalize on her popularity. The novel related the trials of Cecilia Beverley, an orphan whose inheritance depended on her husband's adoption of her surname. Cecilia's wealth and independence fail to ensure her safety and happiness, and she is exploited as a commodity by a society obsessed with money. Burney provides a fictional exploration of women's relationship to money in her own venture into commercial publication. The failure of her heroine's wealth to guarantee her personal agency may reflect Burney's partial alienation from the transaction in which her work was sold by her father.

Burney no longer possessed the luxury of private composition, and, as in the case of *The Witlings*, the new novel was handed about in manuscript to be praised and criticized. Since the work was to be acknowledged by its author, Dr. Burney anxiously oversaw its production as involving the credit of the whole family in its success or failure. Catherine Gallagher argues that despite Dr. Burney's eagerness in urging Burney to publish, he sacrificed his daughter's financial interests in his negotiations with the booksellers Payne and Cadell.[1] Burney received a total of £250 for the work after its publication in 1782, paid in instalments. The payments contingent upon the sale of further editions were delayed, however, by the size of the first edition consisting of two thousand copies; it was exceptionally large for a novel, at a time when first editions of fiction usually consisted of five hundred copies. Contemporary gossip suggested that once more Burney had been the dupe of unscrupulous booksellers. Samuel Johnson calculated that Payne and Cadell would have realized a very large profit of £500 on the first edition alone.[2] Gallagher suggests that Dr. Burney offered his daughter's novel at a "bargain" price to Payne and Cadell, who published his own works, as a personal favour. At the same time, Burney's brother James was courting Thomas Payne's daughter, Sarah. Burney's financial interests may have been sacrificed for the family's corporate good, and like Cecilia, she and her work became objects of exchange within financial and social transactions controlled by men.

The success of Burney's second novel bore unexpected fruit, elevating her social status to such a degree that she attracted a Court appointment, which threatened to put an end to her literary career altogether. In 1786, at the age of thirty-four, Burney entered the service of Queen Charlotte as a Keeper of the Robes, whose duties resembled those of a lady's maid. Burney did not wish for a

---

1 Gallagher 251.
2 By comparison, Thaddeus calculates that Lowndes made a profit of approximately £32 on the first edition of *Evelina* (24).

Court appointment, but was urged to accept it by her father, who hoped to secure royal patronage for the whole family. Burney had been disappointed in her hopes of a marriage proposal from George Cambridge, a clergyman who had been carrying on a desultory courtship with her since 1782. She reluctantly accepted the Court appointment as an alternative settlement for life. Queen Charlotte wished to employ a famous novelist, but her favour was intended to provide a genteel living for the celebrated author, who was thereby relieved of the vulgar need to maintain herself by her pen. Burney makes no mention of thwarted literary ambitions in her journals from the period, yet her frequent anxieties about speculation in the newspapers over her career suggests that she felt the privation. The tragedies she wrote during her time at Court may also be regarded as a tacit rebellion against the decorous restrictions that assumed that financial security would extinguish her desire to write.

Burney's literary ambitions quickly revived following her retirement from royal service on the grounds of ill health in 1791. She attracted the attention of Alexandre d'Arblay, an impoverished French emigré, formerly an officer in the army of Louis XVI, and during their courtship Burney expressed hopes for the commercial potential of her writing. The couple planned to marry but between them had only Burney's income of £120, comprised of a pension from the Queen and the interest of Dr. Burney's investment of the profits of *Cecilia*. Such a sum was barely enough to live on, but Burney was confident that she could augment their income by her writing, and the couple married in 1793. The marriage was a success, and the following year Burney bore her only child, Alexander.

Burney's first attempt at literary self-sufficiency centred upon a production in 1795 of one of her Court tragedies, *Edwy and Elgiva*, which is discussed further below. Burney's other scheme to profit from her pen involved the publication in 1796 of a third novel, *Camilla: or, a Picture of Youth*. The novel traces the fortunes of the Tyrold family, and in particular the experiences of Camilla Tyrold, a beautiful portionless girl, and her sister Eugenia, an heiress who is scarred by smallpox and deformed as a result of a childhood accident. The sisters' trials in the world beyond the safety of the domestic sphere emphasize the enforced passivity and powerlessness of women in making what is often the most important decision of their lives, the selection of a mate. From the haven of her own happy and remarkably egalitarian marriage, Burney explored the limits placed by society upon female desire and self-determination.

Burney decided to publish *Camilla* by subscription in order to maximize her profits. Spurred on by thoughts of providing for her child, Burney laid aside her former scruples about appearing in the public character of a professional author. In a letter to her father dated 13 June 1795, she explained, "I had previously determined, when I *changed my state*, to set aside all my innate & original abhorrences, & regard & use as resources MYSELF, what had always been considered as such by others."[1] Reclaiming her own creative resources from "others" suggests that Burney felt exploited by her previous literary transactions.

Subscription publication allowed Burney to secure public investment in her work in advance, to fund the costs of the novel's production and to provide a surplus to those costs which would be clear profit. Subscribers paid a guinea for the novel and received a promissory note that would allow them to claim a copy upon its publication. Burney treated the venture as a serious business transaction. With the help of her brother Charles she attempted to tender the project to the major booksellers in London, to create a competition that would yield the lowest possible price for the production costs, thus maximizing the profits of the subscription. Burney also determined to retain the copyright and profits of future editions to herself.

Burney's plans to capitalize on her literary talents ran into opposition from family members who were offended by her independent venture. Once more, considerations beyond the strictly financial entered the transaction. Burney's brother James, now married to Thomas Payne's daughter, was angry that his brother-in-law, who had inherited the family bookselling business, was not given first refusal of *Camilla*. Dr. Burney was agitated by Charles's aggressive commercial tactics, and fretted over the consequences of personal affronts taken by powerful booksellers who were excluded from the subscription. In the face of these domestic demands, Burney was obliged to moderate her plan by agreeing to deal with Payne and Cadell, and, in view of her own lack of business expertise, to sell the copyright for £1000, to be added to the profit of £1000 she realized from the subscription. She did not participate in her father's anxieties over her brother's methods. In publishing *Camilla* by subscription Burney combined the methods of the commercial marketplace with

---

1 Berg, D&L, vol. 6, pt. 1, no pagination; after p. 4837.

an exploitation of networks of influence and patronage. Normally, subscriptions were sold by booksellers and were advertised in newspapers and other printed works. Burney did not neglect these commercial resources in her subscription for *Camilla*, but she gave the affair more social *éclat* by arranging for her genteel friends to spread word of the subscription in polite society and to collect money on her behalf. The novel's subscription list, which was printed in the first edition, contained nine Dukes and Duchesses, and Burney gained permission from the Queen to dedicate the work to her. In utilizing the names and patronage of her elevated friends, Burney did what she could to elevate the prestige value of her work, and to diminish the impression of commercial ambitions in her literary production. Nevertheless, *Camilla* was criticized by some of Burney's contemporaries as an artistically flawed work whose literary status had been compromised by her desire for profit.

Towards the end of August 1779 Dr. Burney had written to his daughter attempting to divert her attention from the suppression of her first comedy, *The Witlings*, to the production of a new work of fiction by reminding her that "[i]n the Novel way, there is no danger—& in that, *no Times* can affect you." By the time Burney came to publish her last novel, *The Wanderer, or Female Difficulties*, in 1814, both the genre and the political situation in Britain had changed.

The Wanderer is Burney's most challenging novel. It relates the history of Juliet Granville, an orphan of aristocratic birth and, like Evelina, the product of a secret marriage. Raised in seclusion in France, on the outbreak of the Terror in 1792 Juliet was coerced into marriage with a revolutionary who threatened otherwise to execute her guardian, a Bishop. Juliet consented to the marriage but escaped and fled to England. The novel begins with her flight as a mysterious refugee without name or family. Juliet's attempts to secure a respectable occupation illustrate the difficulties faced by women who are obliged to support themselves. Her trials are illuminated by an explicitly feminist commentary supplied by Elinor Joddrel, a secondary character who espouses radical and feminist philosophies. Juliet's career may reflect some of Burney's own social and economic concerns in occupying the role of professional author. Juliet is rescued by a romance plot which annuls her marriage and recognizes her aristocratic status, but the social and feminist critique in the novel is never controverted.

Burney had been living in France since 1802, and returning to England in 1812 she hastened to arrange the sale of her novel so that she could rejoin her husband in Paris. She again sought to maximize her profits, but her haste made a second attempt at subscription publication impractical. Instead, Burney gambled on the popularity of her name by accepting an offer from Longman and Co. in which payment was contingent on sales. She received £1500 for the manuscript of the novel, with further payments of £500 for the second edition and £250 each for the third through sixth editions. Had the novel passed through all six editions as Burney hoped, she would have realized £3000.

Initially, the novel seemed successful, and the first edition of three thousand copies sold out in a month, with orders taken for a further eight hundred copies. The second edition of a further thousand copies was prepared but five hundred of the orders were countermanded, possibly as a result of a hostile review of the novel by John Wilson Croker in the *Quarterly Review* of April 1814. Burney realized £2000 from *The Wanderer* and she was confident that eventually the novel's merit would be recognized "when read fresh, & free from local circumstances of a mischievous tendency."[1]

Burney was probably correct to assign her novel's comparative failure to "local circumstances." The genre had changed since Dr. Burney praised its independence of political considerations. In the wake of the French revolution and the emergence of radical philosophies in Britain, the novel had been appropriated as a vehicle for political debate. In her dedication to *The Wanderer*, Burney stated her decision to avoid such debates in her work: "I held political topics to be without my sphere."[2] Modern readers may find this comment surprising in view of the revolutionary setting and the spiritual and feminist debates that are featured in the novel, but to Burney, "political" apparently signified the narrowest sense of governmental politics. Contemporary readers seemed to find *The Wanderer* alternately too political, or not political enough. Written in the tradition of Jacobin fiction from the turn of the century, the novel's engagement with radical philosophies seemed out of date to some readers, like the reviewer from the *British Critic*:

> The revolutionary spirit, which displays itself in the sentiments and actions of Miss Elinor Joddrel, is, fortunately for a bleeding world, now no longer in existence: few of our

---

1 FBA to CBjr, 25 October 1814.
2 *The Wanderer*, ed. Margaret Doody et al. (Oxford UP, 1991), 5.

female readers can remember the *egalité* mania, which once infested the bosoms of their sex; and were we disposed to recommend a portrait of a female revolutionist, we should certainly advise them to seek it in the chaste and animated pages of "Modern Philosophers," and not in the over-drawn caricature of Miss Elinor Joddrel.[1]

However, in the *Quarterly Review* the novel was condemned by John Wilson Croker for its failure to criticize the current government in France. Burney attributed the slump in sales to false expectation that the novel would contain "from my long residence in France, Political anecdotes, or opinions."[2] In view of Croker's criticism of Burney's declaration of political neutrality in the novel's dedication, her assumption seems a fair one. To assert the political neutrality of fiction was no longer a tenable position, as readers had come to expect a declared political allegiance in the novel. Even the *British Critic*, which seemed to eschew political debate altogether, recommended Elizabeth Hamilton's parodic *Memoirs of Modern Philosophers* (1800) for a conservative treatment of the radical philosophies that were deplored in the character of Elinor. For the *Quarterly* and the *British Critic*, both of which espoused Tory policies, it was not politics itself but Burney's failure to expound a wholly conservative view that informed their criticisms of her novel. Burney, having been abroad for ten years, may have been unaware of these developments, which had transformed the novel from the safe, domestic, apolitical genre recommended by her father, into an organ of faction. Whether or not this was the reason, Burney never again ventured to write fiction.

The fate of Burney's last novel illustrates the power of the critical reviewing press in Britain. In the mid–eighteenth century, periodical reviews devoted to literary criticism proliferated, striving to define the aesthetic and ideological direction of public taste.[3]

---

1 *British Critic*, ns 1 (Apr. 1814): 374–86 (385–86).
2 FBA to JB, 10–12 July 1815.
3 My account of the critical reviewing press derives from Frank Donoghue, *The Fame Machine: Book Reviewing and Eighteenth-Century Literary Careers* (Stanford UP, 1996); Joseph Bartolomeo, *A New Species of Criticism: Eighteenth-Century Discourse on the Novel* (U of Delaware P, 1994) and Derek Roper, *Reviewing Before the "Edinburgh" 1788-1802* (Methuen, 1978).

Conflict arose, though, in determining a single standard of taste for an increasingly diverse body of readers. The principal reviews in the eighteenth century were the *Monthly Review* and the *Critical Review*. In the nineteenth century, less comprehensive but more detailed criticism was made by the *Edinburgh Review* and the *Quarterly Review*. The impartiality of the reviewing press was frequently challenged. Political, commercial, and personal bias unquestionably influenced the reviews. Marilyn Butler has argued that we should read reviews with care, particularly those from the quarterly publications, as they were increasingly used to expound particular ideological views on art and society, rather than simply to provide information about a text's contents for the reading public.[1]

Burney made it a point of virtue to flout the reviews. In this she was encouraged by Samuel Johnson, who repeatedly told her to despise the opinions of those who judged by rules.[2] By publishing her first novel anonymously, Burney was able to evade considerations of gender in the responses of the reviewing press. Nevertheless, she feared for her novel's reception in the reviews, and prepared for it with a dextrous address in the dedication of *Evelina* to "the Authors of the Monthly and Critical Reviews." Burney addressed them not as patrons of the "supplicating author" but as impartial servants to the reading public, from whom she sought not favour but justice. It is difficult to determine the degree of irony in Burney's address to the reviewers, but her dedication reads like a double bluff, praising their impartial justice which makes any appeal to their favour by flattery or interest a positive insult.[3]

As it turned out, Burney's first work enjoyed an autonomous success; its popularity spread by word of mouth, and was confirmed but not created by the reviews. This early triumph seems to have encouraged Burney's independent attitude towards the reviews of her later works. Even when *Camilla* became the target of criticism,

---

1   See "Culture's Medium: The Role of the Review," *Cambridge Companion to British Romanticism*, ed. Stuart Curran (Cambridge UP, 1993), 120-47.
2   For example, see FB to SEB, 11 January 1779.
3   For an analysis of the dedication to *Evelina*, see Doody's "Beyond *Evelina*: The Individual Novel and the Community of Literature," *Eighteenth-Century Fiction* 3.4 (1991): 359-71, and Gina Campbell's "How to Read Like a Gentleman: Burney's Instructions to her Critics in *Evelina*," ELH 57 (1990): 557-84.

Burney wrote to her father on 8 November 1796 defying the reviews: "There are two species of Composition which may nearly brave them; Politics & Novels: for these will be sought & will be judged by the various Multitude, not the fastidious few." Burney granted primacy to the judgement of her anonymous readers over the assumed authority of the critics. However, she underestimated the increasing influence of ideological agendas in the quarterly reviews, which was demonstrated in the critical reception afforded her last novel.

Burney had been granted a peculiar status as a woman writer whose acknowledged success qualified her to be judged by the standards used for male authors. Reviewers of women's writing generally evaluated it by different, "chivalrous" standards, but in the *Monthly*'s review of *Cecilia*, Samuel Badcock identified Burney's as a special case: "she doth not plead any privilege of her sex: she stands on firmer ground."[1] Over thirty years later, though, reviews of *The Wanderer* by William Hazlitt in the *Edinburgh Review* and by Croker in the *Quarterly Review* expended some effort in tracing the deleterious effects of gender upon Burney's writing. Both critics called on images of the female body to disparage the female author. Hazlitt asserted that women's physical "softness" resulted in an absence of rigour in their mental perceptions, while Croker characterized Burney's last novel as the decayed form of an old woman: "The Wanderer has the identical features of Evelina—but of Evelina grown old; [...] the eyes are there, but they are dim; the cheek, but it is furrowed; the lips, but they are withered."[2] It is curious that these negative critical evaluations of Burney's work as a sign of general female literary incompetence should emerge only after the publication of her last novel. Hazlitt identified faults in Burney's novels, particularly her "humorist" characterizations, as limitations peculiar to her sex, though they could more accurately be regarded as literary modes from a previous age, employed by novelists like Fielding and Smollett whose works had provided models for Burney's fiction. The gender essentialism of these reviews was probably an attempt to promote a conservative revision of cultural conceptions of femininity in the wake of the French Revolution. Whatever their object, these reviews proved that Burney could no longer defy the critical press.

---

1 Samuel Badcock, *Monthly Review*, 67 (Dec. 1782): 453-58 (456).
2 John Wilson Croker, *Quarterly Review*, 11 (Apr. 1814): 123-30 (125-26).

Burney and Eighteenth-Century Theatre

Burney's early fascination with the theatre is recorded in a fragmentary memorandum written by her father and printed in the *Memoirs of Doctor Burney*:[1]

> She had, however, a great deal of invention and humour in her childish sports; and used, after having seen a play in Mrs. Garrick's box, to take the actors off, and compose speeches for their characters; for she could not read them. (2:168)

Once she had learnt how to write, Burney began to produce dramatic works of her own, and mentions farces and tragedies among the works she destroyed in her sacrificial bonfire on her fifteenth birthday. In her early journals Burney recorded her participation in a number of domestic productions of popular comedies. She was a keen actress with a talent for memorization but a nearly paralyzing shyness in performance. Unlike Jane Austen's Fanny Price from *Mansfield Park* (1814), Burney in her youth was able to reconcile her private acting with the demands of feminine propriety by the judicious omission of all that was "exceptionable" from her parts.

Private theatricals were permissible, but active participation in the public theatre threatened the reputation of a respectable woman. Dr. Burney, through his professional duties as a musician, had extensive connexions in the theatrical world, but his daughter had to tread carefully to distinguish herself from the underclass of performers. Before she achieved fame through *Evelina*, Burney befriended a virtuous young actress, Jane Barsanti, but in later life the acquaintance must have seemed too compromising, for Burney obliterated many references in her early journals to this friendship. Queen Charlotte, when told that Burney had thoughts of writing for the stage, responded that she hoped "she may *not*; for though her

---

1 Eighteenth-century drama and Burney's participation in it are discussed in Barbara Darby's *Frances Burney, Dramatist: Gender, Performance, and the Late Eighteenth-Century Stage* (U of Kentucky P, 1997). Doody makes useful evaluations of Burney's plays, and a general account of women's participation in the eighteenth-century theatre can be found in Ellen Donkin's *Getting into the Act: Women Playwrights in London 1776-1829* (Routledge, 1995).

reputation is so high, her Character, by all I hear, is too delicate, to suit with writing for the stage."[1] Novel-writing was evidently permissible, but entry into the public realm of the theatre was potentially compromising for the female author.

Nevertheless, there were strong incentives to write for the stage. Playwriting was potentially much more lucrative than novel-writing, as a play might reap as much as £600 in author's benefits. Competition, however, was fierce, and female playwrights faced particular problems in producing their plays. It was difficult for women to acquire knowledge of production techniques and basic stage mechanics. These could best be learnt by acting oneself, and a number of female dramatists, such as Elizabeth Inchbald, began their careers as players. A respectable woman did not have this resource. Burney had some experience with amateur productions but her stagecraft could only be learnt as a member of the audience. In the production of her novels, Burney had been able to rely upon agents to deliver her finished product to a bookseller. In the case of her tragedy, Burney was limited by considerations of propriety that forbade her fraternization with performers and therefore from participation in the collaborative process of the play's production.

Burney was obliged to rely upon her brother Charles to supervise the production of her tragedy, *Edwy and Elgiva*, at Drury Lane Theatre in 1795. There were problems with the production from the start which demonstrated how dangerous such reliance could be. Charles had attended the first reading of the play but he neglected to tell his sister, who was ill after the birth of her child, that the actors had walked out one by one until he found himself alone. The production on 21 March 1795 was a disaster; it was under-rehearsed and marred by almost constant interruptions by the prompter. John Palmer, who played Aldhelm, improvised most of his part, often to comic effect. Burney, who attended the performance, afterwards maintained that she was not cast down by its failure as the play had not been performed at all, an assertion which was ratified by some of the reviews. Nevertheless, Burney admitted that the play was marred by "*undramatic*" effects, caused by her ignorance of stage business. She was eager to revise the piece in the light of her new knowledge but her literary and commercial ambitions were soon afterwards diverted into a safer channel, the composition of *Camilla*.

---

1   FB to CB and SBP, 1 December 1785.

Burney's final dramatic attempts focused on three comedies, *Love and Fashion*, *The Woman Hater*, and *A Busy Day*, composed between 1798 and 1802. In 1799, Burney reached an agreement with Thomas Harris, the manager of the Covent Garden Theatre, to sell him the rights to *Love and Fashion* for £400, but the death of Burney's sister Susan in 1800 meant that the comedy had to be withdrawn and was never staged.

In attempting to produce this comedy, Burney encountered the same family resistance that had thwarted her hopes for *The Witlings*. At the age of forty-seven, Burney still conducted her theatrical dealings under a veil of secrecy, referring to her play as a piece of furniture and the theatre manager as an "upholsterer." Such subterfuge seems absurd until we consider Dr. Burney's panic on discovering her plans. In a letter dated 11 February 1800 Burney responded to his fears over the possible consequences of a dramatic venture, not submissively, as in the case of *The Witlings*, but with an assertion of her irresistible and innocuous drive to creative activity:

> The combinations for another long work did not occur to me. Incidents & effects for a Dramma [*sic*] did. I thought the field more than open—inviting to me. The chance held out golden dreams. The risk could be only our own for—permit me to say, appear when it will, you will find nothing in the principles, the moral, or the language that will make you blush for me. *A failure*, upon those points only, can bring DIS-GRACE—upon mere control or want of dramatic powers, it can only cause *disappointment*.

In this letter Burney announced a separation between her literary career and her moral life. Failure was not social annihilation if it involved only the text. Burney asserted herself as a professional writer able to distance herself from her productions.

Creativity and the Female Artist in Eighteenth-Century Britain

In the winter of 1778-79, when Frances Burney was writing *The Witlings*, Samuel Crisp, who was privy to the secret of her new project, wrote several letters advising her how best to go about dramatic composition. He was concerned that Burney's personal prudishness would inhibit her comic facility, but even as he deplored the literary limitations imposed by her scruples, he approved the morality that lay behind them. Having explored this dilemma, Crisp rather disingenuously concluded that it was possible, and indeed necessary, for Burney to reconcile the literary need for spirit and humour in a comedy with the constraints imposed upon her play's language and content by the demands of feminine propriety. He chose a memorable image to describe her situation.

> Do you remember about a Dozen Years ago, how you used to dance Nancy Dawson on the Grass plot, with Your Cap on the Ground, & your long hair streaming down your Back,— one shoe off, & throwing about your head like a mad thing?—now you are to dance Nancy Dawson with Fetters on—(19 January 1779)

The Nancy Dawson was a hornpipe, named after the dancer who performed it. Crisp's characterization of Burney's dramatic writing as a dance to be performed in fetters is very revealing of her position as a writer. In writing for a public forum like the theatre, Burney's natural impulses were to be curbed by the expectations of her audience. Nevertheless, the limits that propriety would set upon her gender were not the sole restraints acting upon Burney's writing. As Crisp made clear in the rest of his letter, Burney was also subject to the demands and restrictions inherent in the literary genre of drama. Burney's task was to walk the line between these two sometimes conflicting obligations, to social and to literary decorum. In her defence of her dramatic ambitions written in 1800, however, Burney seemed to envisage the possibility that her creativity could be freed from the limits of social propriety, and be subject only to the restraints of literary decorum. Could the female author ever thus separate her social persona from her professional career? Or would the female artist and her work forever be regarded as one?

In a letter written on 8 December 1778, Crisp analysed the conflicting demands placed upon the female dramatist. Burney responded by writing, "I would a thousand Times rather forfeit my character as a *Writer*, than risk ridicule or censure as a *Female*."[1] We

---

1   FB to SC, *c.* 7 January 1779.

need to be cautious, however, in reading such a letter as a transparent utterance of Burney's views. The sentiments she declared to Crisp may have been affected by his expectations. One might compare this declaration with a letter Burney wrote to her sister Susan on 5 July 1778, describing her fears following the success of *Evelina*. Burney found herself at the pinnacle of fame:

> I see about me, indeed, many Hills of far greater height & sublimity;—but I have not the strength to attempt climbing them;—if *I* move, it must be in *descending*! [...] The wisest Course I could take, would be to bid an eternal adieu to Writing; then would *the Cry* be "'Tis pity she does not go on!—she might do something better by & by;—" &c, &c, *Evelina*, as a First, & a youthful publication, has been received with the utmost favour & lenity,—but would a future attempt be treated with the same Mercy?—No, my dear Susy, quite the contrary,—there would not, indeed, be the same *plea* to save it,—it would no longer be a *Young Lady's first appearance* in public;—those who have met with less indulgence, would all *peck* at any new Book;—& even those who most encouraged the 1st. offspring, might prove Enemies to the 2^{d}., by receiving it with Expectations which it could not answer.— —& so, between either the Friends or the Foes of the *Eldest*, the 2^{d}. would stand an equally bad chance, & a million of *flaws* which were overlooked in the former, would be ridiculed as villainous & intolerable *Blunders* in the latter.—But, though my Eyes Ache as I strain them to look forward,—the temptations before me are *almost* irresistable [...]

The anxiety Burney expressed here in venturing upon a second, acknowledged work was directed not at a possible contravention of feminine propriety in appearing in the public character of an author, but upon the chances of literary success or failure. Her half-formed wish to stand still seems primarily an instinct to protect her literary reputation rather than her social standing. Though she bowed to advice to suppress her first comedy, Burney's confidence in her literary judgement can be seen to increase over her life, as she resisted Crisp's criticisms of the unconventional ending of *Cecilia*, braved the disastrous first night of *Edwy* to emerge full of plans for its improvement, and defied her father in declaring her right to persist in dramatic writing. Burney's determination reveals a stronger conviction in herself and her work than modern readers might perhaps expect from the decorous lady novelist.

Burney's fictional and non-fictional writings occasionally contain descriptions of other female artists.[1] In her journals and letters from 1775, Burney described several meetings with the celebrated opera singer, Agujari. Beth Kowaleski-Wallace has analysed these descriptions to derive an account of Burney's views on art and the female artist. Kowaleski-Wallace argues that in her accounts of the lame, reputedly illegitimate Italian singer who was able to transcend her body and origins by her sublime performances, Burney characterized art as a transcendent sphere, in which class difference and the (female) body ceased to matter to artist and audience alike.[2] Was Burney ever able to make such a transcendence in her own art? Or was her writing nothing more, as Crisp reductively put it, than "sitting still in her Chamber by a good Fire"?[3]

Three years after meeting Agujari, Burney published her first novel anonymously, successfully though temporarily evading the social demands concomitant on her authorship and, briefly, creating a work of art that stood alone, apparently transcending the individual who created it. Burney's persistent drive towards anonymity, or "snugship" as she called it, seems less to be about the personal modesty for which she was alternately praised and blamed, and more like a statement of a philosophy of art, in which she strove to detach her work from its author. In her first publication Burney was able, like Agujari, momentarily to erase her body, her gender, and her class from her work. The experience of publishing *Evelina* embodied an ideal for Burney, in a promise of an unmediated relationship between art and the audience where producers and consumers remained unknown to one another, and works of art sustained themselves by their intrinsic merit. Unfortunately, contemporary critics like Croker linked Burney so closely with her texts that advancing age and infirmity depreciated the perceived literary value of her works, which very nearly died with her.

---

1 For example, consider the portrait of the female musician Juliet in *The Wanderer*.

2 See "A Night at the Opera: The Body, Class, and Art in *Evelina* and Frances Burney's Early Diaries," *History, Gender and Eighteenth-Century Literature*, ed. Beth Fowkes Tobin (U of Georgia P, 1994), 141-58.

3 Letter to Sophia Gast, 23 May 1782, *Burford Papers* 81.

Burney's Life-Writings

Though we might expect social and literary constraints to shape Burney's works in the public literary marketplace, it is easy to suppose that the writings of her private life contained the "real" Burney, unmediated by expectation or restriction. Samuel Johnson pointed out the fallacy of a similar supposition about the private letter, which in the eighteenth century was sometimes idealized as an entirely authentic and transparent form of literary utterance. In his life of Pope, Johnson suggested that writing for a single, known reader might incur more anxiety and demand a more artful self-presentation than writing for a faceless public audience:

> Friendship has no tendency to secure veracity; for by whom can a man so much wish to be thought better than he is, as by him whose kindness he desires to gain or keep? Even in writing to the world there is less constraint; the author is not confronted with his reader, and takes his chance of approbation among the different dispositions of mankind; but a Letter is addressed to a single mind, of which the prejudices and partialities are known; and must therefore please, if not by favouring them, by forbearing to oppose them.[1]

In reading Burney's life-writings, both journals and letters, we must always bear in mind that they seldom remained entirely private.

Burney's life-writings passed through distinct phases. The early journals, written before 1778, were generally composed soon after the events they recorded, and were relatively private. The journal entries were irregular, and covered topics relating to Burney's family and social life, with occasional comments on her readings of literary works. One early entry from July 1768 describes how Burney composed her journals, jotting her entries on a portable piece of paper which she later stitched into a booklet.

After the publication of *Evelina*, there was a slight change of emphasis in Burney's life-writings. In her new public life, Burney was often absent from home, and she composed long journal-letters addressed to her sister Susan, detailing her adventures in the

---

1 "Pope," *The Lives of the Most Eminent English Poets* [...], 4 vols. (C. Bathurst et al., 1781), 4: 153.

great world as a substitute for the more introspective early journals. These journal-letters were read by others, including Samuel Crisp and, on occasion, Burney's father.

In 1786 Burney took up her appointment at Court, and she continued to write journal-letters to Susan, sometimes jointly addressed to the sisters' close friend, Frederica Locke, but the demands of her duties reduced the time available for writing. At this period, Burney composed her journal-letters retrospectively, usually in batches of about one month, from memoranda notes which she made daily. The content of these journals also changed. Rather than recording Burney's social and literary activities, the journal-letters from this period provided an outlet for her growing depression and frustration in her isolated situation at Court. On occasion, Burney wrote Susan separate letters that dealt with private matters, suggesting that her longer journal-letters might still be circulated within the family.

After her retirement from Court and her marriage, Burney's life-writing for a time was directed exclusively into letters to family and friends. She continued to write these kinds of letters until shortly before her death in 1840, but after the death of her husband in 1818, Burney undertook to write a series of formal journals of events in her life, to honour his request that she write an account of her life for the sake of their son and his descendants. Burney did not write a systematic memoir, but concentrated instead on discrete narratives composed long after the events they recorded, including her account of returning to England in 1812 after an absence of more than ten years, and a description of life in Brussels during the Battle of Waterloo. These narratives show a degree of self-consciousness in their composition and revision, and focus on historical as well as personal events.

Burney's earliest surviving journal, written in March 1768, begins with a dextrous address to Miss Nobody. By establishing a cipher as her text's audience, Burney attempted to evade restraints upon her writing, since "To Nobody can I be wholly unreserved—to Nobody can I reveal every thought, every wish of my Heart, with the most unlimited confidence, the most unremitting sincerity to the end of my Life!"

The ideal of perfect self-revelation in the privacy of her journal could not be sustained. In 1768, Burney recorded the admonitions of an old family friend, Dorothy Young, who undertook to instruct Burney on the perils of journal-writing. Miss Young was opposed to self-disclosure in journals, asserting that some personal experiences "ought *not* to be recorded, but instantly forgot." Miss Young gendered this peril as peculiarly feminine in her example of a man reading Burney's journal and discovering an unsolicited and unrequited declaration of love for himself. The journal, in presenting an opportunity to register the female subject and her desires, provided a permanent record of that which ought not to be represented at all within a phallocentric system, but should be "instantly forgot." Miss Young pressed her point that no matter how closely the journal was guarded, restricted to one safe reader, Nobody, the artefact of the text remained available to other readers and so to some degree must engage with the public sphere. Private textual self-revelation crossed the line into social and (implicitly) sexual indecorum. Burney had already suffered the embarrassment of losing a page of her diary, which was discovered by her father, in which she referred to her stepmother's pregnancy. Despite this lapse, Burney argued that her text was sufficiently circumspect to negate these dangers. Miss Young, having examined an entry at random, concurred that Burney's self-inscription was innocuous—which leads us to assume it was not particularly revealing. Burney had evidently chosen to censor herself for the sake of propriety. Her revised philosophy was expressed several years later when she commented in a journal entry upon the elopement of her stepsister Maria Allen: "I dare not commit particulars to paper" (21 May 1772).[1]

Later, Burney's journals acquired an intentional audience. Around 1773, Burney began a correspondence with Samuel Crisp, and he, enjoying her letters, requested to see her journals also. After much persuasion, in 1775 Burney permitted him to borrow her Teignmouth Journal, written in 1773 during a visit to her stepsister. Crisp's request set a precedent that was taken up by other family members and friends, and Burney's life-writings, both letters and journals, acquired a real audience, and entered into a semi-public circulation.

Composing for her new "public" audience, Burney was called upon to shape her writings according to her readers' expectations. Crisp provided her early instruction in letter-writing:

—you cannot but know, *that trifling, that negligence, that even incorrectness* now & then, in familiar Epistolary writing, is the very soul of Genius & Ease & that if your letters were to be

---

1 Berg, JJ, vol. 5, p. 283.

fine labour'd Compositions, that smelt of the *Lamp*; I had as lieve they travelled else where—So, no more of that, Fan, & thou lov'st me—Dash away, whatever comes uppermost; & believe me, You'll succeed better, than by leaning on your Elbows, & studying what to say—(18 April 1775)

Instructions to artlessness are a revealing irony upon eighteenth-century notions of "Nature," and illustrate the paradox at the heart of the familiar letter, which ought to be an authentic expression of the self, though that expression must nevertheless be constrained by notions of prudence and decorum. Hugh Blair, a Scottish divine, analysed epistolary writing as a literary form in his *Lectures on Rhetoric and Belles Lettres*, first published in 1783. Though Blair recommended naturalness and simplicity in the familiar letter, he warned readers that a "slovenly and negligent manner of Writing, is a disobliging mark of want of respect. [...] The first requisite, both in conversation and correspondence, is to attend to all the proper decorums, which our own character, and that of others, demand."[1]

Crisp, too, though he seemed to enjoin spontaneity, was a demanding reader, and employed images of food and eating to figure Burney's letter-writing as the feminine art of cookery, while his reading became the pleasurable act of gourmandizing. Though his replies might consist of the plain homely fare of "Bacon and Greens," Crisp expected Burney's letters to him to be "highly season'd."[2] Since the recipient of a letter had to pay the postal costs, Crisp perhaps had a right to dictate its contents.

These personal and social expectations upon Burney's life-writing transformed her into a chameleon. Samuel Johnson, in his analysis of the familiar letter from his life of Pope, warned that it must be read as a self-serving fiction, conveying a calculated performance of a social persona. Burney's life-writings illustrate this doctrine, as she fitted her letters and journals to their readers by the assumption of a range of dramatic "voices." Her teasing but always deferential letters to Samuel Crisp contrast with her acutely sentimental submission in writing to her father, her easy equality in

---

1 "Lecture 37: Philosophical Writing—Dialogue—Epistolary Writing—Fictitious History," *Lectures on Rhetoric and Belles Lettres*, 2nd ed., 3 vols. (1785), 3: 69.
2 SC to FB, April 1774.

addressing her favourite sister Susan, and the frankly bossy tone she assumed when writing to her younger sister Charlotte. In composing her epistolary novel, *Evelina*, Burney employed some of the dramatic techniques learnt from her experiences in journal and letter-writing. Modern analysts of the letter have concurred that epistolary writing is inherently dramatic in its creation of an artful illusion of a physical presence by the absent correspondent. Barbara Herrnstein Smith argues that the absent letter-writer is an actor, who employs a complex syntax in writing to convey information which, if present, would be supplied by intonation, gestures, and shared physical contexts. Smith suggests that the artful language of the letter supplies this deficiency with description, literary allusion, and graphic substitutions for intonation such as underlining, punctuation and variations in spelling.[1]

The demands presented by Burney's readers were not the only constraints that shaped her journals and letters. Eighteenth-century models of autobiographical and epistolary writing also exerted influences upon Burney's life-writings. She read published correspondence and the works of essayists like Johnson and Blair, and in her personal writings showed her awareness of contemporary debates about journal and letter-writing.

Though the term autobiography was not coined until 1809, some eighteenth-century critics attempted to codify the genres associated with self-inscription. The cornerstone of contemporary generic definitions of autobiographical writing rested upon a conviction in its didactic utility. Samuel Johnson explained in the *Rambler* (no. 60) and the *Idler* (no. 84) that biographical and autobiographical writing should instruct the reader. Johnson rejected philosophic abstractions and historical curiosities as the basis for this kind of writing, and encouraged instead a focus upon the domestic and sensory experiences common to all men, as most useful to readers. Other critics, such as Isaac D'Israeli, took a different approach. In his essay "Some Observations on Diaries, Self-Biography, and Self-Characters" (1796),[2] D'Israeli insisted that to be useful, autobiographical writing must have a "philosophic" focus. He criticized journals from earlier periods for their inclusion of trivial detail; that

---

1 *On the Margins of Discourse: The Relation of Literature to Language* (U of Chicago P, 1978), 23.
2 In *Miscellanies; or, Literary Recreations* (1796), 95-110.

is, anything that was not purely intellectual, or politically or historically significant. Recording "the minutest events of domestic life" was, D'Israeli declared, "giving importance to objects which should only be observable in the history of any other animal, but man" (99). Unlike Johnson, D'Israeli rejected the physical life in favour of the intellectual, but his language in so doing suggestively erased another kind of history—that of woman. D'Israeli's essay made no mention of women diarists, yet his condemnation of trivial detail and descriptions of physical existence like meals and medical treatments tended to exclude from autobiographical writing much of women's experience as unfit for representation.[1] Burney was certainly aware of these restrictions, and on occasion she playfully defied the literary decorum that would exclude this material from her life-writings. She wrote to Samuel Crisp on 22 January 1780 apologizing for relating her domestic rather than literary activities:

> Caps, Hats, & Ribbons make, indeed, no venerable appearance upon Paper;—no more does Eating & Drinking;—yet the one can no more be worn without being *made*, than the other can be swallowed without being *Cooked*,—& those who can niether pay *Milliners*, nor keep *scrubbers*, must either toil for themselves, or go *Capless* & Dinnerless,— —So if you are for an high-polished comparison, *I'm* your man!—

Burney might have defended her inclusion of this homely detail by citing Johnson's recommendation for the representation of domestic experience within life-writing. However, Johnson's commitment to the didactic utility of the genre to some extent impaired the usefulness of his model for the female autobiographer, since it was hardly possible to present female existence as either normative or exemplary.

---

1   Modern theorists of autobiography have suggested that the inscription of self is inherently problematic for women. Domna Stanton, in her essay "Autogynography: Is the Subject Different?" argues that the position of subject is a precarious one for the female autobiographer or diarist, who writes within a phallocentric system in which women are defined solely as objects (*The Female Autograph: Theory and Practice of Autobiography from the Tenth to the Twentieth Century*, ed. Domna Stanton, U of Chicago P, 1987. 3-20).

Eighteenth-century generic models for life-writing thus presented Burney with problems in writing about herself, problems that were specific to her gender. These obstacles to the inscription of a female life were illustrated in the critical responses afforded the published versions of Burney's autobiographical writing. In 1832 Burney published an account of her father's life and career, the *Memoirs of Doctor Burney*. Dr. Burney had left a manuscript memoir of his life, but when she examined it, Burney found it, in her judgment, unfit to print. She destroyed nearly all of Dr. Burney's original text and composed a new account of her father's life. In his hostile review of the *Memoirs* in the *Quarterly Review*, John Wilson Croker accused Burney of destroying her father's manuscript and substituting her own text in order to obtrude her autobiography upon the public. He complained that the title deliberately misled the reader: "instead of being called 'Memoirs of Dr. Burney,' [it] might better be described as 'Scattered Recollections of Miss Fanny Burney and her Acquaintance.'"[1] Croker interpreted Burney's rather strained representation of herself in the third person, under odd denominations like "this memorialist" or "the-then-Bookham-and-afterwards-West-Hamble-female hermit" as a transparent manoeuvre to present while denying herself as the real subject of the *Memoirs*. Burney does seem to have been uneasy about her appearance in the text, and in her preface to the *Memoirs* she made a convoluted apology:

> Not slight, however, is the embarrassment that struggles with the pleasure of these mingled reminiscences, from their appearance of personal obtrusion: yet, when it is seen that they are never brought forward but to introduce some incident or speech, that must else remain untold [...] these apparent egotisms may be something more,—perhaps—than pardoned. (1: viii)

Representation of the female self automatically attracted the charge of egotism, and even posthumously, the publication of Burney's own journals and letters convicted her of a transgression against the social and literary proprieties that would discount female experience. Burney's niece, Charlotte Barrett, who had

---

1   Croker, *Quarterly Review* 49 (Apr. 1833): 97–125 (106).

inherited her aunt's manuscripts, chose to publish a large selection from them. Burney had edited and censored her life-writings before her death, but Barrett revised the material even further, making large excisions and sanitizing her aunt's sometimes robust language.[1] Despite her care, Barrett's edition of *The Diaries and Letters of Madame d'Arblay*, issued from 1842, met with a mixed reception from the critics.

On 3 July 1820, Burney had written to reassure a friend who was contemplating the publication of her great-aunt's private papers not to be troubled by fears of damaging the lady's reputation: "*She*, who did not write for the press, can never be satirized that she did not prepare for it."[2] This remark is sadly ironic in view of some of the responses accorded the published version of Burney's own life-writings. Far from making allowance for the private medium in which they were composed, critics such as Croker arraigned Burney on the charge of vanity, resenting the central position she assumed in her private writings after a lifetime of feminine effacement in her public career. Even Burney's sister Sarah deplored Burney's insistent presence in the *Diaries*. Sarah Burney wrote to Henry Crabb Robinson on 9 December 1842:

> That there is still considerable vanity I cannot deny. In her life, she Bottled it all up, & looked and generally spoke with the most refined modesty, & seemed ready to drop if ever her works were alluded to. But what was kept back, and scarcely suspected in society, wanting a safety valve, found its way to her private journal.[3]

In his review of the *Memoirs of Doctor Burney* in 1833, Croker had suggested that Burney write an account of her own life, rather than attempting to insert it into the biography of her father. However, in the *Quarterly Review* Croker denounced Burney's *Diaries* as rampant egotism, written solely for "the *glorification of Miss Fanny*

---

1 For details of editorial changes made by Burney and others to the manuscript life-writings see Ingrid Tieken-Boon van Ostade, "Stripping the Layers: Language and Content of Fanny Burney's Early Journals," *English Studies* 72.2 (1991): 146–59.

2 FBA to MPW, Berg, ms. letter, no pagination.

3 Williams, Henry Crabb Robinson mss., vol. 1842, letter 201b.

Burney."[1] Though Croker had complained there was an insufficient sense of Dr. Burney in the *Memoirs*, he resented Burney's centrality in her *Diaries*, where she ought, according to Croker, have been a vehicle for the presentation of others, such as the celebrities of her day. Johnson's and D'Israeli's endorsement of the didactic power of textual records of self-contemplation was implicitly restricted to the autobiography of man. The history of that "other animal," woman, was the history of Nobody, a mass of trivial detail with neither importance nor utility. For Nobody to arrogate a subjecthood to herself, and to make herself the theme of her own writing could only be, as Croker put it, "*much ado about nothing*."[2]

Croker's dismissive estimation of Burney's achievements in her published and personal writings did not go unchallenged. In the *Edinburgh Review* for January 1843, Thomas Babington Macaulay's review of the *Diaries* expounded a different view of Burney as an enabling precursor for other women novelists, including Jane Austen and Maria Edgeworth. Modern scholars have increasingly taken their cue from Macaulay rather than Croker. As interest in women's writing, both in published works and in private self-inscriptions, has expanded, Burney's published and personal texts have attracted new scholarly attention. While her novels have been rediscovered as significant contributions to the development of the genre, her life-writings have been re-evaluated by feminist critics such as Julia Epstein.[3] In her earliest surviving journal, Burney had called her life-writings a "*living proof* of my manner of passing my time, my sentiments, my thoughts of people I know, & a thousand other things." Though Burney showed a wry awareness in her journals and letters that she was writing for Nobody, and about Nobody, her insistent inscription of a self that refused decorous obliteration does live on, as a unique record of a female artist, who has now been recognized as Somebody of significance to English literature.

---

1 Croker, *Quarterly Review* 70 (June 1842): 243–87 (245).
2 Croker, 1842: 247.
3 See *The Iron Pen: Frances Burney and the Politics of Women's Writing* (Bristol Classic Press, 1989).

Frances Burney: A Brief Chronology

1752 13 June: FB born at Kings Lynn, third child of Charles
Burney and Esther Sleepe Burney.

1760 Burney family move to London.

1762 death of Esther Sleepe Burney.

1767 13 June: FB burns all her early writings, including *The
History of Caroline Evelyn* and her journals.
2 October: Charles Burney and Elizabeth Allen marry.

1768 FB begins new journal.

1776 December: FB sends first two volumes of *Evelina* to Thomas
Lowndes, a bookseller in the Strand.

1777 September: FB dispatches the third volume of *Evelina* to
Lowndes.
Lowndes offers 20 guineas for *Evelina*.

1778 29 January: First edition of *Evelina* appears.
July: FB meets Hester Thrale and Samuel Johnson.

1779 FB works on a comedy, *The Witlings*.
August: Dr. Burney and Crisp condemn the satire of
Bluestocking circles in *The Witlings*. FB abandons work on
the comedy.

1780 FB begins work on *Cecilia*.

1782 12 July: Publication of *Cecilia*; copyright sold for £250.

1783 26 April: Samuel Crisp dies aged 76.

1784 Hester Thrale marries an Italian musician, Gabriel Piozzi,
and is alienated from FB.
13 December: Death of Samuel Johnson.

1785 FB meets George III and Queen Charlotte.

1786 17 July: FB takes up a place at Court, as Second Keeper of
the Robes to the Queen, with a salary of £200 per annum.

1788 October: The King falls ill and is diagnosed as insane.
FB begins work on her first tragedy, *Edwy and Elgiva*.

1789 March: The King recovers.

1790 FB completes a first draft of *Edwy and Elgiva*, and begins
three other tragedies, *Hubert de Vere*, *The Siege of Pevensey*,
and *Elberta*.

1791 July: FB retires from Court with a pension of £100 per annum.

1792 FB meets Alexandre d'Arblay.

1793 John Philip Kemble, acting manager of Drury Lane Theatre,
accepts *Hubert de Vere* for production. Later it is withdrawn
and *Edwy and Elgiva* accepted in its place.

28 July: FB and Alexandre d'Arblay marry.

19 November: Publication of FBA's pamphlet for charity, *Brief Reflections Relative to the Emigrant French Clergy*.

1794   *Edwy and Elgiva* accepted for production at Drury Lane.

18 December: Birth of FBA's son, Alexander.

1795   21 March: *Edwy and Elgiva* fails at Drury Lane, and is withdrawn after one performance.

1796   12 July: Publication of *Camilla*; copyright sold for £1000.

1798   FBA writes *Love and Fashion*, a comedy.

1799   Thomas Harris, manager of Covent Garden Theatre, offers £400 for *Love and Fashion*, planning to produce it in March, 1800.

1800   January 6: Death of Susan Burney Phillips.

FBA consequently withdraws *Love and Fashion* from production.

FBA begins work on two comedies, *The Woman-Hater* and *A Busy Day*.

1801   October: Peace of Amiens between France and Britain allows ADA to return to France.

1802   FBA and Alexander join ADA. Plans to produce her two new comedies are shelved.

1803   War is resumed between Britain and France, and the d'Arblays are trapped in France for the duration.

1811   Following a diagnosis of breast cancer, FBA submits to a mastectomy.

1812   Peace is declared between Britain and France, and FBA sets out for England.

1813   FBA sells the copyright for her fourth novel, *The Wanderer*, for £1500.

1814   28 March: *The Wanderer* published.

12 April: Dr. Burney dies.

FBA returns to France.

1815   Napoleon escapes from Elba and advances on Paris.

19 March: FBA and ADA flee Paris to Belgium.

2 April: ADA is dispatched to Trèves (Trier) while FBA remains in Brussels.

18 June: Battle of Waterloo.

July: After receiving word that ADA has been wounded, FBA makes a perilous journey across Germany to join him.

October: D'Arblays return to England, making their home in Bath.

1818   3 May: Alexandre d'Arblay dies of rectal cancer.

1819	Alexander ordained as a priest in the Church of England.
1832	November: Publication of FBA's *Memoirs of Doctor Burney*.
1837	19 January: Alexander dies of influenza, aged 43.
1840	6 January: FBA dies of a fever. She is buried in Bath, alongside her husband and son.
1842–46	Charlotte Francis Barrett, FBA's niece, edits her diary and letters for publication.

A Note on the Text

The original manuscripts of Burney's journals and letters are often incomplete. In the final years of her life, Burney censored her own and others' papers, cutting away pages and making smaller obliterations by overscoring the text with heavy loops in black ink. She sometimes rewrote the obliterated or discarded passages. Her editorial work also included some attempts to standardize the punctuation of the text, especially of quotation marks. Burney destroyed materials relating to family scandals such as her brother Charles's expulsion from university. She also expunged nearly all references to money matters in her journals and letters. Surprisingly, Burney did not excise the portions of her writings that related to her thwarted love affairs with George Cambridge and Stephen Digby. She seems not to have thought anything discreditable that related only to her emotional life.

In preparing the printed version of the text I have employed the following conventions.

Ellipses [...] indicate the omission of material. Greetings and signatures have been silently omitted from letters.

I have placed [xxx] to indicate material that is indecipherable, because of tears or cuttings of the manuscript pages, or because Burney has deliberately overscored passages.

Passages within square brackets [ ] contain material that has been obscured in some way. The text within the brackets contains either recovered material, or Burney's own substitution for the obscured passage. In the case where Burney deliberately overscored a passage, I have where possible given the original text, but it should be borne in mind that the obliterated material is difficult to decipher and some of the text may be conjectural. In the case where I have chosen to give the text written later by Burney to substitute for an earlier version, the material is placed within square brackets and annotated with a footnote. It is not always possible to judge exactly when these substitutions occurred, whether an immediate excision and rewriting of a passage, or a revision that occurred many years later.

I have altered the substance of the text as little as possible, and tried to reproduce as exactly as the printed form will allow Burney's own punctuation, capitalization, layout and spelling. Some of these elements are matters of opinion. Burney's letter formation is not always precise enough to tell when she wished to indicate a capital letter. I have rendered underscored material as italics. Burney's revisions to standardize the punctuation were neither systematic nor complete, and so I have chosen to retain the punctuation used in the original text, as far as it is possible to distinguish it from later additions. Burney seldom used the running quotation mark, down the left hand side of quoted text, and so this is omitted from all of the journals and letters for the sake of clarity. However, I chose not to make further corrections to the punctuation and quotation marks because I felt what might be gained in clarity for the modern reader would be at the expense of a sustained sense of the text as a manuscript, rather than as a finished, polished piece of writing.

Italicized material within square brackets, such as [*example*], contains editorial annotations, including summaries of details given in omitted portions of the text and descriptions of concurrent events in Burney's life.

Principal Persons

Charles Burney D. Mus. (1726-1814): FB's father, a professional musician.

Esther Sleepe Burney (1725-62): FB's mother.

Elizabeth Allen Burney (1728-96): FB's step-mother; widow of Stephen Allen.

Children of Charles Burney and Esther Sleepe Burney

Esther (Hetty) Burney (Burney) (1749-1832): married to her cousin, Charles Rousseau Burney.

James Burney (1750-1821): Naval officer, married to Sarah Payne, daughter of the bookseller Thomas Payne the elder.

Frances Burney (d'Arblay) (1752-1840): married to General Alexandre d'Arblay (see below). They had one child, Alexander Charles Louis Piochard d'Arblay (1794-1837), a clergyman.

Susan Burney (Phillips) (1755-1800): FB's favourite sister, married to Molesworth Phillips, Lieutenant-Colonel of the Marines.

Charles Burney Jr. D. D. (1757-1817): a classical scholar, clergyman, and headmaster of Greenwich School.

Charlotte Ann Burney (Francis Broome) (1761-1838): married (1) Clement Francis, a physician (2) Ralph Broome.

Children of Elizabeth Allen's First Marriage

Maria Allen (Rishton) (1751-1820): married Martin Rishton, separated 1796.

Stephen Allen (1755-1847)

Elizabeth Allen (Meeke Bruce) (1761-c.1826)

Children of Charles Burney and Elizabeth Allen Burney

Richard Thomas Burney (1768-1808)

Sarah Harriet Burney (1772-1844)

★★★

Richard Burney (1723-92): FB's uncle, family of the "Worcester Burneys."

FB's cousins:

Charles Rousseau Burney (1747-1819): married to Esther Burney.

Ann Burney (Hawkins) (1749-1819)
Richard Gustavus Burney (1751-90)
James Adolphus Burney (1753-98)
Elizabeth Warren Burney (1755-1832)
Rebecca Burney (Sandford) (1758-1835)
Edward Francesco Burney (1760-1848): artist and portrait-painter.

★★★

Charlotte Francis (Barrett) (1786-1879): FBA's niece; eldest child of Charlotte Burney Francis and Clement Francis. She edited FBA's journals for the press in the 1840s.

★★★

Alexandre-Jean-Baptiste Piochard d'Arblay (1754-1818): An adjutant-general in the army of Louis XVI, d'Arblay had been second-in-command to the Marquis de Lafayette in the war between France and Austria in 1792. Both officers were taken prisoner by their rebellious troops, and were rescued by Austrian forces. D'Arblay fled to England where he joined a colony of aristocratic French emigrés. Though he had been in the army since the age of fourteen, d'Arblay was a cultured man with many literary interests. He respected his wife's work and served as her amanuensis. After the restoration of Louis XVIII, d'Arblay retired with the rank of lieutenant-général, and received the title Comte in recognition of his services.

Samuel Crisp (c.1707-83): A connoisseur and gentleman-amateur musician, Crisp was a friend of CB and later FB. He had theatrical ambitions but financial losses and the failure of his tragedy *Virginia* in 1754 led Crisp to retire to a rural boarding house, Chessington Hall in Surrey, run by a lady in reduced circumstances, Sarah Hamilton, with her niece Kitty Cooke.

Hester Lynch Thrale Piozzi (1741-1821): One of the second-generation Bluestockings, Hester Lynch was the only child of parents of elevated birth but reduced fortune. She was given a liberal education, including Latin, but was married at the command of her parents to a wealthy brewer with whom she had little in common. Mrs. Thrale turned her energies to cultivating literary society, including Johnson, Arthur Murphy and, eventually, FB. After the death of her husband in 1781, Mrs. Thrale fell in love with an Italian musician, Gabriel Piozzi, whom she married in 1784. FB opposed the match on grounds of class and religion, and was alienated from her friend as a result. The two were partially reconciled in 1815.

JOURNALS AND CORRESPONDENCE
OF FRANCES BURNEY

1768

JOURNAL FOR 1768

1. [This strange Medley of Thoughts & Facts was written at the age of 15. for my Genuine & most private amusement.]¹

Fanny Burney

Poland Street, London, March 27ᵗʰ.

To have some account of my thoughts, manners, acquaintance & actions, when the Hour arrives in which time is more nimble than memory, is the reason which induces me to keep a Journal: A Journal in which I must confess my *every* thought, must open my whole Heart! But a thing of th[is] kind ought to be addressed to somebody—I must imagion myself to be talking—talking to the most intimate of friends—to one in whom I should take delight in confiding, & remorse in concealment: but who must this friend be?—to make choice of one to whom I can but *half* rely, would be to frustrate entirely the intention of my plan. The only one I could wholly, totally confide in, lives in the same House with me, & not only never *has*, but never *will*, leave me one secret *to* tell her.² To *whom*, then, *must* I dedicate my wonderful, surprising & interesting adventures?—to *whom* da[re] I reveal my private opinion of my nearest Relations? the secret thoughts of my dearest friends? my own hopes, fears, reflections & dislikes?—Nobody!

To Nobody, then, will I write my Journal! since To Nobody can I be wholly unreserved—to Nobody can I reveal every thought, every wish of my Heart, with the most unlimited confidence, the most unremitting sincerity to the end of my Life! For what chance, what accident can end my connections with Nobody? No secret *can* I conceal from No—body, & to No—body can I be *ever* unreserved. Disagreement cannot stop our affection, Time itself has no power to end our friendship. The love, the esteem I entertain for Nobody, No-body's self has not power to destroy. From Nobody I have nothing to fear, [the] Secrets sacred to friendship,

---

1 Inserted by FBA.
2 FB's sister, Susan.

Nobody will not reveal, when the affair is doubtful, Nobody will not look towards the side least favourable—.

I will suppose you, then, to be my best friend; tho' God forbid you ever should! my dearest companion—& a romantick Girl, for mere oddity may perhaps be more sincere—more *tender*—than if you were a friend [in] propia personae—in as much as imagionation often exceeds reality. In your Breast my errors may create pity without exciting contempt; may raise your compassion, without eradicating your love.

From this moment, then, my dear Girl—but why, permit me to ask, must a *female* be made Nobody? Ah! my dear, what were this world good for, *were* Nobody a female? And now I have done with *preambulation*.

[...]

2.   Monday Night May 30th.

[*FB describes a family party with music.*]
[...]—there, freed from the noise & bustle of the World, enjoy'd the [xxx] *harmony* of chattering—& the melody of Musick!—there, burying each gloomy thought, each sad reflection, in the Hearse of disipation, lost the remembrance of our woes, our cruel misfortunes, our agonising sorrows—& graciously permitted them to glide along the stream of reviving comfort, blown by the gentle gale of new born hopes till they reposed in the bosom of oblivion—then————no! 'tis impossible! this style is too great, too [noble][1] to be supported with proper dignity—the sublime & beautifull how charmingly blended!—Yes! I *will* desist—I *will* lay down my pen while I can with [honour]—it would be miraculous had I power to maintain the same glowing enthusiasm, the same————on my word I can*not* go on—my imagionation is raised *too* high—it Soars above this little dirty sphere—it transports me beyond mortality—it conveys me to the Elysian fields—but my ideas grow confused—I fear you cannot comprehend my meaning—all I shall add, is to beg you would please to attribute your not understanding the sublimity of my sentiments to your own stupidity & dullness of apprehension, & not to any want of meaning.

---

1 Substitution.

After this beautiful flow of expression, refinement of sentiment & exaltation of ideas, can I meanly descend to common life?—can I basely stoop to relate the particulars of common Life?—Can I condescendingly diegn to recapitulate vulgar conversation?—[xxx] I can. !—

[...]

3.   From Lynne Regis[1]

[...]

I am Reading the Letters of Henry & Frances,[2] & like them pro-didgiously. I have Just finish'd M^rs. Rowe's Letters from the Dead to the Living—& moral & Entertaining.[3]—I had heard a great deal of them before I saw them, & am sorry to tell you I was much dis-appointed with them: they are so very enthusiastick, that the religion she preaches rather disgusts & cloys than charms & elevates—& so romantick, that every word betrays improbability, instead of disguising fiction, & displays the Author, instead of human nature. For my own part, I cannot be much pleased without an appearance of truth; at least of possibility—I wish the [story][4] to be natural tho' the sentiments are refined; & the Characters to be probable, tho' their behaviour is excelling. [...]

4.   Tuesday—Cabin.[5]

I have this very moment finish'd Reading a Novel call'd the Vicar of Wakefield. It was wrote by D^r. Goldsmith, Athour of the Comedy of the Good-natured Man—& several Essays His style is [natural & sensible][6] & I knew it again immediately. This Book is of a very singular kind—I own I began it with distaste & disrelish,

---

1   King's Lynn.
2   *A Series of Genuine Letters between Henry and Frances* (4 vols., 1757,1766) by Richard and Elizabeth Griffith.
3   Elizabeth Rowe, *Friendship in Death: in Twenty Letters from the Dead to the Living* (1728) and *Letters Moral and Entertaining, in Prose and Verse* (1729-33). In FBA's *Camilla* Mrs. Berlinton enthuses over the former (Bk. 6, ch. 5).
4   Substitution.
5   A summerhouse in the garden at King's Lynn.
6   Substitution.

having Just Read the elegant Letters of Henry—the beginning of it, even disgusted me—he mentions his wife with such indifference—such contempt—the contrast of Henry's treatment of Frances struck me—the more so, as it is real—while this tale is fictitious—& then the Style of the latter is so elegantly natural, so tenderly manly, so unassumingly rational!—I own, I was tempted to thro' the Book aside—but there was something in the situation of his Family, which [if it did not interest me, at least] drew me on—& as I proceeded, I was better pleased—the description of his rural felicity, his simple, unaffected contentment—& family domestic happiness, gave me much pleasure—but still, [I was not *satisfied*—] a *something* was wanting to make the Book [please] me—[to make me *feel* for the vicar in every line he writes]—nevertheless, before I was half thro' the 1st. volume, I was, as I may truly express myself, *surprised into Tears*—& in the 2^d. Volume, I really sobb'd. It appears to me, to be impossible any person could Read this Book thro' with a dry Eye [& yet, I don't much like it—my sensations on Reading it were woeful and tender—but it is an inconsistent performance all the same—I was affected without being interested, I was moved without being pleased] [xxx] [He advances]^1 many very bold & singular opinions—for example, he avers that murder is the sole Crime for which Death ought to be the punishment—he goes even farther, & ventures to affirm that our laws in regard to penaltys & punishment are *all* too severe. This Doctrine might be contradicted from the very essence of our religion—Scripture—for [xxx] in the Bible—in Exodus particularly, Death is commanded by God himself for many Crimes besides murder. But this Author shews in all his works a love of peculiarity & of marking originality of Character in others; & therefore I am not surprised he possesses it himself. His vicar is a very venerable old man—his distresses *must* move you [tho' the Tale in itself may fail to please.] There is but very little story, the plot is thin, the incidents very rare, the sentiments uncommon, the vicar is contented, humble, pious, virtuous—but upon the whole [the Book has not at all satisfied my expectations—] how far more was I pleased with the genuine productions of Mr. Griffith's pen—for that is the real name of Henry.—[I hear that 2 more volumes are lately published—I wish I could get them—I have read but 2—] the elegance & delicacy of the manner—expressions—style—of

---

1 Inserted by FBA.

that Book are so superiour!—How much I should like to be Acquainted with the Writers of it!—those Letters are doubly pleasing, charming to me, for being genuine—[of which, if their own authors left no record, I have *proof positive* from my Mama, who saw the original Letters, with the post marks on them all, at the publisher's Shop. That Book has] encreased my relish for *minute, heartfelt* writing, and encouraged me in my attempts to give an opinion of the Books I Read. [...]

5.   Cabin—Wednesday afternoon.

[...]—I cannot express the pleasure I have in writing down my thoughts, at the very moment—my opinion of people when I first see them, & *how* I alter, or *how* confirm myself in it—& I am very much deceived in my *fore sight*, if I shall not have very great delight in reading this *living proof* of my manner of passing my time, my sentiments, my thoughts of people I know, & a thousand other things, in future.—there is something to me very Unsatisfactory in passing year after year, without even a Memorandum of what you did, &c. And then, all the happy Hours I spend with particular friends and favourites, would fade from my recollection.—

6.   [Sunday.] July 17

[...]
We Live here, generally speaking, in a very [re]gular way—we Breakfast always at 10, & rise as much before as we please—we Dine precisely at 2 Drink Tea about 6—& sup exactly at 9 [&] I make a kind of rule never to indulge myself in my two *most* favourite persuits, reading & writing, in the morning—No, like a very good Girl I give that up wholly, Accidental occasions & preventions excepted, to [needle][1] work, by which means my Reading & writing in the afternoon is a pleasure I [am not] blamed for, [& does me no harm,] as it does not take the Time I ought to spend otherwise. I never pretend to be so superiour a Being as to be above having and indulging a *Hobby Horse*, & while I keep mine within due bounds & limits, Nobody, I flatter myself, would wish to deprive me of the poor Animal: to be sure, he is not form'd for labour, & is rather lame & weak, but then the dear Creature is faithful, constant, & loving, & tho' he

---

1   Inserted by FBA.

sometimes prances, would not kick any one into the mire, or hurt a single soul for the world—& I would not part with him for one who could win the greatest prize that ever *was* won at any Races. Alas, alas! my poor Journal!—how dull, unentertaining, uninteresting thou art!—oh what would I give for some Adventure worthy reciting—for something which would surprise—astonish you!— [Would to Cupid I was in love!—Shall I never feel that so much desired passion—& are you not sick, my dear, at so foolish a wish? Even myself I balk at writing willful middling nonsense. I have very] lately Read the Prince of Abyssinia[1]—I am almost equally charm'd & shock'd at it—the style, the sentiments are inimitable— but the subject is dreadful—&, handled as it is by Dr. Johnson, might make *any* young, perhaps old, person tremble—O [heavens!] how dreadful, how terrible it is to be told by a man of his genius and knowledge, in so affectingly probable a manner, that true, real happiness is ever unattainable in this world!—Thro' all the scenes, publick or private, domestick or solitary, that Nekaya or Rasselas pass, real felicity eludes their pursuit & mocks their solicitude. In high Life, superiority, envy & haughtiness battle the power of preferement, favour & greatness—[and with or without] them, all is Animosity, suspicion, apprehension, & misery—in Private familys, disagreement, Jealousy & partiality, destroy all domestick felicity & all social chearfulness, & all is peevishness, contradiction, ill will & wretchedness!—And in Solitude, Imagionation paints the World in a new light, every bliss which was wanting when in it, appears easily attain'd when away from it, but the [universal] loneliness of retirement seems unsocial dreary, [misanthropical] & melancholy— & all is anxiety, doubt, fear & anguish! In this manner does Dr. Johnson proceed in his melancholy conviction of the impossibility of all human enjoyments, & the impossibility of all earthly happiness. One thing during the Course of the successless enquiry struck me, which gave me much comfort, which is, that those who wander in the world avowedly & purposely in search of happiness, who view every scene of present Joy with an Eye to what may succeed, certainly are more liable to disappointment, misfortune & unhappiness, than those who give up their fate to chance and take the goods & evils of fortune as they come, without making happiness their study, or misery their foresight.

[...]

---

1 Johnson's *The History of Rasselas, Prince of Abyssinia* (1759).

And so I suppose you are staring at the torn paper, & unconnected sentences—I don't much wonder—I'll tell you how it happen'd. Last Monday I was in the little parlour, which Room my
papa generally dresses in—& writing a Letter to my Grand mama
[Sleepe][1]—You must know I always have the last sheet of my Journal in my pocket, & when I have wrote it half full—I Join it to the
rest, & take another sheet—& so on. Now I happen'd, unluckily, to
take the last sheet out of my pocket with my Letter—& laid it on
the piano forte, & there, negligent fool!—I left it. [Unfortunately
while we were at Mrs. Allen's on Sunday Evening, I wrote about
half a page in which I mention'd poor Susan [xxx] teazing me with
particular questions on a *particular* subject, which related to a *particular* case, concerning Mama—Can you not guess *what*?[2]—[xxx] &
besides this, I mentioned several other little matters—] Well, as ill
fortune would have it, papa went into the Room—took my poor
Journal—Read & pocketed it! Mama came up to me & told me of
it. O Dear! I was in a sad distress—I could not for the Life of me
ask for it—& so *dawdled* & fretted the time away till Tuesday
Evening. Then, gathering courage—"Pray, papa—have—you
got—any *papers* of mine?—" "Papers of yours?—said he—how
should *I* come by papers of yours?—" "I'm sure—I don't know—
but"—"Why do you leave your papers about the House?" asked
he, gravely—I could not say another word—& he went on playing
the Piano Forte. Well, to be sure, thought I, these same dear Journals are most shocking plaguing things—I've a good mind to
resolve never to write a word more.—However, I stayed still in the
Room, working, & looking wistfully at him for about an Hour &
half. At last, he rose to Dress—Again I look'd wistfully at him—he
laugh'd—"what, Fanny, s^d. he, kindly—are you in sad distress?—" I
half laugh'd—"well—I'll give it you, now I see you are in such distress———but take care, my dear, of leaving your writings about
the House again—Suppose Any body else had found it—I declare
I was going to Read it loud—Here—take it—but if ever I find any
more of your Journals, I vow I'll stick them up in the market

---

1 Mother of CB's first wife, FB's own mother, Esther Sleepe Burney.
2 Possibly a reference to EAB's pregnancy. FB's half-brother Richard was
   born in November 1768.

place!" And then he kiss'd me *so* kindly—Never was parent so *properly*, so *well-Judged* affectionate!

I was so frightened that I have not had the Heart to write since, till now, I should not but that————in short, but that I cannot help it!—As to the *paper*, [xxx] [I destroyed it the][1] moment I got it. [...]

8.　　　　Transcript of a lost portion
　　　　from the journal for 1768.

I have been having a long conversation with Miss Young[2] on journals. She has very seriously and earnestly advised me to give mine up—heigho-ho! Do you think I can bring myself to oblige her? What she says has great weight with me; but, indeed, I should be very loath to *quite* give my poor friend up. She says that it is the most dangerous employment young persons can have—that it makes them often record things which ought *not* to be recorded, but instantly forgot. I told her, that as *my* Journal was *solely* for my own perusal, nobody could in justice, or even in sense, be angry or displeased at my writing any thing.

"But how can you answer," said she, "that it *is* only for your perusal? That very circumstance of your papa's finding it, shows you are not so very careful as is necessary for such a work. And if you drop it, and any improper person finds it, you know not the uneasiness it may cost you."

"Well but, dear ma'am, this is an 'if' that may not happen once in a century."

"I beg your pardon; I know not how often it may happen; and even *once* might prove enough to give you more pain than you are aware of."

"Why, dear ma'am, papa never prohibited my writing, and he knows that I *do* write, and *what* I do write."

"I question that. However, 'tis impossible for you to answer for the curiosity of others. And suppose any body finds a part in which they are extremely censured."

"Why then, they must take it for their pains. It was not wrote for *them*, but *me*, and I cannot see any harm in writing to *myself.*"

1　Inserted by FBA.
2　Dorothy (Dolly) Young of King's Lynn, a spinster who had been a close friend of Esther Sleepe Burney.

"It was very well whilst there were only your sisters with you to do anything of this kind; but, depend upon it, when your connections are enlarged, your family increased, your acquaintance multiplied, young and old *so* apt to be curious—depend upon it, Fanny, 'tis the most dangerous employment you can have. Suppose now, for example, your favourite wish were granted, and you were *to fall in love*, and then the object of your passion were to get sight of some part which related to himself?"

"Why then, Miss Young, I must take a little trip to Rosamond's Pond."[1]

"Why, ay, I doubt it would be all you would have left."

"Dear Miss Young!—But I'm sure, by your earnestness, that you think worse of my poor Journal than it deserves."

"I know very well the nature of these things. I know that in journals, thoughts, actions, looks, conversations—*all* go down; do they not?"

The conclusion of our debate was, that if I would show her some part of what I had wrote she should be a better judge, and would then give me her best advice whether to proceed or not. I believe I shall accept her condition; though I own I shall show it with shame and fear, for such nonsense is *so* unworthy her perusal.

I'm sure, besides, I know not what part to choose. Shall I take at random?

JOURNAL FOR 1768

9.   Wednesday, August the 10th.

[...]

Well, my Nobody, I *have* read part of my Journal to Miss Young—& what's more, let her chuse the Day herself, which was our Journey, & the Day in which I have mention'd our arrival, &c. I assure you I quite triumph!—prejudiced as she was, she is pleas'd to give it her sanction,—*if it is equally harmless every where*—nay, says she even approves of it.[...] I am Reading Plutarch's Lives—his own, wrote by Dryden has charm'd me beyond expression—I have Just finish'd Lycurgus[2]—& am as much *pleased* with all his publick

---

1   That is, to drown herself. Rosamund's Pond in St. James's Park was a rendezvous for lovers and a scene of suicides until 1770 when it was filled in.
2   Founder of the Spartan constitution.

Laws, as *dis*pleased with his private ones. There is scarce *one* of the former which is not noble & praiseworthy—&, as *I* think, *very* few of the latter which are not the contrary—the custom of only pre-serving healthy Children, & destroying weak ones—how bar-barous!—besides, *all* his domestick family duties appear strange to me!—but you must consider how very, very, very bad a Judge I am, as I read with nobody, & consequently have nobody to correct or guide my opinion: nevertheless, I cannot forbear sometimes writ-ing what it is.

[...] I read Plutarch's Lives with more pleasure than I can express. I am charmed with them, & rejoice exceedingly that I did not Read them ere now; as I every Day, certainly, am more able to enjoy them. I have Just finished Paulus Amilius, whom I love & honour, most particularly for his fondness for his Children, which instead of blushing at, he avows & glories in: and that at an Age, when almost all the Heros & great Men thought that to make their Chil-dren & Family a *secondary* concern, was the first proof of their superiority & greatness of soul, & when, like Brutus, they co'ld stand with a Countenance firm and unmoved & see their sons exe-cution—At such an age, I say, I think the paternal affections of Paulus Amilius his first & principle glory. Insensibility, of all kinds, & on all occasions, most *moves my imperial displeasure*——however, that of the Ancient Romans was acquired by the false notions they had of true greatness & honour.

[...]

10.   Wednesday, Sept^r

[...]

Certainly I have the most complaisant friend in the world—ever ready to comply with my wishes—never hesitating to oblige, never averse to any concluding, yet never wearied with my beginning—charming Creature.

And pray, my dear Miss Fanny, *who* is this?—

Nobody.

Alas alas! what then is to become of Every body?

How should I know? let every body manage themselves & oth-ers as well as I do Nobody, & they will be "Much the same as God made them!"[1]—And now, Adieu my charmer—[xxx] Adieu

---

1   Unidentified.

then—my fair friend—that's one comfort that I can make you fair or brown at pleasure—Just what I will—a creature of my own forming—I am now [going to] Read the Illiad[1]—I cannot help taking notice of one thing in 3^d. Book—which has provoked me for the honour of the Sex: Venus tempts Hellen [with every] delusion in favour of her Darling,—in vain—Riches—power—honour—Love—all in vain——the enraged Deity threatens to deprive her of her own beauty, & render her to the level with the most common of her sex—blushing & trembling—Hellen immediately yields her Hand.

Thus has Homer proved his opinion of our poor sex—that the Love of Beauty is our most prevailing passion. It really grieves me to think that there certainly must be some reason for the insignificant opinion the greatest men have of Women—At least I *fear* there must.—But I don't in fact *believe* it—[thank God!]

1769

JOURNAL FOR 1769

11.   Saturday [*between February and April*]

[...]

I am in a moralising humour.—How truly does this Journal contain my real & undisguised thoughts—I always write in it according to the humour I am in, & if any stranger was [to think it worth] reading, how capricious—[inconsistent] & whimsical I must appear!—one moment flighty & half mad,—the next sad & melancholy. No matter! it's truth & simplicity are it's sole recommendation, & I doubt not but I shall hereafter receive great pleasure from *reviewing* and almost *renewing* my youth & my former sentiments. Unless, indeed, the latter part of my Life is doom'd to be as miserable as the beginning is the reverse, & then indeed, every Line here will rend my Heart—I sigh from the bottom of it at this dreadful idea I think I am in a humour to write a funeral sermon—Hetty is gone to Ranelagh,[2] & I fancy does not *simpathise* with me!
[...]

---

1 In translation.
2 A fashionable public resort in Chelsea.

What an Age since I last wrote!—I have been wavering in my mind whether I should ever again touch this Journal, unless it were to commit it to the Flames—for this same *Mind* of mine, would fain persuade me that this same *Journal* of mine is a very ridiculous—trifling, & useless affair; & as such, would wisely advise me to part with it for ever—but I felt at the same Time; a regret—a loss of some thing in forbearing to *here unburthen* myself—the pleasure which (in imagination at least) awaits me in the perusal of these sheets hereafter, pleaded strongly in favour of continuing to encrease them—& now that I once more have taken Courage to begin, I think I already feel twice the Content I did while this dear little Book was neglected—

[...]

13.   FRANCES BURNEY TO DR. CHARLES BURNEY
                    23 June 1769, London

[*A poem written by FB and sent to CB at Oxford to commemorate his graduation with a Doctorate in Music from Oxford University.*]

To Doctor Last.[1]

1

O aid me, ye Muses of ev'ry Degree,
O give me the Standish[2] of Mulberry Tree
    Which was cut for the Author of Ferney;
O give me a Quil to the Stump worn by Gray[3]
And Paper which cut was on Milton's Birth Day
    To write to the great Doctor Burney.

---

1   FBA annotates the ms. "A Pun, alluding to the character in the Devil on 2 sticks." *The Devil upon Two Sticks* (1768), by Samuel Foote, was a satire on doctors in three acts, in which a shoemaker, Last, applies to the College of Physicians for a license to practise. "Last" is a term for a shoemaker's model.
2   FBA inserts a note "an Ink Standish cut out of a mulberry Tree planted by Shakespear for Mr. Keate, author of Ferney an Epistle to Voltaire."
3   Thomas Gray, a poet best known for his "Elegy written in a country churchyard" (1751).

2

O Doctor, of Doctor's the Last & the Best,
By Fortune most honour'd, distinguish'd & blest,
  And may you for ever be her nigh!
O smile (if a Doctor's permitted to smile),
Your natural gravity lessen a while
  To Read this, O dread Doctor Burney.

3

For the Letter most kind we to Day did receive
With grateful affection our Bosom's do heave;
  And to see you, O grave sir! how yern I!
'Tis true the Time's short since you last was in Town
Yet both fatter & Taller you doubtless are grown
  Or you'll make but a poor Doctor Burney.

4

For I never can think of a Doctor, not big
As a Falstaf,[1] & not with a full bottom'd Wig
  And the sly air Fame gives an Attorney;
Not more at the Bag did the Citizen's stare
Of Harley,[2] when Harley was made a Lord Mayor,
  Than I at the thin Doctor Burney.

5

O! may Wisdom, which still to good humour
                    gives Birth
May fatness with dignity, goodness with mirth,
  Still attend you, & speed your Town Journey!
And O! till the Hour that Death us shall part
May Fanny a Corner possess of the Heart
  Of the owner of her's, Doctor Burney!

---

1 Sir John Falstaff from Shakespeare's *Henry IV*, Parts 1 and 2.
2 Thomas Harley, Lord Mayor of London, disregarded custom in 1768
   when he wore an informal bag-wig for his installation ceremony, instead
   of the traditional full-bottomed wig.

14.   Mersh—June 29th.
                                           Thursday Night.

[...]
[*FB reports her father's return from Oxford on the previous Sunday.*]
Well,—when Papa had been [in] a short Time, unfortunately a
[new] play called Dr. Last in his Chariot, was mentioned [by my
Cousin, who was with us.][1] Papa looked at me—I looked any
other way—"O you sawcy Girl!" cried he—Charles appeared
curious, I was horidly ashamed—"What do you think, continued
papa [to my Cousin—] do you know this abominable Girl calls me
Dr. Last?—"

Charles & Hetty both Laughed, & papa took out the Letter &
holding it out to me said "come, do me the favour of Reading
this!—" I would fain have torn it, but papa drew it back, & was
going to Read it—I beg'd him not—but *in vain*, & so I ran out of
the Room—but to own the truth, my curiosity prevail'd so far, that
I could not forbear running down stairs again with more speed
than up, & into the next Room [& heard these comments.] I
found, by papa's voice & manner, that he did not appear displeased—tho' he half-affected to be so—he Read it loud—[they all
Laughed very much—] "I assure you, said Papa, 'tis very *good
stuff!*—I Read it to Mrs. Playdel, & she was much pleased—particularly with the last stanza—& to one or 2 of my new Oxford
friends at Breakfast, & we had a very hearty Laugh.—"

This was enough—I ran once more up stairs, & lighter than a
Feather felt my Heart!

[I was monstrously ashamed of appearing at supper—Papa
sawced me not a little—but as I found he was not at all sincerely
angry, I bore it *very tolerably.*]
[...]
O—but one thing has very much vexed me—my Papa had
Read my nonsense to Mrs. Skinner, an intimate acquaintance & a
very clever woman, & she insisted on having a Copy, which papa
desired me to write—. I was horid mad, & beged most earnestly to
be excused; for such trash, however it may serve to Read at the

1   Charles Rousseau Burney.

moment, must be shocking a second Time but Papa would take no denial—"It's very sufficient, said he for the occasion, and for your Age." However I am as much mortified at doing this, as if my first fear had been verified, for I cannot at all relish being thus exposed to a *deliberate* examination.—

[...]

1770

JOURNAL FOR 1770

15.   January 10th:

[...]
In truth, I have a most delightful subject to commence the present Year with—such a one, as I fear I may never chance to meet with again—Yet why should I look into futurity with a gloomy Eye?—But let me Wave all this Nonsense, & tell you, my dear, faithful, ever attentive Nobody,—that I was last Monday, at a Masquerade!

Has Nobody any curiosity to Read an Account of this Frolick? I am sure Nobody has, and Nobody will I satisfy by Writing One. I am so good natured as to prevent Nobody's wishes.

This Masquerade—how does that word grace my Journal!— was, however, a very private one & at the House of M^r. Laluze, a French Dancing master. [He at first intended it only as an Amusement for his own scholars, but afterwards enlarged his plans to inviting almost All his Acquaintance. [...] It is easy to believe that we were niether of us averse to it, though it was some time ere we had my Father's consent, not from his being unwilling to give it, but from our being half afraid to ask it—though we afterwards found that he had thought there would be only Children there, on account of M^r. Laluze's profession,—& to that idea, I fancy we owed our Frolick.]

Hetty had for 3 months thought of nothing but the Masquerade—no more had I.—She had long fixed upon her Dress; my stupid Head only set about one on Friday Evening. I could think of no Character which I liked much, and could obtain; as to Nuns, Quakers, &c, (which I was much advised to) I cannot help thinking there is a gravity & extreme reserve required to support them, which would have made me necessarily so dull & stupid, that I could not have met with much entertainment, & being unable to fix on a *Character*, I resolved at length to go in a meer *fancy Dress*. [In truth, I was so long wavering & irresolute, that I had Time for no other, & at a masquerade every thing is allowable.]

> One Day—and who could do it less in?
> The Masqueraders spent in Dressing.—[1]

It is really true that all Monday we passed in *preparationing* for the Evening, [for my own part, I was really working to the last moment, & my Aunt Anne was assisting me.]
[...]

Hetty went as a Savoyard, with a [Pompadour-Jacket trimed with Blue, and a Blue Coat trimmed with pompadour, a plain Gause Handkerchief tied under her Chin, white shoes & *Blue Roses*, a short Gause Apron very prettily trimed, white mittens, & to complete her a Vielle or] *Hurdy Gurdy*[2] fasten'd round her waist. Nothing could look more simple, innocent or pretty.

My Dress was, a close pink persian *Vest*, [with long close sleeves, to my Wrists, it was] covered with Gause, in loose pleats [behind, & drawn half tight & half loose at the sleeve, *puckered* before, with very small pink Flowers fastened on to look like buttons, it came up high in the Neck, & had a Gause frill round the Waist. My Coat was white silk trimed also with small artificial flowers before, & a Gause train looped up behind, & pink ribband round the Bottom. I had pink silk shoes & Roses, a very small black color[3] about my Neck, &] a little Garland or Wreath of Flowers on the left sight of my Head, [& looped Pearl Earings.

Thus my Dress, being a regular one, has taken twice the Time to describe as Hetty's did.]
[...]

[*A group of visitors to the Burney household admired the masqueraders' dress.*]

The Captain had a fine opportunity for gallantry—to say the truth, those whimsical dresses are not unbecoming. He made a story for me "That I had been *incarcerated* by the Grand Seignor as

---

1 Parody of Swift's "The Lady's Dressing Room" (1730).
2 A musical instrument similar to a barrel-organ, played by turning a handle.
3 Collar.

a part of the Seraglio [& made] prisoner by the Russians in the present War;[1] & that the generosity of the commanding Officer had prevailed with him to grant me my Liberty, & that I had consequently thrown myself into the protection of the bravest and noblest People of Europe, & sought shelter from oppression in this Land of Freedom."

[...]

We called for Miss Strange, & then went to M^r. Lalause, who lives in Leicester Square. Miss Strange had a White sattin Domino [trimed with Blue.] M^r. & M^{rs}. Lalause were niether in *Masquerade*, [but received us in *propria Personae*.] The Room was large, & very well lighted, *but*, when we first went in, not half filled, so that every Eye was turned on each new Comer—I felt extremely awkward & abashed, notwithstanding my mask, [the more so as we were all separated in a moment.] Hetty went in, playing on her *Hurdy Gurdy*, & the Company flocked about her with much pleasure. I was soon found out by Miss Lalause who is a fine Girl, about 16, [& apppears to be very fond of Hetty & me:] she had on a *fancy* Dress, [& except that she had a great deal of silver Braid on it, it was] much in the style of mine. The first mask who accosted me was an Old Witch, Tall, shrivell'd, leaning on a Broom stick, & in short a fear inspiring figure, apparently, by his Walk, a Man. [You must know that my mask had been made by my Cousin (who was also one of the spectators of our curious Dresses) & not quite so well as I expected, but it was finished too late for me to get another. The Witch began] "Thou thinkest, then, that that little bit of Black silk is a mask?—"

I was absolutely confounded, for I thought directly that he meant to Laugh at my mask, but on recollection I believe he was going on with some [thing else,] but I was so unable to rally, that with a silly half Laugh, I turned on my Heel & Walked away.

[O clever, thought I, this is a dismal beginning. However, I grew more courageous after being there some Time.]

I observed a Nun, Dressed in Black, who was speaking with great earnestness, & who discovered by her Voice to be a Miss Milne, a pretty Scotch Nymph I have met at M^{rs}. Strange's. I [addressed myself] to her. She turn'd about & took my Hand & led me into a Corner of the Room—"Beautiful Creature! cried she, in a plaintive Voice, "with what pain do I see you here, beset by this

___

1 The Russo-Turkish war, 1768-74.

Crowd of folly & deceit! O could I prevail on you to quit this wicked world, & all it's vices, & to follow my footsteps!"

"But how am I to account, said I, for the reason that one who so much despises the world, should chuse to mix with the gayest part of it?

"I come but, said she, to see & to save such innocent, beautiful, young Creatures as you from the snares of the Wicked. Listen to me, I was once such as you are, I mixed with the World; I was caressed by it, I loved it—I was deceived!—surrounded by an artful set of flattering, designing men, I fell but too easily into the net they spread for me. I am now convinced of the vanity of Life, & in this peaceful, tranquil state shall I pass the remainder of my Days."

"It is so impossible, said I, to listen to you without being benefitted by your Conversation, that I shall to the utmost of my power *imitate you*, & always chuse to despise the World, & hold it in contempt.—at a *masquerade!*—"

"Alas, said she, I am here meerly to contemplate on the strange follys & vices of mankind—this scene affords me only a subject of joy to think I have quitted it."

We were here interrupted, & parted. After that I had several short conversations with different masks—I will tell you the principal Dresses as well as I can recollect them. [They were]

A Punch, who was indeed very completely Dressed, & who very well supported his Character. The Witch whom I mentioned before was a very capital Figure, & told many Fortunes with great humour. A Shepherd, of all Characters the last, were I a man, I should have wished to have assumed; A Harliquin, who hop'd & skip'd about very lightly & gayly; A Huntsman, who indeed seemed suited for nothing but the company of Dogs, a Gardener, A Persian, 2 or 3 Turks, & 2 Friars—A Merlin, who spoke of spells, magick & charms with all the *mock heroick* and bombast manner which his Character could require. There were also two most jolly looking sailors, & many Dominos, besides some Dresses which I have forgot. Among the Females, two sweet little Nuns in white pleased me most; there was a very complete shepherdess, with the gayest Crook, the smartest little Hat, & most trifling Conversation one might desire; never the less full as clever as her choice of so hackneyed & insipid a Dress led one to expect—you may imagion that she was immediately & unavoidably paired with the amiable shepherd I mentioned before. There were 2 or 3 young pastoral Nymphs to keep her in Countenance; &, I can recollect no other Dresses, save an Indian Queen; & Dominos.

I siezed the first opportunity that offered of again joining my sage monitor the fair Nun—who did not seem averse to honouring me with her Conversation. She renewed her former subject, expatiated on the wicked[ness of mankind] & degeneracy of the World, dwelt with great energy and warmth on the deceit & craft of Man, & pressed me to join her holy Order with the zeal of an Enthusiast [in religion.] [xxx] a pink Domino advanced, & charged her not to instill her preposterous sentiments into my Mind; she answered him with so much contempt that he immediately quitted us.—We were then accosted by the shepherd, who would fain have appeared of some consequence, & aimed at being gallant & agreeable—Poor man! wofully was he the contrary. The Nun did not spare him. "Hence," cried she, "thou gaudy Animal, with thy trifling & ridiculous trappings away—let not this fair Creature be corrupted by thy Company. O fly the pernicious impertinence of these shadows which surround thee!—" "The—the Lady—stammered the poor swain—"the Lady will be—will be more likely—to be hurt—by—by you than—than—" "Yes, yes," cried she, "she would be safe enough were she followed only by such as Thee!" Hetty just then bid me observe a very droll old Dutch man, who soon after joined us—He accosted us in High Dutch— —not that I would Quarrel with any one who told me it was *Low* Dutch!—[Heaven knows] it might be Arabick for ought I could tell! He was very completely Dressed, & had on an exceeding droll old man's mask, & was smoaking a Pipe—He presented me with a Quid of Tobaco, I accepted it very cordially:—the Nun was not disposed to be pleased—she attacked poor Mynheer with much haughtiness—"Thou savage!—hence to thy native Land of Brutes & Barbarians, smoak thy Pipe there, but pollute not us with thy [bestial] coarse attempts at Wit & pleasantry—[Man, go to the Witch, quit this civilised people & seek company suited to thy own jovially vulgar manners, *this* set, believe me, is too polished, too refined to be adapted to your taste!"]

The Dutch man however heeded her not, he amused himself with talking & making signs [of devotion][1] to me, while the Nun [abused], & I Laughed.—At last she took my Hand, & led me to another part of the Room, where we renewed our former Conversation. "You see," she cried, "what a Herd of Danglers flutter

---

1 Inserted by FBA.

around you; thus it once was with me; your form is elegant; your Face I doubt not is beautiful; your sentiments are superior to both: regard these Vipers then with a proper disdain; they will follow you, will admire, Court, caress & flatter you—they will engage your affections—& then they will quit you! it is not that you are less amiable, or that they cease to esteem you; but they are weary of you; novelty must attone in another for every loss they may regret in you:—it is not merit they seek, but variety. *I* speak from experience!"

I could almost have taken my Nun for M^r. Crisp in disguise. "'Tis rather surprising," said I, "that one who speaks with such rigour of the World, & [professes]^1 having quitted it from *knowing* it's degeneracy, & who talks of experience in the style of Age; should have a Voice which is a perpetual reminder of her own Youth; & should in all *visible* respects, be so formed to grace & adorn the World she holds in such contempt."

"Hold," cried she, "remember my sacred order; & remember that we Nuns can never admit to our Conferences that baleful Enemy of innocence, Flattery! Alas, you learn this from Men! Would you but renounce them! what happiness would such a Convert give me!"

["Never yet did I see an example before me, said I, which could possibly be so striking, & never did I feel *more* inclination to quit this seducing World which has incurred your resentment & hatred. The example you just have set is peculiarly engaging & in coming, like you, to masquerades, & entering into the spirit of them to the utmost of my power, depend upon my remembering your precepts, & following your example!"

The Nun had recourse to her former justification.] The Dutchman & the shepherd soon joined us again—the former was very liberal of his tobaco, & supported his Character with much drollery, speaking no English, but a few Dutch words, & making signs. The shepherd seemed formed for all the stupidity of a Dutch man more than the man who assumed that Dress; but *he* aimed at something superior.—[My mask gave me a courage I never before had in the presence of strangers, & I did not spare either of them, though I cannot say I ventured so far as] the Nun, [who] looking

---

1 Substitution.

on her Veil and Habit as a sanction to the utmost liberty of speech [she desired,] spoke to them both without the least ceremony. [Niether did I *wish* to use them as she had done]—All she said to *Me* did honour to the Name she assumed—it was sensible, & delicate, it was *probably* very true; it was *certainly* very well adapted to her apparent character: but when we were joined by men, her exhortations degenerated into [ranting]; which though she might intend the better to support her part, by displaying her indignation against the sex, nevertheless seemed rather suited to the virulency & bitterness of a revengeful woman of the World, than the gentleness & dignity which were expected from the piety, patience & forbearance of a Cloister. "And what," said she to the Dutch man, what can have induced such a savage to venture himself here? Go, seek thy fellow Brutes! the vulgar, bestial society thou art used too, is such alone as thou ought to mix with."

He *jabbered* something in his defence, & seemed inclined to make his Court to me. "Perhaps, said she, "it may be in the power of this fair Creature to reform thee; she may civilise thy gross & barbarous manners." The Dutch man bowed, said *yaw*, & put his Hand on his Heart in token of approbation. "Ay, said the poor shepherd, whose Eyes had the most marked expression of stupidity (if stupidity can be said to have *any* expression) that I ever saw, & his words & manner so exactly coincided with his appearance, that he was meerly an object for Laughter.—He served only for such to *me* at least; for indeed my spirits were not very low. [He affected to Laugh at the Dutch man, who soon after left us. The Nun attacked him openly on his stupidity & advised him to be silent.] [...]

[Refreshments were then brought, & every body was engaged with a Partner; Merlin, a delightful mask, secured Hetty, & the Dutchman my Ladyship. Everybody was then unmasked.][1]
[I] turned hastily round, & saw a [young man] so very like M^r. Young that at the first glance I thought it was him, but what was my surprise at seeing the Dutch man! I had no idea that he was under 50, when behold he scarse Looked three & Twenty. I believe my surprise was very manifest, for Mynheer could not forbear

---

1 Inserted by FBA.

Laughing. On his part he paid me many Compliments, repeatedly & with much civility congratulating himself on his [Choice. Whether pleased or not he could not well help appearing, & he did not spare himself in Words to Paint himself so. But though few things are more agreeable at the moment than Compliments spoke with an air of sincerity, yet] [xxx]

Nothing could be more droll than the first Dance we had after unmasking; to see the pleasure which appeared in some Countenances, & the disappointment pictured in others made the most singular contrast imaginable, & to see the Old turned Young, & the Young Old,—in short every Face appeared different from what we expected. The old Witch in particular we found was a young Officer; the Punch who had made himself as Broad as long, was a very young and handsome man—but what most surprised me, was the shepherd whose own Face was so stupid that we could scarsely tell whether he had taken off his mask or not!

[...]

16.   *FEMALE CAUTION*
        ADDRESSED TO MISS ALLEN.

[*Verses composed by FB around December 1770, when Maria Allen was jilted by her suitor Martin Rishton. They later married.*]

Ah why in faithless Man repose
The peace & safety of your mind?
Why should ye seek a World of woes,
To Prudence and to Wisdom blind?

★

Few of mankind confess your worth,
Fewer reward it with their own:
To Doubt and Terror Love gives birth;
To Fear and Anguish makes ye known.

★

The roseate Cheeks, the sparkling Eyes
Which bright in liquid lustre swim,
Love views but as his destin'd prize
Those Cheeks to fade, those Eyes to dim.

★

Your minds, ingenuous, open, just,
To Love, to Tenderness inclin'd,
  Unguarded, the Deceivers trust,
Nor, till too late, the error find.

★

While They, inur'd to specious art
Seek but their vanity to feed;
  Complete the conquest of the Heart
Then leave that wretched heart to bleed.

★

In vain the Inconstant are accus'd;
In vain the Injur'd may upbraid,
  Mourn their credulity abus'd,
Their sensibility betray'd!

★

The lovely Harriet, gay and fair,
Possest the happiest power to please;
  Her sparkling Eye, her Smile, her Air,
Often sportive, spoke a mind at ease:

★

Till false Alcanor saw the Maid,
And aim'd the conquest of her heart:
  With fatal excellence he play'd
A vile, insinuating part

★

Adieu to Freedom, & to Ease!
The breast that Love admits they leave:
  The wayward Swain's attentions cease;
'Tis His to rove — 'tis Hers to grieve.

★

O, Wiser, learn to guard the heart,
Nor let it's softness be its bane!
  Teach it to act a nobler part;
What Love shall lose, let Friendship gain.

★

Hail, Friendship, hail! To Thee My Soul
Shall undivided homage own;
  No Time thy influence shall control;
And Love and I ... shall ne'er be known.

★

1771

17.   July 3ᵈ.

[...]

[*FB describes a house party at Chessington, where the guests included Jane Barsanti, a soprano singer who had formerly been a pupil of CB. After losing her singing voice, she became an actress.*]

Miss Barsanti has great Theatrical talents; her Voice is entirely lost, but [still] her Mother designs her for the stage, [& as she was his pupil] my Father [consulted them about it, & he went to] beg Mʳ. Crisp would hear her *spout*, while she was at Chesington. To make her acting less formidable to her, Miss Allen[1] & myself proposed to perform with her; & accordingly we got by heart some scenes from the Careless Husband,[2] in which she chose to be Edging—myself Lady Easy—& Miss Allen Sir Charles!—that [good] Girl has so very great a love of sport & mirth, that there is nothing upon Earth she will not do to contribute to it.

We had no sooner fixed upon this scheme, than we were perplexed about the Dressing Sir Charles.—We all agreed that it would be ridiculous for that gallant man to appear in Petticoats, & [Allen] had no idea of *spoiling sport*,—she only determined not to exhibit before Mʳ. Featherstone; [3] as to Mʳ. Crisp, as he was half author of the project, we knew it would be in vain to attempt excluding him,—& Mʳ. Burney could not be avoided—besides, [a Brother!—] his Cloaths she intended to borrow; but unluckily, we found upon enquiry, he had no Wardrobe with him, [& the Cloaths he wore were all his stock.] This quite disconcerted us. Mʳ. Crisp was so tall & large, it was impossible [Allen] could wear any thing of his.—we were long in great perplexity upon this account; but being unwilling to give the frolic up, Allen at length, though very mad at it, resolved upon the only expedient left—to borrow Cloaths of Mʳ. Featherstone. I never met a character so little damped by difficulties as hers—indeed she seldom sees any, &

---

1 Maria Allen, FB's stepsister.
2 By Colley Cibber, first performed in 1704.
3 Probably one of the boarders at Chessington Hall.

when she cannot help it, always surmounts them, [& never submits to be conquered by any, however formidable they may appear.]

To ask this of him, made his being one of the Audience inevitable;—but it was the last resource. Accordingly, [Allen] & Barsanti watched one morning for his coming into the Gallery up stairs, from which all the Bed chambers lead, & addressed themselves to him very gravely, to [beg] the favour of him to lend them a suit of Cloaths. [The man] laughed monstrously, & assumed no small consequence, on their begging him to keep the affair secret, as they intended to surprise the company, for they were obliged to explain the motives of the request. This seemed something like confidence, & flattered him into better temper than we ever saw him in. he led them to his Wardrobe, & [begged] Allen to chuse to her fancy. She fixed upon a suit of dark blue uncut Velvet.—I was in a Closet at the End of the Gallery, not able to compose my countenance sufficiently to join them, till a loud Laugh raised my curiosity.—I found she had just been begging the favour of a Wig; & he produced a most beautiful tye, which he told her his man should dress for her. She then asked for stock, shoes, Buckles, Ruffles, [stockings,] & all with great gravity, assisted by Barsanti, who reminded her of so many things, I thought she could never have been satisfied. M^r. Featherstone enjoyed it prodigiously, sniggering & joking, & resting upon his Crutches to Laugh: for my own part, the torrent of their ridiculous requests, made me every minute march out of the Room [to laugh more freely.]^1 [When every thing was adjusted, & we were all retiring, Barsanti, as if suddenly recollecting herself, returned, & with great gravity, told M^r. Featherstone that Miss Allen was ashamed to tell him, that he had forgot a shirt. I now ran away with all speed, not able any longer to keep with them, both from laughter, & really from shame.]

[...]

On [Sunday] morning, rehearsing our parts, we found them so short that we wished to add another scene, & as there is a good deal of drollery in the quarel[ling scene] between Sir Charles Easy & Lady Graveairs, we fixed upon that, Miss Allen to continue as Sir Charles, & Barsanti to change her Cap, or so, & appear

---

1 Inserted by FBA.

as Lady Graveairs. [It was with great difficulty I prevailed upon them to give up the 1st. scene of the 5th. Act, but I had an insuperable aversion to doing any part, even that of Lady Easy, in such a scene.]^1

While they studdied their parts, Kitty Cooke & myself, as we frequently did, walked out, visiting all the Cottages within a mile of Chesington. Upon our return to Dinner, Barsanti told us she found the *new scene* too long to get in Time, [& said she had given it up.] Miss Allen & I, [being] both sorry, after some deliberation, agreed to perform it ourselves, &, accordingly, [after Dinner,] we hurried up stairs, & made all possible Expedition in getting our parts, resolving not to Act till after supper, [xxx] [not being ready then.] While we were studdying with great diligence, Miss Barsanti ran up [stairs], & told us that M^r. Crisp had informed all the Company of our intention, & that they were [now] very eager for our performance, & declared they would never forgive us if we disappointed them. This flurried me violently, insomuch, that my memory failed me, & I forgot my old part, without seeming to learn my new one. I can, in general, get by Heart with the *utmost facility*, but I really was so much [agitated] that my Head seemed to turn round, & I scarce knew what I was about. [...]

We [all] retired after supper, & could not forbear being highly diverted at seeing [Allen] Dress herself. M^r. Featherstone's cloaths fitted her horribly—the back preposterously broad—the sleeves too wide,—the Cuffs hiding her Hand—yet the Coat hardly long enough—niether was the Wig large enough to hide her Hair; &, in short, she appeared the most dapper, ill shaped, ridiculous figure I ever saw. Yet her Face looked remarkably well.

[Hetty, who was not well, & refused to join us, nevertheless was eager to make us begin]—my [*Terour*] every moment encreased—but in vain—they insisted upon no further delay—& accordingly we descended.—[Hetty first joined our audience, having prepared us a stage.] As we came down, the servants were all in the Hall, & the first object that struck us, was M^r. Featherstone's man, staring in speechless astonishment at the Figure in his master's Cloaths.

Unfortunately for me, I was to appear first, & alone.—I was pushed on,—they clapped violently—I was fool enough to run

---

1 FB may have objected to this scene because in it Lady Graveairs makes an assignation with Sir Charles Easy.

off, quite overset, & unable to speak. I was really in an agony of fear & shame!—& when, at last, [Allen] & Barsanti persuaded me to go on again,—the former, [having,] in the lively warmth of her Temper, called to [them] *not to Clap again, for it was very imperti-nant*;—I had lost all power of speaking steadily, & almost of being understood; & as to action, I had not the presence of mind to attempt it: [surely,] only M^r. Crisp could excite such extreme ter-ror [in me!] My soliloquy at length over, *Edging* entered, with great spirit, & spoke very well. I was almost breathless the whole scene—& O how glad when it was over!—Sir Charles's appear-ance raised outrageous mirth,—[*Horse*] *laughs* were ecchoed from side to side, & nothing else could be heard. She required all her resolution to stand it—Hetty was almost in convulsions—M^r. Crisp hollowed—M^r. Featherstone absolutely *wept* with excessive laughing—& even Mamselle Rosat lent her Elbows on her lap, & could not support herself upright. What rendered her appearance more ridiculous, was that, being wholly unused to Acting, she for-got her Audience, & acted as often with her back to them as her Face—& her back was really quite too absurd [—the full breadth of her height.]^1

I had soon after to make my appearance as Lady Graveairs. To be sure I was in proper spirits for the Part—however, a few excep-tionable speeches, I had insisted upon omitting,^{2} & I was greatly recovered compared to my former appearance. Barsanti, at a sud-den thought, went on & made an apology, "that the *gentlewoman* who was to have performed Lady Graveairs, being taken ill, her place was to be supplied by the Performer of Lady Easy." To be sure it was rather in the Barn style.

I acquitted myself with rather a better grace now, & we were *much applauded*. Not having Performers sufficient for a regular plan, we finished with [such]^3 a short, unsatisfactory scene, that they all called out for *more*.—Allen, intending to carry the affair off with a *joke*, took Barsanti & me each by the Hand, & led us on—but, whether from shame, or what I know not, when *she* had Bowed,

---

1 Inserted by FBA.
2 As Sir Charles's mistress, the part of Lady Graveairs had some mildly salacious remarks, including one speech where she recommends that Sir Charles resort to prostitutes if he desires a compliant mistress.
3 Inserted by FBA.

& *we* had curtsied, she was wholly at a loss, & could not think of a Word to say—so after keeping the Company in a minutes suspence, "in short, cried she, "You know the rest;—" & ran off.

It is easy to suppose laughs were not spared for this ridiculous attempt.

[...]

18.   [Nov^r.4th.]

[...]

I am Reading—I blush to say for the first Time, Pope's works. He is a darling Poet of our Family: it is with exquisite delight I make myself acquainted with him: & in serious truth, I am glad he is new to me.

[...]

19.   Dec^r.8th.

[...]

But now that I am in a scribbling vein, I cannot forbear mentioning that the Reading of Pope's Letters has made me quite melancholy. He laments with such generous sorrow the misfortunes of his friends, that every Line I read, raises his Character higher in my estimation. But it is not possible to find with unconcern, that all his best & dearest friends Die before him. [O] great misery of length of Days, to preserve Life only to know its little value! Pope had but one great end in view, to render this World supportable to him—that was, *Friendship—The peculiar gift of Heaven.*[1]—This did he nobly deserve—& obtain—but for how short a Time!—[...] But in nothing does Pope equally charm me, as in his conduct to his Mother. It is truly Noble. he gives up all his Time, thought & attention to her ease & comfort.—I dare not begin to mention his long friendship with the admirable Swift, because I shall not know where to stop; for the attachment of such eminent Men to one another, has [som]ething in it almost awes me—& at the same time, inexpressibly delights [me].—I must tear myself from this.

[...]

---

1 FB quotes the first line of Johnson's "Ode on Friendship" (1743).

1772

JOURNAL FOR 1772

20.   May 30th.

Maria, Susan & myself [made a successful effort] to see Garrick, last Night, in Richard the Third. We had always longed to see him in all his great characters, though least in this which is *so* shocking [xxx], though not the least, of the praise of his acting. [We rode in chairs,[1] so that we got in the instant we arrived, without the least difficulty. The chair, however tiresome & fatiguing, is the only way for going to the theatre, & I never attempt to *step out*, but in that manner.]

Garrick was sublimely horrible!—[Good Heaven]—how he made me shudder whenever he appeared! it is inconceivable, how terribly great he is in this Character. I will never see him so disfigured again—he seemed so truly the monster he performed, that I felt myself glow with indignation every time I saw him. The Applause he met with exceeds all belief of the Absent. I thought, at the End, they would have torn the House down: Our seats shook under us.

[...]

1773

JOURNAL FOR 1773

21.   Sunday June 13th.

[...]

We [*SEB and FB*] are Reading [some of the][2] best French Works together not regularly, but only such parts as are adapted either to our Capacity or Inclination: we have just finished the Henriade— I am not absolutely in raptures with it—I think Voltaire has made much too free with Religion, in giving Words to the *Almighty*. I

---

1   Covered sedan chairs.
2   Inserted by FBA.

doat on Poetry—but cannot allow of even Poetical License giving Language human to the Divine Power. For which reason, I am more attached to Poetry concerning Fabulous Times—for Jove, Juno, Minerva, Venus—may talk as much as they please—I am never hurt even at their Quarrelling—but a man pretending to belief in revealed Religion,—to presume to Dictate sentiments to his Maker—I cannot think it right. Nay more, he actually makes his God so very a human Creature—as to *give up* his intended proceedings, upon the prayers of Lewis! It is very well for a Jove, or any other Fabulous God, to be softened, enraged, & mutable—but—an all seeing Eye—can it leave any thing for another to represent?—an all wise, all Good Power—can it have any design which is *better* to be laid aside?

[...]

22.   Novr. 24th.

[...]

I have, [xxx], entered into a very particular Correspondance with M^r. Crisp: I write really a Journal to him. & in answer, he sends me most delightful long, & incomparably clever Letters: Animadverting upon all the facts, &c which I acquaint him with, & dealing with the utmost sincerity in stating his opinion, & giving his Advice. I am infinitely charmed with this correspondance—which is not more agreable, than it may prove Instructive.

23.   SAMUEL CRISP TO FRANCES BURNEY
             c. December 1773, Chessington

In consequence of our Agreement, I shall now begin with an instance of the most pure & genuine Sincerity, when I declare to You that I was delighted with your letter[1] throughout—[...] I profess there is not a single word or expression, or thought in your whole letter, that I do not relish—not that in our Correspondence, I shall set up for a Critic, or Schoolmaster, or Observer of Composition—[Damn it] all!—I hate [it] if once You set about framing studied letters, that are to be correct, nicely grammatical & run in smooth Periods, I shall mind them no others than as newspapers of

---

1 Lost.

intelligence; I make this preface because You have needlessly enjoin'd me to deal sincerely & to tell You of your faults; & so let this declaration serve once for all, that there is no fault in an Epistolary Correspondence, like stiffness, & Study—Dash away, whatever comes uppermost—the sudden Sallies of imagination, clap'd down on paper, just as they arise, are worth Folios, & have all the warmth & merit of that sort of Nonsense, that is Eloqu[ence] in Love—never think of being correct, when You write to me—[...]

1774

JOURNAL FOR 1774

24.   February 20th.

What will become of the World if my Annals are thus irregular! Almost two months have [elapsed without my Recording][1] one anecdote! I am really shocked for Posterity!—But for my Pen, all the Adventures of this Noble family might sink to oblivion! I am amazed when I consider the greatness of my Importance, the dignity of my Task, & the Novelty of my pursuit! I [shall] be the 8th. Wonder of the World, if the World had not already, & too prematurely, Nominated so many Persons to that Honour!
[...]
[Thursday Mama took us [FB and SEB] with her to Miss Reid, the celebrated Paintress, to meet Mrs Brooke,[2] the celebrated Authoress.][3]

Miss Reid is shrewd & clever, where she has any opportunity given her to make it known; but she is so very Deaf, that it is a fatigue to attempt her. She is most exceeding ugly, & of a very melancholy, or rather discontented, humour.

Mrs Brooke is very short & fat, & squints, but has the art of shewing Agreeable Ugliness. She is very well bred, & expresses herself with much modesty, upon all subjects.—which in an *Authoress*, a Woman of *Known* understanding, is extremely pleasing.

---

1   Substitution.
2   Frances Brooke (1724–89), novelist, playwright, and co-manager of the Opera House.
3   Inserted by FBA.

[...] [*The party also includes Dr. John Shebbeare, a former medical practitioner.*]

Dr. Shebbeare, who was once put actually in the Pillory for a libel, is well know for political & other writings; he absolutely ruined our Evening, for he is the most Morose, rude, gross, & ill mannered man I was ever in Company with. He aims perpetually at Wit, though he constantly stops short at rudeness—he reminded me of Swift's Lines

> Thinks raillery consists in railing,
> Will tell Aloud your greatest failing.[1]

For he did to the utmost of his power, *cut up* every body, on their most favourite subject: though what most [attracted] his spleen, was *Woman*, to whom he professes a fixed Aversion; & next to her, his greatest disgust is against the *Scotch*—& these two subjects he wore thread bare.—though indeed, they were pretty much fatigued before he attacked them; & all [his] *satire* which he levelled at them, consisted of trite & hackneyed abuse. The only novelty which they owed to him, was from the extraordinary coarseness of Language he made use of. But I shall recollect as much of the conversation as I can, & make the parties speak for themselves. I will begin with M^r. Strange's Entrance, which was soon after our's.

After his Compliments were paid to the *Fair Sex*—he turned to the *Growler*—

"Well, Dr. Shebbeare, & how do *you* do?"

Dr. Shebbeare ... Do? why, as you see, pestered by a parcel of Women.

M^rs. Brooke ... *Women* & the *Scotch* always fare ill with Dr. Shebbeare.

Dr. Shebbeare ... Because they are the two greatest evils upon Earth. The *best* Woman that ever I knew is not to be compared to the *Worst* Man. And as to the Scotch!—there is but *one* thing in which they are clever, & can excell the English;—& that is, they can use both Hands at once to scratch themselves—the English never think of using more than one.

Miss Reid ... Ay, Dr. you only abuse us, because you are sorry that you are not [my] Countryman.

---

1 Cf. "The Furniture of a Woman's Mind" (1727) ll. 19-20.

Dr. Shebbeare ... What, *Envy*? hay? Why it's true enough that they get every thing into their own Hands, & when once they come, they take care never to return—no, no!

Miss Reid ... You was saying, M^{rs}. Brooke, that you did not know till I told you, that Dr. Burney had a Wife;—what do you then think of seeing these grown Up Daughters?

M^{rs}. Brooke ... Why, I don't know how, or why, but I own I was never more surprised than when I heard that Dr. Burney was married.

Dr. Shebbeare ... What, I suppose you did not take him for a Fool?—All Men, who marry, are so; but above all, God help him who takes a Widow!

M^{r}. Strange ... This is a strange Man, M^{rs}. Burney,—but nobody ever minds him.

Dr. Shebbeare ... I don't wonder that Dr. Burney went abroad!—all my amazement is at his ever coming Home! Unless, indeed, he left his understanding behind him: which I suppose was the case.

M^{rs}. Brooke ... I am sure that does not appear from his Tour[1]— I never received more pleasure than from Reading his account of what he saw & did abroad—

Dr. Shebbeare ... I hate Authors! but I suppose one Wit must hate another.

M^{rs}. Brooke ... Those few Authors that *I* know, give me great reason *not* to hate them,—quite the contrary—Dr. Johnson, Dr. Armstrong—and I won't say *what* I think of Dr. Burney;—but for Dr. Armstrong I have a very particular regard. I have known him more than 20 years.

Dr. Shebbeare. What, I suppose you like him for his Intrigues?

M^{rs}. Brooke ... Indeed, I never heard he had any.

Dr. Shebbeare ... What, I suppose you had too many yourself to keep his in your Memory?

M^{rs}. Brooke ... O, Women you know, Dr., never have Intrigues. I wish Dr. Burney was here,—I am sure he would be our Champion.

Dr. Shebbeare ... What, do you suppose he'd speak against himself? I know but too well what it is to be married! I think I have been Yoked for 1 & forty years; & I have wished my Wife under Ground any Time since.

---

1   CB published two musical surveys, *The Present State of Music in France and Italy* (1771) and *The Present State of Music in Germany* (1773).

Mama ... And if she were, you'd marry in a Week!

Dr. Shebbeare ... I wish I was tried!

M^r. Strange ... Why this is a sad man, M^rs. Burney, I think we must toss him in a Blanket.

Dr. Shebbeare ... Ay, with all my Heart! but speak for yourself (to M^rs. Brooke) do you suppose your Husband was not long since tired of you?

M^rs. Brooke ... O—as to that—that is not a fair Question;—I don't ask you if you're tired of *your* Wife.

Dr. Shebbeare ... And if you did, I'd tell you.

Miss Beatson ... Then *I* ask you;—pray, Dr. Shebbeare *are* you tired of your Wife?

Dr. Shebbeare ... I did not say I'd tell *you*. [Bold face.]¹

Mama ... I wish that M^rs. Strange was here;—she'd fight our Battles admirably.

M^r. Strange ... Why do you never Come to see her, Dr.?

Dr. Shebbeare... Because she has so much Tongue, that I expect she'll talk herself to Death, & I don't chuse to be Accessary. [Who are you to have for singer next year?

Mrs Brooke... Rauzini: a most excellent performer.

Dr. Shebbeare ... Ay, it's your Interest to say so.

Mrs Brooke ... Well, I sha'n't Talk to *you*, but I know Dr. Burney's opinion of him.]

M^r. Strange ... What do you think of the Bookseller's Bill, & the state of Literary Property, Dr.?²

Dr. Shebbeare ... Why I don't think at all About it. I have done with Books! I have not written a Line these 20 years—though indeed, I wasted a Pint of Ink last Week.

Mama ... Then I am sure You must have *spilt* it, Dr.

Dr. Shebbeare ... I never knew a Bookseller who was not a scoundrel; I was cheated plaguly about Lydia,³ & the Rascal who sold the Marriage Act promised to share the profits,—yet though I know that there have been 6 Editions, he always Calls it the first.

---

1 Added in different ink.

2 A reference to a petition presented on behalf of booksellers to the House of Commons protesting the ruling which had deprived them of perpetual copyright.

3 *Lydia; or, Filial Piety* (1755) and *The Marriage Act* (1754) were novels by Shebbeare.

Miss Reid ... pray, Dr. have you seen Nelly's last Drawing?[1] She has made *me* Dance a Minuet!

Dr. Shebbeare ... Well said, Nelly! I'll make Thee immortal for that! I'll write thy Life.

M[rs]. Brooke ... She'll make *herself* immortal, by her Works.

★

As to Susy & I, we never presumed to open our Lips, for fear of being affronted! but when we were coming away, Dr. Shebbeare Called out to us "Here!—mind what *I* say—be sure you never marry!"

You are right, thought I, there could not be a greater antidote to that state than thinking of you.

Miss Reid was, I suppose, some what scandalised at this Man's Conversation, as it happened at her House; & therefore before we took leave, she said—"Now I must tell you that Dr. Shebbeare has only been Jesting—he thinks as we do, all the Time."—

"This it is, cried he, to have a friend to lie for one!"

What a strange fancy it was, for such a Man as this to Write Novels! however—I am tired of Writing—& so adieu sweet Doctor Shebbeare—

25.   SAMUEL CRISP TO FRANCES BURNEY
April 1774, Chessington

I tell you what—You are a Jew—an Ebrew Jew—of the line of Shylock, & I shall henceforth call You, Jessica—because you, an overgrown Rich Jew can give me an Entertainment of a hundred Dishes, do you expect the like from such a poor, forked, unbeleiving Christian, as I am?—You riot in Provisions of all Sorts, & have nothing to do, but to choose, or reject; & your Cookery is at your Fingers ends, & to do you Justice has the true relish, & is highly season'd; All this I give You Credit for; I devour the feast you give me, finish the desert, lick up the Jellies & Ic'd Creams to the last drop, & am thankful—but all this wont do it seems—the Mosaic law says—"*An Eye for an Eye, & a Tooth for a Tooth*—"And if I have neither, *then I must have your pound of Flesh says Jessica*—The truth is, Chessington produces nothing beyond Bacon & Greens, with a

---

1   Helena "Nelly" Beatson was Miss Reid's niece. FB had previously praised her untaught talent for drawing.

new laid Egg, or so, & the week round the Meats are pretty near the same; so that I can give you no better than I have Fanny—You say, because I don't like your new Young Acquaintance, Mr. Twiss I am so short[1]—here you are mistaken—I like your *picture* of him, just as in Raphael's School of Athens at the Vatican, I like his picture of the Pope's frightful Dwarf, which for fun, & spite he lugg'd by head & shoulders into that fine Composition—I wont pretend to say, like that Beast Shebbeare, I will make you immortal, for your Pictures; but I shall make a Choice Cabinet Collection of them, & review them often for my own entertainment—
[...]
    Send a minute Journal of every thing; & never mind their being trifles—trifles well dress'd are excellent food; & your Cookery is with me of established reputation
[...]

26.   FRANCES BURNEY TO SUSAN BURNEY
           17-29 September 1774, Chessington

                                              Wednesday Sept[r].
[...]
I have almost, though very undesignedly, occasioned a *grand fracas* in the House, by a ridiculous [joke] which I *sported* for the amusement of Miss Simmons & Kitty. We had been laughing at some of poor Moone's queer phrases, & then I mentioned some of Kitty's own,—her Cousin joined in laughing violently, & as I proceeded from one absurd thing to another, I took Miss Simmons herself to task, upon some speeches she had made; & in conclusion, I told them that I intended to write *a Treatise upon politeness* for their Edification. All this was taken as it was said, *in* [*Joke*,] & we had much laughing in consequence of my scheme, which I accompanied by a thousand flighty speaches.
    After this, upon all indecorums, real or fanciful, I referred to my Book for Instruction—& it became a sort of standard joke among us, to which we made every thing that passed applicable, & Miss Simmons, who enjoyed hearing me *run on*, as she called it, introduced the subject perpetually. Indeed the chief amusement I have made myself when with the two Cousins, has been in indulging

---

1   That is, curt.

[myself] in that kind of Rhodomantide Discourse, that it will be easy to you to recollect some Instances of, [my dear Susy, with all their *ludicrousness*.]

All this did very well among ourselves;—but the Day after the Simmons left us, while we were at Dinner, Kitty blundered out "Good people I tell you what;—*She's* going to write something about politeness, *& that*, & it's to be for all of you, here at *chiss*."

"I'm sure, cried Mlle. Courvoisyois, we shall be very much *obligè* to the lady."

"I'll subscribe to the Book with all my Heart, cried Mlle. Rosat. I beg leave to bespeak the first Copy. I am sure it will be a very useful work."

"She's to tell you all what you're to do, resumed Kitty, & how you're to do this—& all that."

"Exceedingly well defined, Kate. said M^r. Crisp, but pray, Fannikin, what shall you *particularly* treat of?"

"O Sir, cried I, all parts of life! it will be a very comprehensive work.—& I hope you'll all have a *Book*.

"Pray what will it cost?" demanded M^rs. Moone.

"A Guinea a Volume, answered I, & I hope to comprize it in 9 Volumes."

"O lord! exclaimed she, I shan't give *no such money* for it."

"*I* will have 2 Copies, said Mlle. Rosat, let it cost what it will. I am sure it will be exceeding well Executed."

"I don't doubt *in least*, cried Mlle. Courvoisyois, of politeness of Miss Burney—but I should like to see the Book, to see if I should *sought* the same."

"Will it be like Swift's Polite Conversation?" said M^r. Crisp.

"I intend to Dedicate it to Miss Notable,[1] answered I. it will contain all *the newest fashioned* regulations. In the first place, you are never again to Cough."

"Not to *Cough*? exclaimed every one at once, but how are you to help it?"

"As to *that*, answered I, I am not very clear about it myself, as I own I am guilty sometimes of doing it. But it is as much a mark of ill breeding as it is to *Laugh*, which is a thing that Lord Chesterfield has stigmatized."[2]

---

1 Miss Notable is one of the characters in Swift's satiric dialogues, *A Complete Collection of Genteel and Ingenious Conversation* [...] (1738).
2 See Lord Chesterfield's letter to his son, 19 October 1748.

"Lord, well, for my part, said M^rs. Moone, I think there's no fun without it."

"Not for to *Laugh*! exclaimed Courvoisyois, with Hands uplifted—Well, I declare I *did* not *sought* of such a *sing*!"

"And pray, said M^r. Crisp, making a fine affected Face, may you *simper*?"

"You may *smile*, Sir, answered I. but to *laugh* is quite abominable. Though not quite so bad as *sneezing*, or *blowing the Nose*."

"Why, if you don't blow it, cried Kitty, what *are* you to do with it? [don't you think it nastier to let it *run* out perhaps?"]

I pretended to be too much shocked to answer her.

"But pray, is it permitted, said M^r. Crisp, very drily, to *Breathe*?

"*That* is not yet, I believe, quite exploded. answered I, but I shall be more exact about it in my Book, of which I shall send *you Six* Copies. I shall only tell you in general, that whatever is Natural, plain or easy, *is* entirely banished from polite Circles."

"And all is sentiment & *Delicacy*, hay Fannikin?"

"No, Sir, not so, replied I, with due gravity, *Sentiments & sensations* were the *last* fashion; they are now done with—they were *laughed* out of use, just before laughing was abolished. The *present Ton* is *refinement*;—nothing *is to be*, that *has been*; all things are to be *new polished*, & *highly finished*. I shall explain this fully in my Book."

"Well, for my part, cried M^rs. Moone, who [I believe] took every word I said seriously, I don't desire to read *no* such *tiddling* Books. I'm very well as I am."

It's well you think so. thought I.

"Pray ma'am, said Mlle. Rosat, is it within the Rules of politeness to *pick the Teeth*?"

"Provided you have a little *Glass* to look in before you." answered I, & rose to go up stairs to my Father.—

"pray, Ma'am, cried she again, is it polite, when a person talks, if you don't understand them, to look at another as if you said "What nonsense she says!"

"I should imagine not;" answered I, moving [to the Door,] as I found these Questions were *pointed* [against poor Kitty].^1

"Pray is it polite, ma'am, cried Mlle. Rosat again, to make *signs* & to *whisper*?"

"I suppose not." cried I, opening the Door.

---

1 Inserted by FBA.

"And *pray*, cried Kitty colouring, is it *pelite* to be *touchy*? & *has* people any business to suspect, & to be suspicious?"

"O, cried I, these are things that don't come into my Cognisance—" & away I ran.

[...]

JOURNAL FOR 1774

27.   St. Martin's Street.
                                                      Leicester Fields
                                                      Octr 18th.

[...]

The first Opera was performed last Tuesday. The morning before, M^{rs}. Brooke, [who lives in Market Lane,] Called here, & very civilly invited my Mother, Susy & me to [go with her] to the Opera the next Day. [The managers of public places are the only people to whom I care to be obliged, as all *pecuniary* obligations are odious & insupportable.] we were very desirous to hear the new singer, Rauzzini, of whom my Father has said so much in his German Tour, & we agreed to wait upon M^{rs}. Brooke about seven.

Accordingly we went. her House in Market Lane, by means of divers turnings & windings, has a passage to the Opera House. We intended to have sat in her Box, & have seen only her, but when we went, we found she was up stairs with M^{rs}. Yates,[1] & [when she came down,] she immediately asked us to go up stairs with her. This we declined, but she would not be refused, & we were obliged to follow her.

[It is very disagreeable that the Yates are half managers with the Brookes, nor can I understand how a woman of Character & reputation, such as Mrs. Brooke, can have reconcil'd herself to becoming intimate with one whose fame will bear no scrutiny.]

We were led up a noble stair case, that brought us to a most magnificent Apartment [...] Here we saw M^{rs}. Yates, seated like a stage Queen surrounded with gay Courtiers, & dressed with the utmost elegance & brilliancy. What most provoked me was that [a Brother of the Miss Garricks[2] was among the Gentlemen in the

---

1   Mary Ann Yates, a famous tragedienne, whose early life was marked by
    scandalous liaisons. In 1773 she and her husband Richard Yates, an actor,
    became joint managers of the Opera with Frances Brooke.
2   David Garrick's nieces.

Room, it will therefore, in all probability, *travel* to that family, that we visited Mrs. Yates for] as we entered the Room, our Names were announced in an *audible* Voice. All I can comfort myself with, is, that it was only at the *Opera House* we met, & that of *late years* M^rs. Yates has had no harm said of her; [but it was mortifying [xxx] that *her* acquaintance, [xxx] should be inseparably annexed to that of Mrs. Brooke, which we would much rather choose to cultivate.]

Mrs. Yates to a very fine Figure, joins a very handsome Face, though not now in her *premiere jeunnesse*; but the expression of her Face is infinitely haughty & hard.

With an *over done* civility, as soon as our Names were spoken, she rose from her seat hastily, & rather *rushed* towards us, than meerly advanced to meet us. but I doubt not it was meant as the very *pink of politeness.*

[...]

1775

28.   FRANCES BURNEY TO SAMUEL CRISP
                  2 March 1775, London

[...]

[*FB describes a visit by Lucrezia Agujari, a celebrated Italian soprano, known as La Bastardini because of her supposed illegitimate birth.*]

Signora Agujari, detta Bastardini sent very particular Compliments to my Father by Dr. Matty, of the Museum, regretting that she had not seen him when he was abroad, & very much desiring to be Introduced to his acquaintance. It is somewhat remarkable, that this is the second Capital Female singer who has sent to *solicit* my Father's Acquaintance, & both of them by men of learning; for Miss Davies commissioned Dr. Johnson to deliver *her* message of Compliments.

An Evening was accordingly appointed, & M^r. Burney & Hetty came here to meet this *Silver side* lady,[1] who is reckoned, next to Gabriella, the greatest singer in the World.

---

1   Agujari was reputed to have a plate in her side, as a result of a childhood accident. See below, letter FB to SC, 15 March 1775.

Dr. Matty, who is a little, formal man, very civil, & very affected, Handed the Bastardini into the Room. She is of middle stature, & a little Lame; she has a very good Complection, & was *well*, not *absurdly*, Painted, & she has fine, expressive, languishing Eyes, & alltogether is a handsome Woman, & appears about 4 or 5 & Twenty.

She was accompanied by Signor Colla, who is Maître *de Musique à la Cour* at Parma, & who attends her in her Travels, & is, like her, pensioned by the Duke. He is a Tall, thin, spirited Italian, full of fire, & not wanting in Grimace.

[...]

We were all of us excessively eager to hear her sing, but as it was not convenient to offer her her Pantheon price of 50 Guineas a song, we were rather fearful of asking that favour: however, my Father ventured to hint at it to Signor Colla; who told us that she certainly *would* sing—*but* that she had a bad Cold, & slight sore Throat!

As to Signor Colla, he was *so* Civil to my Father! talked so much of his *Fame* abroad, & of the *ardent* Desire which he had of the *Honour* of knowing so *celebrated* a person! It seems he composes for Agujari, who he suffers not to sing any music but his own. He talked of *her* as of the greatest Wonder of the World,—"*c'est une prodige!*"[1] he said that Nature had been so very lavish of it's gifts to her, that he had had hardly any trouble in teaching her; every thing was ready done!

One very ridiculous circumstance I cannot forbear mentioning: Susette had, I know not how, understood by Dr. Maty that Signora Agujari was married to Signor Colla: This she told to Hetty & me, & we therefore concluded that it was only a *foreign* custom, that she still kept her name; as is the case with many other singers. Well, when my sister[2] was asked to play, she pleaded want of Practice, & said to Agujari that she had other Things to mind than Harpsichords.—

"Et qu'avez vous donc, Mademoiselle?" demanded the Bastardini. "Des Enfans!" answered Hetty. "Ah Diable! exclaimed she, (for that is her favourite Exclammation) et vous etes si jeune encore! & Combien avez vous?"

"J'en ai trois." answered Hetty—

"Ah Diable! C'est bien extraordinaire!"

---

1 "She's a prodigy!"
2 EBB.

"Avez *vous* une Enfant?" asked Hetty.—

She stared—& after some Gestures of surprise, said "Moi!—je ne suis pas mariée, moi!"

Hetty was quite confounded,—she begged her pardon, & said "mais en verité j'ai toujours cru que ce monsieur étoit votre epoux!"

"Non, Mlle." answered the Bastardini, "c'est mon Maître."[1] [And looked very dignified.][2]

This was a very ridiculous mistake, however, she took it [very] good naturedly, & without being offended, as it was evident that it was not designed.

Dr. Maty has assured us that she bears an unexceptionable character, & that she is therefore visited by his Wife & Daughters. She has been strongly recommended to him from abroad.

Her Behaviour was very *proper,* & she displayed none of her airs, though it was not difficult to see that she *could* behave otherwise; for she betrayed, perhaps involuntarily, a consciousness of her greatness, superiority & consequence by a thousand little speeches & looks. I believe that she allows *Gabriella* to be a *Rival*; all the rest of the World She holds in Contempt. She has not even the curiosity to *hear* any Singing but her own. She said she had not been once to the opera; & when we asked her if she had ever heard Rauzini, she answered "No! mais on dit qu'il chante *joliment.*"[3]My Father asked her how she liked *Galluci,* a new woman who sings at the Pantheon, as well as Agujari. She answered that she had never heard her! that she went into her own Room the moment she had done singing herself. How conceitedly incurious!

"Mais vous, Monsieur," said she, "vous avez entendu la Gabriella? n'est-ce pas?"

My Father told her that Gabriella was in Sicily when he was in Italy, & therefore he could not hear her. "No?" said she, "mais vraiment c'est dommage!"[4]

---

1 "And what are they, Miss?" "Children!" "The Devil! and you are still so young! and how many do you have?" "I have three." "The Devil! that's quite extraordinary!" "Do you have a child?" "Me!—I am not married!" "... but really, I thought that this gentleman was your husband." "No, Miss, he is my Master."

2 Inserted by FBA.

3 "But they say he sings prettily."

4 "But you, Sir, you have heard Gabriella, haven't you? ... well really, that's a pity!"

My Father then asked if *she* had heard her?

"O no," she said, & Signor Colla added that they two could never be in the same place together. "Two suns," said Dr. Maty, "never appear at once."

"O, ce n'est pas possible!" cried Agujari[, composedly].[1]

After Tea, we went into the Library, & Hetty was prevailed upon to play a Lesson of Bach of Berlin's, upon our Merlin Harpsichord. It was very sweet, & Agujari appeared to be *really* much pleased with it, & spoke highly of the *Taste & Feeling* with which Hetty played. M[r]. Burney sat down next. They all stared [with admiration][2] as usual, at his performance And the Bastar-dini, after thanking him, expressed herself to be *extremely* con-cerned that it was not then in her power to sing, saying it would give her particular pleasure: but she added, that she would come some other Time, & bring some of her best songs, & sing *comme il faut*!

When she went away, she again said, "O! je viendrai absolument!"[3] [...]

JOURNAL FOR 1775

29. [*An undated journal entry from late February 1775 concludes:*]

This Singer is really a *slave* to her Voice; she fears the least Breath of air—she is equally apprehensive of Any heat—she seems to have a perpetual anxiety lest she should take Cold; & I do believe she neither Eats, Drinks, sleeps or Talks, without considering in what manner she may perform those vulgar duties of Life so as to be most beneficial to her Voice. However, there are so few who are gifted with eminent Talents, that it is better to cultivate them even labouriously, than to let them suffer Injury from Carelessness or Neglect.

---

1 Inserted by FBA.
2 Inserted by FBA.
3 "I will certainly come again!" In a letter to SC dated 10 June 1775, FB reports another visit from Agujari in which she finally consented to sing (See *EJ* 2: 154-56).

FRANCES BURNEY TO SAMUEL CRISP
15 March 1775, London

[...]
I was a little shocked to find, soon after I send you my Last Letter,
that Hetty had written to you upon the same Subject, the Bastardini, just before. I am afraid between us, you must be quite tired of
this poor *silver side*. You have doubtless heard the story of the Pig's
Eating half her side, & of it's being repaired by a silver kind of
machine. You may be sure that she has not Escaped the witticisms
of our *Wags* upon this score: it is too fair a subject for Ridicule to
have been suffered to pass untouched. M^r. Bromfield has given her
the nick name of *Argentini*: M^r. Foote has advised her, (or *threatened*
to advise her) to go to the Stamp Office, to have her *side Entered*,
lest she should be prosecuted for secreting silver contrary to Law:
& my Lord Sandwich has made a catch, in Italian, & in Dialogue,
between her & the Pig: beginning *Caro mio porco*—The pig answers
by a Grunt;—& it Ends by his Exclaiming *ah che bel mangiare!*[1] Lord
S. has shewn it to my Father, but he says he will not have it set, till
she is gone to Italy.
[...]

31   SAMUEL CRISP TO FRANCES BURNEY
18 April 1775, Chessington

Tho' Fingers are Crippley & left Arm lame I shall not spare them,
to tell You, You are at last (after a hard fight with You) a tolerable
(not *very tolerable*, observe) good Girl—you make such a Rout
about my sisters seeing what you are pleas'd to call, *your trifling
Stuff*,[2] *&c, &c, &c* that I could beat you—I thought you had more
Taste—but no—'tis not want of Taste; 'tis a Way Young Girls have
got by Habit, & as it were mechanically, of making *mille façons*[3]
without a Shadow of Reason—you cannot but know, *that trifling,
that negligence, that even incorrectness* now & then, in familiar Epistolary writing, is the very soul of Genius & Ease & that if your

---

1 "Ah my beloved pig!" "Ah, what fine eating!"
2 SC had persuaded FB to let his sisters, Ann Crisp and Sophia Crisp Gast,
   read FB's journal from Teignmouth, written in 1773.
3 A great fuss.

letters were to be fine labour'd Compositions, that smelt of the *Lamp*; I had as lieve they [travelled else where][1]—So, no more of that, Fan, & thou lov'st me—Dash away, whatever comes uppermost; & believe me, You'll succeed better, than by leaning on your Elbows, & studying what to say—One thing more, & I have done—rest assur'd, that the unconnected rattle You tax Yourself with, is exactly the same sort of thing, as that *Nonsense*, which we are told, *is Eloquence in Love*—[...]

JOURNAL FOR 1775

32.   May 8th.

This Month is called a *tender* one—It has proved so *to* me— —but not *in* me—I have not breathed one sigh,—felt one sensation,—or uttered one folly the more for the softness of the season.—However—I have met with a youth whose Heart, if he is to be Credited, has been less guarded—indeed it has yielded itself so suddenly, that had it been in any Month—I should not have known how to have accounted for so easy a Conquest.
[...]
[*Visiting EBB's house, FB met Thomas Barlow, a young man aged around 24, probably of merchant family, who was boarding with Mrs. O'Connor, an acquaintance of the Burneys.*]
M[r] Barlow is rather short but handsome, he is a very well [behaved, civil,] good tempered & sensible young man. [He bears an excellent] character, both for Disposition & morals. He has Read more than he has Conversed, & seems to know but little of the World; his Language is stiff & uncommon, he has a great desire to please, but no elegance of manners; niether, though he may be very worthy, is he at all agreeable.
Unfortunately, however, he happened to be prodigiously Civil to me, & though I have met with much more gallantry occasionally, yet I could not but observe a *seriousness* of attention much more expressive than Complimenting.
[...]

---

1 Substitution.

Four Days after this Meeting, my Mother & M^{rs}. Young happened to be in the Parlour, when I received a Letter which from the strong resemblance of the Hand writing to that of M^r. Crisp, I immediately opened & thought came from Chesington but what was my surprise, to see Madam, at the beginning, & at the Conclusion

your sincere Admirer &

very humble serv^t. Thos. Barlow

I Read it 3 or 4 Times before I could credit my Eyes. An Acquaintance so short, & a procedure so hasty astonished me. It is a most tender Epistle & contains a passionate Declaration of Attachment, hinting at hopes of a return, & so forth.[1]

I took not a moment to deliberate.—I felt that my Heart was totally insensible—& felt that I could never consent to unite myself to a man who I did not *very* highly value.

However, as I do not consider myself as an independant member of society, & as I knew I could depend upon my Father's kindness, I thought it incumbent upon me to act with his Concurrence I therefore, at Night, before I sent an answer, shewed him the Letter. He asked me a great many Questions—I assured him that forming a Connection without attachment—(& that I was totally indifferent to the Youth in Question) was what I could never think of. My Father was all indulgence & goodness he at first proposed that I should write him Word that our acquaintance had been too short to authorise so high an opinion as he expressed for me; but I objected to that, as seeming to infer that a *longer* acquaintance might be acceptable. He therefore concluded upon the whole, that I should send no answer at all.

I was not very easy at this determination, as it seemed to treat M^r. Barlow with a degree of Contempt, which his partiality to me by no means merited from myself; & [as] I apprehended it to be possible for him to put, perhaps, *another*, & more favourable interpretation upon my silence. I shewed Hetty the Letter next Day. She most vehemently took the young man's part: urged me to think differently, & above all advised me to certainly Write an answer, & to be of their party, according to my promise, when they went to M^{rs} O Connor's.

---

1 FB omitted the letter from her journal, but it can be read in *EJ* 2: 117-18.

I told her I would speak to my Father again in regard to writing an Answer, which I wished much to do, but could not now without his consent: but as to the Party, I could not make one, as it would be a kind of tacit approbation [&] assent of his further attentions.

I went afterwards to call on my Grandmother; [my] sister followed me, & directly told her & my aunts of the affair. They all of them became most zealous Advocates for M^r. Barlow; they spoke most highly of the Character they had heard of him, & my aunt Anne humourously bid me beware of her & Beckey's fate!

I assured them I was not intimidated, & that I had rather a thousand Times Die an old Maid than be married, except from affection.

When I came Home, I wrote the following Answer which I proposed sending, with my Father's leave.

Miss Burney presents her Compliments to M^r. Barlow; she is much obliged for, though greatly surprised at the good opinion with which on so short an Acquaintance he is pleased to Honour her; she wishes M^r. Barlow all happiness, but must beg leave to recommend to him to Transfer to some person better known to him a partiality which she so little merits.

My Father, however, did not approve of my Writing. I could not imagine why; but have since heard from my sister that he was unwilling I should give a No without some further knowledge of the young man.

Further knowledge will little avail. In Connections of this sort, the *Heart* ought to be heard.

My sister was not contented with giving her own advice; she wrote about the affair to M^r. Crisp, representing in the strongest light the utility of my listening to M^r. Barlow. He has written me such a Letter! God knows how I shall have Courage to answer it. Every body is against me but my beloved Father. [My Mother, indeed, knows nothing of the matter & yet has had a downright Quarrel with me upon the subject, & though Hetty was at first very kind, she has at last also Quarrelled with me. My 2 aunts will hardly speak to me—Mr. Crisp is in a *rage*.]

They all of them are kindly interested in my welfare; but they know not so well as Myself what may make me happy or miserable. To unite myself for Life to a man who is not *infinitely* dear to me, is what I can never, never Consent to. Unless, indeed, I was strongly urged by my Father. I thank God most gratefully he has not interfered.

They tell me they do not desire me to *marry*, but not to give up the *power* of it, without seeing more of the proposer: but this reasoning I cannot give into.—it is foreign to all my Notions: how can I see more of M[r]. Barlow without encourageing him to believe I am willing to think of him?

33.   SAMUEL CRISP TO FRANCES BURNEY
8 May 1775, Chessington

So much of the future Good or Ill of your Life seems now depending, Fanny, that I cannot dispense with myself from giving You (without being call'd upon) my whole sentiments on a subject which I dare say, you already guess at—
[*SC inserts a portion of EBB's letter containing a favourable description of Barlow.*]
Is all this true, Fanny?—if it is, is such a Man, so very determinately to be rejected, because from the overflowings of an innocent, honest mind (I wont call it *ignorant* but) *untainted with* the World, (instead of a thousand pitiful Airs & disguises, mixt perhaps with treachery & design) he with trembling & diffidence ventures to write, what he is unable to declare in person; & forsooth, to raise your indignation to the highest pitch, is so indelicate as to hint, that his intentions aim at MATRIMONY—[God damn my blood Fan, You make me mad!—] if you dont put me in Mind of Moliere's Precieuses Ridicules![1] [...]
[...]—But seriously, Fan, all the ill-founded Objections You make, to me appear strong & invincible marks of a violent & sincere Passion—what You take it into your head to be displeas'd with, as too great a Liberty, I mean, his presuming to write to You, & in so tender & respectful & submissive a strain, if You knew the World, & that villanous Yahoo,[2] call'd Man, as well as I do, You would see in a very different Light—[...] Ah Fany, such a disposition promises a thousand fold more happiness, more solid, lasting, home-felt

---

1   Jean-Baptiste Poquelin (Molière), *Les Précieuses ridicules*, first performed 1659.
2   An imaginary race of brutes described in Swift's *Gulliver's Travels* (1726).

happiness, than all the seducing, exterior Airs, Graces, Accomplishments, & Address of an Artful [worldly man][1] such a man, as this Young Barlow, if ever You are so lucky, & so well-advis'd, as to be united to him, will improve upon You every hour; You will discover in him Graces, & Charms, which kindness will bring to light; that at present You have no Idea, of—I mean if his Character is truly given by Hetty—that is the grand Object of Inquiry—as likewise his Circumstances. This last, as the great Sheet Anchor, on which we are to depend in our Voyage thro' life, ought most minutely to be scrutiniz'd. is he of any profession, or only of an independent Fortune?—if either, or both, sufficient to promise a [really] comfortable [Income,][2] You may live to the Age of your Grandmother, & not meet with so Valuable an offer—Shakespear says,

> There is a Tide in the affairs of Men,
> Which taken at the heighth, leads on to Fortune;
> But being neglected, &c[3]

I forget how it goes on, but the Sense is, (what You may guess,) that the Opportunity is never to be recover'd—the Tide is lost, & You are left in the Shallows, fast aground, & struggling in Vain for the remainder of your life to get on—doom'd to pass it in Obscurity & regret—look around You Fan—look at y[r]. Aunts—*Fanny Burney* wont always be what she is now!—M[rs]. Hamilton once had an Offer of £3000 a Year or near it—a parcel of young Giggling Girls laugh'd her out of it—the man forsooth was not quite smart enough, tho' otherwise estimable—Oh Fany this is not a marrying Age, without a handsome Fortune!—[how happy does Hetty feel herself to have married] [xxx]—Suppose You to lose y[r]. Father—take in all Chances. Consider the situation of an unprotected, unprovided Woman—

Excuse my being so Earnest with You—Assure Yourself it proceeds from my regard, & from (let me say it, tho' it savors of Vanity) a deep knowledge of the World—Observe, how far I go—I don't urge You, hand over head, to have this man at all Events; but for Gods sake, & your own sake, give him & yourself fair Play—dont decide so positively against it—if You do, You are ridiculous to a high degree—[...]

---

1 Substitution.
2 Substitution.
3 Cf. *Julius Caesar* 4.3.217-19.

And so it is all over with me!

& I am to be given up—to forfeit your blessing—to lose your good opinion—to be doomed to regret & the Horrors—*because*—I have not a Mind to be Married.

Forgive me—my dearest M^r. Crisp—forgive me—but indeed I cannot act from *Worldly motives*—you know, & have long known & laughed at my Notions & Character. Continue still to *Laugh* [at me]—but pray don't make *me* Cry—for your last Letter really made me unhappy—I am grieved that you can so earnestly espouse the Cause of a person you never saw—I heartily wish him well—he is, I believe, a worthy young man—but I have [long] accustomed myself to the idea of being an old maid—& the Title has lost all its terrors in my Ears. I feel no repugnance to the expectation of being ranked among the Number.

[...]

Don't imagine by what I say that I have made a *Vow* for a single Life—no. but on the other Hand I have no *objection* to it, & have all my life determined never to marry without having the highest value & esteem for the man who should be my Lord.

Were I ever so well disposed to follow your advice & see more of this Youth—I am convinced he would not let me;—he is so extremely precipitate—I *must* either determine for or against him—or at least, enter into such conditions as I should think myself in honour bound to abide by.

If you ask my objections—I must frankly own they are such as perhaps will only satisfy myself—for I have none to make to his Character—Disposition or person—they are all good; *but*—he is not used to Company or the World—his Language is stiff, studied, & even affected—in short—he does not *hit my fancy*—

I do not like you, Dr. Fell—
The Reason why I cannot tell—But I don't like you, Dr. Fell![1]

[...]

---

1   FB abridges Thomas Brown's quatrain addressed to Dr. John Fell, Dean of Christ Church, Oxford.

FRANCES BURNEY TO SAMUEL CRISP
2 June 1775, London

[...]

If I do *not* see you—I must take this opportunity of entreating &
conjuring you not to use your Influence with my Father for Mr.
B. in case he should mention that personage to you. I have not
Time at present to tell you *all about* it—but a great deal has passed
since I wrote last, & I have suffered the most cruel & terrifying
uneasiness—I am *now* again at peace & hope to continue so.
Should my father happen to speak to you of what I have said,—(as
it is well known that I write very openly to you) I entreat you to
assure him that I have expressed the greatest aversion to forming a
connection with Mr. B. I have not dared to speak so much to the
purpose myself,—for I have been—& I am, determined at all Events
not to oppose *his* will & advice—but I know he wishes only for
my happiness, & I am sensible that I should be wretched for ever
if induced to marry where I have no manner of affection or
regard.—O M^r. Crisp—it is dreadful to me to think of uniting my
Destiny—spending my Time—Devoting my Life—to one whose
face I never desire to see again!

Had I with equal bluntness expressed myself to my Father, I am
certain he would not ever think of M^r. B. more—but—his interference was so unexpected—it silenced, confounded, & frightened
me.

[...]

JOURNAL FOR 1775

36.   June 6th.

[*FB explains the reason for her "terrifying uneasiness."*]
A Week passed after this, without my hearing or seeing any more
of M^r. Barlow & I hoped that he had resigned his pretensions. But
on Saturday morning, while we were at Breakfast, I had a Letter
brought me in a Hand which I immediately knew to be Barlow's.

As it by no means is so high flown as his first, I will Copy it.

Madam,

I have somewhere seen that powerful Deity Cupid, & the invincible Mars habited in a similar manner, & each have in their Train
several of the same dispositioned Attendants: the propriety of which

Thought I own pleased me, for when drawn from the Allegory, it is acknowledged both Love & War are comparative in several particulars; they each require Constancy, & the hope of success stimulate each to perserverance, & as the one is warmed & encouraged by the Desire of Glory so the other is much more powerfully fired & transported by the Charms of the Fair Sex: I have been told that Artifice & Deception are connected to both; but those Qualities I should determine to discard, & substitute in their place an open Frankness, & undisguised Truth & Honour; & for Diligence, Attention, Assiduity & Care, which are essential to both, & which some place in the Catalogue of the Labours of Love, I should have them happily converted to pleasures, in the honour of devoting them to Miss Fanny Burney, if the Destinys auspiciously avert a disagreeable Sequel, for as the bravest General may miscarry, so the most sincere Lover may lose the wished-for Prize; to prevent which, I should continue to invoke my Guardian Genius, that she may ever inspire me with such Principles & Actions as may enable me to reach the summit of my Ambition, in Approveing myself not unworthy the Esteem of your amiable self, & not unworthy—but stop, Oh *ardurous Pen, & presume not*—'till in the front you can place Permission to hope—ascending such sublime heights.

[It has given me great uneasiness that the excessive] hurry of Business has so long prevented me the honour of Waiting on You, & enquiring after your Welfare, which I earnestly wish to hear; but I determine, with your leave, ere long to do myself that pleasure, as methinks Time moves very slowly in granting me an opportunity to declare, in some small degree, (for I could never reach what I should call otherwise) how much I am, with the greatest Respect immaginable, [dear Miss Fanny,]

Your most Devoted & most Obedient servant Tho⁵. Barlow.

***

Notwithstanding I was at once sorry & provoked at perceiving how sanguine this youth chose to be, I was not absolutely concerned at receiving this 2ᵈ. Letter, because I regarded it as a fortunate opportunity of putting an unalterable Conclusion to the whole Affair. However, [as I had begun by asking my Father's advice,] I thought it my duty to speak to my Father before I sent an Answer, never doubting his immediate concurrence.

My Mother, Sukey & I went to the opera that Evening; it was therefore too late when I returned to send a Letter to Hoxton—

but I went up stairs into the study, & told my Father I had received another epistle from M^r. Barlow which I could only attribute to my not answering, as I had wished, his first; I added that I proposed, with his leave, to Write to M^r. B. the next morning.

My Father looked grave, asked me for the Letter, put it in his Pocket unread, & wished me good Night.

I was siezed with a kind of *pannic*—I trembled at the idea of his Espousing, however mildly, the cause of this Young Man:—I passed a restless Night, & in the morning dared not Write without his permission, which I was now half afraid to ask.

About 2 O'clock, while I was dawdling in the study, & Waiting for an opportunity to speak, [we heard a Rap at the Door—& soon after, John came up,] & said "A Gentleman is below, who asks for Miss Burney;—M^r. Barlow."

I think I was never more [mad] in my life—to have taken pains to avoid a private conversation so highly disagreeable to me, & at last to be forced into it at so unfavourable a Juncture,—for I had now *2* Letters from him, both Unanswered, & consequently open to his Conjectures. I exclaimed "[Lord!]—how provoking! what shall I do?"

My Father looked uneasy & perplexed:—he said something about not being hasty, which I did not desire him to explain, [but only said, as I left the Room—

"Well, I must soon tell him I *have* answered his Letter, & so send one tomorrow, & let him think it kept at the Post office." In this determination, I] went down stairs.—I saw my Mother pass into the Back Parlour; which did not add to the *Graciousness* of my Reception of poor M^r. Barlow, who I found alone in the Parlour. I was not sorry that none of the Family were there, as I now began to seriously dread any protraction of this affair.

He came up to me, & with an Air of *tenderness* & satisfaction, began some anxious Enquiries about my Health, but I interrupted him with saying "I fancy, Sir, You have not received a Letter I [have written to you]—"

I stopt—for I could not say which I had *sent!*—

"A Letter?—no, Ma'am!"

"You will have it, then, to-morrow, Sir."

We were both silent for a minute or two, when he said "In consequence, I presume, Ma'am, of the one I—"

"Yes, Sir!" Cried I.

"And pray—Ma'am—Miss Burney!—may I—beg to ask the Contents?"

"Sir—I—it was only—it was merely—in short, you will see it to-morrow."

"But if you would favour me with the Contents now, I could perhaps Answer it at once?"

"Sir, it requires no Answer!"

A second silence ensued. I was really distressed myself to see *his* distress, which was very apparent. After some time, he stammered out—something of *hoping*—& *beseeching*,—which, gathering more firmness, I answered—"I am much obliged to you, Sir, for the good opinion you are pleased to have of me—but I should be sorry you should lose any more Time upon my account—as I have no thoughts at all of changing my situation."

[...]

He remonstrated very earnestly. "This is the severest decision!—[I am persuaded, Ma'am, you cannot be so cruel?]—Surely you must allow that the *social state* is what we were all meant for?—that we were created for one another?—that to form such a resolution is contrary to the design of our Being?—"

"All this may be true,—said I;—I have nothing to say in contradiction to it—but you know there are many odd Characters in the World—& I am one of them

"O no, no, no,—that can never be!—but is it possible you can have so bad an opinion of the married state? It seems to me the *only* state for happiness!—"

"Well, Sir, *You* are attached to the Married Life—*I* am to the single—therefore, *every man in his humour*—do *you* follow *your* opinion,—& let *me* follow *mine.*"

"But surely—is not this—*singular?*—"

"I give you leave, Sir, cried I, laughing, to think me singular—odd—Queer—nay, even whimsical, if you please.

"But, my *dear* Miss Burney, only—"

"I entreat you, Sir, to take my Answer—You really pain me by being so urgent.—"

"That would not I do for the World!—I only beg You to suffer me—perhaps in future—

"No, indeed; I shall never change—I do assure You you will find me very obstinate!"

He began to lament his own Destiny. I grew extremely tired of saying so often the same thing—but I could not absolutely turn him out of the House, & indeed he seemed so dejected & unhappy, that I made it my study to soften my refusal as much as I could without leaving room for future expectations.

[...]

Though I was really sorry for the unfortunate & misplaced attachment which this Young man professes for me, yet I could almost have *Jumped* for Joy when he was gone, to think that the affair was thus finally over.

Indeed I think it hardly possible for a Woman to be in a more irksome situation, than when rejecting [an honest] man who is all humility, Respect & Submission, & who throws himself & his Fortune at her Feet.

[...]

The next Day—a Day the remembrance of which will be never erased from my memory—my Father first spoke to me *in favour* of Mʳ. Barlow! & desired me not to be *peremtory* in the Answer I [was going] to Write.

I scarce made any answer—I was terrified to Death—I felt the utter impossibility of resisting not merely my Father's *persuasion*, but even his *Advice.*—I felt, too, that I had no *argumentative* objections to make to Mʳ. Barlow—his Character—Disposition—situation—I knew nothing against—but O!—I felt he was no Companion for my Heart!—I wept like an Infant—Eat nothing—seemed as if already married—& passed the whole Day in more misery than, merely on my own account, I ever did before in my life,—except upon the loss of my own beloved mother—& ever revered, & most dear Grandmother!

After supper, I went into the study, while my Father was alone, to wish him Good Night; which I did as chearfully as I could, though pretty evidently in dreadful uneasiness. When I had got to the Door, he called me back,—& asked me concerning a new mourning [Gown I had bought for the mourning of Queen Caroline—he desired to know what it would come to, & as our *allowance* for Cloaths is not *sumptuous*, said he would assist] Sukey & me, which he accordingly did, & affectionately embraced me, saying "I wish I could do more for Thee, Fanny!"—

"O Sir!—cried I—*I* wish for Nothing!—only let me Live with you!—"—"My life! cried he, kissing me kindly, Thee shalt live with me for ever, if Thee wilt! Thou canst not think I meant to get rid of thee?"

"I could not, Sir! I could not!" cried I, ["I could not out-live]¹ such a thought—"

I saw his dear Eyes full of Tears! a mark of his tenderness which I shall never forget!

---

1 Substitution.

"God knows—continued he—I wish not to part with my Girls!—they are my greatest Comfort!—only—do not be too hasty!—"

Thus relieved, restored to future hopes, I went to Bed as light, happy & thankfull as if Escaped from Destruction.

I had, however, written my Letter before my Father spoke, & as I had expressly told M^r. Barlow it contained a Refusal, I thought it would be even ridiculous to alter it; [& I rather] determined, if my Father had persisted in desiring it, to *unsay* a rejection, than not to write it after having declared I already had. This is the Copy:

Sir,

I am much concerned to find that my silence to the first Letter with which you honoured me, has not had the Effect it was meant to produce, of preventing your giving yourself any further trouble upon my Account.

The good opinion you are pleased to express of me, however extraordinary upon so short an Acquaintance, certainly claims my Acknowledgements; but as I have no intention of changing my present situation I can only assure You of my good wishes for Your Health & Happiness, & request & desire that you will bestow no further Thoughts, Time, or Trouble upon,

Sir,

Your most humble servant,

F Burney

From that Day to this, my Father, I thank Heaven, has never again mentioned M^r. Barlow.

37.   SAMUEL CRISP TO FRANCES BURNEY
              14 December 1775, Chessington

Don't imagine, that, because my letters are (from necessity, & poverty of matter) shorter than yours, I am therefore insensible, that the Advantage is all on my Side; & that intrinsically a Dozen of one sort would not weigh against One of the Other—& in real Value too, as well as Size—But pray Remember, that when my Lord condescends to visit the humble Curate in his tatterd Cottage, he does not expect a Dinner like his own; but contents himself with the Parson's Ale, & Mutton & Turnips, & this too rather at short Allowance—& all with a real, or feign'd Smile upon his

Countenance—Do you imitate my Lord; for your two last letters are such rich ones, & have made so weighty a ballance against me, that You must either accept Eighteen pence in the pound, or take out a Statute of Bankruptcy against me—[...]

1776

38.   FRANCES BURNEY TO THOMAS LOWNDES
December 1776, London

[*FB's first draft of a letter concerning* Evelina, *written to the bookseller Thomas Lowndes.*]
As an author has a kind of natural claim to a connexion with a Bookseller, I hope that, in the character of the former, you will pardon me, although a stranger, for the liberty I take of requesting you to favour me with an Answer to the following queries.

Whether You will take the trouble of candidly perusing a MS. Novel sent to you without any public Name, or private recommendation?

Whether it is now too late in the year for printing the first volume of the above MS. this season?

And whether if, after reading, you should think it worth printing, you would buy the Copy without ever seeing, or knowing, the Author?

The singularity of this address, you may easily imagine, results from a singularity of situation.

I must beg you to direct you Answer to Mr. King, To be left at the Orange Coffee House till called for.

39.   FRANCES BURNEY TO THOMAS LOWNDES
25 December 1776, London

[*Written in a feigned hand, this letter differs considerably from FB's first draft.*]
As Business, with those who understand it, makes it's own apology, I will not take up your Time with reading Excuses for this address, but proceed immediately to the motives which have induced me to give you this trouble.

I have in my possession a M:S. novel, which has never yet been seen but by myself; I am desirous of having the 2 first volumes printed immediately,—& the publication of the rest, shall depend wholly on their success.

But, sir, such is my situation in Life, that I have objections unconquerable to being known in this transaction;—I therefore must solicit the favour of you to answer me the following queries, which I hope you will not think impertinent.

1st. whether you will give a candid and impartial Reading, to a Book that has no *recommendation* to previously prejudice you in its favour?

Secondly, whether, if, upon perusal, the work should meet with your approbation, you will Buy the Copy, of a Friend whom I shall commission to wait upon you, without every seeing or knowing the Editor?

I shall be obliged to you to direct your answer to Mr. King, to be left at the Orange Coffee House till called for, in the Haymarket.

40.   THOMAS LOWNDES TO FRANCES BURNEY
              25 December 1776, London

Sir,

I've not the least objection to what you propose & if you favour me with sight of your Ms I'll lay asside other Business to read it & tell you my thoughts of it at 2 Press's I can soon make it appeare in print for now is the time for a Novel

41.   FRANCES BURNEY TO THOMAS LOWNDES
              26 December 1776, London

The frankness, with which you favoured me with an answer to my Letter, induces me to send you the M:S. with the firmest reliance upon your candour.

The plan of the first Volume, is the Introduction of a well educated, but inexperienced young woman into public company, and a round of the most fashionable Spring Diversions of London. I believe it has not before been executed, though it seems a fair field open for the Novelist, as it offers a fund inexhaustible for Conversation, observations, and probable Incidents.

The characters of the Sea Captain, and the *would be* French woman, are intended to draw out each the other; and the ignorance of the former, in regard to modern customs, and fashionable modes, assists in marking their absurdity and extravagance.

I shall send you the second volume with all the expedition in my power, if that which is now under your examination, makes you desirous of seeing it.

[*Lowndes replied that he liked the novel and asked her to send the rest.*]

1777

42.   THOMAS LOWNDES TO FRANCES BURNEY
17 January 1777, London

I have read your Novel and cant see any Reason why you shou'd not finish and publish it compleat I'm sure it will be your interest as well as the Booksellers, you may well add One Volume to these & I shall more eagerly print it. I Returnd one in a singular State to a Lady on Thursday who has before favour'd me with the Production of her Pen I w^d. Rather print in July than now to Publish an Unfinished book this I submit to your Consideration and with wishes that you may come into my Way of thinking I'll restore the M^s. to the Gentleman that brought it.

43.   FRANCES BURNEY TO THOMAS LOWNDES
post 17 January 1777, London

I am well contented with the openness of your proceedings, & obliged to you for your advice.

My original plan was, to publish 2 volumes now, & two more next year: I yield, however, to your Experience in these matters, & will defer the publication, till the Work is completed,—though I should have been better pleased to have *felt the pulse* of the public, before I had proceeded.

I will write to you again, when I am ready for the press. In the mean Time, I must beg the favour of a line, directed as before, to acquaint me how long I may delay printing the Novel, without losing the proper season for its appearance.

44.   FRANCES BURNEY TO SAMUEL CRISP
27-28 March 1777, London

[...]
[*FB describes her first meeting with Dr. Johnson at a morning party at home.*]

Hetty, & *Suzette*, for the first Time *in public*, played a Duet, &, in the midst of this performance, Dr. Johnson was announced.

He is, indeed, very ill favoured,—he is Tall & stout, but stoops terribly,—he is almost bent double. His mouth is [in perpetual motion,] as if he was chewing;—he has a strange method of frequently twirling his Fingers, & twisting his Hands;—his Body is in continual agitation, *see sawing* up & down;—his Feet are never a moment quiet,—&, in short, his whole person is in *perpetual motion*.

His Dress, too, considering the Times, & that he had meant to put on his *best becomes*, being engaged to Dine in a large Company, was as much out of the common Road as his Figure: he had a large Wig, snuff colour coat, & Gold Buttons; but no Ruffles to his [Wrist, & Black Worsted Stockings—so, you see, there is another *Worsted Stocking Knave*, besides me,—that's my comfort.]

He is shockingly near sighted, & did not, till she held out her Hand to him, even know Mrs. Thrale. He *poked his Nose* over the keys of the Harpsichord, till the Duet was finished, & then, my Father introduced Hetty to him, as an old acquaintance, & he [instantly] kissed her.[1]

His attention, however, was not to be diverted five minutes from the Books, as we were in the Library; he *pored* over them almost brushing the Backs of them, with his Eye lashes, as he read their Titles; at last, having fixed upon one, he began, without further ceremony, to Read [to himself][2], all the time standing at a distance from the Company. We were very much provoked, as we perfectly languished to hear him talk: but it seems, he is the most silent creature, when not particularly drawn out, in the World.

[...]

JOURNAL FOR 1777

45.

Oh Yes!

Be it known, to all whom it may concern,—c'est à dire, in the first place,—Nobody;—in the 2ᵈ. place,—the same Person;—&, in

---

1 FBA adds "When she was a little Girl, he had made her a present of the Idler."

2 Inserted by FBA.

the third place, *Ditto;*—that Frances Burney, Spinster, of the Parish of S^t. Martin's in the Fields,— — — — —did keep no Journal this unhappy year till she wrote from Worcester to her sister Susan, of the same Parish, & likewise a spinster. There are, who may Live to mourn this,—for my part, I shall not here enumerate all the particular misfortunes which this Gap in Literature may occasion,—though I feel that they will be of a nature the most serious & melancholy;—but I shall merely scrawl down such matters of moment as will be requisite to mention, in order to make the Worcester Journal, which is a delicious morsel of Learning & profound reasoning,—intelligible,—to the 3 persons mentioned above.

★★★

When, with infinite toil & labour, I had transcribed the 2^d. volume [*of Evelina*], I sent it, by my Brother [*CB Jr.*] to Mr. Lowndes. The fear of Discovery, or of suspicion in the House, made the Copying extremely laborious to me; for, in the Day Time, I could only take odd moments, so that I was obliged to sit up the greatest part of many Nights, in order to get it ready. And,—after all this *fagging,* Mr. Lowndes sent me Word that he approved of the Book, but could not think of printing it till it was finished; that it would be a great disadvantage to it, & that he would wait my Time, & hoped to see it again, as soon as it was completed.

Now this Man, knowing nothing of my situation, supposed, in all probability, that I could seat myself quietly at my Bureau, & write on with all expedition & ease, till the Work was finished: but so different was the case, that I had hardly Time to write half a page in a Day; & niether my Health, nor inclination, would allow me to continue my *Nocturnal* scribling, for so long a Time as to write first, & then Copy, a whole volume. I was, therefore, obliged to give the attempt & affair entirely over for the present.
[...]
[I was obliged so much by my dear Father's goodness,][*in permitting FB's visit to the Burney cousins at Worcester*] that, in the fullness of my Heart [at his kind indulgence,] I could not forebear telling him [my scheme in regard to Mr. Lowndes [xxx] I expressed the wish that I might have managed my affairs without any disturbance to himself.] He could not help Laughing; but I believe was much surprised at the communication: he desired me to acquaint him, from Time to Time, how *my work* went on, called himself the *Pere confi-*

dent, & kindly promised to guard my secret as cautiously as I could wish.

[...]

But when I told my dear Father I *never* intended [he] should see my essay, he forbore to ask me its name, or make any enquiries. I believe he is not sorry to be saved the giving me the pain of his criticism. He made no sort of objection to my having my own way in total secresy & silence to all the World. Yet I am easier in not taking the step without his having this little knowledge of it.

46.   THE WORCESTER JOURNAL
           FRANCES BURNEY TO SUSAN BURNEY
                 7 April 1777, Worcester

[...]

[*While staying with her uncle and cousins in Worcester, FB describes a family performance of Arthur Murphy's* The Way to Keep Him.]

Before 5 O'clock, while we were all in the midst of our disorder, Mrs. Bund & her Daughter arrived. They did not know what they came for, & my Uncle & Miss Humphries,[1] who received them, said we were preparing for a droll sort of Concert which we intended to give them.

[...]

You can have no idea what [agitation] every new comer gave me;—I could hardly dress myself,—hardly knew where I was,—hardly could stand. Betsy, too, was very much flurried, & so afraid of being worse, that she forced wine & water, & punch, down her throat till she was almost tipsey. Richard & James gave all their thoughts to their own adornment; Tom Capered about the House in great joy; little Nancy jumped & Laughed; Edward was tolerably Composed;—but Beckey—was in extacy of pleasure,—she felt no fright or palpitation, but Laughed, Danced & sung all Day long delightfully.[2]

[...]

The Band was now got into order for the Overture, & the Company going to be summoned up stairs [...]

I assure you this frightened me so much, that I most heartily

---

1   Sister-in-law of FB's uncle, Richard Burney.
2   Richard, James, Tom, Edward, Betsy (Elizabeth) and Beckey (Rebecca) were FB's cousins. Little Nancy was EBB's eldest daughter, Hannah. A second Nancy, another cousin, acted as prompter.

wished myself 20 miles off;—I was quite sick, &, if I had dared, should have given up the part.

When I came to be Painted, my Cheeks were already of so high a Colour, that I could hardly bear to have any added: but, before I went on, I seemed siezed with an Ague fit, & was so extremely Cold, that my Uncle, upon taking my Hand, said he thought he had touched ice or marble.

At length, they all came up stairs: a Green Curtain was drawn before them, & the overture was played. Miss Humphries did all the Honours, for Nancy was engaged as Prompter, & my Uncle one of the Band.

The Theatre looked extremely well, & was fitted up in a very Dramatic manner: with side scenes,—& 2 figures, of Tragedy & Comedy at each end, & a Head of Shakespear in the middle. We had 4 Changes of scenes. [the play we acted was "The Way to keep Him."][1]

[...]

As soon as the overture was played,—which, you must know, was performed in the *passage*, for we had no Room for an Orchestra in the Theatre,—Edward & Tom were seated at Cards, & the Curtain Drawn. Tom's part was very soon over, & then Betsy entered;—she was much flurried, & yet in very great spirits, & acquitted herself *greatly* beyond my expectations: Edward was, I believe, very little frightened, yet not quite so easy or so excellent as I had imagined he would have been. Indeed the part is extremely unworthy of him, & I fancy he was determined to let it take it's chance, without troubling himself with much exertion.[2]

Take notice, that, from the beginning to the End, no *applause* was given to the play. The Company judged that it would be inelegant, & therefore, as they all said, *forbore*;—but indeed it would have been very encouraging, & I heartily wish they had not practiced such *self denial*!

Next—came *my* Scene;—I was discovered Drinking Tea;[3]—to tell you how *infinitely*, how *beyond measure* I was terrified at my situation, I really cannot;—but my fright was nearly such as I should have suffered had I made my appearance upon a public Theatre,

---

1 Inserted by FBA.
2 Edward played William, a servant to Lovemore, and Tom played another servant. Betsy played Muslin, maid to Mrs. Lovemore.
3 FB played Mrs. Lovemore.

since Miss Humphries & Captain Coussmaker were the only two of the Audience I had ever before seen.

The few Words I had to speak before Muslin came to me, I know not whether I spoke or not,—niether does any body else:—so you need not enquire of others, for the matter is, to this moment, unknown.

Fortunately for me, all the next scene gave me hardly 3 words in a speech, for Muslin has it almost to herself: so I had little else to do than to lean on the Table, & twirl my Thumbs, &, some times, bite my fingers:—which, indeed, I once or twice did very severely, without knowing why, or yet being able to help it.

I am sure, *without flattery*, I looked like a most egregious fool;—for I made no use of the Tea things,—I never tasted a drop,—once, indeed, I made an attempt, by way of passing the Time better, to drink a little, but my Hand shook so violently, I was fain to put down the Cup instantly, in order to save my Gown.

By the way, I have forgot to mention Dresses.

Edward had a Coat Trim'd to have the effect of a rich Lace Livery;—He had a Capital Bag, long Ruffles & so forth.

Tom much the same.

Betsy, as Muslin, had a very showy striped pink & white Manchester, pink shoes, red ribbons in abundance & a short Apron. The Paint upon her very pale Cheeks set her off to the greatest advantage, & I never saw her look nearly so well.

Mrs. Lovemore wore her Green & Grey, which I have trimed with Gause, white Ribbons, Gause Apron, Cuffs, Robins, &c.

The next who made his appearance, was Cousin James,[1]—he was most superbly Dressed, but, as you saw his Cloaths at the music meeting, I will not describe them. His Hair, however, I must not pass unnoticed; for you never saw the most foppish stage Character better Dressed in the *Macaroni*[2] style. Indeed, all our Hairs were done to the astonishment of all the Company.

He entered with an air so immensely conceited & affected, &, at the same Time, so uncommonly bold, that I could scarse stand his *Abord:*[3] &, through out the scene that followed, he acted with such a satisfied, nay, *insolent* assurance of success, that, I declare, had I been entirely myself, & free from fear, he would have wholly dis-

---

1 As Sir Brilliant Fashion.
2 Dandy, fop.
3 Manner.

concerted me: as it was, my flurry hardly admitted of encrease: yet I felt myself glow most violently.

I must assure you, notwithstanding my embarrassment, I found he did the part *admirably*,—not merely *very much* beyond my expectations, but, I think, as well as it *could* be done. He looked very fashionable, very assured, very affected, & very *every way the thing*. Not one part in the piece was better or more properly done: nor did any give more entertainment.

We were, next, joined by Richard:[1] whose *non chalence*, indifference, half vacancy & half absence, excellently marked the careless, unfeeling husband which he represented. Between his extreme unconcern, & Sir Brilliant's extreme assurance, I had not much trouble in appearing the only languid & discontented person in Company.

Richard was in very genteel morning Dress.

A short scene next followed, between Betsy & me, which I made as little of as any body might desire—indeed, I would Challenge all my Acquaintance around, to go through an act more thoroughly to their own dissatisfaction. So that is saying more than every body can, however.

The Act finished by a *solo* of Betsy, which I did not hear, for I ran into a Corner to recover Breath against next Act.

My Uncle was very good natured, & spoke very comfortable things to me,—which I did by no means expect, as at first, he seemed not delighted that Betsy had given me her part. He said I wanted *nothing but exertion*, & charged me to speak louder, & take courage.

"O! cried Edward, that this had but been Lady Betty Modish![2]—

However, since I was so terribly Cowardly, I now rejoice that I had a part so serious & solemn, sad & sorrowful.

Cousin James was prodigiously [facetious] in comforting me, [taking my Hand,] & supporting his *tendresse* yet more strongly off than on the stage. The truth is, he is so very good natured, that the least idea of pity really softens him into downright tenderness.

Richard was entirely occupied in changing his Dress for Lord Etheridge.[3]

---

1   As Lovemore.

2   A comic character from Cibber's *The Careless Husband*.

3   A disguise assumed by Lovemore in which to conduct his affair with the Widow Bellmour.

In the next Act, the widow Belmour made her appearance. Beckey's elegant Figure & [*bred*] Face were charmingly set off, for her Dress was fashionable & becoming: she had on a lilac Negligee, Gause Cuffs trimmed richly with Flowers and spangles, spankled shoes, Bows of Gause & Flowers, & a Cap!—*quite the thing*, I assure you!—full of flowers, frivoleté, spangles, Gause, & long Feathers;—immensely high, & [her Hair][1] delightfully well Dressed. She was in great spirits, & not at all frightened. Her Entrance, I am sure, must be striking, & I was surprised the folks could forbear giving her applause.

[I must, however, frankly own that she did not answer my too high raised expectations in her performance. I thought her unequal to the part, she wanted rather more *coquetry*, & rather more *dignity*, to make it that first rate character it has always been reckoned. Yet she did it *very* prettily, & with infinitely more ease & moderation as to action & Gesture, than, from her general flightiness & gaiety, might be expected. Her appearance was perfectly genteel, nay elegant, & she committed nothing that the severest Judge, could, I believe, call a *fault*, though she did not act up to the full power of the part.]

Betsy changed her Dress entirely for Mignonet,[2] & did the Character very well; though the worse for having another in the same play, as she saved herself very much for Muslin, which she did admirably.

During my reprieve from Business, I thought I had entirely banished my fears, & assumed sufficient Courage to go through the rest of my part to the best of my capacity;—but far otherwise I found it, for, the moment I entered, I was again gone!—knew not where I stood, nor what I said,—a mist was before my Eyes, so strong that it almost blinded me, & my Voice faltered so cruelly, that, had they not all been particularly silent whenever I aimed at speaking, not a word the better would they have been for my presence!—

And all this for pleasure!—but indeed it was too much,—& I have not yet recovered from the [most] painful sensations I experienced that night,—sensations which will always make my recollection of the Way to keep him disagreeable to me.

Fortunately for me, my part & my spirits, in this Act, had great simpathy;—for M^{rs}. Lovemore is almost unhappy enough for a

---

1 Inserted by FBA.

2 Mignionet, the Widow Bellmour's maid.

Tragedy Heroine:—&, I assure you, she lost none of her *pathos* by any giddiness of mine!—I gave her melancholy feelings very fair play, & *looked* her misfortunes with as much sadness as if I really experienced them.

In this Act, therefore, circumstances were so happily miserable for me, that I believe some of my Auditors thought me a much better & more *arttificial* actress than I [really was]—& I had the satisfaction of hearing some few *buzzes* of approbation which did me no harm.

But I would never have engaged in this scheme, had I not been persuaded that my fright would have ended with the first scene: I had not any idea of being so completely overcome by it.

The grand scene between the Widow & Lord Etheridge, Richard & Beckey acquitted themselves extremely well in. If Richard had a fault, it was being *too* easy,—he would have had more spirit, had he been *rather* less *at Home*. His Dress for this part was all elegance.

This Act concluded with the scene that I prevailed with Edward & Betsey to add,—they did it vastly well, & are both, I believe, well pleased that they listened to me.[1]

Again, my Uncle spoke the most flattering things to encourage me, "Only speak out, Miss Fanny, said he, & you will leave nothing to wish;—it is impossible to do the part with greater propriety, or to speak with greater feeling, or more sensibly,—every, the most insignificant thing you say, *comes Home* to me."

You can't imagine how much this kindness from him cheared me. In the third act I recovered myself very decently, *compared* to the 2 first,—but indeed I was very, very far from being easy, or from doing the part according to my own ideas.

So that, in short, I am totally, wholly, & entirely—dissatisfied with myself in the whole performance. Not once could I command my voice to any steadiness,—or look about me otherwise than as a poltroon, either smelling something unsavoury, or expecting to be Bastinadoed.

In the most Capital scene of Mrs. Lovemore, with her Husband, in the third Act, when she is all *Air, alertness, pleasure and enjoyment*,[2] I endeavoured what I could to soften off the affectation of her sudden change of Disposition; & I [*gagged*][3] the Gentleman with as

---

1 An additional scene, probably written by FB.
2 FB quotes Mrs. Lovemore.
3 Hoodwinked.

much ease as my very little ease would allow me to assume. Richard was really charming in this scene; so thoroughly negligent, inattentive & sleepy, that he kept a continual *titter* among the young Ladies;—but, when he is roused from his indifference by Mrs. Lovemore's pretended alteration of Temper & conduct,—he *sung small* indeed!—when *her* flightiness began, you can hardly suppose how *little* he looked,—how mortified!—astonished! & simple!—it was admirably in character, & yet he seemed as if he *really could not help it*,—& as if her unexpected gaity quite confounded him.

Betsy, Beckey & James were all of them very lively, and [really] very clever in all they had to do in this Act.

I am [very,] very sorry that Edward could not have more justice done to those talents which I know only want to be called forth.

At the End of all, there was a faint something in *imitation* of a Clap,—but very faint indeed: yet, though applause would much have encouraged us, we have no reason to be mortified by it's omission, since they all repeatedly declared they *longed* to clap, but thought it would not be approved: & since we have heard, from all quarters, nothing but praise & compliment.

Richard spoke the last speech in a very spirited manner: & he was very delicate & very comfortable to me in our reconciliation, when Mrs. Belmour says "Come, kiss and Friends!—" & *he* adds "It is in *your* power, Madam, to make a reclaimed libertine of me indeed,"—for he excused all the embracing part, & without making any fuss, only took my Hand, which, Bowing over, (*like Sir Charles Grandison,*) he most respectfully pressed to his Lips.

We now all hastened to Dress for Tom Thumb,[1] and the Company went into the Dining Room for some refreshments. Little Nancy was led away by Miss Humphries, who made her take a formal leave of the Company, as if going to Bed, that they might not expect what followed.

The sweet little thing was quite in *mad spirits*, which we kept up by all sort of good things, both Drinking, Eating & flattery: for our only fear was lest she should grow shamefaced, & refuse to make her Entrance.

She flew up to me, "Ay, Cousin Fanny, *I* saw you Drinking your Tea there!—what made you Drink Tea by yourself, before all the Company?—did you think they would not see you?"

---

1 Fielding's farce, first performed in 1730.

You must know she always calls me *Cousin* Fanny, because, she says, every body else does, so she's sure I can't really be *an aunt*.

During the whole performance, she had not the least idea what we all meant, & wanted several Times to join us. especially while I was *weeping*;—"Pray what does Cousin Fanny cry for, aunt Hannah?—Does she cry really, *I say*?—"

But I must now, for your better information, tell you exactly how the Parts in Tom Thumb were cast.

⎰ Lord Grizzle,	
⎱ Noodle,	Mr. Edward Burney.
⎱ Bailiff,	
Doodle,	Mr. Thomas Burney,
⎰ King,	
⎱ Bailiff's Follower,	Mr. Richard Burney.
⎱ A Fighting man,	
And Tom Thumb by	Miss Anna Maria Burney.
Huncamunca,	Miss Fanny Burney,
Cleora,	Miss Beckey Burney,
[Glumdalca, Queen, Giantess,	Mr. James Burney.][1]
And Queen by	Miss Elizabeth Burney.

★★★

Noodle & Doodle, who opened the Farce, were both Dressed very fantastically, in the old English style, & were several minutes practicing antics before they spoke. Edward disguised his voice in this part, & made the Burlesque doubly ludicrous by giving a foppish *twang* to every period: Tom did Doodle vastly well.

Then Entered the King,—which was performed by Richard most admirably, & with a *dignified drollery* that was highly diverting & exceeding clever. Betsey accompanied him; she was [*very*] *well* in the Queen, [—no, she was *better* than *very well*, though by no means excellent.] Their Dresses, though made of mere Tinsel, & all sort of gaudiness, had a charming & most Theatrical effect: their Crowns, Jewels, Trains, &c, were superb.

Next—entered,—Tom Thumb!

[But First,] when the King says

---

1 Inserted by FBA.

But see! our Warrior comes!—the great Tom Thumb!—
The little Hero, Giant killing Boy!—

Then there was an immense *hub a dub*, with Drums & Trumpets, & a Clarionet, to proclaim his approach.

The sweet little Girl looked beautiful as an Angel;—She had an exceeding pretty & most becoming Dress,—made of pink persian, trimed with silver & spangles,—the form of it the same as that of the others, i.e. old English. her mantle was white,—she had a small Truncheon in her Hand, & a *Vandyke* Hat. her own sweet Hair was left to itself.

When she was to appear, I took her Hand, to put her on; but she shrunk back, & seemed half afraid; however, a few promises of good things, caresses & Flattery, gave her courage again, & she strutted on in a manner that astonished us all.

The Company, none of them expecting her, were delighted & amazed beyond measure: a general Laugh & exclammations of surprise went round: her first speech

"When I'm not thank'd at all,—I'm thank'd enough;
I've done my duty, & I've done no more!"

She spoke so loud, so articulately, & with such courage, that people could scarse credit their senses, when they looked at her Baby Face: I declare,—I could hardly help crying, I was so much charmed, &, at the same Time frightened for her: O how we all wished for Hetty!—it was with difficulty I restrained myself from running on with her,—& my Uncle was so agitated, that he began, involuntarily, a most vehement Clap—a sound to which we had hitherto been strangers:—but the hint was instantly taken, & it was echoed & re-echoed by the audience,—

This applause would have entirely disconcerted her, had it been unexpected; but, as we all imagined she could not fail meeting with it, we had accustommed her to it at all Rehearsals: so that she seemed very sensible of the reason of *the Noise*, as she calls it, & highly gratified by it.

The meaning & energy with which this sweet Child spoke, was really wonderful; we had all done our best in giving her instructions, & she had profitted with a facility & good sense that, at her age, I do indeed believe to be unequalled. When the *Ice* was once broken, in regard to Applause, it was not suffered to be again cemented,—but, while behind the scenes, I could not forbear myself leading a Clap to every one of Nance's speeches.

I wish I could give you any idea how sweetly she spoke

> Whisper ye Winds that Huncamunca's mine!
> Echoes repeat that Huncamunca's mine!
> The dreadful Business of the War is o'er,
> And Beauty, heavenly Beauty, crowns my toils!—

But it is impossible,—nor do I expect any body not present to do her the justice she deserves.

At the end of that speech, the Drums & Trumpets again made a racket, & the King, Queen & Tom Thumb marched off in triumph. I caught the dear little Hero in my arms, & almost devoured her. "I wasn't afraid of the people, now, Cousin Fanny; cried she, was I?—no, I wasn't, nor I wasn't ashamed niether;—was I?—"

We gave her all sort of good things to keep up her spirits, & she was so well pleased, that she wanted to go on again immediately;— & such was her innocence, that, without having any notion of connection in the piece, she begged me to accompany her directly "do, now, Cousin Fanny, let's you & I do our scene now,—why won't you, *I say?*—"

After this, Lord Grizzle made his appearance. And here, Edward did shine indeed! he was Dressed very richly, though ridiculously, & was in high spirits; indeed I must own I think he excelled them all, clever as Richard, his only possible Rival, was. He spoke with such solemnity, such tragic pomposity & energy, & gave us such fine & striking attitudes, while his Face preserved the most inviolable gravity, that to enter into the true spirit of Burlesque with greater humour or propriety would be impossible. Among his numerous talents, he has undoubtedly real abilities for the stage.

But I have neglected to mention the entrance of Glumdalca, from my eagerness to speak of little Nancy; yet can nothing in the piece be more worthy of mention, for nothing excited greater merriment.

James was Dressed in a strait Body with long sleeves, made of striped Lutestring, lapelled with Fur, & ornamented with small Bows of Green, Blue, Garnet & yellow; the Back was shaped with Red. His Coat was pompadour, trimmed with white persian; his shoes were ornamented with tinsel, he had a Fan in his Hand, a large Hoop on, & a Cap, made of every thing that could be devised that was Gaudy & extravagant,—Feathers, of an immense height, cut in paper;— streamers of ribbons of all colours,—& old Earings & stone Buckles put in his Hair, for Jewels. We were obliged to keep the Hair Dresser, upon his account, for Sir Brilliant's *Tête* would by no means do for the Giantess,—no, he had the full covering of a modern Barber's Block, Toupee, Chinon, & Curls, all put on at once: The height of his Head, his Cap & Feathers, was prodigious: &, to make him still more violent, he had very high heeled shoes on. His Face was very delicately *rouged*, & his Eye Brows very finely arched;—so that his Face was not to be known. You cannot imagine how impossible it was to look at him thus transformed without laughing,—unless you recollect our infinite *Grinning* when we saw Aunt Nanny in Dr. Prattle.[1] Indeed, there was nothing but Laughter whenever he was on the stage.

The second Act I had myself the Honour of opening, attended by Beckey. My Dress was a good sort enough of Burlesque of Tragedy Dresses, but so made up as to be quite *indescribable*, though of no bad effect. Cleora's was of muslin & pink Gause, & really very pretty,—rather *too* pretty for the purpose. The Curtain was Drawn, & the love sick Huncamunca was discovered, reclining on an easy Chair, & weeping: Cleora standing humbly by her side.

"Give me some music!—see that it be sad!—"

was followed by the *very* sad air of Two Black Birds sat upon a spray,—in which Beckey was accompanied by the *passage Band*, & which gave high diversion to the audience, & great Benefit to *the princess*,—who had Time to become quite easy before she spoke any more.

Indeed, happily for me, my spirits were now entirely restored to me: The seeing the first act, & my being so much interested about Nance, made me quite forget my*self*, &, to my great satisfaction, I found myself forsaken by the Horrors. The extreme absurdity & queerness of my part contributed greatly to reviving me, & I was really in high & happy spirits:—though I must own I had been fain to Drink [a glass of punch] before I began.

The scene that followed went off far beyond my expectations: during Beckey's song, I put myself into all sort of affected attitudes of rapturous attention, & had the pleasure to find each of them produce a Laugh.

---

1 A reference to another family performance of *The Deuce is in Him* (1763), by George Colman the Elder (1732-94), in which CB's sister Ann Burney played Prattle the apothecary.

She then left me, & I had the Honour of a scene with the King,—in which I exerted myself to the utmost of my power, in Tragic pomp & greatness;—and I believe the folks hardly knew me again, for I could hear sundry expressions of surprise from different parts. Indeed, had my extreme terror lasted longer, I should have hated heartily the very thoughts of acting ever after.

The King had not been gone a moment, ere I was visited by Lord Grizzle,—who, kneeling, began

> Oh Huncamunca!—Huncamunca Oh!—

to which came the most haughty of all my speeches,

> "Ha! dost though know me?—Princess that I am!
> That thus of ME you dare to make your Game?

&, I do assure you, it wanted no energy or imperiousness that I could give it. So that my transition to kindness afterwards, in *proposing* to be married in the Fleet, was [so] laughable & ridiculous [that it hit the *general fancy.*]

When we had arranged our plan, & he quitted me to Buy a License, my other Lover, Tom Thumb, entered. O that you could all have heard her say

> Where is my Princess?—where's my Huncamunca?—

She spoke it with a *pathos* that was astonishing.

The tender Princess easily yields to the eloquence of her little Hero, & they are just coming to terms, when the appearance of Glumdalca interrupts them.

And this scene occasions more excess of Laughter than any other throughout the piece: Glumdalca's first speech,

> I need not ask if you are Huncamunca,
> Your Brandy Nose proclaims— —

caused almost a *roar*, & the scornful airs of the two Ladies, while deriding the charms of each other, kept it up as long as we continued together.—But, had you seen little Nancy, standing between James & me, & each of us taking a Hand, & courting her favour,— you would have Laughed [yourself sick.]

I came off, however, victorious, & we left Glumdalca to mourn her slighted Love. Little Nancy, who stood listening for some Time, heard some of them say that *this is Tom Thumb's wedding Day,*— "Am *I* married?" cried she, "O Yes." "*Who* am I married to, then?" "Why to *me*, my love." "O, I'm glad it is n't to Uncle James, then, 'cause he's such an ugly Woman."

The 3^{d}. act had many alterations, in order to lengthen the part of Cleora. Beckey also put [in a speech of her own, which was a pretty good one. She did the part very well, but I must own her acting abilities are not of that superior sort I had been made to expect.]

The Battle scene went off extremely well: but Edward, [*as Grizzle*] while fighting with the Giantess, had his forehead, & the side of his Eye most terribly wounded.

The whole concluded with great spirit,—all the performers dying, & all the Audience Laughing.

The Curtain was then drawn, & we all ran into our Green Room. And here we remained till the Company went down stairs. They had refreshments in the Dining Room.

James changed his Dress, & went to pay his Compliments to his acquaintance: Betsy & Beckey, after some hesitation, followed him: but I begged to be excused, as I knew none of the party, & had been pertly stared at enough. I would have persuaded Richard to make one among them, but he said he *looked so ugly*, (by [means] of Whiskers, & so forth,) that he could not bear to be seen. [He was gallantry itself to me, kissing my Hand, & pouring forth Compliments in abundance, declaring that I was *Capital indeed*—& that he had never seen Mrs. Yates half so great—&c.]
[...]

47.   THOMAS LOWNDES TO FRANCES BURNEY
                11 November 1777, London

[*On 15 September 1777, FB sent the completed ms. of the third volume of* Evelina *to Lowndes. His reply followed.*]
I've read this 3^{d}. Vol & think it better than 1 & 2^{d}. If you please I'll give you Twenty Guineas for the Manuscript and without loss of time put it to Press

48.   FRANCES BURNEY TO THOMAS LOWNDES
                post 11 November 1777, London

I am much gratified by your good opinion of the M.S. with which

I have troubled you; but I must acknowledge that, though it was originally written merely for amusement, I should not have taken the pains to Copy & Correct it for the Press, had I imagined that 10 Guineas a Volume would have been more than its worth.

As yet, the work has been seen by no human Eye but your own & mine; if, however, you think it's value inadequate to this Sum, I would by no means press an unreasonable Demand: I shall, therefore, for the present, only beg the favour of you to deliver the 3ᵈ. Volume to my Friend, who will call for it to-morrow evening. My Intention is to submit it to the perusal of a Gentleman who is much more experienced in authorship business than myself, & to abide by his Decision.

Should his opinion co-incide with yours, as to the Value of the M.S. I will immediately & frankly return you the three volumes upon your own terms,—but if this should not be the case, I will give you no further trouble than that of begging you to receive my apologies & thanks for what you have already taken.

[*There is no surviving response to this letter. It seems unlikely that FB acted on her threat to retrieve the ms., perhaps intending to show it to SC, for she eventually accepted Lowndes's original offer of 20 guineas for the novel, and SC did not see* Evelina *until it was in print.*]

1778

JOURNAL FOR 1778

[...]

49. [*Towards the end of March.*]

This Year was ushered in by a grand & most important Event,—for, at the latter end of January, the Literary World was favoured with the first publication of the ingenious, learned, & most profound Fanny Burney!—I doubt not but this memorable affair will, in future Times, mark the period whence chronologers will date the Zenith of the polite arts in this Island!

This admirable authoress has named her most elaborate Performance "*Evelina, or a Young Lady's Entrance into the World.*"

Perhaps this may seem a rather bold attempt & Title, for a Female whose knowledge of the World is very confined, & whose inclinations, as well as situation, incline her to a private & domestic Life:—all I can urge, is that I have only presumed to trace the accidents & adventures to which a "*young woman*" is liable, I have not pretended to shew the World what it actually *is*, but what it *appears* to a Girl of 17:—& so far as that, surely any Girl who is *past* 17, may safely do? The Motto of my excuse, shall be taken from Pope's Temple of Fame,—

> In every Work, regard the Writer's End;
> None [e'er] can compass more than they intend.[1]

★★★

About the middle of January, my Cousin Edward brought me a private Message from my Aunts, that a Parcel was come for me, under the name of Grafton.[2]

I had, some little Time before, acquainted both my Aunts of my *frolic*: they will, I am sure, be discreet,—indeed, I exacted a *vow* from them of strict secresy;—& they love me with such partial kindness, that I have a pleasure in reposing much confidence in them. & the more so, as their connections in Life are so very confined, that almost all their concerns centre in our, & my Uncle's Family.

I immediately conjectured what the Parcel was, [opened it &] [xxx] found the following Letter.

To Mr. Grafton
    to be left at [Gregg's] Coffee House[3]
          [York street]

M^r. Grafton,
    Sir,
    I take the liberty to send you a Novel which a Gentleman your acquaintance, said you would Hand to him. I beg with Expedition, as 'tis Time it should be published, & 'tis requisite he should first revise it, or the Reviewers may find a flaw. I am sir,
                 Your obed^t. serv^t.
Fleet street, Jan. 7. 1778.   Thos. Lowndes.

---

1 "An Essay on Criticism," ll. 255-56.
2 The pseudonym used by Edward Francesco Burney in his transactions with Lowndes on FB's behalf.
3 Troide suggests that CB may have been the proprietor of Gregg's Coffee House (See Appendix I, *EJ* 3: 457-59).

My Aunts, now, would take no denial to my reading to *them*, in order to make Errata; &—to cut the matter short, I was compelled to communicate the affair to my Cousin Edward,—& then to obey their Commands.

Of course, they were all prodigiously charmed with it.

My Cousin, now, became my Agent with Mr. Lowndes, &, when I had made the Errata, carried it to him.

The Book, however, was not published till the latter End of the Month. [...]

March 26th.

[...]

On Friday se'night, my Mother accompanied my Father to Streatham, on a visit to Mrs. Thrale for 4 or 5 Days. We invited Edward to Drink Tea with us, &, upon the plan of a *frolic*, determined upon going to Bell's circulating Library, at which my Father subscribes for new Books, in order to ask some questions about Evelina; however, when we got to the shop, I was ashamed to speak about it, & only enquired for some Magazines, at the back of which I saw it advertised. But Edward, the moment I walked off, asked the shop man if he had [Evelina.—yes, he said, but not at Home.] [...] I have an exceeding odd sensation, when I consider that it is in the power of *any* & *every* body to read what I so carefully hoarded even from my best Friends, till this last month or two,—& that a Work which was so lately Lodged, in all privacy, in my Bureau, may now be seen by every Butcher & Baker, Cobler & Tinker, throughout the 3 kingdoms, for the small tribute of 3 pence.[1]

The next Morning, Edward Breakfasted here, & we were very [cheerful]. Charlotte, afterwards, accompanied him to Brumpton,[2] & Susan & I settled that we would go thither about noon.

But, when Charlotte returned, *my* plan altered; for she acquainted me that they were then employed in reading Evelina. My sister had recommended it to Miss Humphries,—& my Aunts & Edward agreed that they would save it,[3] without mentioning any thing of the Author!—Edward, therefore, bought, & took it to Brumpton! This intelligence gave me the utmost uneasiness,—I foresaw a

---

1   The price of hiring a volume of the book from a circulating library, rather than buying a copy.

2   Brompton, where FB's aunts lived.

3   That is, conceal the secret of FB's authorship.

thousand dangers of a Discovery;—I dreaded the indiscreet warmth of all my Confidents; & I would almost as soon have told the *Morning Post* Editor, as Miss Humphries. In truth, I was quite sick from my apprehensions, [& seriously regretted that I had ever entrusted any body with my secret.]

I was too uncomfortable to go to Brumpton, & [so] Susan went by herself. Upon her return, however, I was somewhat tranquilised, for she assured me that there was not the smallest suspicion of the Author, & that they had concluded it to be the Work of a *man*! [...]

Finding myself more safe than I had apprehended, I ventured to go to Brumpton to tea. In my way up stairs, I heard Miss Humphries reading,—she was in the midst of Mr. Villars' Letter of consolation upon Sir John Belmont's rejection of his Daughter, &, just as I entered the Room, she cried out "How pretty that is!"—

How much in luck would she have thought herself, had she known *who* heard her!—In a private *confabulation* which I had with my Aunt Anne, she told me a thousand things that had been said in it's praise, & assured me they had not for a Moment doubted that the Work was a *Man's*.

Comforted & made easy by these assurances, I longed for the Diversion of *hearing* their observations, & therefore, (though rather mal *à propos*,) after I had been near 2 Hours in the Room, I told Miss Humphries that I was afraid I had interrupted her, & begged she would go on with what she was reading. "Why, cried she, taking up the Book, We have been prodigiously entertained—" &, very readily, she continued. I must own I suffered great difficulty in refraining from Laughing upon several occasions,—& several Times, when they praised what they read, I was upon the point of saying "*You are very good!*" & so forth, & I could scarce keep myself from making Acknowledgements, & Bowing my Head involuntarily.

However, I got *off perfectly* safely.

Monday, Susan & I went to Tea at Brumpton. We met Miss Humphries coming to Town. She told us she had just finished "Evelina," & gave us to understand that she could not get away till she had done it. We heard, afterwards, from my Aunt, the most flattering praises,—& Richard[1] could talk of nothing else! His Encomiums gave me double pleasure, from being wholly unexpected: for I had prepared myself to hear that he held it extremely

---

1   Richard Gustavus Burney, FB's cousin.

cheap. And I was yet more satisfied, because I was sure they were sincere, as he convinced me that he had not the most distant idea of suspicion, by finding great fault with Evelina herself for her bashfulness with such a Man as Lord Orville: "a Man, continued he, whose politeness is so extraordinary,—who is so elegant, so refined,—so—so—*unaccountably* polite,—for I can think of no Word,—I never read, never heard such Language in my life!—& then, just as he is speaking to her, she is *so confused*,—that she runs out of the Room!"

I *could* have answered him, that he ought to consider the original character of Evelina,—that she had been brought up in the strictest retirement, that she knew nothing of the World, & only acted from the impulses of Nature; & that her timidity always prevented her from daring to hope that Lord Orville really was seriously attached to her. In short, I *could* have bid him read the Preface again, where she is called "the offspring of Nature, & of Nature in her simplest attire:" but I *feared* appearing too well acquainted with the Book, & I *rejoiced* that an *unprejudiced* Reader should make no weightier objection.

Edward walked Home with us; I railed at him violently for having bought the Book, & charged him to consult with me before he again put it into any body's Hands: but he told me he hoped that, as it had gone off so well, I should not regret it. Indeed he seems quite delighted at the approbation it has met with. He was extremely desirous that his Brother should be made acquainted with the Author, telling me that he wished to plead for him, but did not know how.

[...]

[*The following Friday, FB met Edward at a concert.*]

Edward talked only of Evelina, & frequently [hinted his desire that Richard could be of the select party:—] It seems,—to my utter amazement, Miss Humphries has guessed the Author to be *Anstey*, who wrote the Bath Guide![1]—Good God, how improbable,—& how extraordinary a supposition! But they have both of them done it so much Honour that, but for Richard's anger at Evelina's bashfulness, I never could believe they did not [smoak][2] me. I never went to Brumpton, without finding the 3ᵈ. volume in

---

1 In the *New Bath Guide* (1766) Christopher Anstey described fashionable life in Bath in a series of humorous verse letters.
2 Discover.

Richard's Hands; [he talks of it eternally]; he speaks of all the Characters as if they were his Acquaintance; & praises different parts perpetually: both he & Miss H. seem to have it by Heart, for it is always apropos to whatever is the subject of Discourse, & their whole conversation almost consists of quotations from it.

[...]

I now grew very uneasy, lest Miss Humphries & Richard should speak of the Book to my Mother, & lest she should send for it to read, upon their recommendation;—for I could not bear to think of the danger I should run, from my own Consciousness, & various other Causes, if the Book [was] brought into the House: I therefore went, on Saturday morning, to consult with my aunt at Brumpton. She advised me, nay, *besought* me to tell them the real state of the Case at once; but I could not endure to do that, & so, after much pondering, I at last determined to take my chance.

Richard, in Handing me some Macaroons, chose to call them *Macaronies*, & said "Come, Miss Fanny, you *must* have some of these,—they are all *Sir Clement Willoughby's*,—all in the highest style,—& I am sure to be like *him* will recommend them to *you*, for *his* must be a very favourite Character with you;—a Character in the *first style*, give me leave to assure you."

My Aunt could not refrain from Laughing, but he did not notice it; & then ran on in praise of Lord Orville, with whom he seemed so struck, that we all fancied he meant to make him his *Model*, as far as his situation would allow.

Indeed, not only *during* his illness he [moved us all by his] patient & most amiable behaviour, but since his recovery he has *more* than kept his Ground, by having wholly discarded all the foibles that formerly tinged his manners, though they *never*, I believe, affected his Heart.

[...] My aunt pressed me very much to reveal my secret to Richard; but I assured her that I could not think of it. Some Time after, I heard her say, in a low voice, to Susan, "Pray *won't* Fanny tell him?"

"No, I believe not."

"Why then, if *she won't*,—*I* will!"

This intimation [startled] me at first, & then determined me since I *must* be *blab'd*, to speak *myself*, since I might, at least, make my own conditions: &, in an affair so important to me, will never trust to *mere* discretion, but bind my confidents by the most solemn promises.

Soon after, Edward returned to Town; & I seated myself at a Table, to finish a Letter to Betsy. [Sukey] took up Evelina,—which

[is] always at Hand,—Richard said to her "I like that Book better & better; I have read nothing like it, since Fielding's Novels."

[Sukey] laughed,—so did I, but I wrote on. He asked with some surprise, what was the Joke? but, as he obtained no answer, he continued his [favourite topic.] "I think I can't read it too often,—for you are to know I think it very *edifying*. The two principal Characters, Lord Orville & Mr Villars, are so excellent!—& there is something in the character, & manners, of Lord Orville so *refined*, & so polite,—that I *never saw the like* in any Book before: & all his Compliments are so *new*,—as well as elegant—"

"His Character, said Susan, rises vastly in the 3^d. volume; for he hardly appears in the second, it is almost filled with the Branghtons."

"Yes, cried he, with warmth, but then how admirable is all that low humour!—how well done what a mixture of high & low life throughout

"It is pity, cried I, still writing, but you should know the Author,—you like the Book so well."

"O, cried he, very unsuspiciously, there are a great num. of authors unknown at present. Several good things have appeared without any Name to them.

[...]

"But, cried Richard, [...] I am quite lost!—such amazing knowledge of Characters,—such an acquaintance with *high*, & *low* Life,—such universal & extensive knowledge of the World,—I declare, I know not a Man Breathing who is likely to be the Author,—unless it is my Uncle."

All this extravagant praise redoubled my difficulties in making my confession; but he would not let me rest, & followed me about the Room, till I feared Miss Humphries would hear the subject of his earnestness. At last, he brought me a pen & some Paper, & begged me to *write* the name, promising not to read it till I left him. I am sure, by his manner, that if he *had* a suspicion, it was of my Father.

I only wrote, on this Paper, "No Man,"—& then folded it up. He was extremely eager to see it, but I told him he must first make an *oath* of secresy. He put his Hand on his Heart, & promised, by his Honour, to be faithful.

"But this, cried I, won't satisfy me;—you must kiss [the] Bible,—or kneel down, & make a Vow, that you will never tell *any* body in the World."

"Good God! cried he, astonished,—what, not a *sister*?"

"No, not a human Being."

"But, not *Betsy*?—O, pray let me tell *her!*"

"No, no,—not a soul!

"But—sha'n't I Laugh, when I see them reading it?"

"I can't recede,—you must tell *Nobody*,—or not hear it.

"Good God!—Well, I *must* vow, then, to satisfy my curiosity."

"Kneel, then," cried I.—he Laughed, but seemed all amazement; however, he could not kneel, for Miss Humphries looked round; but I made him repeat after me, that he would never communicate what he was to hear, to any human Being, without my leave; & this he protested by all he held sacred on Earth, or in Heaven.

I then gave up my Paper, & ran to the Window He read it with the extremest eagerness,—but still did not seem to comprehend how the affair stood, till he came to the Window,—& then, I believe, my Countenance cleared up his doubts.

His surprise was too great for speech; Susan says he Coloured violently,—but I could hardly look at him. Indeed, I believe it utterly impossible for astonishment to be greater, than his was at that moment.

When he recovered somewhat from it, he came to me again, & taking my Hand, said "I believe I must now kneel indeed! —" & drawing me to the Fire, he actually knelt to me,—but I made him rise almost instantly.

After this,—as if he had forgot all the flattering speeches he had made about the Book, or as if he thought them all *inadequate* to what he *should* have said, he *implored* my forgiveness, for what he called his *Criticisms*, & seemed ready to kill himself for having made them. I know his [partiality][1] to be [so] great, that, had he ever suspected me, I am sure he would offered me nothing short of *Adulation*.

50.   March 30th.

[...]

As to a *Critique*,—it is with fear & fidgets I attend it;—next *Wednesday* I expect to be in one of the Reviews,—oh Heavens, *what* should I do, if I were *known!*—for I have very little doubt but I shall be horribly mauled.

---

1 Substitution.

And—*Mauled*, indeed, I have been!—but not by the Reviewers,—no,—with them I have come off with flying Colours,—but I have had a long & a dangerous Illness [...]

I will Copy the Monthly Review of my Book; In the Critical I have not yet appeared.

But hold,—first, in order, comes
The London review, by *W*. Kenrick;[1]

51.   THE LONDON REVIEW.
                        February 1778

The history of a young lady exposed to very critical situations. There is much more merit, as well respecting stile, character and incident, than is usually to be met with among our modern novels.

52.   THE MONTHLY REVIEW.
                        April 1778

This novel has given us so much pleasure in the perusal, that we do not hesitate to pronounce it one of the most sprightly, entertaining, and agreeable productions of this kind, which has of late fallen under our notice. A great variety of natural incidents, some of the comic stamp, render the narrative extremely interesting. The characters, which are agreeably diversified, are conceived and drawn with propriety, and supported with spirit. The whole is written with great ease and command of language. From this commendation, however, we must except the character of a son of Neptune,[2] whose manners are rather those of a rough, uneducated, country 'squire, than those of a genuine sea-captain.

                        JOURNAL FOR 1778

53.   June 18th.

[*FB went to Chessington to convalesce after her illness.*]
Here I am, & here I have been this Age; though too weak to think of Journalising; however, as I have never had so many curious

---

1 William Kenrick founded the *London Review of English & Foreign Literature* in 1775. He was notorious for his scurrilous attacks on writers.
2 Captain Mirvan.

anecdotes to record, I will not at least *this Year*,—the first of my *appearing in public*,—give up my favourite old Hobby Horse. [...]

My recovery [...] has been *slow & sure*; but, as I could walk hardly 3 yards in a Day at first, I found so much Time to spare, that I could not resist treating myself with a little *private sport* with Evelina,—a young lady whom I think I have some right to make free with. I had promised *Hetty* that *she* should read it to Mr. Crisp, at her own particular request; but I wrote my excuses, & introduced it myself.

I told him it was a Book which Hetty had taken to Brumpton, to divert my Cousin Richard during his Confinement, [& I pretended to know nothing of it myself.] He was so indifferent about it, that I thought he would not give himself the trouble to read it; & often embarrassed me by unlucky Questions; such as, *if it was reckoned clever?* & *what I thought of it?*—& *whether folks laughed at it?* [However,] though I always evaded any direct or satisfactory answer he was so totally free from any idea of suspicion, that my perplexity escaped his Notice. At length, he desired me to begin reading to him. I dared not trust my voice with the little introductory ode, for as *that* is no romance, but the sincere effusion of my Heart, I could as soon read aloud my own Letters, written in my own Name & Character: I therefore *skipped* it, & have so kept the Book out of his sight, that, to this Day, he knows not it is there. Indeed, I have, since, heartily repented that I read *any* of the Book to him, for I found it a much more awkward thing than I had expected: my voice quite faltered when I began it, which, however, I passed off for the effect of remaining weakness of Lungs; &, in short, from an *invincible* embarrassment, which I could not for a page together repress, the Book, by my reading, lost all manner of spirit.

Nevertheless, though he has by no means treated it with the praise so lavishly bestowed upon it from all other Quarters, I had the satisfaction to observe that he was even *greedily* eager to go on with it; so that I flatter myself the *story* caught his attention: &, indeed, allowing for my *mauling* reading, he gave it much [more] credit as I had any reason to expect. But, now that I was sensible of my error in being my own Mistress of the Ceremonies, I determined to leave to Hetty the 3^{d}. Volume, & therefore pretended I had not brought it. He was in a delightful ill humour about it, & I *enjoyed* his impatience far more than I should have done his forbearance.

Hetty, therefore, when she comes, has undertaken to *bring it*.
[...]

To be sure, the concealment of this affair has cost me no few Inventions, & *must* cost me many, many more; but I am so well satisfied of their innocency, & feel so irresistably their necessity, that I do not find they at all affect my conscience. And yet, perhaps no body can have a more real & forcible detestation of falsehood & of [*Equivocating*] than myself; but in this particular case, I have no alternative, but avowing myself for an authoress, which I cannot bear to *think of*, or exerting all my faculties to ward of *suspicion*.

But,—two Days after, I received, from Charlotte, a Letter the most interesting that could be written to me,—for it acquainted me that my dear Father was, at length, reading my Book!!!—

How this has come to pass, I am yet in the dark; but, it seems, the very moment, almost, that my Mother & Susan & Sally left the House, he desired Charlotte to bring him the Monthly Review,— she contrived to look over his shoulder as he opened it, which he did at the account of *Evelina, or a young lady's Entrance into the World*. He read it with great earnestness,—then put it down; & presently after, snatched it up, & read it again. Doubtless his paternal Heart felt some agitation for his Girl, in reading a review of her Publication!—*how* he got at the *name*, I cannot imagine![1]

Soon after, he turned to Charlotte, [& asked if she could go to Fleet Street? but, immediately after, said she could not be back in Time, as he must go out in half an Hour; then,] bidding her come close to him, he put his Finger on the Word Evelina, &, saying *she knew what it was*, bid her write down the Name, & send the Man to Lowndes, as if for herself. This she did, & away went William![2]

He then told Charlotte that he had never known the name of it till the Day before: 'tis strange *how* he got at it!—& added that I had come off vastly well in this Review: except for the *Captain*; Charlotte told him it had also been in Kenrick's review, & he desired her to copy out for him what was said in *both* of them. He asked her, too, whether I had mentioned the Work was by *a Lady*? & When William returned, he took the Books from him, &, the moment he was gone, opened the 1st. Volume,—& opened it upon the *Ode!*—

---

1 Many years later, FBA discovered that SEB had told CB.
2 The Burneys' servant. Lowndes's shop was in Fleet Street.

How great must have been his astonishment, at seeing himself so addressed! Indeed, Charlotte says, he looked all amazement, read a line or 2 with great eagerness,—& then, stopping short, exclaimed "Good God!"—&, as he read on, he seemed quite affected, [again][xxx] & the Tears started into his Eyes: dear soul! I am sure they did into *mine*, nay I even [*slobbered*] as I read the account. I believe he was obliged to go out, before he advanced much further. But the next Day, I had a Letter from Susan, in which I heard that he had begun reading it with Lady Hales & Miss Coussmaker! & that they *liked it vastly!*—I was, indeed, a little startled at this intelligence, but I received, at the same Time, assurances that my Father neither did, nor would betray me, & had only told them it was recommended to him by an acquaintance. Susan, who knew how deeply I should be interested in all that related to this affair, was very particular in her accounts: & highly flattering were all the Comments she transmitted to me.

[...]

54.   Susan Burney to Frances Burney
                 16 June 1778, London

[...]

My dear Dad came in in very good spirits & invited me into his Study—told me he had just [xxx] recollected that he had a Letter to give me from Miss Couss—written when he took leave of her Sunday = "I dare say, s^d. he, she talks to you in it of *the Book*—We've finished Evelina = Indeed!—And....What are your real sentiments of it? = Why *Upon my Soul I think it the best Novel I know except Fielding's*—& in some respects it is better than his—I have been *excessively* pleased wth. it—there are perhaps a few things might have been otherwise—Mirvan's trick upon Lovel is I think carried too far—I don't hate that young man enough, ridiculous as he is, to be pleased or diverted at his having his ear torn by a monkey—there's a something disgusting in it. = but the Capt. is reckoned a Brute by *everybody* = Why that's true—but in this case 'tis a brutality wch. does not make one laugh—Now Mad^e. Duval loss of her curls & all that is very diverting—However *except this instance* I declare I think the Book w^d. *scarce bear an improvement!*—I wish I may die if I do not believe it to be the best Novel in the language—Fielding's excepted—for Smollett's are so d——d *gross* that they are not fit reading for women wth. all their wit—M^r. Villars Character is admirably supported—& rises upon one in every Let-

ter—the language throughout his Letters are *as good as any body need write* (NB. spoken w^{th}. *emphasis* & spirit) I declare as good as I w^d. wish to read!—& every Letter of his seems to me better & better—L^d. Orville's character is just what it ought to be— perfectly Benevolent & upright = And without being *fade*, I think = Oh entirely—there's a *boldness* in it that struck me mightily—He is a Man not *ashamed* of being better than the rest of Mankind—indeed I am excessively pleased wth. him—Evelina is in a new style too—so perfectly natural & innocent—& the scene between her & her father, Sir John Belmont——I protest I think 'tis a scene for a Tragedy—I *blubber'd* = No—did you Sir—? How the *Ladies* must Cry = Oh! I don't think they've recovered it yet—It made them quite ill—'tis indeed wrought up in a most extraordinary manner—I laid the Book down—& c^d. not for sometime get on with it = Oh Miss Coussmaker was distracted about it before—what she will be *now* I can't tell—but she'll be wanting me to tell her *my* opinion of it & I shall scarce know what to say = Oh speak out about it as you w^d. of another Book—*I have*—& if it was to be discovered I sh^d. tell them that I was as much at liberty to admire or criticise as them, for I'm sure I knew as little about it.—However keep snug for poor Fan's sake—tho' I protest that sometime hence I sh^d. think there w^d. be no kind of impropriety in its being known—on the contrary it w^d. do her a great deal of credit—For a young Woman's work I look upon it to be really *Wonderful*!" (His own very words as I hope to live!)
[...]

JOURNAL FOR 1778

55.

[...]
Well, I cannot but rejoice that I published the Book, little as I ever imagined how it would fare; but, hitherto, it has occasioned me no small diversion,—& *nothing* of the disagreeable sort,—but I often think a change *will* happen, for I am by no means so sanguine as to suppose such success will be uninterrupted. Indeed, in the midst of the greatest satisfaction that I feel, an inward *something* which I cannot account for, prepares me to expect a reverse! for the more the Book is drawn into notice, the more exposed it becomes to criticism & annotations.

June 23ᵈ

O—not yet,—not yet, at least, is come the reverse! I have had a visit from my beloved, my kindest Father—& he came determined to complete my recovery by his goodness. I was *almost* afraid—& *quite* ashamed to be alone with him—but he soon sent for me to his little Gallery Cabinet—& then, with a significant smile that told me what was coming, & made me glow to my very forehead with anxious expectation, he said "I have read your Book, Fanny—but you need not blush at it:—it is full of Merit—it is really extraordinary.—" I fell upon his Neck with heart-beating emotion, & he folded me in his arms so tenderly that I sobbed upon his shoulder—so delighted was I with his precious approbation. But I soon recovered to a gayer pleasure, more like his own: though the length of my illness, joined to severe mental suffering from a Family calamity which had occurred at that period, had really made me too weak for a joy mixt with such excess of amazement. I had written my little Book simply for my amusement; I printed it, by the means first of my Brother, Charles, next of my Cousin, Edward Burney, merely for a frolic, to see how a production of my own would figure in that Author like form: but as I had never read any thing I had written to any human being but my sisters, I had taken it for granted that They, only, could be partial enough to endure my Compositions. My unlooked for success surprized, therefore, my Father as much as myself—

56.   FRANCES BURNEY TO THOMAS LOWNDES
                30 June 1778, Chessington

A long and dangerous illness having, for some months past, confined me in the country, it was not till yesterday that I sent to Gregg's to enquire if any parcel had been left there for Mʳ. Grafton.

In the hurry of your Business, & the variety of your concerns, you have probably forgotten that the set of Evelina which you sent to me for the Errata, is incomplete & unbound, & that I begged of you to make it perfect, by sending the 1ˢᵗ. & last sheets.

However, as I have, since, made certain marginal notes that will make it impossible for me to send it to a Book-Binder, I now write to beg the favour of you to let me have a finished set, sent according to the former direction.

I should not give you this trouble, but that I am informed it is by no means customary for an author to *purchase* his own productions, for his own use,—though their value may, probably, be by no one so readily acknowledged.

Sh^d. the Book pass through another Edition, I sh^d. be glad to have Timely notice, as I have many corrections, & some alterations, to propose. I find that no acc^t. has yet appeared in the Critical Review: I am extremely satisfied with what is said in the Monthly & London:—& I heartily hope that that general sale will somewhat more than answer your Expectations.

57.   THOMAS LOWNDES TO FRANCES BURNEY
              2 July 1778, London

I Bound up a Sett for you the first Day I had one & hoped by some means to hear from you The great World send here to buy Evelina A polite Lady said Do Mr. Lowndes give me Evelina Im treated as unfashionable for not having read it I think the impression will be sold by Christmas if mean time or about that time you favour me with any Commands I shall be proud to observe them

58.   SUSAN BURNEY TO FRANCES BURNEY
              post 16 June 1778, London

[...]
[*SEB reports CB's account of* Evelina's *reception at Streatham, home of the Thrales and centre of a literary circle that included Samuel Johnson.*]
I have *such* a thing to tell you s^d. he [my Father][1] about poor Fan! = L^d. Sir, what?—& I immediately suppos'd he had spoke to M^rs. Thrale? = Why to Night, we were sitting at tea—only Johnson— M^rs. Thrale & me—"Madam," cried Johnson, *seesaw-ing* on his Chair—M^rs. Cholm'ley was talking to me last night of a new Novel, wch. she says has a very uncommon share of merit—*Evelina.*—She says she has not been so much entertained this great while as in reading it—& that she shall go all over London in order to discover the author = Good G-d, cried M^rs. Thrale (do you tremble, my dear Fanny?)—why somebody else mentioned that Book to me—Lady Westcote it was I believe—*The modest writer of* Evelina she talk'd to me of. = M^rs. Cholm'ley says she never met so much modesty with so much merit before in any literary performance, s^d. *Johnson*. = Why, s^d. I quite cooly & innocently, somebody

---

1 Inserted by FBA.

recommended it to *me* too—& I read a little of it, wch. indeed seem'd to be above the common place works of this kind = Well, s^d. M^{rs}. Thrale, I'll get it certainly = It will do, s^d. I, for your time of confinement I think = You *must* have it Madam, cried Johnson, for Mrs. Cholm'ley says she shall keep it on her Table the whole summer, that every body that knows her may see it—for she says everybody ought to read it!————

[...]

59.   FRANCES BURNEY TO SUSAN BURNEY
        5 July 1778, Chessington

Don't you think there must be some wager depending, among the *little Curled Imps* who hover over *us* Mortals, of *how much flummery goes to turn the Head of an Authoress?*—Your last communication very near did my business! for, meeting M^r. Crisp ere I had composed myself, I *"tipt him such a touch of the Heroicks,"* as he has not seen since the Time when I was so much celebrated for *Dancing Nancy Dawson*.[1] I absolutely longed to treat him with one of Capt. Mirvan's frolics, & to fling his wig out of the Window.—however, I restrained myself, from the apprehension that they would imagine I had a *universal spite* to that harmless piece of Goods, which I have already been known to treat with no little indignity.[2] He would fain have discovered the *reason* of my skittishness,—but as I could not tell it him, I was obliged to assure him 'twould be lost Time to enquire further into my flights, since *"True no meaning puzzles more than Wit."*[3]—& therefore, *begging the favour* of him to *"set me down an ass,"*[4] I suddenly retreated.

My dear, dear Dr. Johnson!—what a charming Man you are!—why Cousin Charles could not be more worthy & affable—Mrs. Cholmondely,[5] too, I am not merely *prepared*, but *determined* to admire—for really she has shewn so much penetration & sound sense of late, that I think she will bring about a union between Wit

1 A hornpipe from the *Beggar's Opera*, named after the celebrated dancer Nancy Dawson.
2 An allusion to a childhood prank.
3 Pope, "Moral Essays: Epistle to a Lady," l. 114.
4 Cf. "Be sure you write him down an Ass" in Arthur Murphy's two-act farce, *The Apprentice* (1756).
5 Mary Woffington Cholmondeley, a society hostess and member of the Bluestocking circle.

& Judgement, though their separation has been so long, & though their meetings have been so few.—But,—Mrs. Thrale!—She, she is the Goddess of my Idolatry!—*What* an *eloge* is hers!—an *eloge* that not only delights at *first*, but that proves more & more flattering every Time it is considered!—[1]

I often think, when I am counting my Laurels, what pity it would have been had I *popt off* in my last Illness, without knowing what a *person of Consequence* I was!—& I sometimes think, that, were I *now* to have a Relapse, I could never *go off* with so much *Eclat!*—I am now at the *summit* of a high Hill,—my prospects, on one side, are bright, glowing, & invitingly beautiful;—but when I turn round, I perceive, on the other side, sundry Caverns, Gulphs, pits & precipices, that to *look at*, make my Head giddy, & my Heart sick!——I see about me, indeed, many Hills of far greater height & sublimity;—but I have not the strength to attempt climbing them;—if *I* move, it must be in *descending!* I have already, I fear, reached the *pinnacle* of my Abilities, & therefore to *stand still* will be my best policy:—But there is nothing under Heaven so difficult to do!—Creatures who are formed for Motion, *must* move, however great their inducements to forbear. The wisest Course I could take, would be to bid an eternal adieu to Writing; then would *the Cry* be "'Tis pity she does not go on!—she might do something better by & by;—" &c, &c, *Evelina*, as a First, & a youthful publication, has been received with the utmost favour & lenity,—but would a future attempt be treated with the same Mercy?—No, my dear Susy, quite the contrary,—there would not, indeed, be the same *plea* to save it,—it would no longer be a *Young Lady's first appearance* in public;—those who have met with less indulgence, would all *peck* at any new Book;—& even those who most encouraged the 1st. offspring, might prove Enemies to the 2^{d}., by receiving it with Expectations which it could not answer.— —& so, between either the Friends or the Foes of the *Eldest*, the 2^{d}. would stand an equally bad chance, & a million of *flaws* which were overlooked in the former, would be ridiculed as villainous & intolerable *Blunders* in the latter.—But, though my Eyes Ache as I strain them to look

---

1 On 4 July 1778 SEB had written to FB, describing CB's account of HLT's initial response to *Evelina*, of which she said, "I was a little afraid (from the name I suppose), it had been a mere Sentimental business— but there's a vast deal of humour & entertainment in it [...]—It's writ by somebody that knows *the top & the bottom—the highest & lowest* of Mankind—" (Berg, ms. letter, no pagination).

forward,—the temptations before me are *almost* irresistable,—& what you have transcribed from *Mrs. Thrale*—may, perhaps, prove my destruction!—

[...]

60.   FRANCES BURNEY TO DR. CHARLES BURNEY
6 July 1778, Chessington

I have *just* received from Susan an Account of a little *Embarras* you have been in, upon the affair of my *Schtoff*;[1] & I know not how to thank you for the kind manner in which you guard my secret:— indeed, every Soul, but yourself, who is acquainted with it, I have made take a solemn Oath, [*by all they held most sacred,*][xxx] never to reveal it, without my consent. I was sure it would be impossible for me to be too cautious.

But with *You*, the matter has not merely the constrained difference of Duty, but the voluntary one of Inclination, & I should be *ashamed* if I thought *you* had any restriction, but your own Judgement;—for *my* Honour, Interest & Welfare I know are *yours*, & to you, therefore, (though to *you only*,) I willingly commit the same unlimited liberty of concealment or Discovery which, of course, I reserve for myself.

Believe me, my dearest Father, I don't *puff* when I tell you it has always been as much upon *your* account as my own, that I have so earnestly desired to continue *incog.*; for *I*, as *myself*, am Nobody; but as *your* [*Spawn*], I could easily make myself *known*, & have power to *disgrace*, though not to *credit* you,—as I have said already, with *truth*, though not with the *Flowers of poetry*, in the foolish Lines I ventured to insert in my so highly honoured *Wollums*,—& which cost me more Time in deliberating whether or not to *Print* than they did to *write* them,—but I hope their sincerity will make you accept them as *meant*, for I may truly say they *flowed from the Heart*, since I wrote them, in the very fullness of it, in the Dead of the very Night that I owned to you my secret; & my views & intentions relative to it,—all which you took so kindly, that I could not resist making the attempt, as soon as I had *de tort*,—& the very next Day,—I parted with all power of *retreat*, by giving up my M.S.

[...]

---

1 A family joke, for the German pronunciation of "stuff."

61.   SUSAN BURNEY TO FRANCES BURNEY
                    post 6 July 1778, London

[...]
When my Mother was saying something in favour of the Book the other Morn^g. "Oh, s^d. he [*CB*], One might be sure there must be *something* in it by M^rs. Cholmondeley's recommending it so strongly—for such women as she & M^rs. Thrale are *afraid* of praising *à tort et à travers*[1]—& if there is not something more than common, as they know they are liable to have their opinions *quoted*, they are d——lish shy of speaking favourably."—To me, I believe I have already told you, he s^d. you c^d. not have had a greater compliment than the making these two Ladies your Friends—as they were *d— —d severe* & *d——d knowing*—you must excuse the *energy* of the Expression!
[...]

62.   FRANCES BURNEY TO DR. CHARLES BURNEY
                    8 July 1778, Chessington

The *request* you have condescended to make me, I *meant* to anticipate in my last Letter.[2] How good you are, to pave the way for my secret's being favourably received, by sparing your *own* Time & Breath, to gain the Book attention & partiality!—I can't express a third part of either the gratitude or pleasure I feel, upon hearing, from Susy, that you are reading it aloud to my Mother,—because I well know, nothing can give it so good a chance with her, or indeed with *any body*, & I would have given the World you had Read it to M^rs. Thrale,—as she *was* to hear it,—for so *Fortune*, in the shape of M^rs. Cholmley, seemed to decree.
[...]
    My Mother will the sooner pardon my privacy, when she hears that even from *you* I used every method in my power to keep my Trash concealed, & that I even yet know not in what manner you got at the Name of it. Indeed, I only proposed, like my friends the Miss *Branghtons*, a little *private fun*, & never once Dreamt of extending my confidence beyond my sisters.

---

1 At random.
2 CB had requested permission to reveal FB's authorship to HLT and to EAB.

As to M^rs. Thrale,—your wish of telling *her* quite *unmans* me—
I *shook* so, when I read it, that, had any body been present, I must
have betrayed myself,—&, indeed, many of my late Letters have
given me such extreme surprise,—& *perturbation*, that I believe
nothing could have saved me from M^r. Crisp's discernment, had he
seen me during my first reading: however, he has not an idea of the
kind.—

But,—if you do tell M^rs. Thrale,—won't she think it very
strange where I can have *kept Company*, to draw such a family as
the Branghtons, M^r. Brown & some others?—Indeed, (thank
Heaven!) I don't myself recollect ever passing half an Hour at a
Time with any *one* person *quite* so bad;—so that, I am afraid she
will conclude I must have an *innate vulgarity of ideas* to assist me
with such coarse colouring for the objects of my Imagination.
Not that I suppose the *Book* would be better received by her, for
having Characters *very pretty, & all alike*; my only fear, in regard to
that particular, is for poor Miss Bayes!—If I were able to *insinuate
the plot into the Boxes*,[1] I should build my defence upon Swift's
maxim, *that a Nice man is a man of Nasty ideas.*[2]—I should certainly have been more finical, had I foreseen what has happened, or
had the most *remote* notion of being known by *Mrs. Thrale* for the
scribe;—however, 'tis perhaps as well as it is, for these kind of
Compositions lose all Their spirit if they are too scrupulously corrected: besides, if I had been very nice, I must have cleared away
so much, that, like poor M^r. Twiss after his friends had been so
obliging as to give his Book a scourge, nothing but hum drum
matter of Fact w^d. be left.[3] Indeed I never found courage sufficient to ask any advice of the *useful* Confidents I *might* have
made,—you & my Daddy Crisp,—& my fear of Discovery was so
great, that I never found opportunity to read even to the kind
ones, I *did* make, except Esther & Mr Burney—Edward & my
Aunts, Charles, Charlotte—&, far worse, Susan herself never saw
it in MSS. [...]

---

1   FB quotes the hapless dramatist Bayes from the first act of *The Rehearsal*
    (1671) by George Villiers, Duke of Buckingham.
2   *Thoughts on various subjects* (1727).
3   FB refers to Richard Twiss's *Travels through Portugal and Spain*, which in
    an earlier entry she criticised for overcautious editing (See *EJ* 2: 135).

63. August 3ᵈ.

[...]

I now come to last Saturday Evening,—when my beloved Father came to Chesington,—in full Health, charming spirits, & all kindness, openness, & entertainment.

As soon as I was alone with him, he presented me a little parcel; it consisted of my new set of Evelina, which Mr. Lowndes sent to *Mr. Grafton*, & which are charmingly Bound.—He then most affectionately congratulated me upon it's great success, & communicated to me a thousand delightful things relative to it.

[...]

In his way hither, he had stopped [to give Miss Thrale a Lesson] at Stretham: & he settled with Mrs. Thrale that he would call on her again in his way to Town, & carry *me* with him!—& Mrs. Thrale said "We all long to know her."—I have been in a kind of *twitter* ever since, for there seems something very formidable in the idea of Appearing as an *Authoress*! I *ever* dreaded it, as it is a Title which must raise more expectations than I have any chance of answering. Yet I am highly flattered by her invitation, & highly delighted in the prospect of being introduced to the Stretham society.

She sent me some very *serious advice* to write for the *Theatre*, as she says, I so naturally run into conversations, that Evelina absolutely & plainly points out that path to me: & she hinted how much she should be pleased to be *"Honoured with my Confidence."*

[...]

But,—if I *do* go to Stretham, & can muster so much courage, I shall certainly speak *earnestly* to her not to spread my affair any further. My dear Father communicated all this intelligence, & a great deal more, with a pleasure that almost surpassed that with which I heard it: & he seems quite *eager* for me to make another attempt. He desired to take upon himself the communication to my Daddy Crisp; & as the affair is now in so many Hands, that it is possible *Accident* may discover it to him, I readily consented.

Sunday Evening, as I was going into my Father's Room, I heard him say, "the variety of characters,—the variety of scenes, & the *Language*,—why she has had very little Education but what she has given *herself*,—less than any of the others!"—& Mr. Crisp exclaimed "Wonderful!—it's *wonderful!*"—I now found what was going forward, & therefore deemed it most fitting to decamp.

About an Hour after, as I was passing through the Hall, I met my Daddy;—His Face was all animation & archness,—he doubled his Fist at me, & would have stopt me, but I ran past him into the Parlour.

Before Supper, however, I again met him, & he would not suffer me to escape; he caught both my Hands, & looked as if he would have looked me through,—& then exclaimed "Why you little [Hell!]—you young Devil!—a'n't you ashamed to look me in the Face?—you *Evelina* you!—Why what a Dance have you led me about it!—Young Friend, indeed!—O you little [Hell Fire!] What tricks have you served me!"—

I was obliged to allow of his running on with these gentle appellations for I know not how long ere he could sufficiently compose himself, after his great surprise, to ask or hear any particulars of the affair.—& then, he broke out every 3 instants with exclammations of astonishment at how I had found *Time* to write so much *unsuspected*, & how & where I had picked up such various materials.—& not a few Times did he, with *me*, as he had with my Father, exclaim "*wonderful!*"—He has, since, made me read him all my Letters upon this Subject. He said Lowndes would have *made an Estate* had he given me [1100] pounds for it, & that he *ought not* to have given less! "You have nothing to do now, continued he, but to take your pen in Hand, for your Fame & reputation are made; & any Bookseller will snap at what you write." I then told him that I could not but, *really*, & *unaffectedly* regret that the affair was spread to Mrs. Williams'[1] & her Friends—"Pho, said he, if those who are proper Judges of the affair think it right it should be known, why should you trouble yourself about it? *You* have not spread it, there can be no imputation of vanity fall to *your* share, & it cannot come out more to your Honour than through such a Channel as Mrs. Thrale."

[...]

London. August

I have now to write an account of the most *consequential* Day I have spent since my Birth: namely, my Streatham visit.

[...]

---

1 Anna Williams, a blind poet who resided in Johnson's household. Johnson had recommended the novel to her, and told her of FB's authorship.

[*Conversing with HLT.*]

She talked a little while upon common topics, & then,—at last,—
she mentioned Evelina, calling it "*the Book of which I alone was
ashamed.*" And ashamed enough I felt, in Conscience! & I began
[*poking*] among the Books, in order to turn from her.

"Well, said she, it is a sweet pretty Book indeed! & Yesterday at
supper we talked it all over, & discussed all your Characters; but
Mr. Johnson's favourite is Mr. Smith!—he is *so* smart!—he declares
the *fine Gentleman manqué*[1] was never better drawn: & he acted him
all the Evening, saying *he was "all for the Ladies! whatever was agreeable to the Ladies!* & so on; while *I* took up Madame Duval, & told
them I *desired I might hear no more of such vulgar pieces of Fun!*—But
Mr. Johnson repeated whole scenes by Heart!—I declare I was
astonished at him!—O you can't imagine how much he is pleased
with the Book;—he "*could not get rid of the Rogue*", he told me."
[...]

I prevailed upon Mrs. Thrale to let me amuse *myself*, & she went
to obey *her Master's* orders, & Dress. I then *prowled* about, to chuse
some Book, & I saw, upon the Reading Table, Evelina;—I had just
fixed upon a new Translation of Cicero's Laelius, when the Library
Door was opened, & Mr. Seward Entered.[2] I instantly put away my
Book, because I dreaded being thought *studious* & affected. He
offered his service to find any thing for me, & then, in the same
Breath, ran on to speak of the Book with which I had, myself,
favoured the World!—The exact Words he began with I cannot recollect, for I was actually confounded by the attack: I had not any
idea that he knew of the affair; & his abrupt manner of letting me
know he was *au fait* equally *astonished* & *provoked* me: how different from the delicacy of Mr. & Mrs. Thrale!—I was so much
amazed, & so much displeased, that I could not speak a word, & he
then went on with some general praises, & said that I had hit off
the *City Manners* wonderfully.

I doubt not but he expected my thanks!—but I only stammered
out something of my surprise to find the affair *so spread*, & then,
with the coldest gravity, I seated myself, & looked another way.

It could not be very difficult for him, now, to perceive that he
had wholly mistaken *his Game*, & that my *Greediness* for praise was
by no means so *gluttonous* as to make me swallow it when so ill

---

1 Would-be fine gentleman.
2 William Seward, a member of the Thrales' literary circle.

Cooked; but I fancy he imagined I should, of course, be delighted to hear my *own* Book mentioned with Compliments, & so he concluded I should, with much eagerness, Enter upon the subject. [...]

He stayed, talking upon divers matters, till he was obliged to go & Dress for Dinner: & then, before he left me, he offered his service to find me any Book;—I accepted his offer, [& desired him to chuse,] as I did not know where to look, or for what. He spent no little Time ere he could satisfy himself, &, at last, he brought me a Book of Poems by Miss Aiken:[1] I Laughed *inwardly* at this Choice, which seemed *a Bob at the Court*,[2] but took it very chearfully, & said I had long wished to read them.

"But the doubt is, Ma'am, said he, whether they are her own writing." *Another Bob*, perhaps, thought I! however, I felt too innocent of *that* to be hurt. I asked him who *was* suspected as Author? "Why her Brother,—they Live in the same House." Ah, thought I, how kindly willing is the World to make charitable constructions! [...]

[*FB describes Johnson's arrival for dinner.*]

Soon after we were seated, this great man entered. I have so [great] a veneration for him, that the very sight of him inspires me with delight & reverence, notwithstanding the cruel infirmities to which he is subject; for he has almost perpetual convulsive [motions], either of his Hands, lips, Feet, or knees, & sometimes of all together. However, the sight of them can never excite ridicule, or, indeed, any other than melancholy reflections upon the imperfections of Human Nature; for this [man,] who is the acknowledged [Head of Literature] in this kingdom, & who has the most extensive knowledge, the clearest understanding, & the greatest abilities of any Living Author,—has a Face the most ugly, a Person the most awkward, & manners the most singular, that ever were, or ever can be seen. But all that is unfortunate in his *exterior*, is so greatly compensated for in his *interior*, that I can only, like Desdemona to Othello, "*see his Visage in his Mind*."[3] His Conversation is so replete with instruction & entertainment, his Wit is so ready, & his Language at once so original & so comprehensive, that I hard-

---

1 Anna Laetitia Aikin, later Mrs. Barbauld.
2 "Bob" carries a meaning of "taunt," suggesting that FB interpreted Seward's assiduity as a mockery of female authorship.
3 Cf. *Othello*, 1.3.252.

ly know any satisfaction I can receive, that is equal to listening to
him.
[...]

64. [*Back in London, FB recounts EBB's description of a meeting with
Frances Reynolds, sister to Sir Joshua Reynolds.*]

[...] she talked very much, & very highly, of a *new novel called Evelina*; [though without a shadow of suspicion as to the scribbler,]¹ &,
not contented with her own praise, said that Sir Joshua, who began
it one Day when he was too much engaged to go on with it, was
so much caught by it, that he could think of nothing else, & was
quite *absent* all the Day, not knowing a word that was said to him:
&, when he took it up again, found himself so much interested in
it, that he sat up all night to finish it!
[...]
    Sir Joshua, it seems, vows he would give 50 pounds to know the
Author!—I have, also, heard of a Mr Taylor, a Gentleman of Reading, by the means of Charles, who has declared he *will* find him
out!—This intelligence determined me upon going myself to Mʳ.
Lowndes, & finding out what sort of answers he made to such
curious Enquirers as, I found, were likely to address him. But, as I
did not dare trust *myself* to speak, for I felt that I should not be able
to act my part well, I asked my Mother to accompany me: [she was
pleased with the Task, &] determined, as if from a mere idea, yet
earnest curiosity, to *push the matter Home*.
    We introduced ourselves by Buying the Book, for which I had
a Commission from Mrs. Gast. Fortunately, Mr. Lowndes himself
was in the shop; as we found by his air of consequence and authority, as well as his age; for I never saw him before. The moment he
had given my Mother the Book, she asked if he could tell her who
wrote it? "No. he answered, I don't know myself."
    "Pho, Pho, said she, you mayn't chuse to *tell*, but you *must*
know."
    "I don't, indeed, Ma'am, answered he; I have no honour in
keeping the secret, for I have never been trusted. All I know of the
Matter is, that it is a Gentleman of the other End of the Town."
    And *that*, thought I, is *more* than even the *Author* knows! but I
took up an old Book, & turned my back, & seemed not to attend.

---

1 Inserted by FBA.

My Mother made a thousand other enquiries, to which his answers were to the following effect. That, for a great while, he did not know if it was a Man or a Woman; but now, he *knew that much*, & that he was a Master of his subject, & well versed in the manners of the Times. "For some Time, continued he, I thought it had been Horace Walpole's; for *he* once published a Book in this snug manner;[1] but I don't think it is now. I have often people come to enquire of me who it is;—but I suppose he will come out soon, & then, when the rest of the World knows it, *I* shall.—Servants often come for it from the other end of the Town, & I have asked them divers questions myself, to see if I could get at the Author; but I never got any satisfaction."

Just before we came away, upon my Mother's still further pressing him, he said, with a most important Face, "Why, to tell You the truth, Madam, I have been informed that it is a piece of *secret History*; &, in that case, it will never be known!"

This was too much for me; I grinned irrestistably; & was obliged to look out at the shop Door till we came away. How many ridiculous things have I heard upon this subject! I hope that, next, some particular *Family* will be fixed upon, to whom this *secret History* must belong! However, I am delighted to find myself so safe, & that if Sir Joshua, Mr. Taylor, Mrs. Cholmondley, or any other person, enquire of Mr. Lowndes,—they will not be much wiser for his intelligence.

65.   FRANCES BURNEY TO SUSAN BURNEY
          23-30 August 1778, Streatham

[...]
[*As a guest of HLT, FB joins the literary circle at Streatham. HLT and Johnson bring up the subject of a comedy. Later, HLT comes upon FB in the library, and resumes the subject.*]
"O ho, cried she, I have been looking for you; how soon did you & Mr. Johnson part? have you begun your Comedy?"

And then, she proceeded to give me her *serious advice* to actually set about one; she said it was her opinion I *ought* to do it the moment she had finished the Book; she stated the advantages attending Theatrical writing, & promised to *ensure* me success. "I

---

1   *The Castle of Otranto* (1765), published by Lowndes under a false name.

have asked Mr. *Johnson*, added she if he did not think you could write a Comedy,—& *he* said *yes!*"

"O Ma'am, cried I, think of the *poor* Miss Cumberlands!—it would be *my* turn to be *Hissed*, & to be *condoled* with then!"[1]

However, she has frequently *pressed* me to it since, nay, she declared to me *she should never be at rest till I did*.

Indeed, since the Ice *has* been broken, almost every thing that is said has some reference either to Evelina, or to the future plans which they have all formed for me:—so that, to enumerate them would be to write every thing that passes.

[...]

[*Johnson joins them in the library, and insists that FB sit by him.*]

"But, my dear, continued he, with a very droll look, what makes you so fond of the *Scotch?*—I don't like you for *that;*—I hate the Scotch, & so must you. I wish Branghton had sent the Dog to jail!—"[2]

"Why, Sir, said Mrs. Thrale, don't you remember he says he would, but that he should *get* nothing by it?"

"Why ay, true, cried the Doctor, see-sawing very solemnly, that, indeed, is some palliation for his forbearance.—But I must not have you so fond of the Scotch, my little Burney,—make your Hero what you will, but a *Scotchman*. Besides, you *talk* Scotch,— you say *the one*,—my dear, that's not English,—Never use that phrase again."

Now was not this *extremely* good in him? Who would not have concluded the Book must have *abounded* in Errors too widely spread, & too closely weaved into the general work, to allow of his instructing me in any *one?*

"O, cried I, I have written *any* thing that is *ignorant*, but I did not *mean* to be only *Scotch*."

"Perhaps, said Mrs. Thrale, it may be used in Macartney's Letter, & then it will be a *propriety*."

"No, Madam, no! cried he, you *can't* make a Beauty of it!—it is in the 3ᵈ. volume;—put it in *Macartney's* Letter & welcome!—that, or *any thing* that is nonsense."

[...]

---

1 A reference to an incident when the daughters of Richard Cumberland, the playwright, were hissed out of the theatre for the extravagance of their headdresses (See FB's letter to SEB, 21 August 1778, *EJ* 3:88).

2 I.e. Macartney. Johnson was notorious for his virulence against the Scotch.

[The following day, FB recounts Johnson's description of Bet Flint whom he characterizes as a "Wit" alongside the bluestocking Mrs. Montagu. HLT asked who Bet Flint was.]

"O, a fine Character, Madam!—she was *habitually* a Slut & a Drunkard, & *occasionally* [a Whore &] a Thief."

"And, for Heaven's sake, how came *you* to know her?"

"Why, Madam, she figured in the *Literary* world, too!—Bet Flint wrote her own Life, & called herself Cassandra,—& it was in Verse;—it began

> When Nature first ordained my Birth
> [A Diminitive]¹ I was Born on Earth;
> And then I came from a Dark abode
> Into a gay & gaudy World.

So Bet brought me her Verses to correct;—but I gave her half a Crown, & she liked it as well. Bet had a fine Spirit;—She Advertised for a Husband, but she had no success, for she told me no man aspired to her!—Then she hired very handsome Lodgings, & a Foot Boy;—& she got a Harpischord, but Bet could not *play*;—however, she put herself in fine attitudes, & *Drum'd.*"

[...]

"And pray what became of her? Sir?"

"Why, Madam, she stole a Quilt from the Man of the House, & he had her taken up;—but Bet Flint had a spirit not to be subdued,—so when she found herself obliged to go to Jail, she ordered a sedan Chair, & bid her Foot boy [go] before her! However, the Boy proved refractory, for *he* was ashamed, though his Mistress was not."

"And did she ever get out of Jail again, Sir?"

"Yes, Madam; when she came to her Trial,—the Judge,—who Loved a Wench at his Heart,—acquitted her. "So now, she said to me, the Quilt is my own!—& now I'll make a petticoat of it. —" O,—I Loved Bet Flint!—"

Lord, how we all [hollowed!]—[...]

[Later in the week.]

Dr. Johnson was very communicative concerning his present work of the Lives of the Poets;—*Dryden* is now in the Press; & he told us he had been just writing a Dissertation upon Hudibras.

---

1 Substitution.

He gave us an account of *Mrs. Lenox*;[1]—her Female Quixote is very justly admired here: indeed, *I* think *all* her Novels far the best of any *Living* Author,—but Mrs. Thrale says that though her *Books* are generally approved, Nobody likes *her*. I find *she*, among others, waited on Dr. Johnson, upon her commencing writer: & he told us that, at her request, he carried her to *Richardson*: "Poor Charlotte Lenox! continued he;—when we came to the House, she desired *me* to leave her, for, says she, "I am under great restraint in your presence, but if you leave me *alone* with Richardson, I'll give you a very good account of him:" however, I fear poor Charlotte was disappointed, for she gave me no account at all!"

[...]

Some Time after, turning suddenly to me, he said "Miss Burney, what sort of Reading do you delight in?—History?—Travels?—Poetry?—or Romances?—"

"O Sir! cried I, I dread being Catechised by *You*!—I dare not make *any* answer, for I [am sure] whatever I should say would be wrong!"—

"*Whatever* you should say?—how's that?"

"Why not whatever I *should*,—but whatever I *could* say."

He Laughed, &, to my great relief, spared me any further questions upon the subject. Indeed, I was very happy I had the presence of mind to *evade* him as I did, for I am sure the examination which would have followed, had I made any direct answer, would have turned out sorely to my discredit.

[...]

[*Johnson*] said he wished Richardson had been alive, "And then, he added, you should have been Introduced to him,—though, I don't know, niether;—Richardson would have been afraid of her!"

"O yes!—that's a likely matter!" quoth I.

"It's very true, continued he; Richardson would have been really *afraid* of her;—there is merit in Evelina which he could not have borne.—No, it would not have done!—unless, indeed, she would have flattered him prodigiously.—Harry Fielding, too, would have been afraid of her,—there's nothing so delicately finished in *all* Harry Fielding's Works, as in Evelina;—(Then, shaking his Head at me, he exclaimed) O, you little *Character-monger*, you!"

---

1 Charlotte Lennox, a novelist and miscellaneous writer, best known for *The Female Quixote* (1752).

Mrs. Thrale then returned to her charge, & again urged me about a Comedy,—& again I tried to silence her,—& we had a *fine fight* together;—till she called upon Dr Johnson to *back* her,—"Why, Madam, said he, Laughing,—she *is* Writing one!—What a rout is here, indeed!—She is writing one up stairs all the Time.—Who ever knew when she began Evelina? She is working at some Drama, depend upon it."

"True, true, Oh King!" thought I.

"Well, that *will* be a sly trick! cried Mrs. Thrale;—however, you know best, I believe, about That, as well as about every other Thing."

[...]

Dr. Johnson began Laughing very Heartily to himself, & when upon repeated entreaty, he confessed the subject of his mirth, what should it be but an idea that had struck him [that I should write *Stretham, a Farce*—Lord, how I Laughed, & he carried on the notion, &] said I should have *them all* in it, & give a touch of the Pitches & Tattersalls![1]

"O if she does!—cried Mrs. Thrale, if she *inserts* us in a *Coomedy*—we'll serve her trick for trick—she is a young Authoress, & very delicate,—say it will be hard if we can't frighten her into order."

[...]

[*In the evening, when other guests expressed their curiosity about the authorship of* Evelina, *FB was discomposed. Later, HLT teases FB by threatening to reveal her secret.*]

When Mrs. Thrale & I retired, she not only, as usual, accompanied me to my Room, but stayed with me at least an Hour, talking over the affair. I siezed, with eagerness, this favourable opportunity of conjuring her not merely not to tell Mr. *Lort* my secret, but ever after never to tell *any* body. For a great while she only *Laughed*, saying "Poor Miss Burney!—so you thought just to have played & sported with your sisters & Cousins, & had it all your own way!—but now you are *in for* it!— —but if you *will* be an Author & a Wit,—you must take the Consequence!"

["Indeed! cried I, yes, in such a manner as Bet Flint—"]

But, when she found me seriously urgent, & really frightened,—she changed her Note, & said, "O,—if I find you are in *earnest* in

---

1 The Pitches and the Tattersalls were neighbours of the Thrales who had been satirized by FB in previous letters (see *EJ* 3:84; *EJ* 3:123).

desiring concealment, I shall quite *scold* you!—for if such a desire does not proceed from *Affectation,*— 'tis from something *Worse.*"

"No, indeed, cried I, not from *Affectation,*—for my *conduct* has been as uniform in trying to keep snug as my *words*: & I *never* have wavered: I *never* have told *any body* out of my own Family, nor half the Bodies in it.—And I have so long forborn making this request to you, for no other reason in the World but for *fear* you should think me affected."

"Well, I *won't* suspect you of affectation,—returned she,—nay, I *can't,* for you have looked, like your name sake in the Clandestine Marriage, all this Evening, of *50 Colours, I wow & purtest;*[1]—but— when I clear you of *that,* I leave something *worse.*"

"And what,—dear Madam, *what* can be worse?"

"Why an over-delicacy that may make you unhappy all your Life!—Indeed you must *check* it,—you must get the better of it:— for *why* should you *write* a Book, *Print* a Book, & have every Body *Read* & *like* your Book,—& then sneak in a Corner & disown it!"

"My *printing* it, indeed, said I, tells terribly against me, to all who are unacquainted with the circumstances that belonged to it: but I had so little notion of being *discovered,* & was so well persuaded that the Book would never be *heard of,* that I really *thought* myself as safe, & *meant* to be as private, when the Book was at Mr. Lowndes', as when it was in my own Bureau."

"Well,—I don't know what we shall do with you!—it is a *sweet* Book, & it *will* make it's way; but indeed you must blunt a little of this delicacy,—for the Book has such success, that if *you* don't own it—somebody else will!"

[...]

Yet notwithstanding all her advice, & all her encouragement, I was so much *worked*[2] by the certainty of being *blown* so much more than I had apprehended, & by seeing that, in spite of all my efforts at *snugship,* I was in so foul,—I won't say *fair,*—a way of becoming a *downright* & *known* scribbler,—that I was really ill all night & I could not sleep,—&, at 4 in the morning, found myself so very unwell, that I was obliged to get up, & take a dose of nastiness with which Mr. Devaynes had furnished me, but which I had, hitherto, despised & rejected.

---

1   HLT recalls a speech by Mrs. Heidelberg about Fanny Sterling in Colman and Garrick's comedy, *The Clandestine Marriage* (1766), 1.2.
2   That is, worked up.

When Mrs. Thrale came to me the next morning, she was quite concerned to find I had *really* suffered from my panics;—"O Miss Burney, cried she, what shall we do with you?—this *must* be conquered, indeed; this delicacy *must* be got over."

"Don't call it *delicacy*, cried I, when I know you only think it folly."

"Why indeed, said she, Laughing, it is not very *wise!*"

"Well, cried I, if, indeed, I *am* in for it,—why I must seriously set about reconciling myself—yet I never can!"

"We all Love you, said the sweet woman,—we all Love you *dearly* already,—but the Time will come when we shall all be *proud* of you;—so proud we shall not know where to place you!—you must set about a *Comedy*,—& set about it openly; it is the true style of writing for you,—but you must give up all these fears & this shyness,—you must do it without any disadvantages,—& we will have no more of such sly, sneaking, private ways!"

[...]

66.   FRANCES BURNEY TO SUSAN BURNEY
                3 September 1778, Streatham

[...]

O Susy, I had *such* a Conversation with Mrs. Thrale!—We were alone in the Library for I believe 3 Hours [...]

Our Tête à Tête began by comparing Notes about Irene,[1] & picking out favourite passages, & agreeing that, though the Language & sentiments are equally Noble, there was not any reason to wonder that the play all together had no success on the stage. Thence we talked over the Plays we could recollect & discussed their several merits according to our particular Notions,—& when we had mentioned a great number, approving some for *This thing*, & disliking others for *that*,—Mrs. Thrale suddenly said "Now, Miss Burney, if *you* would write a Play, I have a Notion it would hit *my* Taste in *all* things;—do,—you *must* write one;—a *play* will be something *worth* your Time, it is the Road both to Honour & Profit,—& *why* should you have it in your power to gain [these rewards] & not do it?"

"O Ma'am—how *can* you—" But I won't write the Answers, or, rather, *exclammations* with which I interrupted her,—for they *make no effect upon paper!*—

_____

1 Johnson's tragedy, produced in 1749.

"I declare, continued she, I *mean*, & *think* what I say with all my Heart & soul!—You seem to me to have the right & true talents for writing a Comedy,—you would give us all the fun & humour we could wish, & you would give us a scene or 2 of the pathetic kind that would set all the rest off. If you would but *try*, I am *sure* you would succeed, & give us such a Play as would be an Honour to all your Family. And, in the *grave* parts, all your sentiments would be Edifying, & such as would *do good*,—& I am sure *that* would be real pleasure to you."—My dear Susy, I *assure* you I recollect her words as exactly as my memory will allow.

"Hannah More, added she, got near 400 pounds for her foolish play,[1]—& if *you* did not write a better than *hers*, I say you deserve to be *whipped!*—Your Father, I know, thinks the same,—but we will *allow* that *he* may be partial but what can make *me* think it?—& Dr. Johnson;—*he*, of all men, would not say it if he did not think it.

She then rejoiced I had published Evelina as I did, without shewing it to any body; "Because You have proved what are your own real resources, she said, & now,—you have nothing to do but to write a *Play*, [& both Fame & Profit will attend you.] Mr. Johnson, I am sure, will be at your service in any thing in his power,—we'll make him write your Prologue,—we'll make him carry your play to the Manag[ers] we'll do *any* thing for you, & so, I am sure, he readily will! As to *Plot, situation*, & *Character*,—*Nobody* shall assist you in *them*, for nobody *can!*"—In short, my dear Susy, I was ready to *greet*[2] at the kind things she said, & the sweet manner in which she said them [...]

67.   FRANCES BURNEY TO SUSAN BURNEY
          post 16-21 September 1778, Streatham

[...]
[*Johnson hears that Mrs. Montagu*[3] *is to dine with them at Streatham on Wednesday.*]
Dr. Johnson began to see-saw, with a Countenance strongly expressive of *inward fun*,—&, after enjoying it some Time in silence, he suddenly, & with great animation, turned to me, & cried *"Down*

---

1   More's tragedy, *Percy*, was produced in December 1777.
2   Weep.
3   Elizabeth Robinson Montagu (1720-1800), the "Queen of the Blues." She was a society hostess and patron of the arts. The best known of her own writings was her *Essay on the Writings and Genius of Shakespear* (1769).

with her, Burney!—*down* with her!—spare her not! attack her, fight her, & *down* with her at once!—*You* are a *rising* Wit,—*she* is at the *Top*,—& when *I* was beginning the World, & was nothing & nobody, the Joy of my Life was to fire at all the established Wits!—& then, every body loved to halloo me on;—but there is no Game *now*, & *now*, every body would be glad to see me *conquered*: but *then*, when I was *new*,—to vanquish the Great ones was all the delight of my poor little dear soul!—So at her, Burney!—at her, & *down* with her!"

O how we [all hollow'd!] By the way, I must tell you that Mrs. Montagu is in very great estimation here, even with Dr. Johnson himself, when others do not praise her *improperly*: Mrs. Thrale ranks her as the *first of Women*, in the Literary way.

[...]

Wednesday—at Breakfast, Dr. Johnson asked me if I had been reading his Life of Cowley?—"O yes!" cried I. "And what do you think of it?"

"I am delighted with it," cried I;—"& if I was *somebody*, instead of *Nobody*, I should not have read it without telling you sooner [what I]¹ think of it."

"Miss Burney, cried Mr. Thrale, you must get up your Courage for this encounter! I think you should *begin* with Miss Gregory;² & *down* with *her* first."

Dr. J. = No, no,—fly at the *Eagle*!—*down* with Mrs. Montagu herself!—I hope she will come *full* of Evelina!

Again, when I took up Cowley's Life, he made me put it away, to *talk*. I could not help remarking how very like Dr. Johnson is to his writing; & how much the same thing it was to *hear*, or to *read* him.—but that nobody could tell that, without coming to Streatham, for his Language was generally imagined to be laboured & studied, instead of the nice common flow of his Thoughts.

"Very true, said Mrs. Thrale, he *writes* & *talks* with the same ease, & in the same manner;—but, Sir, (to him) if *this Rogue* is like her Book,—how will she *trim* all of us by & by!—*Now*, she *daintys us up* with all the meekness in the World,—but when we are away, I suppose she pays us off finely!"

[...]

---

1 Substitution.
2 Dorothea Gregory, daughter of John Gregory, who wrote *A Father's Legacy to his Daughters* (1774), lived with Mrs. Montagu as her companion.

[*Mrs. Montagu arrives with Miss Gregory.*]

Now don't you want to hear a vast deal about her?—
She is middle sized, very thin, & looks infirm. She has a sensible & penetrating Countenance & the air & *manner* of a Woman [accustomed to being distinguished, & of great parts.]¹ Dr. Johnson, who agrees in this, says that a Mrs. Hervey of his acquaintance, says she can remember Mrs. Montagu *trying* for this same air & manner;—Mr. Crisp has said the same;—however, Nobody can *now* impartially see her, & not confess that she has extremely well *succeeded*.

[...]

[*HLT recommends* Evelina *to them.*]

"And Mr. Johnson, Ma'am, added my kind *Puffer*, says *Fielding* never wrote so *well*,—never wrote *equal* to this Book;—he says it is a better picture of Life & manners than is to be found *any* where in Fielding."

"Indeed? cried Mrs. Montagu, surprised, *that* I did not expect, for I have been informed it is the work of a young lady,—& therefore, though I expected a very pretty Book, I supposed it to be a work of mere Imagination;—& the *Name* I thought attractive;—but *Life & manners* I never dreamt of finding."

[...]

[*Johnson added his praises of* Evelina *during dinner. Afterwards, FB thanks him for the public praise.*]

"You were *very* kind, Sir, cried I, to speak of it with so much favour & indulgence at Dinner,—yet I hardly knew *how* to sit it, *then*,—though I shall be always proud to remember it here after."

"Why it is true, said he, kindly, that such things are disagreeable to sit,—nor do I wonder you were distressed,—yet, sometimes, they are *necessary*."

Was this not *very* kind?—I am sure he meant that the sanction of his good opinion, so publicly given to Mrs. Mongtagu, would, in a manner *stamp* the success of my Book: & though, had I been allowed to preserve the *snugshipness* I had plan'd, I need not have concerned myself at all about it's fate, yet now, that I find *myself* exposed with it, I cannot but wish it ensured from Disgrace.

"Well, Sir, cried I, I don't think I shall mind Mrs. Montagu herself *now*,—after what *you* have said, I believe I should not mind *abuse* from any one."

---

1 Substitution.

"No, no, never mind them! cried he, *resolve* not to mind them."
Mrs. Thrale then told me *such* civil Things!—Mrs. Montagu, it
seems, talked of nothing else, during my retreat, & enquired very
particularly what *kind* of Book it was? "And I told her, continued
Mrs. Thrale, that it was a picture of Life, Manners, & Characters;
But won't she go on? says she, surely she won't stop here? "Why,
said I, *I* [want her to go on in a *new* path,] I want her to write a
Comedy.—"But, said Mrs. Montagu, one thing must be considered; Fielding, who was so admirable in Novel writing, *never* succeeded when he wrote for the stage."

"Very well said, cried D^r. Johnson; that was an Answer which
showed she considered her subject."

So you see, Susy, they make nothing of coupling Fielding & me
together!—very affronting!—

Mrs. Thrale continued—"Well, but, apropos, said Mrs. Montagu,
if Miss Burney *does* write a play, I beg I may know of it, or, if she
thinks proper, *see* it;—& all my Influence is at her service;—we
shall *all* be glad to assist in spreading the Fame of Miss Burney."

O dear Susy!—you can't think how I tremble for what all this
will *end* in!—I verily think I had best stop where I am, & *never*
again attempt writing—for after so much Honour, so much success,—how shall I bear a downfall?—

[...]

[*The forthcoming second edition of* Evelina *is discussed.*]

Mrs. T. = O,—àpropos;—Now you have a new Edition coming
out, why should you not put your Name to it?

F:B. = O [Lord] Ma'am,—I would not for the World!

Mrs. T. = And why not? come, let us have done, now, with all this
Diddle Daddle.

F:B.—No,—indeed, Ma'am, so long as I Live I *never* can consent
to that!

Mrs. T. = Well, but, seriously, Miss Burney, why should you *not*? *I*
advise it with all my Heart; & I'll tell you why;—you want *harden-
ing,*—& how can you get it better than by putting your Name to
this Book, (to begin with,) which *every* body likes, & against which
I have heard *nobody* offer any objection?—You can never write
what will please *more* universally.

F:B. = But *why*, Ma'am, should I be *hardened*?

Mrs. T. = To enable you to bear a little abuse by & by.

F:B. = O [God] forbid I should be tried that way!

Mrs. T. = O, you must not talk so;—*I* hope I Live to see you trim'd
very handsomely.

F:B. = [God] forbid, God forbid!—I am sure I should Hang or Drown myself in such a Case!— —

Mrs. T. = You grieve me to hear you talk so;—is not *every* body abused that meets with success? You must prepare yourself not to mind a few squibs. How is Mr. Johnson abused!—& who thinks the worse of him?

This Comparison made me *Grin*,—& so our Discourse ended. But pray for me, my dear Susy, that Heaven may spare me the Horror irrecoverable of personal abuse!—Let them Criticise, cut, slash, without mercy my *Book*,—& let them *neglect me*,—but may God [xxx] avert my becoming a public Theme of Ridicule! In such a Case, how should I wish Evelina had followed her humble predecessors to the all devouring Flames![1]—which, in consuming *her*, would have preserved her Creatress!—

68.   FRANCES BURNEY TO SUSAN BURNEY
            26 September 1778, Streatham

[...]

A few Days since, at Dinner, Dr. Johnson repeated some verses, & asked Mrs. Thrale whose they were?—She said she knew not: he then asked *me*;—I made the same Answer:—"Miss Burney does not know either, said Mrs. Thrale, yet she is a very good English Classic."

Some Time after, when we were in the Library, he asked me very gravely if I *loved* reading? *Yes*, quoth I:—"Why do you doubt it, Sir?" cried Mrs. Thrale.

"Because, answered he, I never see her with a Book in her Hand. I have taken Notice that she never has been reading whenever I have come into the Room."

"Sir, quoth I, courageously,—I am always *afraid* of being caught Reading, lest I should pass for being *studious*, or *affected*, & therefore, instead of making a *Display* of Books, I always try to *hide* them,—as is the case at this very Time, for I have now your Life of Waller under my Gloves, behind me!—however, since I am *piqued* to it, I'll boldly produce my voucher.—"

[...]

"And *now*, quoth Mrs. Thrale, you must be more careful than ever of not being thought Bookish, for *now* you are known for a

---

1 A reference to FB's destruction of all her mss. on her fifteenth birthday.

Wit, & a belle esprit, you will be *watched*, &, if you are not upon your guard, all the Misses will rise up against you."

Dr. J. = Nay, nay, *now* it is too late! you may read as much as you will now, for you are *in for it*,—you are dipped, over Head & Ears,—in the Castalian stream,—& so, I hope, you will be *invulnerable*.[1]

[...]

69.   THE CRITICAL REVIEW
                  September 1778

This performance deserves no common praise, whether we consider it in a moral or literary light. It would have disgraced neither the head nor the heart of Richardson.—The father of a family, observing the knowledge of the world and the lessons of experience which it contains, will recommend it to his daughters; they will weep and (what is not so commonly the effect of novels) will laugh, and grow wiser, as they read; the experienced mother will derive pleasure and happiness from being present at its reading; even the sons of the family will forego the diversions of the town or the field to pursue the entertainment of Evelina's acquaintance, who will imperceptibly lead them, as well as their sisters, to improvement and to virtue.

If the author of this amusing and instructive novel possess any of Richardson's merits, he labours also under one of his principal faults. The gold is in some places beat out considerably too fine. The second volume deserves few of the solid praises which we with pleasure bestow on the first and the third. The Roman sibyl, after she had burnt part of her work, still persisted in demanding the same price for what remained; we should set a higher value upon this performance had the writer made it shorter————but perhaps, as Swift said of a long letter, he had not time.

[...]

---

1 The Castalian spring on Mt. Parnassus was sacred to the muses. It
   was frequently invoked in images of poetic inspiration, but here
   Johnson endows it with protective qualities like those attributed to
   the River Styx, into which Achilles was dipped to render him
   invulnerable.

70.   SAMUEL CRISP TO FRANCES BURNEY
              11 November 1778, Chessington

[...]
[SC has read FB's journal of her Streatham visit.]
I now proceed to assume the Daddy; & Consequently the Privilege of giving Counsel—Your kind & judicious Friends are certainly in the right, in wishing You to make your Talents turn to
some thing more solid than empty Praise—When You come to
know the World half so well as I do, & what Yahoos Mankind
are, you will then be convinc'd, that a State of Independence is
the only Basis, on which to rest your future Ease & Comfort—
You are now Young, lively, Gay; You please, & the World smiles
upon You:—this is your time—Years & Wrinkles in their due
Season, (perhaps attended with want of health & Spirits,) will
succeed—You will then be no longer the same Fanny of 1778,
feasted, caress'd, admir'd, with all the soothing circumstances of
your present Situation—the Thrales, the Johnsons, the Sewards,
Cholmondelys &c &c &c, who are now so high in fashion, &
might be such powerful protectors as almost to insure Success
to any thing that is tolerable, may then themselves be mov'd
off the Stage—I will no longer dwell on so disagreeable a
Change of the Scene—let me only earnestly urge You to act
vigorously (what I really believe is in your power) a distinguish'd
part in the present one—*"now while it is yet to day, & before the*
night cometh when no man can work"; *"for favour is deceitful, &*
Beauty is Vain."[1]
[...]
   Lastly, if you do resolve to undertake any thing of the Nature
your friends recommend, keep it (if possible) an impenetrable
Secret that you are even about such a Work.—Let it be all your
own till it is finish'd intirely in your own Way—it will be time
enough then to consult such friends as you think capable of judg-
ing & Advising— —if you suffer any one to interfere till then, 'tis
ten to one, 'tis the worse for it—it wont be all of a Piece—in these
Cases, generally the more Cooks, the worse broth; & I have more
than once Observd, those Pieces that have stole privately into the
world, without Midwives, or Godfathers & Godmothers, like your

---

1   John 9:4; Proverbs 31:30.

own, & the Tale of the Tub, & a few others, have far exceeded any that followed—

[...]

71.   SAMUEL CRISP TO FRANCES BURNEY
               8 December 1778, Chessington

[...]
'Tis true; I have more than once, Fanny, whisper'd in Your Ear, a gentle Caution—that You have much to lose—Why is that?—because much You have gain'd—Now You have gone so far, & so rapidly, You will not be allowed to Slacken your pace—this is so far from being meant as a discouragement, that it is intended to animate you.—But it will explain what was in my head, when I threw out those (perhaps *useless*, perhaps *too officious*) hints—I plainly foresaw (what has since happen'd) that, as your next step, You would be Urg'd, strongly Urg'd, by your many Friends & Admirers, to undertake a Comedy.—I think You Capable, highly Capable of it; but in the Attempt there are great difficulties in the way; some more peculiarly, & individually in the way of a Fanny than of most people—I will instantly name these, lest You should Misapprehend.—I need not Observe to *You*, that in most of Our successful comedies, there are frequent lively Freedoms, (& waggeries that cannot be called licentious, neither) that give a strange animation, & Vig[our] to the same; & of which, if it were to be depriv'd, it would lose wonderfully of its Salt, & Spirit—I mean, *such* Freedoms, as Ladies of the strictest Character would make no scruple, openly, to laugh at, but at the same time, especially if they were Prudes, (And You know You are one) perhaps would *Shy* at being *known* to be the Authors of—Some Comic Characters would be deficient without strokes of this kind in Scenes, where Gay Men of the World are got together, they are natural & expected, [& I suppose perfect Characters are out of the Question in a Comedy,][xxx] the business would be might apt to grow *fade* without them.
[xxx]
     Of late Years (I can't tell why, unless from the great Purity of the Age) some very fine-spun, *all*-delicate, Sentimental Comedies have been brought forth, on the English, & more particularly on the French Stage which, (in my Coarse way of thinking, at least,) are such sick things so Void of blood & Spirits! that they may well be call'd *Comedies Larmoyantes!*—and I don't find that they have

been greatly relished by the Public in general, any more than by *my* vulgar Soul—moral, sublime to a degree!

"*We cannot blame, indeed,—but we may Sleep!*"[1]

They put me in mind of a poor Girl, a Miss Peachy (a real, & in the end, a melancholy Story)—she was a fine young Woman; but thinking herself too ruddy & blowsy, it was her Custom to bleed herself (an Art she had learn'd on purpose) 3 or 4 times against the Rugby Races, in order to appear more dainty & Lady-like at the balls, &c.—poor thing!—She lost her Aim!—for when she came, She *appear'd like* a Ghost, & at last became one!—her Arm bled in the night, & in the morning She was past recovery!—I am afraid these fine performances are not pictures of real life & manners— [...]

Excuse these digressions—the sum total amounts to this—it appears to me extremely difficult, throughout a whole spirited Comedy to steer clear of those agreeable, frolicksome *jeux d'Esprit*, on the one hand; and languor & heaviness on the other:—pray Observe, I only say *difficult*—not *impracticable*—at least to your dexterity, & to that I leave it.

I find myself forestall'd by the intelligent M^rs. Montagu in another Observation I was going to make, & which she very justly & judiciously enforces by the instance she gives of Fielding, who tho' so eminent in Characters & descriptions, did by no means succeed in Comedy.

'Tis certain, different Talents are requisite for the two species of Writing, tho' they are by no means incompatible;—I fear, however, the labouring oar lies on the Comic Author.

In these little entertaining, elegant Histories, the writer has his full Scope; as large a Range as he pleases to hunt in—to pick, cull, select, whatever he likes:—he takes his own time; he may be as minute as he pleases, & the more minute the better; provided, that Taste, a deep & penetrating knowledge of human Nature, & the World, accompany that minuteness.—When this is the Case, the very Soul, & all it's most secret recesses & workings, are develop'd, & laid as open to the View, as the blood Globules circulating in a frog's foot, when seen thro' a Microscope.—The exquisite touches such a Work is capable of (of which, Evelina is, without flattery a

---

1 Pope, "Essay on Criticism," l. 242.

glaring instance) are truly charming.—But of these great advantages, these resources, YOU are strangely curtailed, the Moment You begin a Comedy: *There* every thing passes in Dialogue, all goes on rapidly;—Narration, & description, if not extremely Short, become intolerable.—The detail, which in Fielding, Marivaux, Crebillon, is so delightful, on the *Stage* would bear down all patience,—*There* all must be compress'd into Quintessence—The Moment the Scene ceases to move on briskly, & business seems to hang, Sighs & Groans are the Consequence!—Oh dreadful Sound!—in a Word, if the plot, the Story of the Comedy, does not open & unfold itself in the easy, natural unconstrain'd flow of the Dialogue; if that Dialogue does not go on with Spirit, Wit, Variety, Fun, Humour, Repartee &—& all in short into the Bargain—Serviteur![1]—Good bye—t'ye!—

Once more, now, Fanny, don't imagine that I am discouraging You from the Attempt; or that I am retracting, or shirking back from what I have said above—i.e. that I think You highly capable of it:—on the Contrary, I *reaffirm* it—I affirm that in common Conversation I observe in You a ready Choice of words, with a quickness & Conciseness that have often surpriz'd me: this is a lucky Gift for a Comic writer, & not a very common one; so that if You have not the united Talents I demand, I don't know who has;—for if You have your *Familiar*, your *Sprite*, for ever thus at your Elbow, without calling for, surely it will not desert you, when in deep Conjuration raising Your Genius in your Closet—
[...]

1779

72.   FRANCES BURNEY TO SAMUEL CRISP
c. 7 January 1779, London

[...]—just as I received your Letter, I had had information that my Name had got into print,—&, what was yet worse, was printed in a new Pamphlet.

I cannot tell you, &, if I could, you would, perhaps, not believe me, how greatly I was shocked, mortified, grieved & confounded at this intelligence: I had always dreaded as a real Evil my Name's getting into *Print*,—but to be lug'd into a Pamphlet!—

---

1   A salutation, equivalent to "Your servant."

I must, however, now I have gone so far, tell you how it is, lest you should imagine matters worse. This vile Pamphlet is called *Warley* a Satire:[1] it is addressed to the First artist in Europe,—who proves to be Sir Joshua Reynolds.[2] Probably it is to his unbounded partiality for Evelina that I owe this most *disagreeable Compliment*,—for he had been so eager to discover the Author, that, by what I have had reason given me to conjecture, I fancy he has been not a little *Laughed at* since the discovery, for diverse *comique* sort of speeches which he had made [before me.]

So now the Murder's out! but, dear Daddy, don't *belabour* me for my weakness, though I confess I was, for more than a week, unable to Eat, Drink or sleep for vehemence of vexation:—I am, now, got tolerably stout again,—but I have been furiously Lectured for my *folly*, (as, I see, *every body* thinks it,) by all who have known of it. I have, therefore, struggled against it with all my might, & am determined to *aim*, at least, at acquiring more strength of mind.—Yet, after all, I feel very forcibly that I *am* not—that I *have* not been— & that I never *shall* be formed or fitted for any business with the *Public*—yet, now, my best friends, & my Father at their Head, absolutely *prohibit* a retreat;—otherwise, I should be strongly tempted to empty the whole contents of my Bureau into the Fire, & to vow never again to fill it.— —But, had my *Name* never got abroad with my *Book*,—ere this, I question not, I should again have tried *how the World stood affected to me*. Now once again to your Letter.

Why, my dear Daddy, will you use so vile, so ill applied a Word as *officious* when you are giving me Advice?—Is it not, of all favours the most valuable you can confer on me? & don't I know that if you had not somewhat of a *sneaking kindness* for me, you would as soon *bite off your own nose* as take so much trouble about me? I do, most earnestly, seriously & solemnly entreat that you will continue to me this first, best, greatest proof of regard, & I do, with the utmost truth & gratitude, assure you that it is more really flattering to me than all the flummery in the World. I only wish, with all my Heart, you would be more liberal of it.

Every word you have urged concerning the *salt & spirit* of gay, unrestrained freedom in Comedies, carries conviction along with

---

1   By George Huddesford.
2   The fashionable portrait painter (1723-92) who founded the Literary Club in 1764.

it,—a conviction which I feel in trembling! should I ever venture in that walk publicly, perhaps the want of it might prove fatal to me: I do, indeed, think it most likely that such would be the Event, & my poor piece, though it might escape Cat calls & riots, would be fairly *slept off the stage*. I cannot, however, attempt to *avoid* this danger, though I *see* it, for I would a thousand Times rather forfeit my character as a *Writer*, than risk ridicule or censure as a *Female*. I have never set my Heart on Fame, & therefore would not if I *could* purchase it at the expence of all my own ideas of propriety. You who *know* me for a *Prude* will not be surprised, & I hope, not offended at this avowal,—for I should deceive you were I not to make it. If I *should* try, I must e'en take my chance,—& all my own expectations may be pretty easily answered!
[...]

73.   FRANCES BURNEY TO SUSAN BURNEY
                11 January 1779, London

[...]
Dr. Johnson told me that [I ought to be very civil to] Mrs. Cholmondeley, [as she] was the *first* person who publicly praised & recommended Evelina among the Wits. Mrs. Thrale told me that at Tunbridge & Brighthelmstone[1] it was the *universal* topic;—& that Mrs. Montague had pronounced the *Dedication* to be *so* well written, that she could not but suppose it must be the *Doctor's*. "She is very kind, quoth *I*, because she likes one part better than another to take it from me!"

    "You must not mind that, said Dr. Johnson, for these things are always said where Books are successful. There are 3 distinct kind of Judges upon all new Authors or productions;—the first, are those who know no rules, but pronounce entirely from their natural Taste & feelings; the 2^d. are those who *know*, & *judge* by *rules*; & the 3^d. are those who *know*, but are *above* the rules. These last are those you should wish to satisfy: *next* to them, rate the *natural* judges,—but ever despise those opinions that are formed by the *rules*."
[...]
[*On Wednesday 6 January, FB and CB attend an evening party at Mrs. Cholmondeley's. The company include Sir Joshua Reynolds*

---

1 Fashionable resorts.

and Richard Brinsley Sheridan.[1] *Sheridan seats himself between FB and CB.*]

And now I must tell you a little conversation which I did not hear myself till I came Home,—it was between Mr. Sheridan & my Father.

"Good God, Dr. Burney, cried the former, have you no *older* Daughters? can *this* possibly be the authoress of Evelina?—" & then he said abundance of fine things, & begged my Father to Introduce him to me! "Why it will be a very formidable thing to her, answered he, to be introduced to *you!*" "Well then,—by & by,—" returned he.

Some Time after this, my Eyes happening to meet his, he waved the Ceremony of introduction, &, in a low voice, said "I have been telling Dr. Burney that I have long expected to see in Miss Burney a lady of the gravest appearance, with the quickest parts."

I was never much more astonished than at this unexpected address, as, among all my numerous puffers, the Name of Sheridan has never reached me, & I did really imagine he had never deigned to look at my trash.

Of course I could make no *verbal* answer: & he proceeded then to speak of Evelina in terms of the highest praise, but I was in such a *ferment* from surprise (not to say pleasure) that I have no recollection of his expressions. I only remember telling him that I was much amazed he had spared Time to read it,—& that he repeatedly called it a most *surprising Book.* And, some Time after, he added "But I hope, Miss Burney, you don't intend to throw away your Pen?"

"You should take care, Sir, said I, what you say,—for you know not what weight it may have."

He wished it might have any, he said.—& soon after, turned again to my Father.

I protest, since the approbation of the Streathamites, I have met with none so *highly* flattering to me as this of Mr. Sheridan, & so *very* unexpected.

Sir Joshua, then, came up to me, &, after some general conversation, said "Pray do you know any thing of the Sylph?"

---

1 Sheridan (1751-1816) had written the popular comedies, *The Rivals* (1775) and *The School for Scandal* (1777), and had managed Drury Lane Theatre since 1776.

This is a Novel, lately advertised by Lowndes.[1] Mr. Hutton has already been with me to enquire if it was *mine*.

"No." quoth I. "Don't you upon your Honour?"

"Upon my Honour! did you suspect me?"

"Why a friend of mine sent for it upon suspicion.—"

"So did we, said Miss Linley, but I did not suspect after I had *read* it!"

"What is the reason, said Sir Joshua, that Lowndes always advertises it with Evelina?"

"Indeed I know nothing about it."

"Ma'am," cried Mr. Sheridan, turning to me abruptly, you should send & order him *not*,—it is a take in, & ought to be forbid;—(&, with great vehemence he added) it is a most impudent thing in that fellow!"

I assure you I took it quite *koind* in him to give me this advice. By the way, Mrs. Thrale has sent me a message to the same purpose.[2]

Sir Joshua went on with the Conversation. This, by the way, was the first Time he ever spoke to *me* of this so much honoured Book, but, now the subject was once started, he scrupled not to support it. He did not, however, begin any *formal* or *formidable Eloge*, but *dashed* his general Discourse with occasional civilities equally flattering & delicate.

Among other things, he said that "Mr. Sheridan has declared he holds it *superior* to Fielding."

"[God!]—impossible, impossible!"

"Nay, he has indeed,—& he must *really* think so, for he said it publicly at our Club.[3]—But I dare say he has been telling you so himself?"

F:B. No indeed;—but if he *had*, many things are said to *me* that are not to be believed.

Sir Joshua. But what is said at our *Club*, *is* to be believed. It is his real opinion.

F:B. Well!—I begin to think a Proclamation has been issued that all folks are to attack & try the strength of my poor Head!

---

1 *The Sylph* (1779), said to be the work of the Duchess of Devonshire.

2 See below, letter from HLT dated *post* 6 January 1778. Lowndes's advertisement listed *Evelina* after *The Sylph*, tacitly suggesting they were the work of the same author. CB wrote a letter of complaint to Lowndes, and references to *The Sylph* were omitted from later advertisements.

3 The Literary Club, founded by Reynolds in 1764.

—& I fear they are determined Not to leave me short of Moorfields.[1]

[...]

Some Time after, Sir Joshua, returning to his *standing* place, entered into *confab.* with Miss Linley & your slave upon various matters;—during which, Mr. Sheridan, joining us, said "Sir Joshua I have been telling Miss Burney that she must not suffer her Pen to lie idle;—*ought* she?"

Sir Joshua No, indeed, ought she not.

Mr. Sheridan.—Do *you*, then, Sir Joshua, persuade her.—But perhaps you *have* begun some thing?—may we *ask?*—Will you answer a Question candidly?

F:B.—I don't know,—but *as* candidly as *Mrs. Candour*[2] I think I certainly shall!

Mr. Sheridan. What, then, are you about now?

F:B.—Why—twirling my Fan, I think!"

Mr. Sheridan, No, no,—but what are you about *at Home?*—however,—it is not a fair Question, so I won't press it."

Yet he *looked* very inquisitive; but I was glad to get off without any *down right* answer.

Sir Joshua. Any thing in the *Dialogue* way, I think, she *must* succeed in,—& I am sure *invention* will not be wanting,—

Mr. Sheridan. No, indeed;—*I* think, & say, she should write a *Comedy.*

Lord, Susy, I could not believe my own Ears! *This* from Mr. *Sheridan!*

Sir Joshua. I am sure *I* think so; & I hope she *will.*

I could only answer by *incredulous* exclamations.

"Consider, continued Sir Joshua, you have already had all the applause & fame you *can* have given you in the *Clozet,*—but the Acclamation of a *Theatre* will be *new* to you."

And then he put down his Trumpet,[3] & began a violent clapping of his Hands.

I actually shook from Head to foot! I felt myself already in Drury Lane,[4] amidst the *Hub bub* of a first Night.

---

1 Bethlehem (Bedlam) Hospital for the insane.
2 A character in Sheridan's *School for Scandal.*
3 Ear-trumpet, a hearing-aid.
4 Drury Lane Theatre was one of only two theatres in London granted year-long licenses by Parliament. The other was Covent Garden Theatre.

"O No! cried I, there *may* be a *Noise*,—but it will be just the *reverse*,"—And I returned his salute with a Hissing.

Mr. Sheridan joined Sir Joshua very warmly.

"O Sir! cried I, *you* should not run on so,—you don't know what Mischief you may do!

Mr. Sheridan. I wish I *may*,—I shall be very glad to be accessory.

Sir Joshua. She has, certainly, something of a knack at Characters;—*where* she got it, I don't know,—& *how* she got it, I can't imagine,—but she certainly *has* it. And to throw it away is—

Mr. Sheridan. O she *won't*,—she will write a Comedy,—she has promised me she will!

F:B. O Good God!—if you both run on in this manner, I shall—

I was going to say *get under the Chair*, but Mr. Sheridan, interrupting me with a Laugh, said "Set about one?—very well, that's right!"

"Ay, cried Sir Joshua, that's *very* right.—And *you*, (to Mr. Sheridan,) would *take* any thing of *Her's*,—would you not?—*Unsight unseen?*"

What a *point blank* Question! who but Sir Joshua would have ventured it!

"*Yes*; answered Mr. Sheridan, with quickness,—& make her a Bow & my best Thanks into the Bargain!"

Now, my dear Susy, tell me, did you ever hear the *fellow* to such a speech as this!—it was all I could do to sit it.

"Good God, Mr. Sheridan, I exclaimed, are you not Mocking me?"

"No, upon my Honour! this is what I have *meditated* to say to you the first Time I should have the pleasure of seeing you."

To be sure, as Mrs. Thrale says, if folks *are* to be spoilt,—there is nothing in the World so *pleasant* as spoiling! But I *never* was so much astonished, & *seldom* have been so much delighted as by this attack of Mr. Sheridan. Afterwards he took my Father aside, & formally repeated his opinion that I should write for the Stage, & his desire to see my Play,—with encomiums the most flattering of Evelina.

Consider Mr. Sheridan as an *Author* & a *Manager*, & really this conduct appears to me at once generous [xxx] & uncommon. As an *Author*, & one so high, & *now* in his first Eclat, to be so lavish of his praise—is it not [rare][1]?—As a *Manager*, who must, of course,

---

1 Substitution.

be *loaded* with Pieces & recommendations, to *urge* me to write, & to promise to *thank* me for my Writing, instead of making a favour & a difficulty of even *looking* at it,—is it not truly good-natured & liberal-minded?

And now, my dear Susy,—if I *should* attempt the stage,—I think I may be fairly acquitted of presumption, & however I may fail,— that I was strongly pressed to *try* by Mrs. Thrale,—& by Mr. Sheridan,—the most successful & powerful of all Dramatic living Authors,—will abundantly excuse my temerity.

In short,—this Evening seems to have been *decisive*, my many & encreasing scruples *all* give way to encouragement so warm from so experienced a Judge, who is himself *interested* in not making such a request *par pure complaisance*.

[...]

74.   HESTER THRALE TO FRANCES BURNEY
        post 6 January 1779, Streatham

Though your Papa kindly told me the time of our meeting was not now long to be delayed, yet I cannot help writing just to express my Wishes that you would chide Lowndes for advertising his Novel called the *Sylph* in the Manner he does, for I find every body is falling apace into the Snare, and fancying it your Book, because Evelina is oddly included in the Advertisement.—It is a common Trick as the D^r. can inform you, and they have served Mr. Johnson so before now; but *your* Reputation as an Author is young yet & cannot carry Weight.[1] Excuse me my sweet Friend, but after many silly Enquiries & Hints from People I have seen, this Morning's Post brought me a Letter from a Lady forty Miles off, from which I take Leave to copy for your use the following Paragraph.

I want your opinion of the Sylph; if as 'tis said it is written by *your* Miss Burney—very well; but was She my Daughter, I think I should feel sorry at her Age to see her so

---

1   *The Sylph* threatened to damage FB's reputation because it was a scandalous novel, depicting a number of extra-marital affairs, and a husband who attempted to sell his wife to his friends to liquidate his gambling debts.

perfectly acquainted with the *warm* Passions supposed incident to our Sex which I should rather wish her to be ignorant of—at least for a *few Years*.

Now do my lovely Girl get your Papa to huff the Man for making your Reputation contribute to sell his nasty Novels; & pray see all the Shows, and divert yourself a great deal before you come *home* to rusticate at Streatham. I wish you would bring some *Work* with you; Sheridan has really behaved with great politeness, pity to let it cool I think, & M^r. Johnson says so too. The Stage is certainly the high Road to Riches and to Fame, and the *broad Wheeled Waggons* which have gone over it lately, will only have rolled it smooth I hope, for our elegant *Vis a Vis*.[1]
[...]

75.   SAMUEL CRISP TO FRANCES BURNEY
              19 January 1779, Chessington

[...]
I long of all things, Fannikin, to see *Warly*, & [xxx] the Continuation of your Journal (for I have copied & will faithfully return by the first opportunity your last)—if You answer me, You have not Continued it, You are unpardonable & I advise You to set about it immediately, as well as You can, while any traces of it rest in your Memory—it will one day be the delight of your Old age—it will call back your Youth, your Spirits, your Pleasures, your Friends, whom you formerly lov'd, & who lov'd You. (at that time, alas, probably, long gone off the Stage—) & lastly, when your *own* Scene is clos'd, remain a Valuable Treasure to those that come after You:— but I will not *suppose* You have *not* Continued it—you *can't* be so wanting to yourself.—*this* is what I require:—the whole in all it's detail.—not bits & scraps of 3 Characters at a time, as You talk of— that won't satisfy my Maw.—as to your *vexations*, Child, I don't mind it of a Pin—Fram'd as You are, I know that must come first, before You could be Easy.—People that are destin'd to live in the Midst of the World, must & ought to be innoculated, before they can go about in safety—You talk of being *Slept off the Stage*— Would You wish Your Book to die such a Death? there is no Alternative—if it lives, it's fate & yours are inseparable, &, the Names of

---

1 Face to face: a light carriage for two people, seated facing each other.

Evelina & Burney must & will go together, so that, your discontent at what has happen'd, to me seems strangely ill-founded; & your fantastic sickly Stomach is to recoil, forsooth, because You cannot compass impossibilities!

Well—I have been ruminating a good deal on the Obstacles & difficulties I mention'd in my last, that lye directly across YOUR Path (as a Prude—): in the Walk of Comedy—on the most mature Consideration, I do by no means retract the general Principle that produced those observations; I will never allow You to sacrifice a *Grain* of female delicacy, for all the Wit of Congreve, & Vanbrugh,[1] put together—the purchase would be too dear; but this much I will assert, & can prove by several instances; viz, that Light principles may be display'd [(where the Characters require it)] without *Light expressions*: And *that* is the Rock a Female must take Care to steer clear of—Vice must not talk *unlike itself*; but there is no necessity, it should show all it's filth—a great deal of management & dexterity will certainly be requisite to preserve, Spirit & Salt, & yet keep up Delicacy—but it *may* be done; & You, can do it, if any Body—Not but that [xxx]—Do you remember about a Dozen Years ago, how you used to dance Nancy Dawson on the Grass plot, with Your Cap on the Ground, & your long hair streaming down your Back,—one shoe off, & throwing about your head like a mad thing?—now you are to dance Nancy Dawson with Fetters on—there is the difference—yet there is certainly a nameless Grace & Charm in giving a loose to that Wildness & friskyness sometimes—[xxx]

I am very glad You have secur'd Mʳˢ. Montagu for your Friend—her Weight & Interest are powerful; but there is one particular I *do* not relish; tho' she means it as a mark of Favour & distinction—it is, where she says— "If Miss Burney *does* write a Play; I beg I may know of it, &, (if she thinks proper) *see* it."—["& all my Interest is at her service"]—Now, Fanny, this same *seeing it* (in a profess'd Female Wit, Authoress, & *Maecenas*[2] into the Bargain) I fear, implies too much *interference*—implies, *advising, correcting altering*, &c &c &c—not only so; but in so high a Critic, the not submitting to such grand Authority, might possibly give a secret, con-

---

1 William Congreve's (1670-1729) and Sir John Vanbrugh's (1664-1726) popular comedies, written in the closing years of the seventeenth century, reflected the bawdy tastes of the Restoration age.
2 Patron.

ceal'd lurking Offence—Now, d'ye see, as I told You once before, I would have the whole be *all your own—all of a Piece*—& to tell you the truth, I would not give a pin for the advice of the ablest Friend, who would not suffer me at last to follow *my own* Judgment, without resentment—[...]

76.　　　　　HESTER THRALE: *THRALIANA*
10 February 1779

[...]—Our Miss Burney is big with a Comedy for next Season; I have not yet seen the *Ebauche*,[1] but I wish it well: Can I help wishing well to every thing that bears the name of *Burney*? The Doctor is a Man quite after my own Heart, if he has any Fault it is too much Obsequiousness, though *I* should not object to a Quality *my* Friends are so little troubled with. [...] his Daughter is a graceful looking Girl, but 'tis the Grace of an Actress not a Woman of Fashion—how[2] should it? her Conversation would be more pleasing if She thought less of herself; but her early Reputation embarrasses her Talk, & clouds her Mind with Scruples about Elegancies which either come uncalled for or will not come at all: I love her more for her Father's sake than for her own, though her Merit cannot as a Writer be controverted. The Play will be a good one too I doubt not—She is a Girl of prodigious Parts—
[...]

77.　　　　FRANCES BURNEY TO SUSAN BURNEY
February 1779, Streatham

[...]
[*FB reports a conversation with a clergyman, Mr. Davis, who asks if she assists in the education of her half-brother, Richard Burney. FB answers in the negative.*]
"No?—don't you know Latin, Ma'am?"
　"No, indeed! not at all!"
　"Really?—Well, *I had heard* you did."
　I wonder, my dear Susy, what *next* will be said of me! Yesterday, at Night, I told Dr. Johnson the enquiry, & added that I attributed it to my being at *Streatham*, & supposed the folks took it for grant-

---

1　Outline.
2　HLT adds a note "The Burneys are I believe a very low Race of Mortals."

ed nobody would be admitted there, without knowing *Latin* at least.

"No, my dear, no, answered he; the Man thought it because you have written a *Book*; he concluded that a *Book* could not be written by one who knew no Latin. And it is strange that it *should*, but perhaps you *do* know it,—for your shyness, & slyness, & pretending to know nothing, never took *me* in, whatever you may do with others. *I* always knew you for a *Toadling!*"

At our usual Time of *absconding*, he would not let us go, & was in high good humour;—& when, at last, Mrs. Thrale absolutely refused to stay any longer, he took me by the Hand, & said "Don't *you* mind her, my little Burney,—do *you* stay, whether she will or not." So away went Mrs. Thrale, & left us to a Tête à Tête.

Now I had been considering that perhaps I *ought to* speak to him of *my* [new *Castle*,—][1] lest, hereafter, he should suspect that I *preferred* the counsel of Mr. Murphy: I therefore determined to take this opportunity, &, after some general nothings, I asked if he would permit me to take a great liberty with him? He assented with the most encouraging smile. And then, I said "I believe, Sir, you heard part of what passed between Mr. Murphy & me the other Evening, concerning—a—a comedy,—now,—if I *should* make such an attempt,—would you be so good as to allow me,— any Time before Michaelmas, to put it in the Coach for you to look over as you go to Town?"

"To be sure, my dear!—What, have you begun a Comedy, then?"

I told him how the affair stood. He then gave me advice which just accorded with my wishes,—viz—not to make known that I had any such intention;—to keep my own Counsel,—not to *whisper* even the *Name* of it [to my Bedfellow],—to raise no expectations [of it,] which were *always* prejudicial, &, finally, to have it *performed* while the Town knew nothing of whose it was.

I readily assured him of my hearty concurrence in his opinion; but he somewhat distressed me, when I told him that Mr. Murphy *must* be in my confidence, as he had *offered* his services, by desiring *he* might be the *last* to see it.

What I shall do, I know not, for he has, himself, begged to be the *first*. Mrs. Thrale, however, shall guide me between them. He

---

1 Substitution. FB refers to *The Witlings*. HLT had previously introduced FB to the playwright Arthur Murphy, who offered his help with the comedy.

spoke highly of Mr. Murphy, too, for he really loves him. He said he would not have it in the Coach, but that *I* should read it to him;—however, I could sooner drown or hang!—When I would have offered some apology for the attempt, he stopt me, & desired I would never make any, "For, said he, if it succeeds, it makes it's *own* apology, if not,—" "If *not*, quoth I,—I cannot do worse than Dr. Goldsmith, when *his* play failed,—*go home & Cry!*—"[1]

He Laughed,—but told me, repeatedly, (I mean *twice*, which, for him, is very remarkable,) that I might depend upon all the service in his power; & he added it would be well to make Murphy the last Judge "for *he* knows the stage, he said, & *I* am quite ignorant of it." And afterwards, grasping my Hand, with the most affectionate warmth he said "I *wish* you success! I *wish* you well! my dear little Burney!"

Indeed I am *sure* he does.

[...]

But I forgot to mention that, when I told Dr. Johnson Mr. Murphy's kind offer of examining my *Plan*, & of the several rules he gave me,—& owned that I had already gone too far to avail myself of his obliging intention,—he said "Never mind, my dear,—ah! *you'll* do without,—*you* want no rules!"

[...]

78.   SAMUEL CRISP TO FRANCES BURNEY
        ante 15 May 1779, Chessington

[*FBA annotated the letter:* "My affrighted refusal to let a part of my Streatham Journal be copied—My dearest Mr. Crisp saw not the difference or danger in any communications from the time I was dubbed Authour, to what existed before or he would not have talked of lessened confidence— never was mine lessened in *Him.*"]

You are a Jew, Fannikin, an Ebrew Jew—so you won't trust me to take a copy of y.[r] 2.[d] part!—Now, you must know, in this 1.st part, I have so manag'd it, that if a stranger was to get possession of it, they could never find out who are meant—nothing but Initial letters—M.[r] T—M.[rs] T—for the Master & M.[rs] St. for Streatham D. J.

---

1   Oliver Goldsmith (1728-74), essayist and dramatist, was convinced that his comedy, *The Good Natured Man*, had failed upon its first performance in 1768, because the audience hissed at one scene. Afterwards, when alone with Samuel Johnson, Goldsmith broke down in tears. To Johnson's astonishment, Goldsmith himself subsequently related the story to his friends.

for D^r. Johnson, M^r. S. for Seward—Lady L. Lady Ladd—( ) for Evelina, or the Book—y^r self Miss B. D. B. your Daddy & so forth—now add to this my solemn promise, that no Soul, without your particular, individual, separate leave, shall ever see or hear this manuscript—on these Conditions if you refuse, you are a most accomplish'd Jew, & have lost all that Confidence in me, which you once had—for in very many of the former letters of our ancient Correspondence, there were a hundred particulars, that would never bear the light, any more than Streathamism—nevertheless if you still adhere to Circumcision, you shall be obey'd —[...]

79.   FRANCES BURNEY TO SUSAN BURNEY
            21-27 May 1779, Brighton

[...]

[*FB accompanied the Thrales on their summer visit to Brighton. HLT reported that Murphy wanted to see FB's play, and persuaded her to give him the 1st act to read, rather against her will.*]

As he could not stay to sleep here, he had only Time, after Dinner, to finish the 1st. Act. He was pleased to commend it very liberally; he has pointed out 2 places where he thinks I might enlarge, but has not criticised one *word*, on the contrary; the Dialogue he has honoured with high praise.

So far is well,—what may be yet to come I know not. Further particulars I shall write to my dear Padre himself.

O—but—shall I tell you something?—Yes, though you won't care a fig,—but I have had my first Lesson in Latin, [xxx] Dr. Johnson tutored Miss Thrale while I was with you, & was set off for Litchfield before I came; but Mrs. Thrale attended the Lecture, & has told me every word of it she could recollect: so we must both be ready for him against his return. I heartily wish I rejoiced more sincerely in this *Classical plan*; but the truth is, I have more fear of the malignity which will follow it's being known, than delight in what advantages it may afford. All *my* delight, indeed, is that this great & good man should think me worthy his instructions.
[...]

80.   FRANCES BURNEY TO SUSAN BURNEY
            post 26 June 1779, Streatham

[...]

Mrs. Thrale told me that Dr. Johnson was talking to her & Sir Philip Jennings of the amazing progress made of late years in Literature by the Women. He said he was himself all astonished at it,

& told them he well remembered when a Woman who could spell a common Letter was regarded as all accomplished,—but that *now*, they vied with the men in *every* thing.

"I think, Sir, said my friend Sir Philip, the young lady we have here is a very extraordinary proof of what you say."

"*So* extraordinary, Sir, answered he, that I know none like her,— nor do I believe there *is*, or there ever *was* a *Man* who could write *such* a Book so young."

They both stared,—no wonder, I am sure!—& Sir Philip said "What do you think of *Pope*, Sir? could not *Pope* have written such a one?"

"Nay, nay, cried Mrs. Thrale, there is no need to talk of *Pope*,— a Book may be a clever Book & an excellent Book, & yet not want a *Pope* for it's Author. I suppose he was no older than Miss Burney when he writ Windsor Forest;[1] & I suppose *Windsor Forest* is not equal to Evelina!"

"Windsor Forest, repeated Dr. Johnson, though so delightful a Poem, by no means required the knowledge of Life & manners, nor the accuracy of observation, nor the skill of penetration necessary for composing such a Work as Evelina: He who could *ever* write Windsor Forest, might as well write it Young as Old. Poetical abilities require not *age* to mature them; but Evelina seems a work that should result from long Experience & deep & intimate knowledge of the World; yet it has been written without either. Miss Burney is a real Wonder. What she is, she is intuitively. Dr. Burney told me she had had the fewest advantages of any of his Daughters, from some peculiar circumstances. And such has been her timidity, that he himself had not any suspicion of her powers."

"Her modesty," said Mrs. Thrale—(as she told me) is really beyond bounds. It quite provokes me. And, in fact, I can never make out how the Mind that could write that Book could be ignorant of its value."

"That, Madam, is another Wonder," answered my dear—dear Dr. Johnson, "for Modesty with her is neither pretence nor decorum; 'Tis an ingredient of her Nature; for she who could part with such a Work for Twenty pounds, could know so little of it's worth, or of her own, as to leave no possible doubt of her native humility."

---

1 Pope claimed to have written the first part of "Windsor Forest" at the age of sixteen. He finished the poem by the age of twenty-five, which was FB's age at the publication of *Evelina*. HLT's analogy is more apt than it first appears.

My kind Mrs. Thrale told me this with a pleasure that made me embrace her with gratitude: but the astonishment of Sir Philip Clerke at such an *eloge* from Dr. Johnson was quite, she says, comical. [...]

81.   SUSAN BURNEY TO FRANCES BURNEY
            3 August 1779, Chessington

[*SEB describes the initial reading of* The Witlings *at Chessington, while FB was at Streatham.*]

Tuesday August 3ᵈ.—Yesterday was appointed for the perusal of your Piece—Mʳ. Crisp had I found spoke of it to Mʳˢ. Gast, & as Kitty was to be of the Party I delivered her your Message, wᶜʰ. was very *acceptable.* We all assembled soon after Breakfast into Mʳˢ. Gast's Room—& My Father, pleased he said to see *so respectable an Audience,* began the Piece.

The Witlings—"Good"—sᵈ. Mʳ. Crisp—"Good—I like the Name—the Dramatis Personae too pleased him, & the name of *Codger* occasion'd a general Grin. As He has now got the play in his own Room & I cannot therefore refer to it I must be more concise in my accᵗ. than I shᵈ. otherwise wish to be—but the Milliners Scene & indeed all the first Act diverted us *extremely* all round—"It's *funny*—It's *funny* indeed"—sᵈ. Mʳ. C. who you know does not love to throw away praise—the Second Act I think much improved, & its being more compressed than when I first heard it gives to the whole more *Zest*—it did not flag at all in the reading.—The 3ᵈ. is charming—& they all went off wᵗʰ. great Spirit—Here my Father's voice was so tired that we were obliged to stop—much against Mʳˢ. Gast's inclination—but I thought it was all for the best, as we had had no rests between the Acts, & we cᵈ. not indeed have got thro' a whole Act before Dinner.[...]—the fourth act was upon the whole that wᶜʰ. seemed least to exhilarate or interest the Audience, tho' Charlotte laugh'd till she was almost black in the face at Codger's part, as I had done before her—The fifth was more generally felt—but to own the truth it did not meet all the advantages one could wish—My Father's voice, sight, & lungs were tired—yʳ. writing, tho' neat, dazzled his Eyes more than printing wᵈ. have done, & occasion'd him, latterly as he grew fatigued, some difficulty in reading—& being entirely unacquainted wᵗʰ. what was coming notwithstanding all his good intentions, he did not always give the Expression you meant shᵈ. be given—Yet he exerted himself in the warmest manner throughout the

Piece to give it force & Spirit—&, except this Act, I believe only yourself w^d. have read the play better.

For my own part the Serious part seem'd even to *improve* upon me by this 2^d. hearing, & made me for to cry in 2 or 3 places—I wish there was more of this Sort—so does my Father—so, I *believe*, does M^r. Crisp—however their sentiments you are to hear fully from themselves, wch. will make me the less eager to write them—Codger & Jack too seem Characters which divert every body, & w^d. yet more I sh^d. imagine in a public Representation.
[...]

82.   FRANCES BURNEY TO DR. CHARLES BURNEY
              c. 13 August 1779, London

The fatal knell then, is knolled!—& down among the Dead Men sink the poor Witlings,—for-ever & for-ever & for-ever!—[1]

I give a *sigh* whether I will or not to their Memory, for, however worthless, they were *mes Enfans*, & *one must do one's Nature*, as Mr. Crisp will tell you of the Dog.

You, my dearest Sir, who enjoyed, I really think, even more than myself the astonishing success of my first attempt, would, I believe, even more than myself, be hurt at the failure of my second;—& I am sure I speak from the bottom of a very honest Heart when I most solemnly declare that upon *your* Account any disgrace would mortify & afflict me *more* than upon my own,—for what ever appears with your *knowledge*, will be naturally supposed to have met with your *approbation*, & perhaps with your *assistance*;—& therefore, though all *particular* censure would fall where it *ought*, upon *me*,—yet any *general* censure of the *whole*, & the *Plan*, would cruelly, but certainly, involve *you* in it's severity.

Of this I have been sensible from the Moment my *Authorship-ness* was discovered,—& therefore, from that Moment, I determined to have no *opinion* of my own in regard to what I should henceforth part with out of my own Hands. I would, long since,

---

1 FB replies to a joint letter from CB and SC, since lost, concerning *The Witlings*, in which they rejected the play in terms which can be gathered from FB's response. CB wrote to FB on 29 August explaining his objections (see below). HLT reported that CB liked the play (see *Thraliana* 1: 381) but SC was anxious and seems to have convinced CB that staging it would present a threat to CB's own career as well as to FB's, if it should alienate the female wits.

have Burnt the 4th. Act, upon your disapprobation of it, but that I waited, & was by Mrs. Thrale so much *encouraged* to wait, for your finishing the Piece.

You *have* finished it, now,—in *every* sense of the Word;—*partial* faults may be corrected, but what I most wished was to know the general effect of the Whole,—& as *that* has so terribly failed, all petty criticisms would be needless. I shall wipe it all from my Memory, & endeavour never to recollect that I ever writ it.

You bid me open my Heart to you,—& so, my dearest Sir, I will,—for it is the greatest happiness of my life that I *dare* be sincere to you,—— I expected many Objections to be raised, a thousand errors to be pointed out, & a million of alterations to be proposed,—but—the *suppression of the piece* were words I did *not* expect,—indeed, after the warm approbation of Mrs. Thrale, & the repeated commendations & flattery of Mr. Murphy, how could I?—

I do not, therefore, pretend to *wish* you should think the decision for which I was so little prepared has given me no disturbance,—for I must be a far more egregious Witling than any of those I tried to draw to imagine you could ever credit that I writ without some remote hope of success *now*, though I literally did when I composed Evelina. But my mortification is not at throwing away the Characters, or the contrivance;—it is all at throwing away the *Time*,—which I with difficulty stole, & which I have Buried in the mere trouble of *writing*.

What my Daddy Crisp says, "that it would be the best *policy*, but for pecuniary advantages, for me to write no more—" is exactly what I have always thought since Evelina was published;—but I will not *now* talk of putting it in practice,—for the best way I can take of shewing that I have a true & just sense of the *spirit* of your condemnation, is not to sink, sulky & dejected, under it, but to exert myself to the utmost of my power in endeavours to produce something less reprehensible. And this shall be the way I will pursue, as soon as my Mind is more at ease about Hetty & Mrs. Thrale,[1]—& as soon as I have *read* myself into a forgetfulness of my old Dramatis persona,—lest I should produce something else as *Witless* as the last.

Adieu, my dearest, kindest, truest, best *Friend*,—I will never proceed so *far* again without your counsel, & then I shall not only save

---

1 They had both been ill.

myself so much useless trouble, but *you*, who so reluctantly blame, the kind pain which I am sure must attend your disapprobation. The World will not always go well, as Mrs. Sap.[1] might say, & I am sure I have long thought I have had more than my share of success already.

[...]

[*FBA annotated this letter:*]

The objections of Mr. Crisp to the MS. Play of the Witlings was its resemblance to Moliere's *Femmes scavantes*— & consequent immense inferiority. It is, however, a curious fact, & to the author a consolatory one, that she had literally never read the *Femmes scavantes* when she composed The Witlings.

83.   FRANCES BURNEY TO SAMUEL CRISP
               c. 13 August 1779, London

Well!—God's above all!—& there are *plays* that *are* to be saved, & *plays* that are *not* to be saved!—so good Night Mr. Dabler!—good Night Lady Smatter,—Mrs. Sapient, Mrs. Voluble,—Mrs. Whee-dle—Censor,—Cecilia—Beaufort,—& you, *you great Oaf*, Bobby!—good Night! good Night!—

And good *Morning*, Miss Fanny Burney!—I hope, now, You have opened your Eyes for some Time, & will not close them in so drowsy a fit again—at least till the full of the Moon.—

I won't tell you I have been absolutely *ravi* with delight at the fall of the Curtain,—but I intend to take the affair in the *tant mieux*[2] manner, & to console myself for your Censure by this great-est proof I have ever received of the sincerity, candour, &, let me add, *esteem* of my dear Daddy.—And, as I happen to love *myself* rather more than my *play*, this consolation is not a very trifling one.

As to all you say of my *rep.* & so forth, I perceive the kindness of your endeavours to put me in humour with myself, & prevent my taking *huff*,—which, if I did, I should deserve to receive, upon any future trial, *hollow* praise from *you*,—& the *rest* from the *Public*.

As to the M.S. I am in no hurry for it.—Besides, it ought not

---

1 Mrs. Sapient, one of the Bluestocking ladies in *The Witlings*.
2 "So much the better."

to come till I have prepared an *ovation*, & the *Honours of conquest* for it.

The only bad thing in this affair,—is that I cannot take the comfort of my poor friend Dabler, by calling you a *crabbed fellow,*—because you write with almost more kindness than ever;—niether can I, (though I try hard) persuade myself that you have not *a Grain of Taste in your whole composition.*

This, however, seriously, I do believe that, when my two Daddys put their Heads together to concert for me that Hissing, groaning, catcalling Epistle they sent me, they felt as sorry for poor little Miss Bayes[1] as she could possibly do for herself.

You see I do not attempt to repay your frankness with the art of pretended carelessness,—but though I am somewhat disconcerted just now, I will promise not to let my vexation Live out another Day. I shall not *browse* upon it,—but, on the contrary, drive it out of my thoughts by filling them up with things *almost* as good of other people's.

[...]

Adieu, my dear Daddy,—I *won't* be mortified, & I *won't* be *downed,*—but I will be *proud* to find I have *out* of my own family, as well as in it, a Friend who loves me well enough to speak plain truth to me.

[...]

84.   DR. CHARLES BURNEY TO FRANCES BURNEY
           c. 29 August 1779, Chessington

[...] yours[2] is rather serious, & requires care in preaching an answer— —I am glad the objections all fall on the Blue Stocking-Club-party—as my chief & almost only quarrel was with its Members. As it is, not only the whole piece, but the *plot* had best be kept secret, from every body. As to finishing another upon a *new Story,* in a *hurry,* for next winter, I think it *may* be done, & w^d. be not only feasible but desirable at any other time than the present— — But public affairs are in such terrible Confusion, & there is so little likelihood of people having more money or more spirits soon, that I own myself not eager for you to come out with any kind of play, *next Winter.* Many Scenes & Characters might otherwise be

---

1 See note 1, p. 146.
2 A letter from FB, now missing.

preserved, & perhaps save you time— —though I am not sure of it— —for the adjusting, fine-drawing, & patching neatly is tedious work—

[...] I had not read, or even opened your Letter, when we last Conversed on the subject— —& I believe you wondered at my taking no Notice of your new Project— —indeed it was what at first struck me as the most feasible & desirable. But the Combined Fleets had not then frighted the whole Nation[1]— —But all this is no reason why you sh^d. not write—tho' it is one against doing anything of such Consequence to your Fame &c—in *a hurry*— — Don't fear that the Author of Evelina will be soon forgotten!— Come out When you will something Good, & pleasing, will be expected—you have resources sufficient for writing a great deal— —only, for the stage, I w^d. have you very Careful, & very perfect— —that is, as far so as your own Efforts, & the best advice you can get, can make you. In the Novel way, there is no danger—& in that, *no Times* can affect you.

1780

85.   FRANCES BURNEY TO SAMUEL CRISP
              22 January 1780, London

[...]
You make a *comique* kind of Enquiry about my *incessant & uncommon Engagements,*—Now, my dear Daddy, this is an Enquiry I feel rather *small* in answering,—for I am sure you expect to hear something respectable in *that sort of way*, whereas I have nothing to ennumerate that *commands attention*, or that will make a *favourable report*.—For the truth is, my *uncommon* Engagements have only been of the *visiting system*, & my *incessant* ones only of the *Working party*;—for perpetual Dress requires perpetual replenishment, & that replenishment actually occupies almost every moment I spend out of Company. "*Fact! Fact!*" I assure you,—however paltry, ridiculous or inconceivable it may sound. Caps, Hats, & Ribbons make, indeed, no venerable appearance upon Paper;—no more does Eat-

---

1   On 16 June 1779, Spain declared war, joining the Franco-American alliance against Britain.

ing & Drinking;—yet the one can no more be worn without being *made*, than the other [can be swallowed][1] without being *Cooked*,—& those who can niether pay *Milliners*, nor keep [*scrubbers*], must either toil for themselves, or go *Capless* & Dinnerless,— —So if you are for an high-polished comparison, *I'm* your man!— Now instead of Furbelows & Gewgaws of this sort, my dear Daddy probably expected to hear of Duodecimos, Octavos or Quartos![2]—Helas! I am sorry that is not the case,—but not one word, no, not one syllable did I write to any purpose from the Time You left me at Streatham, till Christmas, when I came Home. But now I have something to communicate concerning which I must beg you to give me your opinion.

As my Play was settled in it's silent suppression, I entreated my Father to call on Mr. Sheridan in order to prevent his expecting any thing from me, as he had had a good right to do from my having sent him a possitive Message that I should, in compliance with his exhortations at Mrs. Cholmondeley's, try my fortune in the *Theatrical line*, & send him a Piece for this Winter. My Father did call, but found him not at Home,—niether did he happen to see him till about Christmas. He then acquainted him that what I had written had entirely dissatisfied me, & that I desired to decline for the present all attempts of that sort.

Mr. Sheridan was pleased to express great concern,—nay more, to protest he would not *accept* my refusal;—he beg'd my Father to tell me that he could take no denial to *seeing* what I had done,— that I could be no fair Judge for myself;—that he doubted not but it would please;—but was *glad* I was not satisfied, as he had much rather see pieces before their Authors were contented with them than afterwards, on account of sundry small changes always necessary to be made by the Managers, for Theatrical purposes, & to which they were loath to submit when their writings were finished to their own approbations. In short, he said so much that my Father, ever easy to be worked upon, began to waver, & told me he wished I would shew the play to Sheridan at once.

This very much disconcerted me,—I had taken a sort of disgust to it, & was myself most earnestly desirous to let it Die a quiet Death. I therefore *cooled* the affair as much as I conveniently could, & by evading from Time to Time the Conversation, it was again

1 Inserted by FBA.
2 Standard volume sizes; hence a reference to books.

sinking into it's old state,—when again Mr. Sheridan saw my Father, & asked his leave to call upon me himself.

This could not be refused.

Well,—I was now violently *fidgetted*,—& began to think of *alterations*,—&, by setting my Head to Work, I have actually new written the 4th. Act from beginning to end except one scene:—Mr. Sheridan, however, has not yet called;—& I have so little Heart in the affair, that I have now again quite dropt it.

Such is the present situation of *my politics*. Now I wish you much to write me your private opinion what I had best do in case of an emergency:—Your Letters are always sacred, so pray write with your usual sincerity & openness.—I know you too well to fear your being offended if things should be so managed that your Counsel cannot be followed: it will, at any rate, not be thrown away, since it will be a fresh proof of your interest in my affairs.

My Notions I will also tell you; they are:—in case I *must* produce this piece to the Manager—

To entirely omit all mention of the *Club*;—

To curtail the parts of Smatter & Dabler as much as possible;—

To restore to Censor his £5000—& not trouble him even to *offer* it;—

To give a *new* friend to Cecilia, by whom her affairs shall be retrieved, & through whose means the Catastrophe shall be brought to be happy;—

And to change the Nature of Beaufort's connections with Lady Smatter, in order to obviate the unlucky resemblance the *adopted Nephew* bears to our *Female Pride of Literature*.[1]

This is all I have at present thought of,—& yet, if I am so allowed, even these thoughts shall all turn to Nothing,—for I have so much more Fear than hope, & Anxiety than pleasure in thinking at all of the Theatre, that I believe my wisest way will be to *shirk*—which if, by *evasive & sneaking means* I can, I shall.

[...]

86.   SAMUEL CRISP TO FRANCES BURNEY
            23 February 1780, Chessington

Our letters cross'd each other: I did not receive Yours till the day after mine was sent off; otherwise I should not have then omitted,

---

1 To Mrs. Montagu, who, like Lady Smatter, had adopted her nephew as her heir.

what You seemed to require—my Notions on the Subject of M^r.
Sheridan's importunity—[xxx] my great Scruple all along has been
the Consideration of the great Stake You are playing for—how
much You have to lose; & how unequal your delicate & tender
Frame of Mind would be, to sustain the Shock of a failure of Success, should that be the Case—You cant easily imagine how much
it goes against me to say any thing that looks like discouragement
to a spirit, already too diffident, & apprehensive Nothing but so
rooted a regard for my Fannikin, & her peace and happiness, as I
feel, at this instant, could ever have prevail'd on me to have us'd that
freedom with her, which tho' all Authors pretend to insist on, from
the friends they consult; yet Ninety nine out of a hundred are
offended at; & not only so, but bear a secret grudge & Enmity, for
the Sincerity, they have demanded, & in some measure extorted—
I myself have met with, & smarted for, some instances of this kind;
but that shall not hinder me from delivering my real Sentiments to
those I love, when calld upon; & particularly my own Creature
Fannikin for I think I know her generosity too well, to suspect her
of taking amiss what can proceed from no Motive but Friendship,
& fidelity—Well then—this is my Idea.

The play has *Wit* enough, & enough—but the Story & the incidents dont appear to me interesting enough to seize & keep hold
of the Attention & eager expectation of the generality of Audi-
ences—this, to me, is its Capital defect—

The Omissions You propose are right, I think; but how the
Business of the Piece is to go on, with such Omissions & Alterations as You mention, it is impossible for me to know—what You
mean to leave out,—*the Club & a larger Share of Smatter & Dabler*,
seems to have been the main Subject of the play—Cecilia's loss, &
unexpected restoration of her fortune, is not a new Incident by any
means—however any thing is preferable to Censor's interfering in
the business, by his unaccountable generosity.

Now, as to the very great importance, & indeed (to my thinking) the indispensable necessity of an interesting Plot or Story; let
me recommend to You, to borrow or get from the Circulating
Library, *An Apology for the Life of M^r. Colley Cibber*[1]—.This book
has chance thrown in my way since I wrote last to You; & in run-

---

1 Cibber (1671-1757), an actor and dramatist, was a leading figure on the
Restoration and early eighteenth-century stage. His *Apology* (autobiography) was published in 1740.

ning it over I very unexpectedly met with a full & Copious detail of all my very thoughts, on this subject, to a most minute exactness—[...]

What to advise, I profess, I know not—only thus much—I should have a much greater deference for the Opinion of Sheridan than of Murphy;—I take him in himself to be much deeper; & he is besides deeply interested in the fate of whatever he brings forward on his own Stage—upon the whole, as he [is] so pressing to see what You have done, I should almost incline to consent—[xxx]^1

[...]

87.   SAMUEL CRISP TO FRANCES BURNEY
                27 April 1780, Chessington

[...]
I am very glad You are now with them [*the Thrales*] in the midst of the Bath Circle; Your time could not be better employed; for all your St Martin's Daddy wanted to retain You for some other purposes—You are now at School—the great School of the World; where swarms of new Ideas, & new Characters will continually present themselves before You,

—————————————— *"which You'll draw in,*
"As We do Air, fast as 'tis ministred."^{2}

[...]
The Portion You allow'd me, of your Tunbridge & Brighton Journal I suck'd in with much pleasure & Avidity—why, You have began already; & make good what I have said above—you take down whatever you see—
[...]
— M^{rs}. Montague too!—how it flatters me, to have my Idea of her, formed above thirty years ago confirm'd by this Instance!—I believe I have told You of several Letters the Dutchess of Portland showed me of hers formerly (for I had no acquaintance with herself) so full of affectation, refinement, attempts to Philosophize talking Metaphysics, in all which particulars she so bewilder'd &

---

1 Nothing came of this plan to revise *The Witlings*.
2 Cf. *Cymbeline*, 1.1.45.

puzzled herself & her readers, & showd herself so superficial, nay really ignorant in the Subjects she paraded on; that in my own private mind's pocket Book, I set her down for a vain, empty, conceited pretender, & little else!—I know I am now treading on [holy] Ground!—therefore, *Mum*, for your Life! or rather, for *my* Life!—Were M^{rs}. Thrale to know of my presumption, & that I dare to [vent] such desperate Treason to her Play-mate, what would She say to me!

You take no Notice of several particulars I want to hear of—Your un-beautiful, clever Heroine, beset all round for the sake of her great Fortune—what is become of her?[1]—I am persuaded, she'd make her *own* Fortune, whatever were the Fate of her Hunters—the Idea is new, & striking, & presents a large Field, for unhackney'd Characters, Observations, Subjects for Satire & Ridicule, & numberless Advantages you'd meet with, by Walking in such an untrodden path Have you yet met with Colley Cibber, & read the Passage I recommended to You?

I cant say, I am sorry your Affair with M^r. Sheridan is at present at a stand—in the mean time, the Refusal coming from yourself, & not the Manager, tells highly in Your favour—your Coyness will tend to enhance your Fame greatly in Public Opinion—"*'Tis Expectation makes the blessing dear*"[2]

[...]

88.   FRANCES BURNEY TO SUSAN BURNEY
                4 June 1780, Bath

[...]

[*During an evening party at Mrs. Lambart's, a sister of Sir Philip Jennings Clerke, FB meets the strange Miss White.*]

Miss White is young & pleasing in her appearance, not pretty, but agreeable in her Face, & soft, gentle & well bred in her manners. Our conversation, for some Time, was upon the common Bath topics,—but when Mrs. Lambart left us,—called to receive more Company, we went, insensibly, into graver matters.

As I soon found, by the looks & Expressions of this young lady that she was of a *peculiar cast*, I left all choice of subjects to herself,

---

1 This suggests that FB was evolving a plot for a new novel, elements of which would later be divided between *Cecilia* and *Camilla*.

2 Sir John Suckling, "Against Fruition" (1646), l. 23.

determined quietly to follow as she led. And very soon, & I am sure I know not how, we had for topics the follies & Vices of Mankind,—& indeed she spared not for lashing them!—The *women* she rather excused than defended, laying to the Door of the *Men* their faults & imperfections;—but the *Men*, she said, were *all* bad,—*all*, in one word, & without exception, *Sensualists*.

I stared much at a severity of speech for which her softness of manner had so ill prepared me,—& she, perceiving my surprise, said "I am sure I ought to apologise for speaking *my* opinion to *you*,— *you*, who have so just & so uncommon a knowledge of human Nature,—I have long wished ardently to have the honour of conversing with you,—but your Party has, altogether, been regarded as so formidable, that I have not had courage to approach it."

I made, as what could I do else? disqualifying speeches, & she then led to discoursing of happiness & misery;—the *latter* she held to be the *invariable* lot of us all,—& "*one* word, she added, we have in our Language, & in all other, for which there is never any essential necessity,—& that is *pleasure*." And her Eyes filled with Tears as she Spoke.

"Good God, cried I, how you amaze me! I have met with *Misanthropes* before, but never with so complete a one,—& I can hardly think I hear right when I see how young you are."

She then, in rather indirect terms, gave me to understand that she was miserable *at Home*,—& in *very direct* terms that she was wretched *abroad*, & openly said that to affliction she was Born, & in affliction she must die, for that the World was so vilely formed as to render happiness *impossible* for it's Inhabitants.

There was something in this freedom of repining that I could by no means approve, & as I found by all her manner that she had a disposition to even *respect* whatever I said, why I now grew very serious, & frankly told her that I could not think it consistent with either truth or religion to cherish such notions.

"One thing, answered she, there is which I believe *might* make me happy,—but for that I have no inclination;—it is an amourous disposition. But that I do not possess; I can make myself no happiness by Intrigue."

"I hope not, indeed!" cried I, almost confounded by her extraordinary notions & speeches;— "but surely there are worthier subjects of happiness attainable,—"

"No, I believe there are not,—& the reason the Men are happier than us, is because they are more sensual.

"I would not *think such thoughts*," cried I, clasping my Hands with an involuntary vehemence, "for Worlds!—"

The Miss Caldwells then interrupted us, & seated themselves next to us,—but Miss White paid them little attention at first, & soon after none at all, but, in a low voice, continued her Discourse with me; recurring to the same subject of happiness & misery, upon which, after again asserting the folly of ever hoping for the former, she made this Speech—

"There may be, indeed, *one moment* of happiness,—which must be the finding one worthy of exciting a Passion which one should dare own to himself! *That* would, indeed, be a moment worth Living for! but that can never happen,—I am sure not to *me*,—the Men are so low, so vicious,—so worthless!—no, there is not one such to be found."

What a strange Girl! I could do little more than listen to her, from surprise at all she said.

"If, however, she continued, I had *your* talents, I could, bad as this World is, be happy in it—there is nothing, there is nobody I envy like *you*;—with *such* resources as yours, there can never be *ennui*; the Mind may always be employed, & always be gay. O if I could Write as *you* write!—"

"*Try*," cried I, "*that* is all that is wanting,—*try*, & you will soon do much better things."

"O no,—I *have* tried,—but I cannot succeed."

"Perhaps you are too diffident. But is it possible you can be serious in so dreadful an assertion as that you are *never* happy? Are you sure that some *real* misfortune would not shew you that your present misery is *imaginary*?"

"I don't know," answered she, looking down,—perhaps it is so,—but in that case, 'tis a misery so much the harder to be cured."

"You surprise me more and more," cried I;—"is it possible you can so rationally *see* the disease of a disordered Imagination, & yet allow it such power over your Mind?"

"Yes, for it is the only source from which I draw any Shadow of felicity! Sometimes, when in the Country, I give way to my Imagination whole Days,—& then I forget the World & it's cares, & feel some enjoyment of existence."

"Tell me what is *then* your Notion of felicity? whither does your Castle-Building carry you?"

"O—quite out of the World,—I know not where,—but I am surrounded with *Sylphs*,—& I forget every thing besides!"

"Well,—you are a most extraordinary Character indeed! I must confess I have seen *nothing like you!*"

"I hope, however, *I* shall find something like myself,—&,

like the magnet rolling in the Dust, attract some metal as I go."

"That you may *attract* what you please, is of all things most likely;—but if you wait to be happy for a friend resembling *yourself*, I shall no longer wonder at your despondancy."

"O! cried she, raising her Eyes in extacy, *could* I find such a one!—Male or Female,—for Sex would be indifferent to me, with such a one I would go to *Live* directly."

I half Laughed,—but was perplexed in my own mind whether to be *sad* or *merry* at such a speech.

"But then, she continued, after *making*—should I *lose* such a friend—I would not survive!"

"Not survive? repeated I; what can you mean?"

She looked down, but said nothing.

"Surely you cannot mean, said I, *very* gravely indeed, to put a violent end to your Life?"

"I should not, said she, again looking up, hesitate a Moment."

I was quite thunderstruck,—& for some Time could not say a Word;—but when I *did* speak, it was in a style of exhortation so serious & earnest I am ashamed to write it to you lest you should think it too much.

She gave me an attention that was even *respectful*, but when I urged her to tell me by what *right* she thought herself entitled to *rush unlicensed on Eternity*, she said—"By the right of believing I shall be *extinct*."

Good God, I really felt *horror'd*!

"Where, for Heaven's sake, I cried, where have you picked up such dreadful reasoning?"

"In *Hume*, said she;—I have read his Essays repeatedly."[1]

"I am sorry to find they have power to do so much mischief; you should not have read them, at least, till a man equal to Hume in *abilities* had answered him. Have you read any more Infidel Writers?"

"Yes,—Bolingbroke,—the divinest of all Writers!"[2]

"And do you read nothing upon the *right* side?"

---

1 David Hume's *Essays on the Principles of Morality and Natural Religion* (1751).
2 Henry St. John, Viscount Bolingbroke was a Deist. Deists argued that God had withdrawn from the world after Creation, so that all events in the physical universe were the product of mechanistic determinism rather than the active intervention of providence.

"Yes,—the *Bible*, till I was sick to Death of it, every Sunday Evening to my Mother."

"Have you read Beattie on the immutability of Truth?"[1]

"No."

"Give me leave, then, to recommend it to you. After *Hume's Essays*, you *ought* to read it. And even, for *lighter* reading, if you were to look at Mason's Elegy on Lady Coventry, it might be of no disservice to you.—"

And then I could not forbear repeating to her from that beautiful Poem

> Know, vain *Sceptics*, know, th'almighty Mind
> That Breath'd on Man a portion of his Fire,
>   Bad his free Soul, by Earth nor Time confin'd,
> To HEAVEN, to IMMORTALITY aspire!
>
> Nor shall the pile of Hope his Mercy rear'd
> By vain Philosophy be e'er destroy'd;
>   ETERNITY—by all or *wish'd*, or *fear'd*,
> Shall be by All or *suffer'd,*—or *enjoy'd!*...[2]

This was the chief of our Conversation,—which indeed made an Impression upon me I shall not easily get rid of, a young & agreeable *Infidel* is even a shocking sight,—& with her romantic, flighty & unguarded turn of Mind, what could happen to her that could give surprise?

Poor misguided Girl! I heartily indeed wish she was in good Hands. She is in a very dangerous situation with ideas so loose of Religion, & so enthusiastic of Love. What, indeed, is there to restrain an Infidel, who has no belief in a future state, from sin & evil of *any* sort?

[...]

Thursday. [8 June 1780]

[*FB visits Bath Easton, home of Sir John and Lady Miller, and meets the mysterious Miss White again.*]

[...]

---

1 James Beattie's *Essay on the Nature and Immutability of Truth* was published in 1770 as antidote to Hume's philosophy.

2 Final lines of William Mason's "Elegy on the Death of a Lady" (1760), about the celebrated beauty, Maria Gunning, who had married the Earl of Coventry.

She begged to know if I had written any thing else. I assured her *never*; "The *Sylph*, said she, I was told was yours."

"I had nothing at all to do with that or any thing else that ever was *published* but Evelina;—*You*, I suppose, read the *Sylph* for it's *name's* sake?"

"No; I never read Novels,—I hate them; I never read Evelina till I was quite persecuted by hearing it talked of. Sir Charles Grandison I tried once,—but could not bear it,—Sir Charles for a *Lover*!—no Lover for *me*!—for a *Guardian*, or the *Trustee* of an Estate he might do very well,—but for a *Lover*!—"

"What,—when he *Bows upon your Hand*! would not that do?"

"O Lord no!—when he goes so far, I think he ought to go further!" & *gaity* is no word for the *wantonness* with which she spoke this.

Upon my word—I began to be quite disgusted with this new acquaintance, & half ashamed of being thus selected for her private sentiment hearer;—however, she kept me by her side a full Hour, & we again talked over our former Conversation; & I enquired what had *first* led her to seeking Infidel Books?—*Pope*, she said, he was himself a *Deist*, she believed, & his praise of *Bolingbroke* made her mad to read his Works,—& then the rest followed easily. She also gave me an account of her private & domestic Life; of her *misery* at Home, her search of Dissipation, & her incapability of happiness.

Poor Girl! I am really sorry for her,—she has strong & lively parts, but I think her in the high road of lasting destruction! She waits but to *Love* in order to be infamous, & she thinks about *Religion* only to persuade herself there is none!—I recommended to her all the good Books I could think of,—& scrupled not to express warmly & most seriously my surprise & horror at her way of thinking. It was easy to me to see that she attended to my opinions with curiosity, & yet easier to discover that had she not respected me as Author of a Book she happened to be fond of, she would have rallied them unmercifully; however, that consideration gave weight to what I said, & evidently disposed her to be pleased with me.

[...]

89.   FRANCES BURNEY TO SAMUEL CRISP
                     9 August 1780

[...]

I am extremely gratified by your approbation of my Journal. Miss Brisk, I do assure you, exists *exactly* such as I have described her. I never mix Truth & Fiction;—all that I relate in Journalising is *strictly*, nay *plainly* Fact: I never, in all my Life, have been a sayer of the Thing that is not,[1] & *now* I should be not *only* a knave, but a Fool also in so doing, as I have other purposes for Imaginary Characters than filling Letters with them. Give me credit, therefore, on the score of Interest & common sense, if not of Principle! *There I had you again, my Lad!*—But, however, the World & especially the great World, is so filled with absurdity of various sorts,—now bursting forth in impertinence, now in pomposity, now giggling in silliness, & now yawning in dullness, that there is no occasion for *invention* to draw what is striking in every possible species of the ridiculous. [...]

1781

90.   FRANCES BURNEY TO ESTHER BURNEY
            7-8 January 1781, Chessington

[...]
I go on but indifferently,—I don't write as I did, the certainty of being known, the high success of Evelina, which, as Mr. Crisp says, to fail in a 2^d. would *tarnish*,—these thoughts worry & depress me,—& a desire to do more than I have been able, by writing at unseasonable Hours, & never letting my Brains rest even when my *Corporeal machine* was *succumbent*,—these things, joined to a Cold, have brought on a Fever [...]

91.   FRANCES BURNEY TO SUSAN BURNEY
            3 February 1781, Chessington

You are very good & sweet for accepting my excuses about not writing, & promising still to let me hear from you; indeed, but for that promise, I *should* write, in spite of all inconvenience & labour,—for *labour* it now is to me to take up a pen, because one way or other my Hand scarce rests an Hour in the whole Day. Whenever this Work is done—if ever that Day arrives, I believe I shall not write another word for 3 years! however, I really believe

---

1   Cf. Swift's *Gulliver's Travels* (1726), part 4, ch. 5.

I must still publish it *in part*, for I begin to grow horribly tired, &
yet am by no means *near* any thing *bordering* upon an end. And the
eternal fagging of my Mind & Brains does really much mischief to
my Health—
[...]   *firing*

92.   FRANCES BURNEY TO SUSAN BURNEY
                    February 1781, Chessington

[...]
[*CB urged haste in FB's composition of* Cecilia *in order to secure the pub-
licity of a tandem publication with the 2nd volume of his* History of
Music. *However, in February an illness brought on by overwork obliged
FB to stop writing.*]
My illness has been very unlucky,—I believe, indeed, I over harrass
myself, & that, instead of making me write more, *bothers*, & makes
me write less,—yet I cannot help it,—for I know my dear Father
will be disapointed, he will expect me to have just *done*, when I am
so behind hand as not even to see Land!—yet I have written a great
deal,—but the Work will be a long one, & I cannot without ruin-
ing it make it otherwise.
[...]
    I have not yet settled about my return; the truth is it is Time, but
I am *afraid* of seeing my Father. Think of a whole Volume not yet *settled*, not yet begun!—& that so important a one as the last!—O that
I could defer the publication, & relieve my Mind [from] this vile
solicitude which does but shackle it, & disturbs my rest so abom-
inably, that I cannot sleep half the night for planning what to write
next Day,—& then next Day am half dead for want of Rest!—
[...]

93.   FRANCES BURNEY TO SUSAN BURNEY
                    May 1781, Streatham

[...]
[*After the death of Henry Thrale on 4 April, FB joined HLT at
Streatham. FB reports a conversation with HLT.*]
"Why you know Mr. Crutchley[1] yesterday called me out of the

---

1   Jeremiah Crutchley, one of the executors of Mr. Thrale's will, and
    rumoured to be his illegitimate son.

Room to tell me a secret: well, this was to shew me a paragraph he had just read in the news-paper, & do, ma'am, says he, have the news paper burnt, or put some where safe out of Miss Burney's way, for I am sure it will vex her extremely."

Think if this did not terrify me pretty handsomely!—I turned sick as Death,—she gave me the Paper, & I read the following Paragraph.

"Miss Burney, the sprightly Writer of the elegant Novel Evelina, is now domesticated with Mrs. Thrale in the same manner that Miss More is with Mrs. Garrick, & Mrs. Carter with Mrs. Montague."[1]

The preparation for this had been so very alarming, that little as I liked it, I was so much afraid of something still worse, that it really was a *relief* to me to see it: & Mrs. Thrale's excess of tenderness & delicacy about it was such as to have made me amends for almost any thing. I promised, therefore, to take it *like a man*, & after thanking her with the sincerest gratitude for her infinite kindness, we parted to Dress.

It is, however, most insufferably impertinent to be thus dragged into print, notwithstanding every possible effort & caution to avoid it. There is nothing, merely concerning myself, that can give me greater uneasiness, for there is nothing I have always more dreaded, or more uniformly endeavoured to avoid. In spite, therefore, of all that I could do to either be or seem indifferent about it, it weighed heavily upon my Mind the whole Day, & made me so uncomfortable I could hardly rally my spirits at all.

[...]

94.   HESTER THRALE: *THRALIANA*
                          7 July 1781

[...]

What a Blockhead D^r. Burney is, to be always sending for his Daughter home so! what a Monkey! is not She better and happier with me than She can be any where else? Johnson is enraged at the silliness of their Family Conduct, and M^rs. Byron disgusted: I confess myself provoked excessively but I love the Girl *so* dearly— & the D^r. too for that matter, only that he has such odd Notions of superiority in his own house, & will have his Children under his

---

1 I.e. in a relation of patroness and dependent.

Feet forsooth rather than let 'em live in Peace, Plenty & Comfort any where from home. If I did not provide Fanny with every *Wear*able, every *Wish*able indeed, it would not vex me to be served so; but to see the Impossibility of compensating for the Pleasures of S*ᵗ: Martins Street*, makes me at once merry & mortified.

D*ʳ*: Burney did not like his Daughter should learn Latin even of *Johnson* who offered to teach her for Friendship, because then She would have been as wise as himself forsooth, & Latin was too Masculine for Misses—a narrow Souled Goose-Cap the Man must be at last; *agreable* and *amiable* all the while too beyond allmost any other human Creature.

[...]

1782

95.   SAMUEL CRISP TO SOPHIA GAST
25 January 1782, Chessington

[...]
Don't communicate to any one a single word about Fanny's Book, which in a few months I suppose will come out. You see how triumphantly she goes on. If she can coin gold at such a Rate, as to sit by a warm Fire, and in 3 or 4 months (for the real time she has stuck to it closely, putting it all together, will not amount to more, tho' there have been long Intervals, between) gain £250 by scribbling the Inventions of her own Brain—only putting down in black and white whatever comes into her own head, without labour drawing singly from her own Fountain, she need not want money.
[...]

96.   FRANCES BURNEY TO SUSAN BURNEY PHILLIPS[1]
25 February 1782, London

[...]
My Work is too long in all Conscience for the hurry of my *people* to have it produced. I have a thousand million of fears for it; the mere Copying, *without* revising & correcting, would take *at least* 10

---

1   SEB married Molesworth Phillips on 10 January 1782.

weeks, for I cannot do more than a Vol. in a Fortnight, unless I scrawl short Hand, & rough Hand, as badly as the original. Yet my dear Father thinks it will be *published* in a Month!—Since you went, I have Copied 1 Vol. & a *1/4*—no more!—O I am sick to think of it!—Yet not a little reviving is my Father's *very* high approbation of the first volume, which is all he has seen. I totally forget whether, in my last, I told you I had presented it to him? but I am sure you would never forget, for the pleasure you would have felt for me, had you seen or heard him reading any part of it—he is quite *infatuated* with fondness for it,—not only beyond my most sanguine hopes, but almost beyond credibility. Would you ever believe, bigotted as he was to Evelina, that he now says he thinks this a superior design, & superior execution!—& told me, the moment he had done, that he not only liked it better than any thing of mine, but better than any thing of ANY body's, *by G——* !—... you can never half imagine the delight & astonishment this has given me. It is answering my *first* wish, & *first* ambition in life. And though I am certain, & though he thinks himself, it will never be so popular as Evelina, *his* so warm satisfaction will make me amends for almost any mortification that may be in store for me. [...]

97.   FRANCES BURNEY TO SUSAN BURNEY PHILLIPS
February 1782, London

[...]
[*FB gives an account of a rout she attended at the house of Mr. Paradise, where she was introduced to Lady Say and Sele by Mrs. Paradise.*]
"Miss Burney, Lady Say & Seal desires the Honour of being introduced to you."

Her Ladyship stood by her [*Mrs. Paradise's*] side. She seems pretty near 50, at *least* turned 40,—her Head was full of Feathers, Flowers, Jewels, & gew gaws, & as high as Lady Archers, her Dress was trimmed with Beads, silver, persian, *sashes*, & all sort of fine fancies; her Face is thin & fiery, & her whole manner spoke a lady *all alive*.

"Miss Burney," cried she, with great quickness & a look all curiosity, "I am very happy to see you,—I have longed to see you a great while,—I have read your Performance, & I am quite delighted with it. I think it's the most elegant Novel I ever read in my life. Such a style!—I am quite surprised at it! I can't think where you got so much invention."

You may believe this was a reception not to make me very loquacious!—good Heaven! I did not know which way to turn my Head.

"I must introduce you," continued her Ladyship, to my sister,—she'll be quite delighted to see you,—she has writ a Novel herself!—so you are sister Authoresses! A most elegant thing it is, I assure you,—almost as pretty as yours,—only not quite so elegant. She has writ *two* Novels,—only one is not so pretty as the Other. But I shall insist upon your seeing them. One is in Letters, like yours, only yours is prettiest. It's called the Mausoleum of Julia!"

What unfeeling things, thought I, are *my* sisters! I'm sure I never heard them go about thus praising *me*!

Mrs. Paradise then again came forward, & taking my Hand, led me up to her Ladyship's sister, Lady Hawke, saying aloud, & with a courteous smirk "Miss Burney, ma'am, Authoress of Evelina."

"Yes," cried my friend, Lady Say & Seal, who followed me close, "it's the Authoress of Evelina! So you are sister Authoresses!"

Lady Hawke arose & courtsied. She is much younger than her sister, & rather pretty; extremely languishing, delicate, & pathetic; apparently accustomed to be reckoned the Genius of her Family, & well contented to be looked upon as a Creature dropt from the Clouds!

I was then seated between their Ladyships, & Lady S. & S., drawing as near to me as possible, said,—"Well,—& so you wrote this pretty Book!—& pray did your Papa know of it?"

"No, ma'am, not till some months after the Publication."

"So I've heard!—it's surprising!—I can't think how you invented it! there's a vast deal of invention in it. And you've got so much humour, too!—now my sister has no humour,—her's is all sentiment,—you can't think how I was entertained with that old Grandmother & her son!—"

I suppose she meant Tom Branghton for the *son*.

"Lord, how much pleasure, you must have had in writing it!—had not you?"

"Y———e———s, ma'am."

"So has my sister,—she's never without a Pen in her Hand,—she can't help writing for her life;—when Lord Hawke is Travelling about with her, she keeps writing all the way!"

"Yes," said Lady Hawke, "I really can't help writing. One has great pleasure in writing the things,—has not one, Miss Burney?"

"Y———e———s, ma'am."

"But your Novel," cried Lady Say & Seal, "is in such a Style!—

so elegant!—I am vastly glad you made it end happily. I hate a Novel that don't end happy."

"Yes," said Lady Hawke, with a languid smile, "I was vastly glad when she married Lord Orville! I was sadly afraid it would not have been."

"My sister intends," said Lady Say & Seal, "to print her Mausoleum, just for her own friends & acquaintances."

"Yes," said Lady Hawke, "I have never printed yet."

"I saw Lady Hawke's name," quoth I to my *first* friend, "[ascribed]¹ to the play of "Variety"."²

"Did you indeed!" cried Lady Say, in an extacy,—"Sister!—do you know Miss Burney saw your name in the news papers about the Play!—"

"Did she?" said Lady Hawke, smiling complacently, "But I really did not write it: I never writ a Play in my life."

"Well," cried Lady Say, "but do pray repeat that sweet part that I am so fond of,—you know what I mean,—Miss Burney *must* hear it,—out of your Novel, you know!"

Ly. H. "No, I can't,—I have forgot it."

Ly. S. "O no,—I am sure you have not,—I insist upon it."

Ly. H. "But I know you can repeat it yourself,—you have so fine a memory,—I am sure you can repeat it."

Ly. S. "O but I should not do it Justice!—that's all, I should not do it justice!"

Lady Hawke then bent forward, & repeated

"If, when he made the declaration of his Love, the sensibility that beamed in his Eyes was felt in his Heart, what pleasing sensations, & soft alarms might not that tender avowal awaken!

"And from what, ma'am," cried I, astonished, & imagining I had mistaken them, "is this taken?"

"From my sister's Novel!" answered the delighted Lady Say & Seal, expecting my raptures to be equal [to her own]³ "it's in the Mausoleum!—did not you know that?—Well, I can't think how you can write these sweet Novels!—And it's all just like that part!—Lord Hawke himself says it's all Poetry!—For *my* part, I'm sure I never could write so. I suppose, Miss Burney, you are producing another? A'n't you?"

---

1 Substitution.
2 A comedy by Richard Griffith. The play had also been attributed to FB.
3 Inserted by FBA.

"No, ma'am."

"Oh, I dare say you are! I dare say you are writing one at this very minute!"

Mrs. Paradise now came up to me again, followed by a square man, middle aged, & *hum drum*, who, I found, was Lord Say & Seal, afterwards from the Kirwans, for though they introduced him to me, I was so confounded by their vehemence & their manners, that I did not hear his Name.

"Miss Burney, said Mrs. P.—"Authoress of Evelina!"

"Yes," cried Lady Say & Seal, starting up, "'tis the Authoress of Evelina!"

"Of *what?*" cried he.

"Of Evelina!—You'd never think it!—she looks so young!—to have so much invention, & such an elegant *Style!*—Well, I could write a *Play*, I think, but I'm sure I could never write a *Novel*."

"Oh yes, you could if you would try;" said Lady Hawke, [xxx] "O no, I could not!" answered she, "I could not get a *style!*—that's the thing, I could not tell how to get a *style!*—& a Novel's nothing without a *style*, you know!"

"Why no," said Lady Hawke, "that's true. But then you write such charming Letters, you know!"

"Letters?" repeated Lady S. & S. simpering, "—do you think so?—do you know I wrote a long Letter to Mrs. Ray just before I came here!—this very afternoon!—quite a long Letter!—I did, I assure you!"

Here Mrs. Paradise came forward with another Gentleman, younger, slimmer, & *smarter*, & saying to me "Sir Gregory Page Turner," said to him, "Miss Burney,—Authoress of Evelina" At which Lady Say & Seal, in fresh transport, again arose, & rapturously again repeated "Yes,—*she's Authoress of Evelina!*—Have you read it?"

"No,—is it to be had?"

"Oh dear yes!—it's been printed these 2 years!—you'd never think it!—But it's the most elegant Novel I ever read in my life! writ in such a *Style!*"

"Certainly," said he, very civilly, "I have every inducement to get it. Pray where is it to be had?—*every* where, I suppose?"

"O *no* where, I hope!" cried I, wishing at that moment it had been never in human *ken*.

My *square* friend, Lord Say & Seal, then putting his Head forward, said very solemnly, "*I'll purchase it.*"

Lady Say & Seal then mentioned to me an hundred *Novels* that I had never heard of, asking my opinion of them, & whether I knew the Authors: Lady Hawke only occasionally & languidly joining in the discourse. And then, Lady S. & S, suddenly arising, begged me not to move, for she should be back again in a minute, & flew to the next Room.

I took, however, the first opportunity of Lady Hawke's casting down her Eyes, & reclining her delicate Head, to make away from this terrible set,—& just as I was got by the Piano Forte, where I hoped Pacchierotti would soon present himself, Mrs. Paradise again came to me, & said, "Miss Burney, Lady Say & Seal wishes vastly to cultivate your acquaintance, & begs to know if she may have the Honour of your Company to an Assembly at her House next Friday? And I will do myself the pleasure to call for you, if you will give me leave."

"Her Ladyship does me much honour, but I am unfortunately engaged." was my answer [...]

98.   MORNING HERALD
                             12 March 1782

[*A ms. copy of these verses was found among CB's papers in 1822, showing corrections and changes that indicated they were his own composition, probably intended to promote interest in FB prior to the publication of* Cecilia.]

ADVICE *to the* HERALD.
HERALD wherefore thus proclaim,
Nought of WOMAN but the *shame*?
Quit—oh quit at least a while,
Perdita's[1] too luscious smile,
Wanton *Worsley*, stilted *Dally*,[2]
Heroines of each black–guard alley;
Better sure record in story,
Such as shine their sex's glory! —
HERALD! haste, with me proclaim
Those of literary fame.
Hannah More's pathetic pen
Painting high th'impassion'd scene;

---

1 Mary Robinson (1758-1800), an actress who had been mistress of the Prince of Wales.
2 Lady Worsley was a notorious adulteress; Dally referred to Mrs. Grace Dalrymple Elliot, "Dally the Tall," a courtesan.

Carter's[1] Piety, and Learning,
Little *Burney's* quick discerning;
Cowley's[2] neatly pointed wit,
Healing those her satires hit.
Smiling *Streatfield's*[3] iv'ry neck,
Nose, and notions—*a la Greque!*
Let *Chapone*[4] retain a place,
And the mother of her grace,[5]
Each art of conversation knowing,
High bred, elegant *Boscawen*:
Thrale, in whose expressive eyes,
Sits a soul above disguise,
Skill'd with wit and sense t'impart,
Feelings of a generous heart.
Lucan,—Leveson,—Greville,—Crew,[6]
Fertile-minded *Montague!*
Who makes each rising art her care,
"And brings her knowledge from afar!"[7]
Whilst her tuneful tongu[e] defends,
Authors dead, and absent friends;
Bright in genius, pure in fame—
HERALD, haste, and these proclaim!

---

1   Elizabeth Carter (1717-1806), the most erudite of the Bluestockings, published a translation of Epictetus from the Greek in 1758.
2   Hannah Cowley (1743-1809), a dramatist.
3   Sophia Streatfield, a Greek scholar and member of HLT's circle.
4   Hester Mulso Chapone (1721-1801), essayist and poet best known for her conduct work, *Letters on the Improvement of the Mind* (1773).
5   Frances Boscawen, mother of the Duchess of Beaufort.
6   Other Bluestockings. Margaret Bingham, Countess of Lucan, was an amateur painter and friend of Mrs. Delany. Frances Leveson-Gower was another daughter of Frances Boscawen. Frances Greville was wife of CB's patron Fulke Greville, godmother to FB, and mother to Frances Crewe, a leading society hostess.
7   Cf. Job 36:3.

99.   FRANCES BURNEY TO SAMUEL CRISP
            15 March 1782, London

Your Letter,[1] my dear Daddy, which I have just received, has given
me so much uneasiness that I may as well answer it immediately, as
I can do nothing for thinking of it.

The Conflict scene for Cecilia, between the Mother & son, to
which you so warmly object, is the VERY scene for which I wrote
the whole Book! & so entirely does my plan hang upon it, that I
MUST abide by its reception in the World, or put the whole
behind the Fire.

You will believe then, with the opinion I have of your judgment, & the anxious desire I have to do nothing quite contrary to
your approbation, if I can now be very easy. I would it were in my
power to defer the whole publication to another spring,—but I am
sure my Father would run crazy if I made such a proposal.

Let me not, however, be sentenced without making my defence,
& at least explaining to you my own meaning in the part you censure.

I meant in Mrs. Delvile to draw a great, but not a perfect Character: I meant, on the contrary, to blend upon paper, as I have frequently seen blended in life, noble & rare qualities, with striking &
incurable defects. I meant, also, to shew how the greatest virtues &
excellencies, may be totally obscured by the indulgence of violent
passions, & the ascendancy of favourite prejudices.

This Scene has yet been read by no human Creature but yourself & Charlotte, who would not let me rest till I let her go through
the Book: upon Charlotte's opinion you will easily beleive I put no
great reliance, but yet I mention to you the effect it had on her,
because, as you told me about dear Kitty Cooke, the natural feelings of untaught hearers ought never to be slighted,—& Dr. Johnson has told me the same a thousand Times: Well—she prefers it to
any part of the Book, & cried over it so vehemently, that she could
Eat no Dinner, & had a violent Head ache all Day.

I would rather, however, have had one good word from you,
than all the Tears of the Tender, & all the praises of the civil.

The Character of Mrs. Delvile struck you in so favourable a
light, that you sunk, as I remember I privately noticed to myself,
when you mentioned her, all the passages to her disadvantage pre-

---

1   Lost.

vious to this conflict. Else it would have appeared to you less inconsistent, for the way is paved for it in several places. But indeed you read the whole to cruel disadvantage: the bad writing, the haste, the rough Copy, all were against me. Your anger at Mrs. Delvile's violence & obduracy is nothing but what I *meant* to excite;—your thinking it *unnatural* is all that disturbs me.

Yet, when I look about me in the World, such strange inconsistencies as I see, such astonishing contrariety of opinions, & so bigotted an adherence of all *marked* Characters to their own way of thinking, I really know not how to give up this point.

Another thing gives me some comfort: the part you have selected to like the best, Vauxhall, is what I read to you myself, & the whole of the residence at Delvile Castle, which I also read to you, I remember well you were pleased with more than with any other part of the Book. I cannot, therefore, but hope the bad Copy, & difficulty of reading, did me as much mischief as the bad & unequal composition.

[...]

100.   FRANCES BURNEY TO SAMUEL CRISP
6 April 1782, London

Heartily do I thank you, my ever dear Daddy, for your kind & Honourable dealing with me.[1] A [*Flogging*] do you call this? believe me, I am, *as yet*, so far from being *intoxicated with success*, that I read it with gratitude & Wonder!—for I expected much more severity & when I received your Letter, I was almost *sick* with painful *prognostics* of your disapprobation.

I shall do the utmost in my power to profit from your criticisms, but I can speak to no particulars till I come to the places themselves. [I shall never, however, *start myself* your objections to my other Daddy, but when ever his & yours are the same *naturally* I will not hesitate a moment. Mean time, I [xxx] softening, altering, *modifying* in such a manner, all you dislike, that I am not without hopes he will have no *reason* to make the same objections.] With respect, however, to the great point of Cecilia's Fortune, I have much to urge in my own defence, only now I can spare no Time, & I must frankly confess I shall think I have rather written a *Farce* than a *serious History*, if the whole is to end, like the hack Italian

---

1   SC had written a letter to FB containing criticisms of *Cecilia*, now lost.

Operas, with a jolly chorus that makes all parties good, & all parties happy!—The people I have ever met with who have been fond of *Blood & Family*, have all *scouted Title* when put in any competition with it: How, then, should these proud Delviles think a new created Peerage any equivalent for calling their sons sons, for future Generations, by the name of Beverley? Besides, I think the Book, in its present conclusion, somewhat *original*, for the Hero & Heroine are neither plunged in the depths of misery, nor exalted to *unhuman* happiness,—Is not such a middle state more natural? more according to real life, & less resembling every other Book of Fiction?

Besides, my own *End* will be lost, if I change the conclusion, which was chiefly to point out the absurdity & short sightedness of those *Name-compelling* Wills, which make it always *presumed* a woman marries an *Inferior*, since *he*, not *she*, is to leave his own Family, in order to be incorporated into hers. You find, my dear Daddy, I am prepared to fight a good Battle here, but I have thought the matter much over, & if I am made give up this point, my whole plan is rendered abortive, & the last page of ANY Novel in Mr. Noble's Circulating Library, may serve for the last page of mine, since a *Marriage*, a *Reconciliation*, & some sudden expedient for great *Riches*, concludes them all alike. In every thing else you have pointed out, I shall either *wholly* change, or *greatly* alter. And I *will* be *very* diligent to improve & mend the whole. Pray if any thing more occurs to you, write it [...]

101.   HESTER THRALE: *THRALIANA*
                    19 May 1782

[...]
[*HLT maintains that the Duchess of Devonshire styled her verses after translations from Horace, without reference to life.*]
She had no Notion of writing from her own Sensations—She would write as *others* had written—& when Pope begun, he was it seems all of the same Opinion.

Here is Fanny Burney quite in the contrary Extream: Her new Novel called *Cecilia* is the Picture of Life such as the Author sees it: while therefore this Mode of Life lasts, her Book will be of value, as the Representation is astonishingly perfect: but as nothing in the Book is derived from Study, so it can have no Principle of duration—Burney's Cecilia is to Richardson's Clarissa—what a Camera Obscura in the Window of a London

parlour,—is to a view of Venice by the clear Pencil of Can-
naletti.

[Cecilia *was published in July 1782.*]

102.   SAMUEL CRISP TO FRANCES BURNEY
            July 1782, Chessington

I deferr'd a return of my most sincere thanks & acknowledgements, both for your highly agreable present, & your two kind
Short notes, till I had twice read over, & thoroughly (nay, severely)
consider'd the first.—Don't be surpriz'd at so harsh an Adverb—I
was resolv'd to put myself in the place of an uninfluenc'd, yawning
fastidious Reader; that takes up a new Book, with careless indifference expecting from a Novel advertis'd, nothing more than the
Usual common Place trash they abound with—this State of mind
I endeavour'd at; divesting myself, as well as I could, of all remembrance of the Work, & all Partiality for the Author, to do this com-
pleatly, was indeed impossible; but still it was something, to be continually saying to myself, after I had read a Chapter;—how will this
go down?—what will the multitude, who care not a straw for
Author, or Bookseller, or anything but their own immediate
amusement, say of it?—These were my Queries to myself—If I
could have given a positive, & certain answer to them; that answer
would have determin'd the fate of the Book, & the Character of
the Authors Abilities: for these are the people,—(not a few, nay,
even a numerous partial set of Friends) that ultimately can, & do
decide—the Tribunal of the Inquisition itself is not more inflexible
than I endeavour'd to be on this Occasion—every other mode of
proceeding is only delusive, & what is call'd making ones Market
at home—What was the Result of these, my Meditations?—to
enter into particulars would be endless: but the sum total amounts
to this—a full, unlimited Confirmation of my warm approbation
of the whole Work together; & a positive declaration of the
improvements it has receiv'd, beyond all Expectation:—greatly, &
judiciously compress'd; long Conversations curtaild: several incidents much better manag'd; & the winding up of the bottom
beyond all Compare, more happy, more judicious more satisfactory.—Many particulars, which I did not quite relish, are soften'd off
to a degree, that if I do not perfectly concent to, I hardly know
how to condemn,—particularly in the instance of Old Delvile—
in whom (without departing from his original Character, which

would have been unpardonable) You have found means, fairly accounted for, to melt down some of that senseless, obstinate, inherent Pride; which if still kept up to its heigth would have render'd miserable, those who ought to have been dearest to him, & have establish'd him (which would have been a great impropriety) without any necessity (*young Delvile's Father, & the excellent Mrs Delvile's Husband*) the most hateful of Beings.

These my dear Fannikin, without the least Favor or Affection, are my sincere Sentiments; & if I know myself, would be such, if I had by Chance met with the Book without any Name to it—& at the same time, to evince my Sincerity & that you may not think I mean, Sycophant-like, to turn about & recant, in order to swim with the Wind & Tide, that brings you, (as I hear) Clouds of Incence from every Quarter—to avoid this scandalous Imputation, I do declare, that I must adhere to my former Sentiments on some parts of the Work—particularly the loss of Cecilia's Estate—But don't think I pretend to set up against the Public Voice, my trumpery Objection; which even, if well founded, would be a mere dust in the ballance—so much at present for Caecilia.

Now Fannikin, I must remind You of your promise—which was to come to y^r loving Daddy, when You could get loose—look ye Fan, I don't mean to cajole You hither, with the expectation of amusement, or entertainment—you & I know better, than to hum, or be humm'd in that manner—if you come here, come to Work— Work hard—Stick to it—this is the harvest time of your Life— your Sun shines hot—lose not a moment then, but make your hay directly—*touch the yellow Boys*—*grow Warm*—make the Booksellers *come down handsomely*—*count the ready*—*the Chink*—do but secure this one Point, while it is in your Power, & *All things else shall be Added unto thee.*[1] I talk'd to your Doctor Daddy on the subject of Disposing of your money;[2] & we both agreed in the project of a well-secur'd Annuity; & in the mean time, till that could be procur'd, that the ready should be Vested in the 3 p Cent Annuities, that it might produce something; & he promised to advance [to make even money.][3]

---

1 SC combines Briggs's jargon with a biblical allusion, cf. Matthew 6:33.
2 The profits of *Cecilia*.
3 Inserted by FBA.

103.   EDMUND BURKE[1] TO FRANCES BURNEY
                29 July 1782, Whitehall

I should feel exceedingly to blame if I could refuse to myself, the
natural satisfaction, & to you, the just but poor return of my best
thanks for the very great instruction & entertainment I have
received from the new present you have bestowed on the publick.
There are few, I believe I may say fairly, there are none at all, that
will not find themselves better informed concerning human
Nature, & their stock of observation enriched by reading your
Cecilia. They certainly will, let their experience in Life & manners
be what it may. The arrogance of age must submit to be taught by
youth. You have crowded into a few small volumes an incredible
variety of Characters; most of them well planned, well supported,
& well contrasted with each other. If there be any fault in this
respect, it is one, in which you are in no great danger of being imitated. Justly as your Characters are drawn, perhaps they are too
numerous:—but I beg pardon;—I fear it is quite in vain to preach
oeconomy to those who are come young to excessive & sudden
opulence. I might trespass on your delicacy if I should fill my Letter to you with what I fill my conversation to others. I should be
troublesome to you alone, if I should tell you all I feel & think, on
the natural vein of humour, the tender pathetick, the comprehensive & noble moral, & the sagacious observation, that appear quite
throughout that extraordinary performance. In an age distinguished by producing extraordinary Women, I hardly dare to tell
you where my opinion would place you amongst them.—I respect
your modesty, that will not endure the commendations which your
merit forces from every body.

104.   FRANCES BURNEY TO DR. CHARLES BURNEY
                4 August 1782, Ipswich

[...]
But now, dearest Sir, let me call for your congratulations,—You
have sent me many encouraging anecdotes concerning Cecilia, I
have now one to give you in return that, Dr. Johnson's single

---

1 A literary critic and Whig MP, Burke (1729-97) renounced his reformist
   sympathies after the French Revolution, expounding his new political
   philosophy in *Reflections on the Revolution in France* (1790).

approbation excepted, outweighs them all; & as the chief pleasure I take in this success comes from the kind pleasure you so generously, so sweetly take in it, I cannot but hope I shall communicate as much joy as I feel, when I tell you I have had a Letter from Mr. Burke!—& *such* a Letter! ... O, dearest Sir, for elegance of praise no such a one was ever written before. I long to send it you, but have no Frank.[1] Did I not say well when I said Mr. Burke was like *You*—for who, except You or He could, at a Time of Business, disappointment, care & occupation such as His now, have found leisure to read with such attention, & to commend with such good nature, a Work so totally foreign to every thing that just now can come Home to his Business & bosom? he is, indeed, a delightful Creature, & as sweet in his disposition as he is rare in his abilities. I could not, for some time, believe my own Eyes when I looked at his signature.[...]

105. FRANCES BURNEY TO SAMUEL CRISP
5 August 1782, Ipswich

Thanks, my dear Daddy, for your very kind Letter; I need not, I am sure, tell you how highly it gratified me, for the weight which your opinion has with me, I have always rather *proved* than *professed*: & from the moment you peeped into *my* Room at Chesington, with "*Annikin! Annikin!*—may I come in?—" "Yes!—" = "*It will do! it will do!*— —*" & O from the moment I heard those welcome Words, from the severest of *all* my Judges, I took inward courage, & my hopes grew comfortable, & lessened my apprehensions very forcibly & expeditiously; though I cannot say they ever gave me a promise of *such* success as last Tuesday's post brought me, in a Letter from Mʳ. Burke!!!—
[...]
   How good you are to take so much thought & trouble about my *finances*! I am delighted with the plan of the 3 pr. cents;—but I must own I cannot at present set about writing,—I know my own forces, & I must not, by over-rating them, risk the loss of the good will & partiality which, at this Time, seem almost universally grant-

---

1   A cover sheet addressed and signed by a Member of Parliament. Parliamentary privilege allowed MPs to send and receive letters free of expensive postal charges, and they were apt to abuse this privilege by giving pre-addressed sheets to friends.

ed me. You know not how much, &, lately, how wholly Cecilia has occupied my mind; some of the latter part having only been written while the press was waiting,—every Character in that Book is now so strongly [fixed] in my imagination, & the style & manner of the composition is so familiar to me, that though I could with ease write 5 more Volumes upon the same subject, & with the same Characters, I could not, as yet, so far divest myself of the hold they now have upon me, as to form or execute any Work decently varied from the last. I have, indeed, as you know, another already planned & begun, but I have forgotten even my own intentions for its continuation. I must, therefore, dissipate, & drive Cecilia, Delviles, Harrels, Briggs, & Belfields, out of my Head, before I can pretend to write any thing more, with any hope of producing any thing at all new. I entreat you, meantime, not to whisper to any mortal my *ugly scheme*, as I mean to go on with it, as soon as my mind, memory, & faculties can expel their present possesors, & will find they have again free play.[1]

[...]

106.   FRANCES BURNEY TO SUSAN BURNEY PHILLIPS
16 August 1782, Chessington

[...]
[*FB reports a meeting with her publisher Mr. Payne.*]
in which I expressed some surprise at the behaviour of Cadell,[2] & in which *he* expressed much contrition in having ever spoke with him, & promised to call upon him immediately, & remonstrate. This expostulation, since my leaving Town, has succeeded, for Payne has himself brought from Cadell a Draught for £100. [...] I

---

1   FB concluded her letter with another injunction, "*pray* be scrupulously careful of my Ugly plan." To this FBA added the footnote "This *Ugly* plan became, afterwards, a part only, of The Picture of Youth, or Camilla; under the character of Eugenia. My beloved & revered Mr. Crisp did not live to see its execution!" Despite her promise of a prompt beginning for the new novel, in a subsequent letter to SBP dated *c.*25 December 1782 (Berg, ms. letter) FB wrote "I have nothing in the *writing way* to put it upon, [*an excuse to join SBP at Chessington*] as I have nothing in my mind or my Head of that sort,—but don't say so to Daddy, who will only rave,—but it is most true indeed."
2   Cadell had evidently delayed the payment of his share (£100) of the copyright price.

find they printed 2000 of Cecilia, as Payne himself owned. This was not fair, as the £50 was *jockeyed* out of me by surprise, *after* the Bargain had been settled with my Father, & as Evelina had, at first, only 500.[1]

[...]

107.   THOMAS LOWNDES TO DR. CHARLES BURNEY
                5 September 1782, Fleet Street

I came on *Tuesday* to buy your Second Volume Quarto [*of CB's* History of Music] and with design to mention *Cecilia*. As I found you out of Town, I now write my Business. On *Evelina's* being published, Mr. *Cadell* said, he wished he had known he could have got the Copy; and, I doubt not, has circumvented you with unbecoming Art.—In respect to *Evelina*, the two first Volumes were sent to get my Opinion; I answered, that the Author had Ability, and if the *Marybone* Scene was abridged, and the City Visits lessened, the Work would appear more lively; and, if the Author would write a third Volume, replete with Modern Characters, I should be glad to see it when finished. About six Months afterwards the whole was brought by a plain-dressed young Gentleman, who did not chuse to mention the Author. I named a Sum, which was accepted and paid, and he afterwards said the Writer was contented with it. I printed 500, and afterwards a Second Edition of 500, and they being nearly sold, I put into your Hands a Bank Note,[2] as Compliment for a Lady whom I had found out to be of your Acquaintance. About that Time, I told Mrs. *Burney*, who genteely received my Visits, that if the Lady, who had sent me *Evelina*, would write on any Subject, I should be proud to receive it, and would compliment her with a Sum worthy her Acceptance. When I published *Mount* [*H*]*enneth*, I sent it as a moral and entertaining Work to Miss *Burney*.—On my Determination to print *Evelina* a third Time, I prevailed on Mr. *Mortimer* to make me three Drawings.[3] I told him

---

1   Though the agreed price for the copyright was £250, FB had been manoeuvered into consenting that the final £50 should not be paid until the novel reached a second edition. She had not realised, however, that the first edition would be so much larger than that of *Evelina*, which seemed to put the final payment in jeopardy. The second edition appeared in 1783.
2   For an additional £10.
3   The illustrations appeared in the fourth edition, published in 1780.

the Author did not chuse to be known, but was an accomplished young Lady in genteel Life. I begged he would make *Evelina* as elegant as his Mind could conceive. I engaged Mr. *Bartolozzi* and two eminent Artists to do the Engravings; I meant this as a Compliment to the Lady-Author. The Plates cost me Seventy-three Pounds. I shewed you the Drawings and Proofs before Publication. T. *Payne* is a worthy honest Man, the other[1] may have some Envy, and is offended, because I have taken Pains to prevent him smuggling the Advertising Money he has been entrusted with by me and Company. If your Copy had been worth £10,000 I could have raised it as soon as any Man in the Trade, and my Character is as fair as any Merchant's of *London*. At a Meeting of Booksellers this Day, I was asked, Why I had not *Cecilia*? I answered, I did not know, but I would tell them soon.—I beg you'll tell me the Reason.

108.   FRANCES BURNEY TO THOMAS LOWNDES
16 September 1782, Surrey

The Author of Evelina is much surprised that Mr. Lowndes should trouble himself to enquire any Reason why he did not publish Cecilia: she is certainly neither under Engagement or Obligation to *Any* Bookseller whatever, and is to no one, therefore, responsible for chusing and changing as she pleases.

109.   FRANCES BURNEY TO SAMUEL CRISP
15 October 1782

Thanks, my dear Daddy, for your kind & wise counsel,[2] which I shall follow implicitly, [& I shall most earnestly charge Mr. Payne, when I see him, to say nothing of *corrections* or of the *Author*, in his Advertisements.] Dr. Johnson, after a long mental calculation, which his consummate knowledge both of figures & Books enabled him to do very acurately, assured me that the Booksellers of Cecilia must, from the 1st. Edition, supposing it at the 2000, make £500. This is surely a profit immense, to come so early as from July to October. [Mr. Payne *had*, I am certain, [xxx] intentions *to do the genteel thing* against the 2d. Edition, for which he requested of me a new Chapter. But I fancy Mr. Cadell has dissuaded him,

---

1   Cadell.
2   Given in a letter now lost.

as he said no more about the matter.] The little,[1] therefore, I shall do will be merely on my own account, for *they*, as you well say, have by no means any claim upon me. [I believe, however, as *you* do, that Mr. Payne has been drawn in.]

[...]

110. FRANCES BURNEY TO SUSAN BURNEY PHILLIPS
28 October 1782, Brighton

[*FB joined the Thrale family in Brighton.*]
[...] you would suppose me some Thing dropt from the skies. Even if Richardson or Fielding could rise from the Grave, I should bid fair for supplanting them in the *popular Eye*, for being a *fair female*, I am *accounted quelque chose extraordinaire* [...]

111. FRANCES BURNEY TO SUSAN BURNEY PHILLIPS
26 October–20 November 1782, Brighton

[...]
Monday, Nov. 4th.
[...]
The Day after our first appearance at the Rooms on Sunday Evening, Mrs. Thrale came into my Chamber & said "I have a secret to tell you,—you know I told you you might set up for a Beauty when you fail for a Wit, & now it's done for you at once, for Harry Cotton comes & tells me how all the men admired you at the Rooms."

"This is a *secret* indeed!" quoth I,—but the truth is, that the people, hearing I am an Author & seeing me neither as wrinkled as Mrs. Montagu, as old as Mrs. Carter, as fat as Miss More, nor as deformed as Mrs. Chapone know not where to stop in their *personal* preference, because these are the only folks with whom they make my *personal* comparisons.

[...]
Sunday, Nov. 10th.
[...] Lady De Ferrars drew a Chair next mine, & began talking of Cecilia: "We have plagued my Lord, said she, to Death about it, because he always says that old Delvile was in the right not to give up a good family name;—but I was never so glad as when I found

---

1 Of corrections for the second edition.

the old Gentleman's own name was my Lord de Ferrars, for *he*, you know, is a *Compton*,—so I told him I was sure it was *himself*, & he *owned* that if he had been a *Delvile*, he should have done the same with a *Beverley*."

Is not *this* triumph for me, my dearest Susy?—pray let my Daddy Crisp hear it, & *knock under*. Mr. Bewley, too, shall be told it, who has made the same objection with my Daddy, to the *improbability* of relinquishing a fortune for a name. Neither my Daddy, my Father, nor Mr. Bewley are *here* judges to oppose to Lord De Ferrars, who, *being* a man of Rank, & having a cherished *Name* himself, is more fit to decide upon *this* question than wit, understanding, judgment, or general knowledge, can make *any* others, who have not the power to so well feel the *temptation* of family pride in exciting such obstacles to reason & happiness. I never meant to *vindicate* old Delvile, whom I detested & made detestable, but I always asserted that, his Character & situation considered, he did nothing that such a man would hesitate in doing. Mrs. Thrale has, since, met Lord De Ferrars, & talked over all the Book to him, & he told her that he thought its great merit was the *reasonableness of the Delvilian Distress with respect to changing their Name!*
[...]

112.   FRANCES BURNEY TO SUSAN BURNEY PHILLIPS
        2 December 1782 - 3 January 1783, London

[...]
[*At a party FB converses with Edmund Burke for the first time.*]
After many most *eloquent* compliments upon the Book, too delicate either to shock or sicken the nicest Ear, he very emphatically congratulated me upon its most universal success;—said he was now *too late* to speak of it, since he could only eccho the voice of the whole Nation, & added, with a Laugh, "I had hoped to have made some merit of my enthusiasm, but the moment I went about to hear what others say, I found myself merely one in a multitude!"

He then told me, that, notwithstanding his admiration, *he* was the man who had *dared* to find some faults with so favourite & fashionable a Work: I entreated him to tell me what they were, & assured him nothing would make me so happy as to correct them under his direction. He then enumerated them: & I will tell you what they are, that you may not conclude I write nothing but the fairer part of my adventures, which I really always relate very honestly, though *so* fair they are at this Time, that it seems hardly possible they should not be dressed up.

The Masquerade he thought too long, & that something might be spared from Harrel's grand assembly; he did not like Morrice's part at the Pantheon, & he wished the conclusion either more happy or more miserable: "for in a work of imagination, said he, there is no medium."

I was not easy enough to answer him, or I have *much*, though perhaps not *good* for much, to say in defence of following Life & Nature as much in the conclusion as in the progress of a Tale; & *when* is Life & Nature *completely* happy or miserable?

[...]

"But, said he, I have one other fault to find, & a far more material one than any I have mentioned."

"I am the more obliged to you. What is it?"

"The *disposal* of this Book!—I have much advice to offer you upon that subject;—why did not you send for your own friend out of the City? *he* would have taken care you should not part with it so much *below par.*"

He meant Mr. Briggs.

[...]

[*Reviews of* Cecilia *began to appear in December 1782.*]

113.   THE CRITICAL REVIEW
                      December 1782

IN this elegant performance the incidents are ingeniously contrived, and artfully conducted; the characters are natural, well drawn, and well supported; the style, in general, easy, correct, and agreeable: it is amusing, interesting, and instructive; draws us on insensibly from page to page, and keeps up our constant attention from beginning to end. It is supposed to be written by miss Burney, author of Evelina, and daughter of the ingenious Dr. Burney, so well known in the literary world by his excellent History of Music.

[...]

Though the performance before us has many beauties, as our readers must perceive by the extract which we have given [*omitted*], it is not without a few blemishes and defects: amongst these is, in our opinion, its extraordinary length. If the five volumes had been reduced to four, the circle, though smaller, would have been more complete; and there are some conversations in the course of the work, which, perhaps, might have been shortened. The harangues of Mrs. Belfield, however natural, as well as the dialogues of Mr. Hobson and Mr. Simkins, though humourous and characteristic, seem to interrupt more interesting business. Cecilia's conduct, in sacrificing so large a fortune to gratify the pride of the Delvile family, is an example which we would by no means wish to propose as an object of imitation for the fair sex: nor do we entirely approve of the conclusion, as we are of opinion that the pride and ostentation of old Delvile ought, in justice, to have been punished; and the haughty slave convinced of his folly, by feeling in his own person the destructive consequences of his inhumanity.

The few blemishes we have discovered seem, however, to proceed from an ebullition of genius, and a facility of composition; and it is proper to observe, that the purest lessons of morality are every where inculcated, and no improper scenes presented to the reader; a fault which may be too often discovered in the most celebrated novel-writers.

Upon the whole, we think it but justice to class this work among the first productions of the kind; and recommend it to our readers as worthy their attention, and replete with instruction and rational amusement.

114.   [SAMUEL BADCOCK] THE MONTHLY REVIEW
December 1782

THE great and merited success of Evelina hath encouraged the fair Author to the present undertaking—in which we are at a loss, whether to give the preference to the design or the execution: or which to admire most, the purity of the Writer's heart, or the force and extent of her understanding. We see much of the dignity and pathos of Richardson; and much of the acuteness and ingenuity of Fielding. The attention is arrested by the story; and in general, expectation is gratified by the several events of it. It is related in a style peculiarly nervous and perspicuous, and appears to have been formed on the best model of Dr. Johnson's.
[...]
We have thus far dealt only in praise—and it is as sincere as we ever paid to literary merit. Totally unconnected with the Author, and even unknown to her by name, the Writer of this Article is only concerned to discharge the debt of justice: he will call it *rigid* justice; for he hath no motive to be lenient. The Author of Cecilia asks no undue lenity: she doth not plead any privilege of her sex: she stands on firmer ground; and with a spirit superior to solicitation or fear, may meet the decision of impartial criticism.
[...]

115.   CHARLOTTE BURNEY TO FRANCES BURNEY
                    1782, London

[...]
I called on Miss Reynolds yesterday & she had just finished Cecilia; she says it has almost killed her, for that she was so eager & interested that she sat up so late at nights & cried so much she is almost
blind, & "besides, she added, I was so tied down to it, I could n't
bring myself even to go to a certain place when I wanted!" it
diverts me to hear how the people all *complain* about it!—She then
enquired How long you were to stay at Chiswick? & when I told
her a fortnight or three weeks.
     "Well, cried she, I dare say she will meet with an offer before
she returns; but however, I am certain she will have more offers
than ever were heard of to come to *one* person before the winter
is out; for I told M^r. Barry the other night, & I thought so all the
time I was reading it, that if I was the first Duke in the land upon
reading *that* Book I sh^d. certainly go the instant I had done it &
make her an offer! for I look upon it, that in reading Cecilia's character I am reading *hers*."—
[...]

1783

116.   FRANCES BURNEY TO SUSAN BURNEY PHILLIPS
            4 January—*post* 20 January 1783, London

[...]
Saturday, Jany. 11th.
[...]
[*FB attends HLT to the Opera, where she meets Mr. Jermingham in the
coffee room.*]
"Have you read, he said, the new Book that has had such a run in
France, "Les Liasons dangereuses?—"[1]
     "No, answered I, not much pleased at the name, I have not even
heard of it."

---

1   By Pierre-Ambroise-François Choderlos de Laclos (1741-1803), published in 1782.

"Indeed?—it has made so much noise in France I am quite surprised at that. It is not, indeed, a work that recommends very strict morality, but *You*, we all know, may look into *any* work without being hurt by it."

I felt hurt *then*, however, & very gravely answered "I cannot give *myself* that praise, as I never look into any Books that *could* hurt me."

He Bowed, & smiled, & said *that was* "*very right*," & added—"This Book is written by an officer; & he says there are no characters nor situations in it that he has not himself seen."

"That, then, cried I, will with me always be a reason to as little desire seeing the Officer, as his Book."

He looked a little simple at this, but pretended to approve it very much. However, I fancy it will save him the trouble of enquiring into my reading any more. I was really provoked with him, however, & though he was most obsequiously civil to me, I only spoke to him in answer, after this little Dialogue.

[...]

[*FB and Mrs. Chapone pay a call upon Mrs. Mary Granville Delany and her friend the Dowager Duchess of Portland. The Duchess, one of the original Bluestockings, explained that she was at first resistant to reading* Cecilia.]

"The reason, continued she, I held out so long against reading them, was remembering the cry there was in favour of Clarissa & Sir Charles Grandison, when *they* came out; & those I never could read!—I was teized into trying both of them, but I was disgusted with their tediousness, & could not read Eleven Letters, with all the effort I could make: so much about my Sisters & my Brothers, & all my Uncles & my Aunts!—"

"But if your Grace had gone on [with Clarissa][1] said Mrs. Chapone, the latter part must certainly have affected you."

"O I hate anything so dismal! Every body that *did* read [*it*] had melancholy faces for a Week! *Cecilia* is as pathetic as I can bear,—& *more*, sometimes;—yet, in the midst of the sorrow, there is a spirit in the Writing, a fire in the whole Composition, that keep off that heavy depression given by Richardson. Cry, to be sure, we did,—O Mrs. Delany, shall you ever *forget* how we cried?—but then we had so *much* Laughter to make us amends!—we were never left to *sink* under our concern."

---

1 Inserted by FBA.

"For my part, said Mrs. Chapone, when I *first* read it, I did not cry at all; I was in an agitation that half killed me,—that shook all my nerves, & made me unable to sleep at nights, from the suspense I was in; but I could not Cry for excess of eagerness;—the *second* Time, however, when I knew the *sum total*, I cried at the distress ready to break my Heart! Oh that quarrel of Simkins with the Coach man!—I cannot, *now*, think of that moment for poor Cecilia without *trembling!*"

"I only wish, said the Dutchess, Miss Burney could have been in some corner, amusing herself with listening to us, when Lord Weymouth, & the Bishop of Exeter, & Mr. Lightfoot, & Mrs. Delany, & I, were all discussing the point of the *Name!*—so earnest we were, she *must* have been diverted with us. Nothing the nearest our own Hearts could have been debated more warmly. The *Bishop* was quite as eager as any of us. But what cooled us, a little, at last, was Mr. Lightfoot's thinking we were seriously going to quarrel, & while Mrs. Delany & I were disputing about Mrs. Delvile, he very gravely said "Why, Ladies, this is only a matter of *imagination!*—it is not a *fact!* Don't be so earnest!"

"Ah, ma'am, said Mrs. Delany, how hard your Grace was upon Mrs. Delvile! so elegant, so sensible, so judicious, so charming a Woman—"

"O I hate her! cried the Dutchess,—resisting that sweet Cecilia!—*coaxing* her, too, all the Time, with such hypocritical flattery—"

"O no, cried Mrs. Chapone, indeed she is no hypocrite, she shews, in all things but that *Name*, how really & unaffectedly fond she is of Cecilia."

"Ah! said the Dutchess, that silly Name!—"

"I shall never forget, said Mrs. Delany, your Grace's earnestness when we came to that part where Mrs. Delvile bursts a blood Vessel; down dropt the Book, & just with the same energy as if your Grace had heard some real & important news, you called out "I'm glad of it with all my Heart!""

"*I* have heard many people, said Mrs. Chapone, of high family themselves, say that nothing could have been so *base* & so *dirty* as for the Delviles to give up their Name: & others say nothing could be so preposterous as Cecilia's giving up her Fortune to gratify them:—but, for my part, I always say that where the Husband of her Choice was in question, all that could have been *base* & *dirty* would have been keeping the fortune in preference to him."

"Well, said Mrs. Delany, *I* am for the good *husband*; but yet,— methinks I am very sorry for the fortune too! Lord Weymouth says *his* only fault is that Mrs. Delvile, whom he admires most, does not appear again in the conclusion; why then, my Lord, said I, I can only infer from that, that when you have read 5 volumes, your Lordship is dissatisfied not to have a sixth!"

"What disputes, too, said Mrs. Chapone, there are about Briggs!—I was in a Room some time ago where somebody said there could be no such Character,—& a poor little mean City man, who was there, started up, & said "But there is, though, for *I'se* one myself!"

"Mr. Lightfoot declares, said the Dutchess, that he knows the very man."

"He diverts me extremely," said Mrs. Delany.

"And me too, I am sure! said Mrs. Chapone, & I can never either see or hear of a Lobster, a Breast of mutton or a Crab, without Laughing."

"Nothing so much amuses & charms *me*, said the Dutchess, as Miss Larolles & Mr. Meadows: they are incomparable! That Journey on the Road, which made me half crazy with anger when I began it, grew so extremely entertaining as I went on, that I never Laughed so much at any thing I ever read,—but when Miss Larolles loses her little Dog!—& when she applies to Mr. Meadows to shoot the Highway man!—I could not *read* for Laughing!— [...]

"The Harrels,—o then the Harrels!" cried Mrs. Delany.

"If you speak of the *Harrels*, & of the *morality* of the Book, cried the Dutchess, with a solemn sort of voice, we shall indeed never give Miss Burney her due! So striking, so pure, so genuine, so instinctive!—"

"Yes, cried Mrs Chapone, let us complain how we will of the torture she has given our nerves, we must all join in saying she has *bettered* us by every line."

"*No* Book, said Mrs. Delany, ever *was* so *useful* as this, because none other so *good*, was ever so much *read*."

"It should be read, cried the Dutchess, with energy, for-ever! it should be the *study of youth*! both for precept & example I know nothing to compare with it. It seems to me, indeed, in *all* respects, one of the first Books in the World! And it ought to be put in every *Nursery*, it is so innocent & so pure, & if *I* had the care of any young people, it should be the first Book I would put in their Hands."

I think, my dear Susy, I need now write no more! I could, indeed, *hear* no more, for this last so serious praise, from Characters so respectable, so moral, & so aged, quite affected me; & though I had wished a thousand times, during the discourse, to run out of the Room, when they gave me this solemn sanction to the meaning & intention of my writing, I found it not without difficulty that I could keep the Tears out of my Eyes: & when I told what had passed to our sweet Father, *his* quite ran over!

[...]

117.   FRANCES BURNEY TO SUSAN BURNEY PHILLIPS
11-12 July 1783

[...]
I have always forgot to mention to you a Poem by young Hoole, called Aurelia, or the Contest.[1] He sent it me,—& I soon found the reason. His Aurelia runs through the hackneyed round of folly & dissipation, & then appears suddenly to her, in a vision,

—— the Guardian Power, whose secret sway,
The wiser Females of the World obey.

This Guardian Power tells her what he has done for his favour-ites; that he gave to *Dudley's Wife*[2]

A nobler fortitude than Hero's reach,
And virtue, greater than the Sages teach.—

Then, skipping suddenly to modern times, that He instructed

Streatfield, the learn'd, the gay, in blooming years—

to assist the Poor, to attend the sick, & watch over her dying old Tutor, Dr. Collier.—Then, that *He* directed

Carter's piercing Eyes
To roll inquisitive through starry skies;—

---

1 A heroi-comical poem in four cantos by Samuel Hoole.
2 Alice Dudley, wife of Sir Robert Dudley, self-styled Duke of Northum-berland and Earl of Warwick. In 1645 Alice was created Duchess of Dud-ley in her own right, after her husband repudiated her to marry his mis-

that *He*

> —to *Chapone* th'important task assign'd
> To smooth the Temper, & improve the mind.

that *He* told *More*

> to guide unthinking youth,—&c.

And then he says

> *I* stood, a favouring Muse, at *Burney's* side
> To lash unfeeling Wealth, & stubborn pride,
> Soft Affectation, insolently vain,
> And wild Extravagance with all her sweeping train;
> Led her that Modern Hydra to engage,
> And paint a Harrel to a mad'ning Age:
> Then bad the Moralist, admir'd & prais'd,
> Fly from the loud applause her talent rais'd.

And then the Coterie concludes with M^rs. Montagu. What think you of this our Guardian Genius?
[...]

118.   FRANCES BURNEY TO FRANCES BROOKE
              c. October 1783, London
[...]
[*Frances Brooke, fresh from the success of her ballad-opera* Rosina *(1782), proposed that she and FB together start a new periodical. FB declined.*]
I should be very happy to enter into any plan with Mrs. Brooke, & I think myself much honoured by her very flattering proposition: but I must frankly own I am at present so little disposed for writing, that I am certain I could produce nothing worth reading. I have bid adieu to my Pen since I finished Cecilia, not from *disgust*, nor *design*, but from having fairly *written all I had to write*: it was the same for 2 or 3 years after I had done with Evelina;[1] & I am as unwilling now as I was then, to deal hardly with an empty Brain. If any thing again occurs to me, I shall again venture to try its suc-

---

1   Not strictly true, as FB began *The Witlings* soon after the publication of *Evelina*.

cess;—if nothing—it is surely more judicious, & *certainly* most pleasant to myself, to remain perfectly quiet.

I must beg you, therefore, to pardon my declining your kind offer, though I shall always hold myself indebted for your attention to me.

[*HLT married Gabriel Piozzi on 23 July 1784, and immediately quarreled with FB, putting an end to their friendship, which FB never ceased to regret. HLT had been infatuated with Piozzi, a musician, for some time, and her friends and family argued vehemently against the match on the grounds of class and religion. HLT's passion made her an object of ridicule in society. FB has been blamed for her part in the affair, urging against the match and taking the side of HLT's daughters whose own social position and marital prospects were endangered by their mother's mésalliance. However, FB seems to have acted out of a genuine regard for HLT's welfare, though the standards by which she judged the situation would not be used now.*]

1785

119.   FRANCES BURNEY TO DR. CHARLES BURNEY &
SUSAN BURNEY PHILLIPS
1 December 1785, Windsor

[...]
[*Mrs. Delany, with whom FB was staying in Windsor, reports a conversation with the King and Queen.*]
Nevertheless, they talked of me, she says, a good deal, & the King asked many questions about me. There was a new play, he told Mrs. Delany, coming out,—"And it is said to be Miss Burney's,— —" Mrs. Delany immediately answered that she knew the report must be untrue. "But I hope she is not idle? cried the King,—I hope she is writing something?"

What an opportunity, my dear Father, for the speech Mr. Cambridge[1] told you he longed to make,—that *Miss B. had no time to*

---

1   Richard Owen Cambridge, a man of letters with an independent fortune. His son, the clergyman George Cambridge, appeared to be courting FB.

write, for she was always mending her Cloaths!—What Mrs. Delany said I know not; but he afterwards enquired what *she* thought of my writing a Play?—

"What, said he, do you *wish* about it, Mrs. Delany?"

Mrs. Delany hesitated,—& the Queen then said "*I* wish what I know Mrs. Delany does,—that she may *not*; for though her reputation is so high, her Character, by all I hear, is too delicate, to suit with writing for the stage.—"

Sweet Queen!—I could have kissed the hem of her Garment for that speech,—& I could not resist writing it.—

Mrs. Delany then said "Why *my* opinion, is what I believe to be Miss Burney's own,—that it is too public & hazardous a style of writing for her quiet & fearful turn of mind."

[...]

Decr. 16th. Friday.

[...]

[*FB meets the King for the first time, and notes the ceremonious manners his presence requires.*]

The Christmas Games we had been shewing Miss Dewes, it seemed as if we were still performing; for our manner of standing reminded me of nothing but Puss in the Corner. At one corner, close to the Door, was posted Miss Port;[1]—at the opposite corner, close to the wainscoat, stood Mr. Barnard;[2]—at just an equal distance from him, close to a window, stood myself;—Mrs. Delany, though seated, was at the opposite side to Miss Port,—& his Majesty kept pretty much in the middle of the Room. The little Girl, who kept close to me, did not break the order; & I could hardly help expecting to be beckoned, with a *Puss! Puss! Puss!* to change places with one of my neighbours.

This idea, afterwards, gave way to another more pompous. It seemed to me we were *acting a Play*; there is something so little like common & real life, in every body's standing, while talking, in a Room full of Chairs, & standing, too, so aloof from each other, that I almost thought myself upon a Stage, assisting in the representation of a Tragedy, in which the King played his own part, of The King; Mrs. Delany that of a venerable confident; Mr. Barnard, his respectful Attendant; Miss Port, a suppliant virgin, waiting encour-

---

1 Mary Ann Port, great-niece of Mrs. Delany.
2 Bernard Dewes, an attendant of the King, and nephew of Mrs. Delany. Miss Dewes was his daughter.

agement to bring forward some petition; Miss Dewes, a young
orphan, intended to move the Royal compassion; & myself,—a
very solemn, sober, & decent *Mute*.
[...]

120.   FRANCES BURNEY TO ESTHER BURNEY BURNEY
               17 December 1785, Windsor

[...]
Now I know what you next want is to hear accounts of Kings,
Queens, and such Royal Personages.—O ho! do you so?—Well,—
—
    Shall I tell you a few matters of fact?—or had you rather a few
matters of etiquette? = O, matters of Etiquette, you cry,—for matters of fact are short & stupid,—& any body can tell, and every
body is tired with them.—
    Very well, take your own Choice.—
    To begin, then, with the beginning.
    You know I told you, in my last, my various difficulties what
sort of preferment to turn my thoughts to, & concluded with just
starting a young budding notion of decision, by suggesting that a
handsome Pension for nothing at all would be as well as working
night and day for a Salary.
    This blossom of an idea, the more I dwelt upon, the more I
liked: Thinking served it for a Hot-house, and it came out into full
blow as I ruminated upon my Pillow. Delighted that thus all my
contradictory & wayward fancies were overcome, & my Mind was
peaceably settled what to wish & to demand, I gave over all further
Meditation upon Choice of Elevation, & had nothing more to do
but to make my election known.
    My next business, therefore, was to be presented. This could be
no difficulty; my coming hither had been their own desire & they
had earnestly pressed its execution. I had only to *prepare myself for
the rencounter.*
    You would never believe—you, who, distant from Courts &
Courtiers, know nothing of their ways,—the many things to be
studied for appearing with a *proper propriety* before crowned
Heads. Heads without Crowns are quite other sort of rotundas.
Now, then, to the Etiquette. I enquired into every particular,
that no error might be committed. And as there is no saying
what may happen in this mortal life, I shall give you those
instructions I have received myself, that, should you find

yourself in the Royal presence, you may know how to comport yourself.

Directions for Coughing, sneezing, or moving,
before the King and Queen.

In the first place, You must not Cough. If you find a cough tickling in your throat, you must arrest it from making any sound: if you find yourself choking with the forbearance, you must choak: But not cough.

In the 2^d. place, you must not sneeze. If you have a vehement Cold, you must take no notice of it; if your nose-membranes feel a great irritation, you must hold your breath; if a sneeze still insists upon making its way, you must oppose it by keeping your teeth grinding together; if the violence of the repulse breaks some blood-vessel, you must break the blood-vessel: But not sneeze.

In the 3^d. place, you must not, upon any account, stir either hand or foot. If, by chance, a black pin runs into your Head, you must not take it out: If the pain is very great, you must be sure to bear it without wincing; If it brings the Tears into your Eyes, you must not wipe them off; If they give you a tingling by running down your Cheeks, you must look as if nothing was the matter. If the blood should gush from your Head by means of the black pin, you must let it gush; If you are uneasy to think of making such a blurred appearance, you must be uneasy; but you must say nothing about it. If, however, the agony is very great, you may, privately, bite the inside of your Cheek, or of your lips, for a little relief; taking care, meanwhile, to do it so cautiously as to make no apparent dent outwardly. And, with that precaution, if you even gnaw a piece out, it will not be minded; only be sure either to swallow it, or commit it to a corner of the inside of your mouth till they are gone,—for, You must not spit.

I have many other Directions, but no more paper: I will endeavour however, to have them ready for you in Time. Perhaps, meanwhile, you would be glad to know if I have myself had opportunity to put in practice these receipts?—

How can I answer in this little space?— —

[...]

1786

121. FRANCES BURNEY TO SUSAN BURNEY PHILLIPS
post 14 January 1786

[*FB discusses her financial situation with Richard Owen Cambridge.*]
[...] then I acquainted him that the Cecilia he had honoured with such approbation, now supplied me wholly with *Pin Money*: "'Tis but a little matter, said I to tell; but I think it the most certain method I can take to show my sense of the trust you place in me about *your* affairs." He was much pleased with the intelligence, & eagerly said "I know it must be so pleasant to you to *find yourself* in any thing,—*George* takes such delight in having lightened *me* of finding him.—And because I feed his Horses in the Country, he wants, now, to be at the whole expence of manuring my fields,—*do*, Sir, he says, let *me* do that!—I only tell you this, to let you see what the difference is between him & Charles, who is as amiable, all the while, as he knows *how* to be, but who costs me a hundred a year, constantly, in keeping his Horses, without even thinking of it,— though he would not *ask* me for Twenty pounds, for the World!—"

I could hardly help looking very *ungravely* at this immediate allusion to *George,* by way of *understanding* my satisfaction in *finding myself* in any thing. But, soon after, he opened upon a new subject; & told me, once more, he could wish I would write a Play [xxx] I sighed—[xxx] & from the bottom of my Heart, at the idea of such an adventure; & told him the fears I had of it were almost unconquerable;—*so,* he kindly said, were *his,*—& yet, this *General's*[1] late advantages from the Drama had quite new set his wishes afloat. I was tempted, then, to tell him a little speech of the Queen's, which I will write you, as I know I have given you no account of my last Scene with her,—It was the first Day of this year,—the King & Queen were at Mrs. Delany's, & Lady Louisa Clayton, & no one else,—I happened to be in the Room when the King entered, &, as he spoke to me, stayed. In the course of the Evening he suddenly came up to me, & Bowing with a significant half smile, he said "I am very happy to find you are to give us a Play Miss Burney!—"
I stared,—& he added—"stay—it's in the *News-papers,*—so it *must*

---

1 General John Burgoyne (1722-92), veteran of the American war, wrote a successful comedy, *The Heiress,* first produced in January 1786.

be true!—" I assured him it was news to *me*, & he went on, laughing, about it, for some time—but the Queen, addressing herself to Mrs. Delany, very seriously said "I hope *not*, Mrs. Delany!—I should be very *sorry* for it.—Miss Burney's *name* is *every where*—but her Character is as delicate as if it were *no where;*—& I should be sorry to have her write for so *public a thing* as the Stage.—"

This kind Mr. Cambridge heard this sweet speech of the Queen with a pleasure that glistened in his Eyes,—but still could not give up the idea, though he did not urge it. "'Tis so *provoking*, he cried, that you should be *able* to gain money so easily, yet let it alone,—you could write a play so well!—General Burgoyne got 600 pound for his,—& *you*, to be sure—yet where's the end of such wishes? When you had 600, I should wish you 6000,—& then, I should want to see you with *sixty* thousand,—for who would make a better use of riches?—" I could not answer this—who could?
[...]
[*In June 1786, FB received an offer of a place at Court. Despite her misgivings, on 17 July 1786 she entered the service of the Queen as Second Keeper of the Robes.*]

122.   FRANCES BURNEY TO SUSAN BURNEY PHILLIPS
24 July 1786, Windsor

Once more I take up my Pen, to give my beloved Susan a Journal of my proceedings. I have [xxx] been advised against it, but I do not see why; A simple account of inoffensive actions can have no more to fear from the reader than from the listener; & while I never make the most distant allusion to politics, to the Royal family's private transactions or opinions, nor to any State affairs of any kind, I see not why I must be deprived of my long accustomed confidence in the Dearest & Sweetest of Sisters, whose never failing discretion, honour, & fidelity have always called for my trust from the earliest time I have had any thing to communicate.
[...]
Monday, July 17th.
[*FB describes travelling to Windsor to take up her appointment. Waiting with CB at Mrs. Delany's house in Windsor, FB sent word to the Queen of her arrival.*]
[...] A verbal answer came, that I was to go to the Lodge immediately.

Oh my dear Susan! in what an *agony* of mind did I obey the summons! I was still in my travelling Dress, but could not stay to change it. My Father accompanied me,—Mrs. Delany anxiously, & full of mixed sensations, gave me her blessing,—we walked; the Queen's Lodge is not 50 yards from Mrs. Delany's Door. My dear Father's own courage all failed him in this little step; for as I was now on the point of entering,—probably for-ever!—into an entire new way of life, & of fore-going by it all my best hopes— all my most favourite schemes—& every dear expectation my Fancy had every indulged of happiness adapted to its taste,—as now, all was to be given up,—I could disguise my trepidation no longer,—indeed I never had *disguised*, I had only forborn *proclaiming* it,—but my dear Father now, sweet soul, felt it all, as I held by his Arm, without power to say one word, but that if he did not hurry along, I should drop by the way. I heard in his kind voice that he was now really alarmed; he would have slackened his pace, or have made me stop to breathe: but I could not, my breath seemed gone, & I could only hasten with all my might, lest my strength should go too. [...] My dear Father endeavoured here to compose my spirits,— but I could have no other command over them than to forbear letting him know the afflicted state of all within, & to suffer him to keep to his own conclusions, that my emotion was all from fear of the approaching Audience.

Indeed was it not!—I could hardly even think of it. All that I was *resigning*—there, & there only went every fear, & all reluctance.—

[...] [*CB departed after FB's brief audience with the Queen.*]

We spent a short time together,—in which I assured him I would, from that moment, take all the happiness in my power, & banish all the regret. I told him how gratifying had been my reception, & I omittted nothing I could think of to remove the uneasiness that This Day seemed first to awaken in him. Thank God! I had the fullest success; his hopes & gay expectations were all within call, & they ran back at the first beckoning.

[...]

I now took the most vigorous resolutions to observe the promise I had made my dear Father. [While the least opening to sweeter prospects had been in view,[1] my repugnance & my distaste

---

1 I.e. marriage to George Cambridge. FB may have hoped that her Court appointment would spur him to make a proposal, but if so she was disappointed.

had been unconquerable: but] now all was over, & "finally, though not happily, settled," to borrow my own words,—I needed no monitor to tell me it would be foolish, useless, even *wicked* not to reconcile myself to my destiny.

The many now wishing for just the same—O could they look within me!—

I am *married*, my dearest Susan,—I look upon it in that light,—I was averse to forming the union, & I endeavoured to escape it; but my friends interfered,—they prevailed—& the knot is tied. What, then, now remains, but to make the best Wife in my power? I am bound to it in Duty, & I will strain every Nerve to succeed. [...]

123.   FRANCES BURNEY TO SUSAN BURNEY PHILLIPS
10 August–September 1786, Windsor

[...]
How very long since I have spoken to my ever dearest Susan in this only way that is left me for talking to her!—I dare not own the real present Date of this,—nor enter into why so long I have left off writing; I will keep this account of myself free from all latent discussions, leading to past scenes & feelings of what sort soever, that are not in the progressive & necessary order of my life's actual & immediate incidents from the opening of this Journal on the 17. of July, —86. When disposed irresistably,—as *will* happen at times,—to retrospection of thought, I throw it away,—& my pen is a stranger to all writing but of indispensable necessity, till I am again able to confine all retrospection to action & circumstance.

My Pocket Book, however, is constantly filling; every Morning before I breakfast, I write minutes of the preceding Day, that so, sooner or later, my beloved Susan may know all that befalls me.[1]
[...]

124.   FRANCES BURNEY TO SUSAN BURNEY PHILLIPS
1–30 November 1786, Windsor
[...]
Wednesday, Novr. 29th.
[...]
The Queen in looking over some Books while I was in waiting

---

1 FB now composed her journal-letters retrospectively, from memoranda notes made daily.

one Morning, met with *The Mysterious Mother*, Mr. Walpole's Tragedy: which he printed at Strawberry Hill, & gave to a few friends, but has never suffered to be published.[1] I expressed, by looks, I suppose, my wishes, for she most graciously offered to lend it me. I had long desired to read it, from so well knowing, & so much liking the Author: & he had promised me, if I would come a second time to Strawberry Hill, that I should have it: excursions of that sort being now totally over for me!—I was particularly glad of this only chance for gratifying my curiosity.

[...]

[*FB planned to read the play with Mr. Smelt, Deputy Governor to the Princes, and his wife, but to her chagrin they were joined by M. de Guiffardière, the French reader to the Queen and Princesses, and M. de Luc, a Swiss geologist and another of the Queen's readers.*]

A difficulty now arose about the Reader, which had not presented itself to me before. My intention had all been for Mr. Smelt, to whom I instantly offered the Book: but he declared the deserved fame of Mr. De Guiffardiere for reading, especially any thing Dramatic made it not pleasant to him to exhibit in his presence. Mr. De Guiffardière instantly applied to *me*, protesting he would not read English while I was by:—& frankly adding that if the play were *French* he would make no scruple.

This excuse was allowed him by no one, as his pronunciation of our Language is such as to have persuaded almost every body that, though of a foreign family, he is English Born. Before a Reader whom I had heard famed by the highest Powers, I assured them all, in my turn, I could not prevail with myself to stand foremost; & I entreated Mr. Smelt to accept the office at once. He pleaded the natural hoarseness of his voice as a defect not to be overcome in dramatic reading:—& thus we went on, losing the best part of our Evening, by mutual fears of one another; till at last Mrs. Smelt, with a sensible & good-humoured scolding, told her Husband that if he resisted any longer, she would read herself, in defiance of her asthmatic complaints.

This determined him, & the Curtain drew up.

The opening of the play contains a description of *Superstitious fear* extremely well, & feelingly, & naturally depicted: it begins, too,

---

1 FB had met the author and wit Horace Walpole (1717-97) on 19 June 1783. She visited his home, Strawberry Hill near Twickenham in 1786, and gave an account of it and its eccentric owner in *Memoirs of Doctor Burney* (3:64-70).

in an uncommon style, promising of interest & novelty:—but my praise will soon be done! swallowed up all in the heaviest censure. A few Scenes only had we read, when a summons by a Page called away Mr. Smelt to the King. For once I saw him sorry to go; & sorry myself I am always to lose him. I now begged Mr. De Guiffardiere to take the Play: He protested he would not; urging me to read it myself, & pretending that—notwithstanding his Daily habits of reading, in *many* Languages, to their Majesties & their Circle, he could not possibly bring himself to read English to little me!—

I next proposed shutting up the Play for another opportunity, when we could again have Mr. Smelt.

Mrs. Smelt would not listen to this, &, at length, we came, most unwillingly on both sides, to a compromise: Mr. De Guiffardiere was to take the men, & myself the females.

"Who would believe it, cried he, laughing, as he took the Book, that I should dare undertake to read an English Play before Miss Burney!—"Yet he acknowledged, afterwards, that in preaching an English sermon upon some occasion abroad, he had been taken for an English man by all the congregation.

His reluctance, however, was real, though so unnecessary, for I soon found he did not do himself justice, giving none of the energy of his own Character to any of the Personages of the piece.

When the "fair Females" appeared,—I used every possible means to induce him to go on;—but all in vain; he was positive in his claim,—uncontrollable in his desire.

Thus compelled, I took the Book: & I read through the first female Scene; very ill & tamely; but, with all his *Englishising*, he is still too much of a Foreigner not to be civil where occasion is inviting, And *who else* therefore, he said, *could have read that?*—But I was now relieved, for honest Mrs. Smelt confessed my voice was so low, that she had not heard a word!—Mr. De Guiffardière was now compelled in his turn, & he kept close to his task till Mr. Smelt was allowed to come back to us.

They then read in turn till the whole was finished.

Dreadful was the whole! truly dreadful! a story of so much horror, from attrocious & voluntary guilt, never did I hear![1] Mrs. Smelt

---

1 *The Mysterious Mother* relates the story of a man who unbeknownst to himself has an incestuous relationship with his mother and, years later, falls in love with and marries a young woman who is both his sister and his daughter.

& myself heartily regretted that it had come in our way, & mutually agreed that we felt ourselves *ill-used* in having ever heard it. She protested she would never do herself so much wrong as to acknowledge she had suffered the hearing so wicked a tale, & declared she would drive it from her thoughts as she would the recollection of what-ever was most baneful to them.

For myself, I felt a sort of indignant aversion rise fast & warm in my Mind against the wilful Author of a story so horrible: all the entertainment & pleasure I had received from Mr. Walpole seemed extinguished by this lecture, which almost made me regard him as the Patron of the vices he had been pleased to record.

Mr. De Luc had escaped from the latter part of this hateful Tragedy, protesting, afterwards, he saw what was coming, & would not stay to hear it out.

Mr. Smelt confessed, with me, it was a lasting Disgrace to Mr. Walpole to have chosen such a subject, & thought him deserving even of punishment for such a painting of Human wickedness: & the more, as the Story through-out was forced & impossible.

But the whole of all that could be said on this subject was summed up in one sentence by Mr. De Guiffardiere, which, for its masterly strength & justice brought to my mind my ever revered Dr. Johnson.—"Mr. Walpole, cried he, has chosen a plan which nothing can equal the abomination—but the absurdity!—"
[...]

125.   FRANCES BURNEY TO SUSAN BURNEY PHILLIPS
             1-31 December 1786, Windsor

[...]
Just about this time, I put a finishing stroke to an affair which cost me a very unexpected disturbance: I had a Letter from Mr. Foss, the Attorney, & Husband to Mrs. [xxx] sister,—written in the Name of Messrs. Cadell & Payne, to inform me that Cecilia was then printing in Ireland, or Scotland, I forget which,—illegally; & that they desired me to sign a Letter, which Mr. Foss enclosed, in which I threatened, jointly with these Booksellers, to prosecute to the utmost extent of the Law any person or persons who should dare thus pirate my work.—

Equally astonished & dissatisfied at such a demand, I wrote for answer that I had wholly done with the Book, that I would enter into no prosecution for any consideration, & that I wished them well through a business that was entirely their own.—

To this refusal succeeded fresh applications:—I was made so uneasy, that I confided in Mr. Smelt, & begged his counsel. He happened to be present when one of the Letters came to me. He advised me by no means to give way to a request so big with consequences which I could not foresee, &, since the property & the profit were now alike made over to them, to persevere in leaving to their own sole conduct so disagreeable a contest.

I did very thankfully follow this advice: but they next had recourse to my Father, & offered to *indemnify* me of all costs, if I would only give them my Name & sanction.

My Name & sanction were just what I most wished to keep to myself: but so importunate they continued, that my Father asked the opinion of Mr. Batt:—He said he conceived that they had actually a claim to my concurrence in prosecuting any false Editors!—I was quite confounded—but a softer paper was drawn up than the first,—&, little as I liked it, I was obliged to admit Mr. Foss one Thursday at S^t. James's & to sign myself,—with the utmost reluctance—their assistant in their proceedings.—

I know not when I have been more astonished than in finding myself in a situation so unlike any into which I had ever meant to place myself.

Thank God I have heard nothing of the matter since! I flatter myself, therefore, that this signature fierce as it was constrained, has frightened those who have received as much as it did her who writ it.—Otherwise,—to be involved in a prosecution,—a Law suit,— I know few things indeed that could more heartily have disturbed me.

★★★

A most troublesome Letter, also, arrived to me from Ireland. A Mrs. Lemman wrote me her whole history, which was very lamentable, if true, but which concluded with requesting me to pay her Debts, amounting to about 30 or 40 pounds, & to put her & her Family into some creditable way of Business:—otherwise, as I was now her sole resource, she must inevitably put an end to her existence.

I wrote an immediate answer, to assure her I had no power to comply with her demand, & frankly to own that if my power were greater, my claims nearer Home must first be satisfied: I was sorry at a reliance so misplaced, but as we were wholly strangers to each other, I could never suppose myself a resource on which she had placed much dependance:—And I concluded with a severe—I thought it *right*—reprehension of her threat, assuring her that I held such an Action in too much horrour to suffer it to move my compassion at the expence of my prudence, &, indeed, ability: & I strongly advised her to take an opposite method in the next plan she formed, than that of using a menace that must rob her of pity by provoking displeasure.

To this I added such counsel as her Letter enabled me to draw out for her,—& sent it off.—

Soon after, came another Letter from the same Person;—she told me she had just read Cecilia, & was satisfied who ever could write it, must save & deliver her,—& she added that she was then compiling her own Memoirs, & would mention to the world, in the highest terms, all I would do for her.—

Simple artifice!—to suppose flattery so grossly promised could so dearly be bought!—vexed was I, however, to have written at all, to a person who then was in the act of committing to the Press probably what-ever she could gather!—I made no further answer,—I only wish, now, I had a Copy of what she has already. Doubtless her threat originated from a scheme like that she supposes in Mr. Harrel!—she thought where Cecilia had been frightened, I also must give way,—She forgot that she was no wife of my earliest friend,—no Guardian to myself,—that I saw not the Instrument of Death in her Hand,—& that I possessed not £3000 a year from which to borrow her release!—

[...]

Saturday, December 23^d.

[...]

[*The Queen visits FB's apartment.*]

The Queen, when in my Room, looked over all my Books—a thing pretty briefly done! as I have scarce any of my own, but a few Dictionaries, & such works as have been the gifts of their own Authors!—my Father's most delightful Library, as I then told her, with my free access to it, had made it a thing as unnecessary, as, in fact, it would have been impracticable, for me to buy Books of my own. I believe she was a little disappointed; for I could see by her manner of turning them over, she had expected to discover my own choice & taste in the collection I possessed.

[...]

[*FB reports being paid her second quarter's salary by Thomas Mathias, Treasurer's clerk to Queen Charlotte.*]

If you will not laugh at me too much, I will also acknowledge that I liked Mr. Mathias all the more for observing him as awkward

& embarrassed how to present me my *salary*, as I felt myself in receiving it.—There is something, after all, in *money, by itself money*, that I can never take possession of without a secret feel of something like a degradation: Money in its *effects*, & its *produce*, creates far different & more pleasant sensations.—But here,—it made me feel so like—what I *am*, in short,—a *servant!*—we are *all* servants, to be sure, in the *Red Book*,[1]—but still—

[...]

1787

126.   FRANCES BURNEY TO SUSAN BURNEY PHILLIPS
1 March 1787, St James

[...]

[*FB describes a visit to the theatre with the royal party.*]
Once, about this time, I went to a Play myself, which surely I may live long enough, & never forget!—It was *Seduction*,[2] a very clever piece, but containing a dreadful picture of vice & dissipation in high life: written by Mr. Miles Andrews:—with an Epilogue—! O such an Epilogue! I was listening to it with uncommon attention, from a Compliment paid in it to Mrs. Montagu, among other female Writers,—but imagine what became of my attention, when I suddenly was struck with these lines—or something like them—

> Let sweet Cecilia gain your just applause,
> Whose every passion yields to Reason's Laws—

★★★

To hear, wholly unprepared & unsuspicious, such lines in a Theatre,—seated in a Royal Box,—& with the whole Royal family & their Suite immediately opposite me,—was it not a singular circumstance? to describe its embarrassment would be impossible:—my whole Head was leaning forward, with my Opera Glass in my

---

1   The register containing the names of holders of state office and recipients of state pensions.
2   By Thomas Holcroft. The epilogue, by Miles Andrews, contains a couplet:
    And oft let soft *Cecilia* win your praise;
    While Reason guides the clue, in Fancy's maze.

Hand, examining Miss Farren, who spoke the Epilogue:—instantly I shrunk back,—so astonished, & so ashamed of my public situation, that I was almost ready *to take to my Heels & run,*—for it seemed as if I were there purposely,—in that conspicuous place,—

"To sit attentive to my own applause—"[1]

The King immediately raised his Opera Glass to look at me, laughing heartily,—the Queen's presently took the same direction
[...]

127.   FRANCES BURNEY TO SUSAN BURNEY PHILLIPS
                    1-31 July 1787, Windsor
[...]
July 7th.
[...]
M. De La Blancherie has a scheme of a periodical work that I do not think likely to succeed.[2] He by no means strikes me to have abilities equal to supporting such an undertaking, after its first novelty is over.

He *invited* me to Paris, & with a torrent of compliments acquainted me I was *expected* there; & then followed another torrent upon other expectations.

Dry was the Gulph into which these torrents poured—no Stream met them, no emotion stirred them,—& so they soon grew stagnant.

Indeed I often wonder with myself if ever while I live this right Hand will find other employment than writing to *you.*
[...]

1788

128.   FRANCES BURNEY TO SUSAN BURNEY
                    1-7 January 1788, Windsor
[...]
Sunday, Jany. 6th.
[...]

---

1 Cf. Pope, "Epistle to Dr. Arbuthnot" (1735), l. 210.
2 Flammès-Claude-Catherine-Pahin Champlain de Lablancherie, a French man of letters.

[FB learns with trepidation of HLTP's publication of Anecdotes of the Late Samuel Johnson, *containing HLTP's letters to and from Johnson. FB worries that some of her own letters might be included in the work.]*

At noon, to day, the Queen sent one of the Princesses to fetch her a *blue Book*—when it came, she opened the Title-page, & bid me look at it,—it was this dreaded Correspondence!—sick I turned indeed,—& knew not how to endure waiting during an Hour, without discovering whether I was even personally free from being involved in this strange publication.—Before the Queen, however, left her small Dressing Room, in which she powders, for her larger one, I ventured to carry it off, while she was employed in reading Letters: for I am accustomed to convey to the larger Room whatever she can spare when the powdering begins,—& there, notwithstanding the presence of Mrs. Schwellenberg,[1] I retired with the Book to a window—&, trembling so that I could scarce turn over the Leaves, I made my fearful examination;—& most thankful am I to find that the Correspondence is dropt, in the Press, from the year 77,—so that it reaches not to my acquaintance in the family.

My sickness went off,—but a sadness remained which still infests me,—poor, lost Mrs. Thrale!—I can use for her no other words—form for her no other ideas!

[...]

129.   FRANCES BURNEY TO SUSAN BURNEY PHILLIPS
8-12 January 1788, Windsor

[...]
Wednesday, Jany. 9th.
[...]
[FB writes of HLTP's published correspondence.]

With what a sadness have I been reading! what scenes has it revived! what regrets renewed!—

How universally, through-out all her actions, does this dear & unfortunate lady prove that want of judgement which has led her into so many errors & difficulties! These Letters have not been more improperly published in the whole, than they are injudi-

---

1 Juliana Schwellenberg, a German woman who was the other Keeper of the Robes. She was an irascible, domineering colleague.

ciously displayed in their several parts: she has given *all, every word*, & thinks that, perhaps, a justice to Dr. Johnson, which, in fact, is the greatest injury to his memory: for as he wrote them in kindness, for her perusal, not in care, for that of the Public, the far greater part are wholly uninteresting, &, under any other name, would never be read.

The few she has selected of her own, do her, indeed, much credit; she has there discarded all that were trivial & merely local, & given only such as contain something instructive, amusing, or ingenious.

About 4 of the Letters, however, of my ever-revered Dr. Johnson, are truly worthy his exalted powers: one is upon Death, in considering it's approach as we are surrounded, or not, by Mourners; another upon the sudden & premature loss of poor Mrs. Thrale's Darling & only son; & two others, upon the Chances of improvement in the course of 12 years, after 30; which he weighs very deeply, & rejects very deciseively. These, with some admirably spirited Letters from the Hebrides, are all, I think, that I could ever have consented to see in print: nor even these in the life Time of the Person to whom they were addressed.

Our Name once occurs,—how I started at its sight!— 'tis to mention the party that planned the first visit to our House [...]

What has somewhat, however, alarmed [me] is to see an *of Volume First*, in the last page;—another Volume must come forward to so much nearer a period. Yet I hope—I *must* hope she will not bring forth one, she knows so reluctant to such an [exposition]!— [...]

[*Mrs. Schwellenberg informs FB*] that in the Second Volume, I, also, was mentioned! Where she may have heard this, I cannot gather; but it has given me a sickness at Heart inexpressible. It is not that I expect severity; for at the Time of that Correspondence—at all times, indeed, previous to the Marriage with Piozzi, if Mrs. Thrale loved not FB—where shall we find faith in words, or give credit to actions? But I dread *any* thing, *every* thing that brings me forward into Print:—& most of all, into a Coterie so much warred against by the rest of the world.—The innate & early averseness—*terror* I [might] truly call it,—which I conceived of any *printed notice*, seems almost a part of my being, for panegyric no more succeeds to reconcile me to it, than censure would, I believe, to harden me—

And, [xxx] her present resentment, however unjustly incurred, of my constant disapprobation of her conduct, may prompt the lamented Victim of her own uncontrolled passions, to add some note, or other mark, to point out her change of sentiments.—but let me try to avoid such painful expectations—at least, not to dwell upon them.—[1]

[...]

130.   FRANCES BURNEY TO SUSAN BURNEY PHILLIPS
May-June 1788

[...]
But I must mention a laughable enough circumstance, Her Majesty enquired of me if I had ever met with Lady Hawke? O yes, I cried, & Lady Say & Seale too!—"She has just desired permission to send me a Novel of her own writing,"—answered her Majesty.
   "I hope, cried I, 'tis not the Mausoleum of Julia!"[2]
   —But *yes*, it proved no less!—And this she has now published, & sends about!—you must remember Lady Say & Seale's quotation from it?—Her Majesty was so gracious as to lend it me, for I had some curiosity to read it. 'Tis all of a piece,—all Love, Love, Love, unmixt & unadulterated with any more worldly materials!—
[...]

131.   FRANCES BURNEY TO SUSAN BURNEY PHILLIPS
30 July-4 August 1788, Cheltenham

[...]
[*Mr. Digby*[3] *and Miss Planta*[4] *take tea with FB.*]
We then talked much upon Letter Writing, perfectly agreeing in holding it the first of all enjoyments in the absence of those first in our affections. He has many correspondents, for he has many

---

1 When FB read the 2nd volume of HLTP's correspondence in March 1788, she was relieved to find nothing more alarming than a general mention of the Burney family.
2 The novel seems to have been privately printed as no trace of it remains. FB recounted her meeting with Lady Hawke in a letter to SBP dated February 1782.
3 Stephen Digby, formerly Groom of the Bedchamber was at this time Vice-Chancellor to the Queen. He was a widower and conducted a sentimental flirtation with FB while at Court, but in 1790 he married Charlotte Gunning, greatly to FB's chagrin.
4 Margaret Planta, governess to the Princesses.

friends, & loves to keep up a constant intercourse with them. 'Tis a rule with him to destroy his Letters, almost as soon as they are answered.

Here, certainly, we agreed not so perfectly!— But, in the course of this *Epistolary* discussion, some speeches dropt from him, that I could not but understand as implying some desire that *we*, also, should correspond, upon his leaving the party. This would be a point not to be settled without some consideration, even with Mr. Digby. I felt so strongly it would require equal delicacy, with regard to *Him*, to decline, & reflection, with regard to *myself*, *not* to decline such a scheme, that I made, with some quickness, such general sort of answers, as could neither be construed into refusal nor compliance.

Nor have I yet weighed the matter; how should I like to know what occurs to my two dear Friends!—[though]¹ probably my decision must long enough be made ere I hear their opinions. This is often very vexatious to me: yet, however late they arrive, I am always eager to see how our notions have agreed or varied.

For Heaven's sake, however, my dearest Friends, do not imagine my hesitation on this point to proceed from any idea of any *possible* misconstruction with such a Man as Mr. Digby, for I should think any such fear equally *ridiculous & impertinent*. I am fully aware his superiority in family & situation would keep the World in order, as much as his high & excellent Character would satisfy myself:—but I think, though there could not be censure, there might be a laugh,—and I have a sort of constitutional repugnance to running *any risk* whatever.

★★★

When Miss Planta came in, to Tea, he put up his Budget [*of family letters*], & took one of the Letters, which he had read to me in part, & which was from Mrs. Harcourt, with whom his son Charles spends his present Holydays, & very carefully burnt it in the Candle, over the Hearth, picking up all that fell, till the whole was completely consumed: & then saying "See, Miss Burney, when *You* send me any Letters how safe they will be!"

"Yes, cried I, I see what will be their fate!—"

"*You* do not, cried he, returning, burn your Letters?"

1 Substitution.

I was too fairly detected for evasion; but I assured him I kept none dishonourably; none that I was bid destroy.

He then said he thought it a bad and dangerous custom to keep them.

"But what fortitude, cried I, does it not require to burn them, when they are written by those we wish to write them!—"

"And what, cried he, is to become of *yours*, if any thing happens?—Think but how they will be seized!—every body will try to get some of them,—what an outcry there will be!—*Have you seen Miss Burney's Letters?—Have you got any?—I have a bit!—& I have another!—& I!—and I!*—will be the cry all round.—"

No, no, I assured him I was not quite so inconsiderate of consequences: All my Papers would fall into the Hands of one of the most honourable Characters in the World, *though* a pretty near Relation of mine,—a certain Sister, in whose discretion & delicacy I had a reliance the most perfect. And I was sure, I said, I might depend upon the Queen that they should be safely transmitted to her. I could not, therefore, conceive there could be either danger or crime, so situated, in retaining them.

He did not, however, quite acquit me; his sincerity is proof against every thing but the fullest conviction: & he told me it was commonly a mere visionary notion that of reading over Letters in future times: those times [generally] brought their own Letters, & avocations, & all such hoards were as generally useless, as they were frequently hazardous.

O could he see *my* hoards, what a conflagration would he make for me!—However, he has really, by his reasoning, wrought upon me a resolution to take a general review of my manuscript possessions, & to make a few gentle flames, though not to set fire to the whole.

[...]

132.   FRANCES BURNEY TO SUSAN BURNEY PHILLIPS
1-31 October 1788, Kew

Tuesday, 14. This Evening I had again one of my old news-paper vexations: I observed my Beaus softly communicating something one from the other,—but, just as they were retiring to the Concert Room, Col. Goldsworthy marched up to my Tea Table, & hastily saying "There, ma'am!—" he put a news paper on the Table, & hurried out of the room with the greatest speed.—

I read this paragraph.

The literary silence of Miss Burney at present is much to be regretted; no novelist of the present time has a title to such public commendation as that lady; Her characters are drawn with originality of Design, & strength of Colouring, & her Morality is of the purest & most elevated sort.—

You will say, perhaps, *Why* be vexed?—*why*, my dearest Friends, because *every* mention alarms me,—I know not what may follow,—& the original repugnance to being known returns with every panic.—Indeed, the more, & the longer, I look around me, the greater appears the danger of *all public notice!*—Panegyric is as near to Envy, as Abuse is to Disgrace.—

[...]

Sunday—Oct. 19.

[...]

[*The King becomes ill, so the Court postpones its return from Kew to Windsor.*]

We are to stay here some time longer—& so unprepared were we for more than a Day or two, that our distresses are prodigious, even for Cloaths to wear:—& as to Books—there are not 3 amongst us!—& [for Company]¹ only Mr. De Luc & Miss Planta. And so,—in mere desperation for employment—I have just begun a *Tragedy!*²—We are now in so spiritless a situation, that my mind would bend to nothing less sad, even in fiction. But I am very glad something of this kind has occurred to me: it may wile away the tediousness of this unsettled—unoccupied—unpleasant period.—

[...]

Thursday 23ᵈ. [Oct]

[...]

The King continues to mend, thank God. Saturday we hope to return to Windsor. Had not this *Composition* fit seized me, *society-less* & *Bookless*, & *viewless* as I am, I know not how I could have wiled away my being.—But my Tragedy goes on, & fills up all vacancies.

[...]

[*The King's illness returned, and was diagnosed as insanity, though modern experts believe it was porphyria, whose intense pain could produce the King's symptoms. Whatever the cause, the King's physical and mental inca-*

---

1 Inserted by FBA.
2 *Edwy and Elgiva.*

pacity threw the country into a political crisis. Efforts were made to conceal the King's condition, but the Opposition, with the backing of the Prince of Wales, moved for the declaration of a Regency.]

1789

133.   FRANCES BURNEY TO SUSAN BURNEY PHILLIPS
1-18 January 1789, Kew

[...]
Tuesday, Jany. 13th.
[...]
[*Mr. Digby joins FB for tea.*]
In the course of conversation that followed, Mrs. Carter was named: Mr. Smelt is seriously of opinion her ode is the best in our Language:[1] I spoke of her very highly,—[...]

Learning in Women was then our theme: I rather wished to hear, than to declaim, upon this subject; yet I never seek to disguise That I think it has no recommendation of sufficient value to compensate its evil excitement of envy & satire.

He [*Digby*] spoke with very uncommon liberality on the female powers & intellects, & protested he had never, in his commerce with the World, been able to discern any other inferiority in their parts than what resulted from their pursuits:—& yet, with all this, he doubted much whether he had ever seen any woman who might not have been *rather better* without than with the learned Languages,—one only excepted.

He was some time silent, & I could not but suppose he meant his Correspondent, Miss Gunning;[2]—but, with a very tender sigh, he said "And she—was my Mother!—who neglected nothing else, while she cultivated Latin, & who knew it very well,—& *would* have known it very superiorly, but that her Brother, disliked her studying, & one Day—burnt all her Books!—"

---

1   Probably Carter's *Ode to Wisdom*, which Richardson inserted in *Clarissa*.
    See *Clarissa* (Penguin, 1985) letter 54, Clarissa Harlowe to Miss Howe,
    24 March.
2   Digby's future wife, Charlotte Gunning, was renowned for her classical
    education.

This was the famous unaccounter of Millions![1]—so perhaps he was *in the habit* of *burning Books!*—certainly of not *keeping* them!—However, I ventured not to say this, though Mr. Digby most liberally, censured the narrowness of his proceeding.

This anecdote led to one, in return, from myself. I told him, briefly, the history of Dr. Johnson's most kind condescendsion in desiring to make me his Pupil, & beginning to give me regular lessons of the Latin Language: & I proceeded to the speedy conclusion; my great apprehension, *conviction*, rather, that what I learnt of so great a Man could never be *private*, & that he himself would contemn concealment, if any progress should be made,—which to me was sufficient motive for relinquishing the scheme, & declining the high honour, highly as I valued it, of obtaining such a Master.—"And this, I added, though difficult to be done without offending, was yet the better effected, as my Father himself likes & approves all accomplishments for women better than the Dead Languages."

[...]

134.   FRANCES BURNEY TO SUSAN BURNEY PHILLIPS
1–9 February 1789, Kew

[*During the King's illness, the Court was sequestered at Kew.*]
Monday, 2ᵈ. What an Adventure had I this morning! one that has occasioned me the severest personal terror I ever experienced in my life.

Sir Lucas Pepys[2] still persisting that exercise & Air were absolutely necessary to save me from illness, I have continued my walks, varying my Gardens from Richmond to Kew, according to the accounts I received of the motions of the King. For this I had her Majesty's permission, on the representation of Sir Lucas.

This morning, when I received my intelligence of the King, from Dr. John Willis, I begged to know where I might walk in safety? In Kew Garden, he said, as the King would be in Richmond.

---

1   Henry Fox, first Lord Holland, father of Charles James Fox (1749-1806). FB jokes about the statesman's reputation for peculation.
2   The King's doctors were Sir Lucas Pepys, and two specialists in the treatment of the insane, the Rev. Francis Willis, who was also a physician, and his son Dr. John Willis.

"Should any unfortunate circumstance, I cried, at any time, occasion my being seen by His Majesty, do not mention my Name, but let me run off, without call or notice."

This he promised. Every body, indeed, is ordered to keep out of sight.

Taking, therefore, the time I had most at command, I strolled into the Garden; I had proceeded, in my quick way, nearly half the round, when I suddenly perceived, through some Trees, two or three figures. Relying on the instructions of Dr. John, I concluded them to be workmen, & Gardeners;—yet tried to look sharp,—& in so doing, as they were less shaded, I thought I saw the Person of his Majesty!

Alarmed past all possible expression, I waited not to know more, but turning back, ran off with all my might.—But what was my terror to hear myself pursued!—to hear the voice of the King himself, loudly & hoarsely calling after me "Miss Burney!—Miss Burney!—"

I protest I was ready to die,—I knew not in what state he might be at the time, I only knew the orders to keep out of his way were universal, that the Queen would highly disapprove any unauthorised meeting, & that the very action of my running away might deeply, in his present irritable state, offend him.

Nevertheless, on I ran,—too terrified to stop, & in search of some short passage, for the Garden is full of little labyrinths, by which I might escape.

The steps still pursued me, & still the poor hoarse & altered voice rang in my Ears:—more & more footsteps resounded frightfully behind me,—the Attendants all running, to catch their eager Master, & the voices of the two Doctor Willis's loudly exhorting him not to heat himself so unmercifully.

Heavens how I ran!—I do not think I should have felt the hot lava from Vesuvius—at least not the hot Cinders, had I so run during it's Eruption. My feet were not sensible that they even touched the Ground.

Soon after, I heard other voices, shriller though less nervous, call out "Stop! Stop!—Stop!—"

I could by no means consent,—I knew not what was purposed,—but I recollected fully my agreement with Dr. John that very morning, that I should decamp if surprised, & not be named.

My own fears & repugnance, also, after a flight & disobedience like this, were doubled in the thought of not escaping; I knew not to what I might be exposed, should the Malady be then high, & take the turn of resentment.

Still, therefore, on I flew,—& such was my speed, so almost incredible to relate, or recollect, that I fairly believe no one of the whole party could have overtaken me, if these words, from one of the Attendants, had not reached me "Dr. Willis begs you to stop!—"
"I cannot!—I cannot!—" I answered, still flying on,—when he called out "You *must*, ma'am,—it hurts the King to run.—"
Then, indeed, I stopt!—in a state of fear really amounting to agony!—I turned round,—I saw the two Doctors had got the King between them, & about 3 Attendants of Dr. Willis's were hovering about. They all slacked their pace, as they saw me stand still,—but such was the excess of my alarm, that I was wholly insensible to the effects of a *race* which, at any other time, would have required an Hour's recruit.

As they approached, some little presence of mind happily came to my command; it occurred to me that, to appease the wrath of my flight, I must now shew some confidence; I therefore faced them as undauntedly as I was able,—only charging the nearest of the Attendants to stand by my side.

When they were within a few yards of me, the King called out "Why did you run away?—"

Shocked at a question impossible to answer, yet a little assured by the mild tone of his voice, I instantly forced myself forward, to meet him—though the internal sensation which satisfied me this was a step the most proper, to appease his suspicions & displeasure, was so violently combatted by the tremor of my nerves, that I fairly think I may reckon it the greatest effort of personal courage I have ever made.

The effort answered,—I looked up, & met all his wonted benignity of countenance, though something still of wildness in his Eyes. Think, however, of my surprise, to feel him put both his Hands round my two shoulders, & then kiss my Cheek!—I wonder I did not really sink, so exquisite was my affright when I saw him spread out his arms!—Involuntarily, I concluded he meant to crush me:—but the Willis's, who have never seen him till this fatal illness, not knowing how very extraordinary an action this was from him, simply smiled & looked pleased, supposing, perhaps, it was his customary salutation!

I have reason, however, to believe it was but the joy of a heart unbridled, now, by the forms & proprieties of established custom, & sober Reason. He looked almost in *rapture* at the meeting, from the moment I advanced; & to see any of his Household thus by accident, seemed such a near approach to liberty & recovery, that who can wonder it should serve rather to elate than lessen what yet remains of his disorder?—

He now spoke in such terms of his pleasure in seeing me, that I soon lost the whole of my terror, though it had threatened to almost lose *me*: astonishment to find him so nearly *well*, & gratification to see him so pleased, removed every uneasy feeling, & the joy that succeeded, in my conviction of his recovery, made me ready to throw myself at his feet to express it.

What a Conversation followed!—When he saw me fearless, he grew more & more alive, & made me walk close by his side, away from the Attendants, & even the Willis's themselves, who, to indulge him, retreated. I own myself not completely *composed*, but *alarm* I could entertain no more.—

Every thing that came uppermost in his Mind he mentioned; he seemed to have just such remains of his flightiness, as heated his imagination, without deranging his Reason, & robbed him of all controul over his speech, though nearly in his perfect state of mind as to his opinions.

What did he not say!—He opened his whole Heart to me,— expounded all his sentiments, & acquainted me with all his intentions.

[...]

[*The King recovered by the end of March, ending the Regency crisis.*]

1790

135.   FRANCES BURNEY TO SUSAN BURNEY
           PHILLIPS & FREDERICA LOCKE[1]
               March 1790, Windsor

[...]

In one of our Windsor excursions at this time, while I was in her Majesty's Dressing Room, with only Mr. De Luc present, she suddenly said "Prepare yourself, Miss Burney, with all your spirits—for to night *you* must be Reader,— —"

---

1   Frederica Locke, wife of William Locke of Norbury Park. Both were
    close friends of FB and SBP.

She then added that she recollected what she had been told by my most honoured Mrs. Delany, of my reading Shakespeare to her, & was desirous that I should read a Play to herself & the Princesses:—& she had lately heard, from Mrs. Schwellenberg, *nobody could do it better, when I would.*

I assured her Majesty it was rather *when I could*, as any reading Mrs. Schwellenberg had heard must wholly have been better or worse according to my *spirits*, as she had justly seemed to suggest.

This was an amazing panic to me, in expectation, for the rest of the Day;—it was rendering the lecture a sort of *shewing off* truly tremendous, when I considered not only the *presence*, but the *expectation*,—& that perhaps the Lady in waiting might also attend in which case I had no chance to escape the added fatigue of standing the whole time—a doom much better suited to the gigantic & stout M. De Guiffardiere, than to little lank F.B. However, there was no resisting; & I combatted in my Mind the first disagreeability, with the consciousness of the far greater succeeding satisfaction, in an office so congenial to my inclinations, than in any other to which I could be called.

The moment Coffee was over, the Princess Elizabeth came for me. I found her Majesty knotting, the Princess Royal, Drawing, Princess Augusta spinning, & Lady Courtdown I believe in the same employment, but I saw none of them perfectly well.

"Come, Miss Burney, cried the Queen, [in a manner the most condescending], how are your spirits?—How is your voice?"

"She says, Ma'am, cried the kind Princess Elizabeth, she shall do her best!—"

This had been said in attending her Royal Highness back. I could only confirm it, & that *chearfully*,—to hide *fearfully.*

I had not the advantage of chusing my Play; nor do I know what would have been my decision had it fallen to my lot: Her Majesty had just begun Colman's works, & *Polly Honeycomb* was to open my Campaign.[1]

"I think, cried the Queen, most graciously, Miss Burney will read the better for drawing a Chair & sitting down."

"O yes, Mama! I dare [say][2] so!" cried Princess Augusta & Princess Elizabeth, both in a moment.

---

1 *Polly Honeycombe* (1760), a one-act play attacking contemporary fiction by George Colman the elder.
2 Inserted by FBA.

The Queen then told me to draw my Chair close to her side. I made no scruples! God knows I needed not the addition of standing! but most glad I felt in being placed thus near, as it saved a constant painful effort of loud reading.

"Lady Courtdown, cried the Queen, you had better draw nearer,—for Miss Burney *has the misfortune* of reading rather low at first!—"

Nothing could be more amiable than this opening Accordingly, I did, as I had promised, *my best*, & indifferent as that was, it would rather have surprized you, all things considered, that it was not yet worse. But I exerted all the courage I possess, &, having often read to the *Queen*, I felt how much it behoved me not to let her surmize I had any *greater* awe to surmount.

It is but a vulgar performance; & I was obliged to omit, as well as I could [do that] *at Sight*, several circumstances very unpleasant for reading, & ill enough fitted for such Hearers.

It went off pretty flat. Nobody is to comment, nobody is to interrupt; & even between one act & another, not a moment's pause is expected to be made.

I had already been informed of this etiquette by M. De Guiffardiere & Miss Planta; nevertheless, it is not only oppressive to the Reader, but loses to the Hearers so much spirit & satisfaction, that I determined to endeavour, should I again be called upon, to introduce a little break into this tiresome & unnatural profundity of respectful solemnity. My own embarrassement, however, made it agree with me, for the present, uncommonly well.

Lady Courtdown never uttered one single word the whole time! Yet is she one of the most loquacious of our establishment. [But such is the settled etiquette].[1]

The Queen has a taste for conversation, & the Princesses a good humoured love of it, that doubles the regret of such an annhihilation of all Nature & all pleasantry. But what will not prejudice & Education inculcate! they have been brought up to annex silence to respect, & conformity to decorum: to talk, therefore, unbid, or to differ from any given opinion even when called upon, are regarded as high improprieties, if not presumptions.

They none of them do justice to their own minds, while they enforce this subjection upon the Minds of others. I had not experienced it before; for when reading alone with the Queen, or lis-

---

1 Inserted by FBA.

tening to her reading to me, I have always frankly spoken almost whatever has ocurred to me. But there I had no other examples before me, & therefore I might innoffensively be guided by myself.

And her Majesty's continuance of the same honour, has shewn no disapprobation of my proceeding: but here,—it was not easy to make any decision for myself: to have done what Lady Courtdown forebore doing would have been undoubtedly a liberty.

So we all behaved alike: & easily can I now conceive the disappointment & mortification of poor Mr. Garrick, when he read *Lethe* to a Royal Audience.[1] It's tameness must have tamed even him; & I doubt not he never acquitted himself so ill. [...]

136.   FRANCES BURNEY TO SUSAN BURNEY
         PHILLIPS & FREDERICA LOCKE
                 August 1790

[...]
Know, then, fair ladies—about the middle of this August—90— The author [of Cecilia & Evelina][xxx] finished the rough first Draught & Copy of her first Tragedy.

What species of a composition it may prove, she is very unable to tell: she only knows it was an almost spontaneous work,—& soothed the melancholy of Imagination for a while,—though afterwards it impressed it with a secret sensation of horrour, so like real woe, that she believes it [xxx] contributed to the injury her sleep received about this period.

Nevertheless—whether well or ill, she is pleased to have done something, at last: she had so long lived in all ways as nothing.

You will smile, however, at my next trust—but scarce was this completed, as to design & scenery I mean, for the whole is in its first rough state, & legible only to herself—scarce, however, had this done with Imagination, to be consigned over to correction— when Imagination seized upon another subject, for another Tragedy.[2]

The first, therefore, I have deposited in my strong Box, in all its imperfections, to attend to the other: I well know, *correction* may

---

1 FB related Johnson's account of this incident in a letter to SC dated 27–28 March 1777 (See *EJ* 2: 227-28).
2 Probably *Hubert de Vere*.

always be summoned: *Imagination* never will come but by choice. I received her, therefore, a welcome Guest,—the best adapted for softening weary solitude, where only covetted to avoid irksome exertion.

[...]

[*Worsening health now led FB to contemplate retirement from her place at Court, after her father had given his consent. In October 1790 she composed a letter to the Queen to signify her intention, but personal timidity and a reluctance to disappoint her father's and brothers' hopes of royal patronage delayed her presentation of the letter of resignation until December.*]

137.   HORACE WALPOLE TO FRANCES BURNEY
October 1790

[*FB was engaged in negotiations with Philip Columb, a servant of Walpole's, over a disputed bequest from a late servant of her own. Walpole wrote to FB on matters of business and concluded his letter:*]

As this will come to you by my servant, give me leave to add another word on your most unfounded idea that I can forget you, because it is almost impossible for me even to meet you: Believe me, I heartily regret that privation, but would not repine, were your situation, either in point of fortune or position, equal in any degree to your merit—but were your talents given to be buried in obscurity? *You have retired from the World, to a Closet at Court*—where, indeed, you will still discover Mankind, though not disclose it; for if you could penetrate its characters in the earliest glimpse of its superficies, will it escape your piercing Eye, when it shrinks from your inspection, knowing that you have the Mirror of truth in your pocket?!—I will not embarrass you by saying more, nor would have you take notice of or reply to what I have said—judge, only, that feeling Hearts reflect, not forget.—Wishes that are empty look like vanity:—my vanity is to be thought capable of esteeming you as much as you deserve, & to be reckoned though a very distant, a most *sincere* Friend—&, give me leave to say

Dear madam your most obed. h^ble. s^tt.   Hor. Walpole—1

---

1 FB sent a copy of Walpole's letter to her sister SBP, commenting that his panegyric had encouraged CB in his resolution to free FB from her servitude at Court.

1791

138.   FRANCES BURNEY TO SUSAN BURNEY
           PHILLIPS & FREDERICA LOCKE
                    May 1791

[...]

Sunday May 1st. to Saturday May 7th.

Let me have the pleasure, for once, to begin with mentioning something that I know my dear partial Readers will read with satisfaction: last Month I commenced a new work:[1] I finish nothing; I can get time to read & revise nothing; but a spirit of composition has fortunately assailed me, in this suspensive period, which from time to time amuses my solitude, & beguiles my weariness. The melancholy life I lead in this perpetual conflict how to lead any other, would else, I think, since your absences & Charlotte's, quite have consumed me.

But I can go on with nothing—my mind is uneasy & unsettled, & my inventive faculties fly from matter to matter, softening, soothing, & lightening my lonely Hours, but never arriving at what might stand any chance to better those of any other. Three Works which I have now in hand seize me capriciously; but I never reprove them; I give the play into their own direction, & am sufficiently thankful, in this wearing waste of existence, for so being seized at all.

[...]

139.   FRANCES BURNEY TO SUSAN BURNEY
           PHILLIPS & FREDERICA LOCKE
                    June 1791

[...]

[*M. Guiffardière spoke with FB after an evening tea party.*]
He was eager to enquire of me *who was Mrs. Lenox?*[2] He had been reading, like all the rest of the World, Boswell's Life of Dr. Johnson,[3] & the preference there expressed of *Mrs. Lenox* to all other females, had filled him with astonishment, as he had never even heard her name.

---

1 Probably *The Siege of Pevensey.*
2 See note, p. 155.
3 Published 16 May 1791.

These occasional sallies of Dr. Johnson, uttered from local causes & circumstances, but all retailed verbatim by Mr. Boswell, are
filling all sort of readers with amaze, except the small party to
whom Dr. Johnson was known, & who, by acquaintance with the
power of the moment over his unguarded conversation, know how
little of his solid opinion was to be gathered from his accidental
assertions.

The King, who was also now reading this work, applied to me
for explanations without end. Every night, at this period, he
entered the Queen's Dressing Room, & detained her Majesty's
proceedings by a length of discourse with me upon this subject. All
that flowed from himself was constantly full of the goodness &
benevolence of his character; & I was never so happy as in the
opportunity thus graciously given me of vindicating, in instances
almost innumerable, the serious principles & various excellencies
of my ever most revered Dr. Johnson, from the clouds so frequently involving & darkening them, in narrations so little calculated for
any Readers who were strangers to his intrinsic worth, and therefore worked upon & struck by what was faulty in his Temper &
manners.

I regretted not having strength to read this work to Her Majesty
myself. It was an honour I should else have certainly received: for
so much wanted clearing! so little was understood!—However, the
Queen frequently condescended to read over passages & anecdotes
which perplexed or offended her; & there were none I had not a
fair power to soften or to justify. Dear & excellent Dr. Johnson! I
have never forgot nor neglected his injunction, given me when
ill—to stand by him, & support him, & not hear him abused, when
he was no more, & could not defend himself!—but little—little did
I think it would ever fall to my lot to vindicate him to his King &
Queen.—

[...]

Her Majesty, the Day before we left Windsor, gave me to understand my attendance would be yet one more fortnight requisite,
though no longer. I heard this with a fearful presentiment I should
surely never go through another fortnight, in so weak & languishing & painful a state of Health. However, I could but accede—
though I fear with no very courtly grace.

So melancholy, indeed, was the state of my mind, from the
weakness of my frame, & the never-ending struggles for the rest I
sighed after, That I was never alone but to form scenes of *foreign
woe*, when my own disturbance did not occupy me wholly. I

began—almost whether I would or not—another Tragedy![1] The other three all unfinished! not one read!—& one of them, indeed, only generally sketched as to plan & character.—But I could go on with nothing; I could only suggest & invent. And the other work which I have mentioned is of *another* sort—in a style my dear friends all around will most wish me to cultivate:[2] but that was not dismal enough,—& away it went, from Pen, Hand, & Head, to give place to a plan of the deepest Tragedy, which first had occurred to me in the worst part of my illness in January, but which I had not thought of since my quitting my room.

The power of Composition has to me, indeed, proved a solace, a blessing!—When incapable of all else, that, unsolicited, unthought of, has presented itself to my solitary leisure, & beguiled me of *myself*, though it has not, of late, regaled me with gayer associates.

[...]

[*FB was released from her duties at Court in July 1791 and returned to live with her father, EAB and her half-sister SHB, now based in rooms in Chelsea College. The Queen granted FB a pension of £100 per annum, demonstrating that she had not forfeited royal favour by her resignation.*]

140.   FRANCES BURNEY TO SUSAN BURNEY
         PHILLIPS & FREDERICA LOCKE
         October 1791, Chelsea

[...]
I have never been so pleasantly situated at Home since I lost the sister of my Heart & my most affectionate Charlotte. My Father is almost constantly within, & considerations there now are that occasion much an *almost* total sparing of reproach for one who indulges herself with resorting to his apartment.[3]

Indeed—I now live with him wholly; he has himself appropriated me a place, a seat, a desk, a table, & every convenience & comfort, & he never seemed yet so earnest to keep me about him. We read together, write together, chat—compare notes, communicate projects, & diversify each other's employments. He is all goodness,

---

1 Probably *Elberta*.
2 Possibly an early version of *Camilla*.
3 Reproach from EAB, who seems to have been jealous of CB's children from his first marriage.

gaiety, & sweetest affection,—& his society & kindness are more precious to me than ever.

Fortunately, in this season of leisure & comfort, the Spirit of Composition proves active. The Day is never long enough, & I could employ two pens almost incessantly in merely scribbling what will not be repressed. This is a delight to my dear Father inexpressibly great: & though I have gone no further than to let him know, from time to time, the *species* of Matter that occupies me, he is perfectly contented, & patiently waits till something is quite finished, before he insists upon reading a Word. This "suits my humour well," as my own industry is all gone, when once its intent is produced.

My little Ballad, indeed, *Willy*,[1] he was eager to see, conceiving it finished: but, upon reading it over myself, I found it much wanted revisal, in some places, though, in general, I have left it just as you have read it: but I have now added some Stanzas, & new written the denoüment, which my dearest Susanna most justly thought too abrupt, & which I had been entirely dissatisfied with myself, & I have prevailed with him to let me lock it up, till I have done something else, &, by forgetting it, in some measure enable myself to read it, again, as if it were the work of another Person.

For the rest, I have been going on with my third Tragedy.[2] I have two written,—but never yet have had opportunity to read them, which, of course, prevents their being corrected to the best of my power, & fitted for the perusal of less indulgent Eyes—or, rather, of Eyes less prejudiced.

Believe me, my dear Friends, in the present composed & happy state of my mind, I could never have suggested these Tales of Woe;—but having only to connect, combine, contract, & finish, I will not leave them undone. Not, however, to sadden myself to the same point in which I began them, I read more than I write, & call for happier themes from others, to enliven my mind from the dolourous sketches whence I now draw of my own.

The Library & study, in which we constantly sit, supply such delightful variety of food, that I have nothing to wish.—Thus, my beloved Sisters & Friends—you see me, at length, enjoying all that

---

1 A poem written by FB in 1787. The original has been lost, though a copy in French translation survives. It narrates the rescue of two children by a dog (See *HFB* 224-25).

2 *The Siege of Pevensey.*

peace, ease, & chosen recreation & employment, for which so long I sighed in vain, & which, till very lately, I had reason to believe, even since attained, had been allowed to me too late. I am more & more thankful every Night—every morning—for the change in my destiny, & present blessings of my lot.—& you, my beloved Susan & Fredy, for who prayers I have so often applied in my sadness, suffering & despondence,—afford me now the same community of thanks & acknowledgements.—

[...]

1792

141.   FRANCES BURNEY TO SUSAN BURNEY
         PHILLIPS & FREDERICA LOCKE
         October 1792, Aylsham

[...]

[*On a visit to the agriculturalist Arthur Young and his wife, FB meets François-Alexandre-Frédéric de la Rochefoucauld, Duc de Liancourt, a refugee from France. She reports a conversation between the Duc de Liancourt, SHB and herself.*]

Sarah spoke of Me. Brulard,[1]—&, in a little *malice*, to draw him out, said *her sister knew her very well!*—

The Duc, with Eyes of fire at the sound, came up to me—"Comment! Mademoiselle!—Vous avez connû cette coquine de Brulard?"[2] And then, he asked me what I had thought of her?

I frankly answered, that I had thought her *charming*: gay, intelligent, well bred, Well-informed, & amiable.

He instantly drew back, as if Sorry he had named her so roughly, & looked at Sally, for thus surprising him: but I immediately continued, that I could now no longer think the same of her, as I could no longer esteem her; but I confessed my surprise had been inexpressible at her duplicity.

He allowed that, some years ago, she might have a better chance than now of captivation, for the deeper she had immersed in

---

1   Stéphanie-Félicité Brûlart, comtesse de Genlis. FB had met and been charmed by her during her visit to England in 1785, but her reputation, as the long-standing mistress of Philippe "Egalité," duc d'Orléans, to whose children she was governess, meant that she was not generally received and FB did not keep up the acquaintance.

2   "How is this, Miss? You are acquainted with that slut de Brulard?"

politics, the more she had forfeited of feminine attraction. "Ah! he cried, with her talents—her knowledge—her parts—had she been modest, reserved, gentle— — what a blessing might she have proved to her Country!—but she is devoted to intrigue & cabal, & proves its curse!—"

He then spoke with great asperity against all the *femmes de lettres* now known; he said they were commonly the most *disgusting of their sex*, in France, by their arrogance, boldness, & mauvaises moeurs.[1] He [even] named M^e. de Stahl, Daughter of M. Neckar, as one of the most offensively presumptuous women in the world, though of distinguished talents.[2]

[...]

1793

142.   FRANCES BURNEY TO DR. CHARLES BURNEY
                16-19 February 1793, Mickleham

[...]

Mad^e. de Stahl, Daughter of M. Necker, & wife of the Sweedish Ambassadour to France, is now head of the little French Colony in this neighbourhood. M. de Stahl, her Husband, is at present suspended in his Embassy, but not recalled; & it is yet uncertain whether the Regent Duke of Sudermania, will send him to Paris, during the present horrible Convention, or order him home. He is now in Holland, waiting for commands. M^e. de Stahl, however, was *unsafe* in Paris, though an Ambassadress, from the resentment owed her by the *Commune*, for having received & protected in her House various destined victims of the 10th. of August, & of the 2^d. September.[3][...]

---

1 Loose morals.
2 Anne Louise Germaine Necker, daughter of the statesman and financier, Jacques Necker. She had married Eric-Magnus, Baron of Staël-Holstein, who was the Swedish Ambassador to France. Her salon in Paris was a forum for constitutional debate. Her writings, including novels, plays, and moral and philosophical essays, reflected her reformist sympathies, and influenced developments in European philosophy and literature.
3 The September massacres in France, involving the summary execution of political and other prisoners, began on 2 September 1792.

She is a woman of the first abilities, I think, I have ever seen. She is more in the style of Mrs. Thrale than of any other celebrated Character; but she has infinitely more depth, & seems an even *profound* politician & metaphysician. She has suffered us to hear some of her works in MSS. which are truly wonderful, for powers both of thinking & expression. She adores her Father—but is much alarmed at having had no news from him since he has heard of the massacre of the martyrred Louis[1]—& who can wonder it should have overpowered him? She is enthusiastic in the highest degree about your FB—& for a reason extremely amiable—since it is the reflexion of her filial affection, from the pleasure with which she records that, since the miseries which have befallen the unhappy King, & after writing his defence, M. Neckar fell into a state of dejection that incapacitated him from every sort of pursuit till somebody put Cecilia into his hands, which he had never found time to read, or perhaps inclination; it caught him, however, & "*soothed* & *regaled*" him, she said, when nothing else could touch or interest or amuse him.—" I own I was not *very* much displeased at this circumstance.

Ever since her arrival, she has been pressing me to spend some time with her, before I return to Town—she wanted Susan & me to pass a month with her; but finding that impossible, she bestowed all her entreaties upon me alone; & they are grown so urgent, upon my preparation for departing, & acquainting her my *furlough* of absence was over, that she not only insisted upon my writing to you, & telling why I deferred my return, but declares she will also *write herself*, to ask your permission for the visit. She exactly resembles Mrs. Thrale in the ardour & warmth of her temper & partialities. I find her impossible to resist, & therefore, if your answer to her is such as I conclude it must be, I shall wait upon her for a week. She is only a short walk from hence, at Juniper Hall.

There can be nothing imagined more charming, more fascinating than this Colony. Between their Sufferings & their *agrêmens*, they occupy us almost wholly. [...]

M. d'Arblay is one of the most singularly interesting Characters that can ever have been formed. He has a sincerity, a frankness, an ingenuous openness of nature that I had been injust enough to think could not belong to a French Man. With all this, which is his *Military portion*, he is passionately fond of literature, a most delicate

---

1 Louis XVI was executed on 21 January 1793.

critic in his own language, well versed in both Italian & German, & a very elegant Poet. He has just undertaken to become my *French Master*, for pronunciation, & he gives me long daily lessons in reading. Pray expect wonderful improvements! In return I hear him in English,—& for his Thême this Evening, he has been writing an English address *à M^r. Burney*, (ie. M. le Docteur) joining in M^e De Stahl's request. I cannot send it you, because it is a precious morsel of elegant broken English, & I must keep it amongst my treasures: but I will produce it when I return for your entertainment.

[...]

143.   DR. CHARLES BURNEY TO FRANCES BURNEY
19 February 1793, Chelsea

Why Fanny! What are you ab^t. & where are you? I shall write *at* you, not knowing how to write *to* you, as Swift did to the flying & Romantic L^d. Peterborough.[1]

I had written the above, after a yesterday's Glimmering, & a feverish night, as usual, when behold! a Letter of requisition for a further Furlow!—I had long Histories ready for narration, *de vive voix*, but my time is too short & my eyes & head too weak for much writing this morning. I am not at all surprised at your acc^t. of the captivating powers of Mad^e. de Stahl. It corresponds with all I had heard ab^t. her, & with the opinion I formed of her intellectual & literary powers on reading her charming little Apologie de Rousseau.[2]—But as nothing human is allowed to be perfect, she has not escaped censure. Her house was the centre of Revolutionists previous to the 10th. of Augt. after her Father's departure. & she has been accused of partiality to M. de Narbonne[3]—But perhaps all may be Jacobinical malignity—However, unfavourable stories of her have been brought hither—and the Burkes & M^{rs}. Ord have repeated them to me. But, you know that M. Necker's administra-

---

1 A reference to Swift's correspondence with Charles Mordaunt, 3rd Earl of Peterborough, whose duties as admiral, general, and diplomat required constant travel (see *JL* 2: 20n.).

2 *Lettres sur le caractère et les écrits de J.-J. Rousseau* (1788).

3 Louis-Marie-Jacques-Almaric, comte de Narbonne-Lara, former minister of war to Louis XVI. He was a friend of ADA, and had a long-standing affair with Mme. de Staël.

tion & the conduct of The Nobles who first joined in the violent measures that subverted the anc^t. establishm^{ts}. by the abolition of Nobility & ruin of the Church, during the 1st. National Assembly are held in greater horror by aristocrats than even the members of the present Convention.[1]

I know this will make you feel uncomfortable—but it seemed to me *right* to hint it to you—If you are not absolutely *in the House* of Mad^e. de S. when this arrives, it w^d. perhaps be possible for you to waive the visit to her by a compromise, of having something to do for Susey—& so make the *addendum* to your stay under *her* roof. [...]

[*FB complied with her father's instructions with regard to Mme. de Staël, but her relationship with d'Arblay continued unabated, though CB disapproved the Frenchman's constitutionalist politics. Mutual language instruction provided a forum for an exchange of essays between FB and d'Arblay, which soon became a species of correspondence. D'Arblay was socially far above FB but as a refugee from France he was wholly destitute, and unlikely to secure any employment in England. Their union seemed impracticable with only FB's income to live on, for of that she could only be certain of £20 per annum derived from the investment of the profits of* Cecilia, *since the Queen's pension of £100 per annum depended on continuing royal favour which might be withdrawn if FB were to ally herself with a Frenchman of moderate reformist sympathies. Nevertheless, in April 1793 d'Arblay declared his attachment and FB admitted it was reciprocal. She planned to supplement their income by writing, in order to make their union possible. The Queen consented to continue the pension, and CB grudgingly gave his consent to the union after the intervention of William Locke on the couple's behalf. FB and d'Arblay were united in two ceremonies, Protestant and Roman Catholic, on 31 July and 1 August, 1793. FB was attended at both ceremonies by SBP and her brother James, as CB refused to attend. Mr. Locke gave the couple a piece of ground near his home, upon which they would later build Camilla Cottage from the proceeds of FBA's third novel.*]

---

1 CB, strongly conservative and a monarchist himself, blamed the French constitutionalists' efforts to instigate mild reforms for paving the way to revolution.

144. FRANCES BURNEY D'ARBLAY TO DR. CHARLES BURNEY
20 October 1793, Great Bookham

[*CB joined Mrs. Crewe in a scheme to produce charity tracts in aid of the emigrant French clergy. FBA relates the completion of her contribution to the cause,* Brief Reflections Relative to the Emigrant French Clergy.]
My dearest Father will think I have been very long in doing the little I have done,—but my Mind is so anxiously discomfitted by the continued suspence with regard to M. D'Arblay's proposition & wish[1]—that it has not been easy to me to weigh completely all I could say—& the fear of repeating what has already been offered upon the subject, has much restrained me, for I have seen none of the tracts that may have appeared.

However, it is a matter truly near my Heart, & though I have not done it rapidly, I have done it with my whole Mind, &—to own the truth, with a species of emotion, that has greatly affected me, for I could not deeply consider the situation of these venerable men without feeling for them to the quick. If what I have written should have power to procure them *one more guinea*, I shall be paid.
[...]
If you think what I have drawn up worth printing, I should suppose it might make a little 6^d. paper, to be sold for the same purpose it is written. Or will it only do to be printed by the expence of the acting Ladies, & given Gratis? You must judge of this.[2]
[...]

145.   BRIEF REFLECTIONS RELATIVE TO THE
EMIGRANT FRENCH CLERGY:
EARNESTLY SUBMITTED TO THE HUMANE CONSIDERATION
OF THE LADIES OF GREAT BRITAIN
1793

[*FBA's pamphlet was prefaced by the following "Apology."*]
HOWEVER wide from the allotted boundaries and appointed province of Females may be all interference in public matters, even in the agitating season of general calamity; it does not thence

---

1 ADA was still in quest of some remunerative employment; at this time a scheme to offer his services to assist a British expedition intended to support Royalist forces at Toulon. The plan came to nothing.
2 The pamphlet, published by Cadell on 19 November 1793, was sold for one shilling and sixpence, with profits devoted to the relief of the clergy.

follow that they are exempt from all public claims, or mere passive spectatresses of the moral as well as of the political œconomy of human life. The distinct ties of their prescriptive duties, which, pointed out by Nature, have been recognised by reason, and established by custom, remove, indeed, from their view and knowledge all materials for forming public characters. The privacy, therefore, of their lives is the dictate of common sense, stimulated by local discretion. But in the doctrine of morality the reverse is the case, and their feminine deficiencies are there changed into advantages: since the retirement, which divests them of practical skill for public purposes, guards them, at the same time, from the heart-hardening effects of general worldly commerce. It gives them leisure to reflect and to refine, not merely upon the virtues, but the pleasures of benevolence; not only and abstractedly upon that sense of good and evil which is implanted in all, but feelingly, nay awefully, upon the woes they see, yet are spared!

It is here, then, in the cause of tenderness and humanity, they may come forth, without charge of presumption, or forfeiture of delicacy. Exertions here may be universal, without rivality or impropriety; the head may work, the hand may labour; the heart may suggest, indiscriminately in all, in men without disdain, in women without a blush: and however truly of the latter to withdraw from notice may be in general the first praise, in a service such as this, they may with yet more dignity come forward: for it is here that their purest principles, in union with their softest feelings, may blend immediate gratification with the most solemn future hopes.——And it is here, in full persuasion of sympathy as well as of pardon, that the Author of these lines ventures to offer her countrywomen a short exhortation in favour of the emigrant French Clergy.

[*Despite its esoteric subject matter, FBA's pamphlet commanded unusual attention from the critical press as her first foray into print after a silence of over ten years. It was favourably mentioned in the* Monthly Review *12 (Dec. 1793): 455, the* British Critic *2 (Dec. 1793):450, and in the* European Magazine *25 (Jan. 1794): 32, but the* Critical Review *questioned the political bias of the project.*]

146.   THE CRITICAL REVIEW
           March 1794

[...]
Madame d'Arblay, for that is the name she will for the future illustrate, prefaces her remarks by disclaiming *all interference in public*
matters, even in the agitating season of general calamity, as unbecoming
in a female: The writer of Cecilia is not a common female, and we
are confident the public will be gratified by hearing her sentiments
on any subject to which she has turned her thoughts. Were it not
so, the apology would scarcely serve; for it is hardly possible to
touch on the subject she has chosen, without discovering adherence to some political party, and Madame d'Arblay shews that she
has decidedly chosen hers.
[...]
    In all that can be urged concerning the call for charity towards
these unfortunate men, we entirely agree with our author; but we
think she is mistaken in the estimate of their merits, when she
represents them as actuated entirely by religious principle, and
"preferring the most baneful rage of consummate barbarity to
uttering one deviating word." Neither the presumption drawn
from the knowledge of human nature, nor the actual circumstances of the present contest, nor the previous character of the
French clergy, will allow us to suppose that, as a body, their
motives were so pure. The slightest observation will shew how
intimately their emoluments and their power were connected
with the political system they adhered to, and having once chosen their party, it was not in their power to avoid being involved
in the ruin which overwhelmed it. This is not said by any means
to check our pity for the destitute, but to qualify our veneration
for the martyrs.
[...]
    Upon the whole, whatever remarks we may have made upon
either the style or the sentiments of this animated charity sermon,
as it may properly enough be called, our advice to the amiable
author may all be comprehended in two words, *Write on.*

147. FRANCES BURNEY D'ARBLAY TO DR. CHARLES BURNEY
9 May 1794, Great Bookham

[...]

The other Day, M. d'Arblay picked up a Critical Review at Mr. Cooke's, with an article on the *Reflexions*: so I find I am too Aristocratic for them—however, it seems done by some one who has a sort of *personal* kindness for me, as so much praise & encouragement is mixt with an evident dissatisfaction with the little work itself.

[...]

148. FRANCES BURNEY D'ARBLAY TO DR. CHARLES BURNEY
10 August 1794, Great Bookham

[...]

[*FBA writes to CB after his visit to the d'Arblays' rural retreat.*]
You spirited me on in all ways, for this week past I have taken *tightly* to the *grand ouvrage*.[1] If I go on so a little longer, I doubt not but M. d'Arblay will begin settling where to have a new shelf for arranging it! [...]

We think with *very* great pleasure of accepting yours & my Mother's kind invitation for a few Days. I hope, & mean, if possible, to bring with *me* also a littel sample of something less in the dolourous style than what always causes your poor shoulders a little Shrug.

Apropos—(*did not you hear a Gun go off?*) Mr. Lock, to whom I had delivered my historic dismality[2] to read at Mr. Angerstein's, & thence forward to Greenwich,[3] as I told you, is sanguine about it beyond my most daring hopes, & equally to those of my far more intrepid Companion. He has made but one critique, & that upon a point indifferent to me, & which I shall yield *without a pang*. He pronounces peremtorily upon its success—however, I am

---

1 FBA adds a note "Camilla—then lately begun."
2 FBA adds a note "Edwy & Elgiva a Tragedy *once* acted!" This was more likely to be a reference to *Hubert de Vere*, which was first offered to the acting manager of Drury Lane Theatre, John Philip Kemble. Later, it was replaced with *Edwy and Elgiva*, which FBA thought more dramatic.
3 To CBjr who handled the negotiations with Kemble for the production of FBA's tragedy.

prepared for its failure, knowing the extreme uncertainty of all public acts. [...]

149. FRANCES BURNEY D'ARBLAY TO ALEXANDRE D'ARBLAY
16 December 1794, Great Bookham

[*An unfinished letter written before the birth of FBA's only child, Alexander.*]
The moment of danger now fast approaching—presses upon probability to end in Death—If so—O Husband of my Heart! read some consolation for the loss of Her who so truly knew to appreciate you, in this last Farewell—which, solemnly as in the aweful epoch of life's final dissolution, announces her tenderness to have sprung first from just admiration of your noble Character,—& to have lived encreasing to her latest breath from the softest gratitude for your invariable kindness, & goodness, united with the warmest delight in the dear & constant view of the chaste the innocent, the exemplary tenour of your conduct, & the integrity, the disinterestedness, the unaffected nobleness of your principles & sentiments.—Heaven bless you, my d'Arblay! here & hereafter! here, with the continuance of the same worth that alone gives true superiority, & hereafter—with the recompence of eternal life & bliss!— & with—O may be such the bounty of God!—with a re-union with Her who fondly sees herself the Wife of your bosom!— beloved as she loves!—

I leave you no injunctions—I ever held Death-Bed requests cruel from short-sighted Mortals, who ill can judge what events & circumstances may render them impracticable—improper—& even baneful—.

And why recommend to you what will become at once the first care & first joy of your life, our Child?—Ah! Merciful Heaven! if
[*Fragment breaks off here. Despite her misgivings, FBA was safely delivered of a healthy son on 18 December.*]

1795

150.   ALEXANDRE D'ARBLAY TO JAMES BURNEY
22 March 1795, Greenwich[1]

Your Sister, my dear James, would be very obliged to you if you
may copy for her what is said in the news papers concerning her
Tragedy. She receives from all parts the intelligence that all the
papers have acquainted the Public with her *Secret*.[2] [...]
[*PS. by FBA.*]
I am dying to see these paragraphs *Pray, pray* copy them—[3]

151.   MORNING ADVERTISER
Monday 23 March 1795
[...]
Edwy and Elgiva is a beautiful Poem—it is nothing more. To
interest the feelings, to excite emotions, is the business of Tragedy;
this indeed constitutes its *essence*. *Here*, however, there is nothing of
the kind; we listen without anxiety, we behold without alarm;
the affections are unmoved, the passions are unawakened, there
is nothing to raise the curiosity, nothing to point the attention;
no subtle involution of character, no necessary diversity of incident. What then is its merit?—diction, purity of sentiment,
and elegance of phrase. But what is Tragedy without its
essentials?—a pillar without a base, a superstructure without a
foundation.
[...]
[*The review mentions the unfortunate effect of inadvertent humour in some
lines such as "Bring in the Bishop!" (1.7.1), "Bishop" being a mulled
wine served in taverns.*]
The Acting was disgraceful to the Company, and shamefully
injurious to the Author. Surely there was no *intention* to affect the
Piece by such proceedings—it may, however, be shrewdly *suspected*.

---

1 The d'Arblays were staying with CBjr at Greenwich in order to attend
   the *première* of *Edwy and Elgiva* at the Drury Lane theatre on Saturday 21
   March 1795.
2 I.e. her authorship. FBA had hoped to remain anonymous in her theatrical venture.
3 Hemlow presents a summary of the reviews in *JL* 3: 366-67.

After Kemble, Bensley, and Mrs. Siddons,[1] we except none—the Prompter was heard unremittingly all over the House. If the Piece was *accepted*, it should have been *played*.

[...]

152.

FRANCES BURNEY D'ARBLAY TO
MARY PORT WADDINGTON[2]
15 April 1795, Great Bookham

[...]

Let me give you the short History of my Tragedy fairly & frankly.

I wrote it not, as your Acquaintance imagined, *for the Stage*, nor yet *for the Press*—I began it at Kew Palace—at the very time our beloved mutual tie, your revered A[*unt*] D[*elany*] was there on a visit to Mr. Smelt:[3] &, at odd Moments, I finished it at Windsor; without the least idea of any species of publication.

Since I left the Royal Household, I ventured to let it be read by my Father, Mr. & Mrs. Lock, my Sister Phillips, & .... of course, M. d'Arblay: & not another human Being.—Their opinions led to what followed—& my Brother Dr. Charles shewed it to Mr. Kemble while I was on my visit to my Father last October. He instantly & warmly pronounced for its acceptance, but I knew not when Mr. Sheridan would see it, & had not the smallest expectation of its appearing this year. However—just 3 Days before my beloved little Infant came into the World, an Express arrived from my Brother, that Mr. Kemble wanted the Tragedy immediately, in order to shew it to Mr. Sheridan, who had just heard of it, & had spoken in the most flattering terms of his good will for its reception.

---

1 John Philip Kemble played Edwy, Robert Bensley Dunstan, and Sarah Siddons Elgiva. The worst performer was John Palmer, who played Aldhelm.

2 Mrs. Delany's great-niece, whom FB had befriended at Windsor. The two remained friends for many years, until MPW quarrelled with FBA in 1832 on account of a true but mortifying hint contained in the *Memoirs of Dr. Burney* that Mrs. Delany had received financial aid from the Duchess of Portland.

3 Hemlow notes that this places the beginning of the composition of *Edwy* in October or November 1786 (*JL*, 3: 98n.), which contradicts accounts in FB's letters from the Court period in which she records beginning the play in October 1788, during the King's sequestration at Kew.

Still, however, I was in doubt of its actual acceptance, till 3 Weeks after my confinement, when I had a visit from my Brother, who told me he was the next morning to read the Piece in the Green Room.

This was a precipitance for which I was every way unprepared, as I had never made but one Copy of the Play, & had intended divers corrections & alterations:—absorbed, however, by my new Charge, & then growing ill, I had a sort of indifference about the matter, which, in fact, has lasted ever since.

The moment I was then able to hold a pen, I wrote two short Letters to acknowledge the state of the affair to my Sisters—& to one of these, I had an immediate laughing answer—informing me *my confidence* was somewhat of the latest, as the Subject of it *was already in all the news-papers!*—I was extremely chagrined at this intelligence—but, from that time, thought it all too late to be the herald of my own Designs. And this, added to my natural & incurable dislike to enter upon these egoistical details unasked, has caused my silence to my dear Marianne—& to every Friend I possess. Indeed, speedily after, I had an illness so severe & so dangerous, that for full 7 Weeks the Tragedy was neither named nor thought of by M. d'A. or myself—

It was not my *Health enabled me to go to Town*—I was too much indisposed to make a single visit there, even to my sisters—I merely went, ONE NIGHT, to alight at the Theatre, where I was met by my Sister Phillips, with whom, & M. d'A. & my Brother Dr. C. I sat, snug & retired & wrapt up in a Bonnet & immense Pelice, in Mr. Sheridan's Box to see Mrs. Siddons & Mr. Kemble in *Edwy & Elgiva*. [...]

The Piece was represented to the utmost disadvantage, save only Mrs. Siddons & Mr. Kemble,—for it was not written with any idea of the stage, & my illness & weakness & constant *absorbment* in the time of its preparation, occasioned it to appear with so many *undramatic* effects, from my inexperience of Theatrical requisites & demands, that when I saw it, I perceived myself a thousand things I wished to change The Performers, too, were cruelly imperfect, & made blunders I blush to have pass for mine,—added to what belong to me—the most important Character, after the Hero & Heroine, had *but 2 lines* of his part by Heart! he made all the rest at random—& such nonsense as put all the other actors out as much as himself—so that a more wretched performance, except Mrs. S.[*iddons*] Mr. K.[*emble*] & Mr. Bensley, could not be exhibited in a Barn. All this concurred

to make it very desirable to *withdraw the Piece for alterations*—
which I have done.

[...]

153. Dr. Charles Burney to Frances Burney d'Arblay
7 May 1795, Chelsea

[...]

M[r]. C.[*umberland*] expressed his sorrow at what had happened at
D.[*rury*] L.[*ane*] & said that if he had had the honour of knowing
you sufficiently, he w[d]. have told you d'avance what w[d]. happened,
by what he had heard, *behind the Scenes*. The Players seem to have
given the play an ill name—But he says if you w[d]. go to work
again, by reforming this, or work with your best powers at a new
Plan, & w[d]. submit it to his inspection, he w[d]. from the experience
he has had risk his life on its success—This Conversation I thought
too curious not to be mentioned.

[...]

154. Frances Burney d'Arblay to Dr. Charles Burney
13 May 1795, Great Bookham

[...]

The Conversation with Mr. C.[*umberland*] astonished me. I certainly think his experience of stage effect, & his interest with players, so important, as almost instantly to wish putting his sincerity
to the proof. How has he got these two Characters, one of Sir *Fretful Plagiery*, detesting all works but those he owns, & all authors but
himself,—the other, of a Man too perfect even to know or conceive the vices of the World, such as he is painted by Goldsmith in
Retaliation?[1] And which of these Characters is true? I am not at all
without thoughts of a future revise of Edwy & Elgiva, for which I
formed a plan on the first Night, from what occurred by the
repr[esen]tation: but then—I want Mr. Palmer to be so obliging as
to leave the Stage!—Though every body agrees he would not dare,
after what has already passed, play the same part a second time. Let
me own to you, when you commend *my bearing so well a theatrical*

---

1   Cumberland was caricatured as Sir Fretful Plagiary in Sheridan's *The
    Critic* (1779), in contrast to his portrait by Goldsmith in *Retaliation: A
    Poem* (1774).

drubbing, I am by no means enabled to boast I bear it with conviction of my utter failure: the Piece was certainly not heard, & therefore not really judged. The Audience *finished* with an UNMIXED clap
on hearing it was withdrawn *for alterations*, & I have constantly considered myself in the *Publicly accepted* situation of having at my own
option to let the Piece die, or attempt its resuscitation,—its *reform*,
as Mr. Cumberland calls it. And should this be my ultimate act, it
will be worth thinking of that he has made such a proposition.
However, I have not given one moment to the matter since my
return to the Hermitage.

[I have not, however, neglected equally the other,[1] & less have
done because you so strongly recommended to me: but that will
be a great work—I mean in bulk—& very long in hand.—] [...]

155. FRANCES BURNEY D'ARBLAY TO DR. CHARLES BURNEY
18 June 1795, Great Bookham

[...]
[*FBA discusses her plan to print her new novel by subscription.*]
[M. d'Arblay gives completely into the idea of Mrs. Crewe that
the scrip[2] must be but *a Guinea* & prefers both worse paper, &
acknowledgement & certainty of the work, to making it more.

James has sent me a most exact compendium of the printing
expence, which amuses us both: they will swallow so much, that, at
first, we were near drawing back from the project. Upon further
reflexion, we still see, that if the success resembles that of its
predecessors, it will answer well in the course of a few years,
though it will be so short of a *Bookseller's bargain* at the beginning
unless, indeed, there is such a subscription as my Mother seems to
augur.]

I like well the idea of giving *no name at all*,—Why should not
I have my mystery, as well as Udolpho?[3]—but......now don't fly Dr.
Burney!—I own I do not like calling it a *Novel*: it gives so simply
the notion of a mere love story, that I recoil a little from it. I mean
it to be *sketches of Characters & morals, put in action*, not a Romance.
I remember the Word *Novel* was long in the way of Cecilia, as I

1 *Camilla.*
2 Subscription.
3 A reference to Ann Radcliffe's (1764-1823) gothic novel, *The Mysteries of
   Udolpho* (1794).

was told, at the Queen's House. And it was not permitted to be read by the Princesses, till it was sanctioned by a Bishop's recommendation,—the late Dr. Ross of Exeter. Will you, then, suffer *mon amour propre*[1] to be saved by the proposal's running thus—[as we both gain in thinking your objection to the title may be well founded—]

★★★

Proposals
for Printing by Subscription,
In Six Volumes duodecimo
A NEW WORK
By
The Authour of Evelina & Cecilia.
The subscription will be one Guinea, to be paid at the time of subscribing.   &c

★★★

[omit, since you think it useless, the promise of signing.—]
[...]
    [I am very glad you concur with Mr. Lock against wire paper & Hot presses.[2] Yet surely paper & type should be good & clear & *respectable*.

    I must write directly to Charles to speak to Mr. Cadell, & to James to Mr. Payne, to settle about raising subscriptions, as the Proposals cannot be printed till that is settled. And in truth the case is already far too far advanced, for wasting time. [xxx] I suppose my Mother will question Rob[in]son. I hear the Bookseller's profits for the subscription are 10 per cent. To this of course, we agree.]

    Mrs. Crewe does the Work & its Authour much honour by offering to take a Book,—indeed I am sensibly flattered by her kindness. Mrs. Lock—will keep one, of course; &, Miss Cambridge answers for Mrs. Boscawen. Mrs. Montagu, I fancy, may also be counted.[3] To such Characters I shall be happy to owe obliga-

---

1   My self-respect.
2   Used in the production of the most expensive, high quality books.
3   The ladies undertook to solicit subscriptions from their acquaintance, collect the money, and keep accounts of the transactions.

tion....& can more be said by *Hermits*, who would prefer all difficulties, to a debt of gratitude not highly seasoned with esteem & regard?

[...]

156.   FRANCES BURNEY D'ARBLAY TO
         MARY PORT WADDINGTON
         19 June 1795, Great Bookham

[...]
I have a long Work which a long time has been in hand, that I mean to publish soon—in about a year.—Should it succeed like Evelina & Cecilia, it may be a little portion to our Bambino—we wish, therefore, to print it for ourselves, in this hope: but the expences of the Press are *so* enormous, so raised by these late Acts to be tremendous,[1] that is out of all question for us to afford it. We have therefore been led, by degrees, to listen to counsel of some friends, & to print it by subscription. This is in many—MANY ways unpleasant & unpalatable to us both—but the real chance of real use & benefit to our little darling overcomes all scruples, & therefore—to work we go!....You will feel, I dare believe, all I could write on this subject,—I once *rejected* such a plan, formed for me by Mr. Burke, where Books were to be kept for me by Ladies, not Booksellers,—the Duchess of Devonshire, Mrs. Boscawen, & Mrs. Crewe—but I was an Individual then, & had no cares of *Times to come*—now,—Thank Heaven! this is not the case,—&, when I look at my little Boy—who is very sweet—I assure you *seriously*—! when I look at his dear innocent, yet intelligent Face, I defy any pursuit to be painful that may lead to his good.— [...]

157. FRANCES BURNEY D'ARBLAY TO DR. CHARLES BURNEY
         6 July 1795, Norbury Park

[...]
Now as to the NEW WORK—my dearest Father, I am most happy to let you into my secret, for I see it will be a *concord*; it *is* of the same species as Evelina & Cecilia: new *modified*, in being more

---

1 Pitt's Stamp Act of 23 April 1795 placed a heavy duty on paper, increasing printing expenses and incidentally serving as an indirect censorship of the press.

multifarious in the Characters it brings into action,—but all *wove* into *one*, with a one *Heroine* shining conspicuous through the Group, & that in what Mr. Twining so flatteringly calls *the prose Epic style*, for so far is the Work from consisting of detached stories, that There is not, literally, one Episode in the whole plan, [my Dear Sir, which you may make as public as you please, though I would rather you would keep to yourself all you can of detail. Should you like to see any more mss before it is finished? If so, I will prepare against Susan's return from our ½ first Book—& 2 half books] [xxx]

[...]

I will make my Work the best I can, my dearest Father. I will neither be indolent, nor negligent, nor avaricious. I can never half answer the expectations that seem excited! I must try to forget them, or I shall be in a continual quivering. [...]

[*FBA attempted to tender her work to the major booksellers in London, in order to get the lowest possible price for production costs, but her plan proved untenable. JB's wife, Sarah Payne Burney, took offence that her brother Thomas Payne the younger (who had inherited his father's bookselling business) was not given priority in the negotiation. CB worried that playing the booksellers off against one another would antagonize powerful men within the trade. Eventually, the booksellers Payne, Cadell, and Davies formed an association to negotiate for the novel, thwarting FBA's hopes of establishing a competition between them.*]

158.   FRANCES BURNEY D'ARBLAY &
     ALEXANDRE D'ARBLAY TO CHARLES BURNEY JR.
              7 July 1795, Great Bookham

[*By FBA*]
How completely unfortunate, my dearest Charles, that you were too much hurried to *undertake me* when I addressed you, which was when *all* was open for counsel & assistance!—yours came so late, we were fearful to disoblige All that had preceded—& now—that you are so kindly willing to *auctioneer* for us, we receive Letters to assure us such a step will breed absolute *family dissention!*— This is hard, & strange!—I thought my *Brain* work as much fair & individual property, as any other possession in either art or nature: but we cannot resolve upon offending the Paynes—upon hurting James—upon bringing discomfort upon our darling & already so

unhappy Suzanna![1]—I need say no more to your affectionate & brotherly Heart—. We prefer all disadvantages to this danger.

Were it *not* so, those who first offered now coalesce, to *prevent* competition!!!—but were it *not* so, I would entreat you to *make a round* of enquiry, before you struck your Hammer, that might render the coalition immaterial.

We are terribly chagrined—but must do the matter with the best grace we can assume, since our objects & rewards are 2 persons so dear to us, & the avoiding risking their peace with their connexions.—I beg earnestly you will write immediately, to say you have received this. My Father prefers our closing with Mr. P[ayne].

God bless you my dear Brother. We shall always repine this business was not in your Hands exclusively from the beginning. [...]

P.S. My dearest Charles don't let our *sensations* thus frankly avowed be further spread than to yourself, or the sacrifice we make will answer no purpose

[*CBjr eventually succeeded in negotiating a deal with the association of Payne, Cadell and Davies. The exclusion of G.G. and J. Robinson annoyed CB as the latter was his friend and publisher of CB's own works.*]

159.   FRANCES BURNEY D'ARBLAY WITH
        ALEXANDRE D'ARBLAY TO CHARLES BURNEY JR.
            15 July 1795, Great Bookham

[...]
I must now Answer your queries about the Work itself.

It is to all intents & purposes a Novel,—but I annex so merely to that title, in a general sense, a staring Love Story, that I hate so to call it.—However, the words at the opening of this page leave You to do as you will. The Name of my Heroine is Ariella.[2] I had meant to burst it forth upon the Public in a blaze at the end,—but here, also,—as above.

If you will give a Title, I should chuse, YOUTH, or ARIELLA.

This is no more *un*straighway than the two *ors* to Cecilia, & Evelina, of *or* Memoirs of an Heiress, & *or* A young lady's Entrance into life.

---

1 SBP's marriage to Molesworth Phillips was breaking down.
2 Formerly Betulia, later changed to Camilla.

[...]

I entreat, with whomsoever you deal, you will enquire whether it will be *better* or *worse* to curtail the Work. If we print ultimately for ourselves, according to our original plan, we always meant to make 4 *Udolphoish* volumes,[1] & reprint the Edition that succeeds the subscription in 6 volumes duod^{mo}. common, for a raised price.

The *Work* will be better for *not* being lopped, as it's materials are fertile, & I must otherwise cut off short some purposes now very principle in my perspective.

[...]

160. FRANCES BURNEY D'ARBLAY TO DR. CHARLES BURNEY
21 July 1795, Great Bookham

[...]

[I have just received a message from Mrs. Boscawen, that she has now more cash in her House belonging to me than she chuses to keep there in these bad times!—£60!—Is it not interesting?

But,—she declares she will deliver her Cash & her List only *to Dr. Burney!*—

So, my dearest Father, I hope, as that is a challenge not very unflattering to *insist* on a visit from you, you will not be cruel,— Pray let us know what I must say?]

I had heard of such uncommon exertions from her, & of her principal Agent, Miss Cambridge, that I had written to beseech not to have my Book a *burthen*, & that the *name*, & honour of such a Book keeper, was all I desired; Miss Cambridge writ me for answer—

"Mrs. Boscawen laughs at the notion of *her* & *I* sitting with our hands before us upon such a business.—She says she will not *accept* such a sinecure, though you so graciously offer it.—"

Indeed, she has proved her words.

Her Daughter, the Duchess of Beaufort, has just sent her in a list of Nine Dukes & Duchesses!—where in the World can she have ferretted out nine such who would subscribe?

[But can we not learn of the advertisement in any newspaper? It seems only known where spread by *our Book keepers*.]

How grieved I am you do not like my Name!²—the *prettiest in*

---

1 Ann Radcliffe's *Mysteries of Udolpho* (1794) was printed in four unusually long volumes (See JL 3:126n.).

2 FBA adds a note, "the Name, then, was *Ariella*. changed afterwards to *Camilla*."

Nature! I remember how many people did not like Evelina, & called it *affected & Missish*, till they read the Book,—& then they got accustomed in a few pages, & afterwards it was much approved. I must leave it for the present untouched, for the force of the name attached by the idea of the Character, in the author's mind, is such, that I should not know how to sustain it by any other for a long while. In Cecilia & Evelina 'twas the same: the Names of all the personages annexed with me all the ideas I put in motion with them. The Work is so far advanced, that the personages are all, to me, as so many actual acquaintances, whose memoirs & opinions I am committing to *paper*.

[...]

1796

161. FRANCES BURNEY D'ARBLAY TO ALEXANDRE D'ARBLAY[1]
3 February 1796, Great Bookham

[...]
Yesterday I wrote 14 Pages! & $^1/_2$. I won't tell you how late I sat up. You were very good to exact no promises. Come back, & keep me in better order.—

I long for to-morrow's post.

I am very careful of myself, I assure you, except in the one article of writing late—but—it is so delicious to stride on, when *en verf!*

Yet we played a full Hour at Where's My Baby? Where's My Baby?—

[...]
[Camilla *was published on 12 July 1796.*]

162. FRANCES BURNEY D'ARBLAY TO DR. CHARLES BURNEY
WINDSORIANA PART II
5-6 July 1796, Windsor

[...]
[*At Windsor, FBA presented specially-bound copies of* Camilla *to the King and Queen.*]
This led to a little discourse upon the business, in which the King's countenance seemed to speak a benign interest; & the Queen then

---

1 ADA was staying with JB in London.

said "This Book was begun *here*, Sir." which already I had mentioned.

"And what did you write of it here? he cried;—how far did you go?—did you finish any part? or only form the— —skeleton?"

Just that, Sir; I answered; the skeleton was formed here, but nothing was completed. I worked it up in my little Cottage."

"And about what time did you give to it?"

"*All* my time, sir!—from the period I planned publishing it, I devoted myself to it wholly;—I had no Episode—but a little baby!—My subject grew upon me, & encreased my materials to a bulk—that, I am afraid, will be still more laborious to wade through for the Readers, than the Writer!—"

[...]

163.   FRANCES BURNEY D'ARBLAY TO DR. CHARLES BURNEY
WINDSORIANA PART IV
6 July 1796, Windsor

[...]
[*FBA discusses the novel with the Princesses Mary, Sophia and Amelia.*]
"There have been so many *bad* books published of that sort, said Princess Mary, that every body should be glad of a good one." "Yes, said Princess Sophia, & the Writers are all turned Democrats, they say."

I now explained that *Politics* were, *all ways*, left out: that once I had had an idea of bringing in such as suited *me*,—but that, upon second thoughts, I returned to my more native opinion they were not a *feminine* subject for discussion, & that I even believed, should the little work sufficiently succeed to be at all generally read, it would be a better office to general Readers to carry them wide of all politics, to their domestic fire sides, than to open new matter of endless debate.

[...]

164.   DR. CHARLES BURNEY TO CHARLES BURNEY JR.
3 August 1796, Chelsea

[*CB relates reaction of his publisher Robinson to* Camilla.]
It was always my opinion, that if Robinson had no share in Camilla, he w^d. be a formidable enemy to her & her mother. I had, a few days ago the mortification to find that my apprehensions were but too well founded. Calling in Pater-noster Row on other business,

when Camilla was mentioned, R. was frank enough to tell me, that "there was but one opinion about it—M^{rs}. d'Arblay was determined to fill 5 Volumes—& had done it in such a manner as w^d. do her no credit—He had seen the critical reviewers that morning, & they did not like it—"they had said that the book w^d. be praised in the M[onthly]. Review by D^r. Charles B.— & that's all the praise it w^d. get."—I bounced a little—& s^d. if they (the crit. R——s abused it, They w^d. disgrace themselves more than the work—that so far from wanting materials to fill the 4 Vol^s. she promised in her proposals, she was obliged to make her subscribers a present of a huge 5th.Vol. to wch. they had no title—and so far from being inferior to her 2 former Novels wch. had been so favourably rec^d., & gone through so many editions, if I was not superannuated & totally ignorant of my own language, and unable to judge of thought & style, this was far superior to both; & contained, besides the merit of the fable & Characters, innumerable new & deep reflexions wch. no other novel that had ever come to my knowledge c^d. boast. It w^d. be cruel if a work of such intrinsic merit were to be stigmatized & blasted merely because M^r. R. is not proprieter of the Copy-right. He has now the Crit. R. so entirely under his own management & direction, that every work is abused or^1 according to his fiat. It seems as if something sh^d. be done to prevent or counteract this impending mischief. You know [Chatham], one of Robinson's reviewers & advisers—He has spoke well of the book to the younger T. Payne—But I fear Godwin has spoken of it to R. in the manner he mentioned to me, if not his own invention. The work if it has fair play must do credit, not only to Fanny, but to us all—I never felt so zealous for the defence of any of her writings; but I see nothing I can do in the present Case, except to put you, James, & T. Payne on your guard.—Griff (Jemm says) whose family is reading & full of the book, is perfectly well disposed—I wish you w^d. draw up an Article for the M.R.—The Crit. R——s will give you the credit of it by whomever & in whatever manner it is done—& it w^d. be a worthy action that you will long think of with pleasure, to preserve & augment the fame of such a Sister, & such a work. Griff, if you give him a hint before it is put into other hands, will, I dare say gladly accept your offer.—I w^d. not recommend to you such

---

1 A word is missing at this point in the manuscript.

a task, if not stimulated by the peculiar intrinsic merit of the work.[1]

[...]

[*Reviews of* Camilla *began to appear in August.*]

165. [MARY WOLLSTONECRAFT][2] THE ANALYTICAL REVIEW
August 1796

THE celebrity which miss Burney has so deservedly acquired by her two former novels, naturally roused the expectation of the public for the promised production of madame d'Arblay.

A mind like hers could not be supposed to stand still, and new combinations of character are continually ripening to court the fickle.

As a whole, we are in justice bound to say, that we think it inferiour to the first-fruits of her talents, though we boldly assert, that Camilla contains parts superiour to any thing she has yet produced.

In her former works dramatical exhibitions of manners of the comic cast certainly excel the displays of passion; and the remark may with still more propriety be applied to the volumes before us.

The incidents, which are to mark out the errours of youth, are frequently only perplexities, forcibly brought forward merely to be disentangled; yet, there are many amusing, and some interesting incidents, though they have not a plot of sufficient importance to bind them together.

The illustrating sentiments are often excellent, and expressed with great delicacy, evincing the sagacity and rectitude of the author's mind, reflecting equal credit on her heart and understanding. In the style, it is true, there are some indications of haste; but it would be almost invidious to point them out, when so large a proportion is written so well.

[...]

---

1 CBjr frequently wrote for the *Monthly Review*, but it seems that either he or Ralph Griffiths, the editor, resisted CB's plan to have CBjr write the review of *Camilla*, and the task was given to William Enfield. Hemlow discusses this letter in *JL* 3: 368.

2 The miscellaneous writer and radical feminist, best known for her *Vindication of the Rights of Women* (1792).

[...]

In the present work, Mrs. D'Arblay, (formerly known as Miss Burney,) with equal judgment and modesty, pursues the track in which she has already acquired so much deserved reputation; without suffering herself to be diverted from her native bent by an affectation of excelling in different kinds of writing, and without catching the infection of that taste for the marvellous and the terrible, which, since the appearance of her former productions, has, with some writers, become the fashion of the day. [...]

Such a command of the language of character, as appears through all Mrs. D'Arblay's novels, is an excellence which affords ample compensation for occasional negligences. Yet we cannot but regret that a work of such uncommon merit, and so elaborate in its object and extent, was suffered to make its appearance, before it passed under the correction of some friend, who might have saved us the pain of noticing the following verbal and grammatical inaccuracies:—*Scarce* for *scarcely*, in almost every page.—"*Nor* have I *no* great disposition," &c.—"A man and horse *was* sent off."—"An *admirable* good joke."—"Has *strove*."—"Was it *me* that fled?"—"Not *equally* adroit *as* Henry."—"*Almost nothing*," for *scarcely any thing*; a Scotticism.—"The owner of the horse *laid* dead."—"One of the horses *laid* dead."—"She *laid* down in her cloaths"—"Where *laid* the blame?"—"Desirous to know *if*"—for *whether*; an inelegant expression which every where occurs. [...]

[*The final paragraph of the review was written by Ralph Griffiths.*]

The great merit of the work, however, consists in more important characteristics; and we may principally recommend it to the world as a *warning* "picture of youth;"—as a guide for the conduct of young females in the most important circumstances and situations of life. In this view, the truly *Reverend* Mr. Tyrold's *Sermon*, addressed to his daughter Camilla, deserves marked commendation: but were it not, as it is, too long for us to copy, we should think it scarcely fair to detach so large and lustrous a brilliant; and to break it into pieces would indeed be *diminishing* its value.

167. FRANCES BURNEY D'ARBLAY TO DR. CHARLES BURNEY
14 October 1796, Great Bookham

[...]

But I meant to have begun with our thanks for my dear kind Father's indulgence of our extreme curiosity & interest in the sight of the Reviews. I am quite happy in what I have escaped of greater severity, though my Mate cannot bear that the palm should be contested by Evelina & Cecilia, his partiality rates the *last* as so much the highest. So does the News paper I have mentioned, of which I long to send you a Copy. But those immense men whose single praise was Fame & Security, who established, by a Word, the two elder sisters, are now silent—Dr. Johnson & Sir Joshua are no more—& Mr. Burke is ill, or otherwise engrossed. Yet,—even without their powerful influence, to which I owe such unspeakable obligation, the *essential* success of Camilla *exceeds* that of the Elders:[1] the sale is truly astonishing,—Charles has just sent to me that 500 only remain of 4000!—& it has appeared barely 3 Months!—

The first Edition of Evelina was of 800.[2]—The second of 500— & the 3ᵈ. of 1000.—What the following have been I have never heard. The sale from that period became more flourishing than the generous Publisher cared to announce. Of Cecilia the first Edition was reckoned *enormous* at 2000.—& as a part of payment was reserved for it, I remember our dear Daddy Crisp thought it very *unfair*. It was printed, like this, in July, & sold in October,—to every one's wonder. Here, however, the Sale is encreased in rapidity more than a third. Charles says

Now heed no more what Critics thought 'em
Since this you know—All People bought 'em.—

[...]

---

1 FBA realized around £1000 from the subscription, and later sold the copyright of the work for another £1000.
2 Lowndes, in a letter dated 27 January 1779, puts the first edition at 500.

168. FRANCES BURNEY D'ARBLAY TO DR. CHARLES BURNEY
8 November 1796, Great Bookham

[*On 2 November CB wrote to FBA expressing his anger at the criticisms of* Camilla *in the* Monthly Review.]
I had intended writing to my dearest Father by a *return of Goods*; but I find it impossible to defer the overflowings of my Heart at his most kind & generous indignation with the Reviewer. What Censure can ever so much hurt as such compensation can heal? And, in fact, the praise is so strong, that, were it neatly put together, the writer might challenge my best Enthusiasts to find it insufficient the truth, however, is, that the criticisms come forward, & the panegyric is entangled, & so blended with blame, as to lose almost all effect. What of *verbal* criticisms are fair, I shall certainly & gladly attend to in the second edition: but most of them are of another class, & mark a *desire* to find them that astonishes me; for I have no consciousness of any enemy, & yet only to enmity can attribute the possibility of supposing "A man & Horse *was* sent off—" could be other than an error of the press. A Chambermaid, *now adays*, would have written *were.* "An *admirable* good joke," also, is the cant of Clermont, not of the Author; who might as well be accountable for the slip slops of Dubster. "*Nor* have I *no* great disposition"—must be an *invention*, I should think. Certainly I never wrote it, whether it be in the Book or not. I had not time for an errata—which might, methinks, have been observed, in some candid supposition that, otherwise, a few of the verbal errours might have been corrected.[1]

The Reviews, however, as they have not *made*, will not, I trust, *mar* me. Evelina made its way all by itself: it was well spoken of, indeed, in all the Reviews, compared with general Novels; but it was undistinguished by any quotation, & only put in the Monthly Catalogue, & only allowed a short single paragraph. It was circulated only by the general public, till it reached through that unbiassed medium, Dr. Johnson—and thence it wanted no patron. This circumstance made me easy about Cecilia, which, however, was extremely well treated, though not by them, but by Mr Burke brought forward to the high station its supporters have claimed for

---

1   Hemlow notes that FBA's attribution of the errors to the printers will not stand investigation, for a number of the errors can be seen, uncorrected, in the ms. of the novel (*JL*, 3: 221-22n.).

it. Camilla, also, will live or die by more general means. Works of this kind are judged always by the *many*: works of science, History & philosophy & voyages & travels, & poetry, frequently owe their fate to the sentiments of the first Critics who brand or extol them.

Miss Cambridge asked me, early, if I should not take some care about the Reviews? No, I said, none. There are two species of Composition which may nearly brave them; Politics & Novels: for these will be sought & will be judged by the various Multitude, not the fastidious few. With the latter, indeed, they may be Aided, or injured, by Criticism; but it will not stop their being read, though it may prejudice their Readers. They want no Recommendation for being handed about but that of being new, & they frequently become established, or sink into oblivion, before that high Literary Tribunal has brought them to a trial. She laughed at my composure; but, though I am a good deal chagrined, it is not broken. If I had begun by such a perusal, I might indeed have been disturbed: but it has succeeded to so much solace & encouragement, that it cannot penetrate deeply. [...]

1797

169. FRANCES BURNEY D'ARBLAY TO DR. CHARLES BURNEY
26 February 1797, Great Bookham

[*FBA responds to CB's proposal that she contribute to Mrs. Crewe's scheme for a new anti-Jacobin periodical.*]
I hardly know whether I am most struck with the fertility of the ideas Mrs. Crewe has started, or most gratified by their direction: certainly I am flattered where most susceptible of pleasure when a mind such as her's would call me forth from my retirement to second views so important in their ends, & demanding such powers in their progress. But though her opinion would give me *courage*, it cannot give me *means*: I am too far removed from the scene of public life to compose any thing of public utility in the style she indicates. The "manners as they rise,"[1] the morals, or their deficiencies, as they preponderate, should be viewed, for such a

---

1 Cf. Pope, "An Essay on Man," Epistle 1. 14.

scheme, in all their variations, with a diurnal Eye: For though it may not be necessary this *Gentleman-Author*[1] should be a frequenter himself of public places, he must be sufficiently in the midst of public people to judge the justice of what is communicated to him by his correspondents. The Plan is so excellent it ought to be well adopted, & *really* fulfilled. Many circumstances would render its accomplishment nearly impossible for *me*;—wholly to omit politics would mar all the original design;—yet what would be listened to unabused, by a writer who is honoured by a testimony such as mine of having resigned royal service without resigning royal favour? Personal abuse would make a dreadful breach into the peace of my happiness—though censure of my works I can endure with tolerable firmness: the latter I submit to as the public right, by prescription; the former I think authorised by no right, & recoil from with mingled fear & indignation. I could mention other embarrassments as to politics—but they will probably occur to you, though they may escape Mrs. Crewe, who is not so well versed in the history & strong character of M. d'Arblay[2] [...]

170.   FRANCES BURNEY D'ARBLAY TO
            MARY PORT WADDINGTON
            2 June 1797, Great Bookham

[...]
[*FBA responds to MPW's complaint about the inequality of their correspondence.*]
And now—what shall I tell you?—you ask me *What information any of my late Letters have given you, except of my health & affection?*—None, I confess!—yet they are such as all my other friends have borne with, since my writing weariness has seized me, & such as I still, & upon equally *shabby morsels of paper*, continue to give them.
[...]
    It appears to me—perhaps wrongly—you have wrought yourself into a fit of fancied resentment against a succession of *short* Letters, which could only have been merited by Letters that were *unfriendly*. You forget, meanwhile, the numerous Letters, I have, at various epochs, received from yourself not merely of half pages, but

---

1   The character of Sir Hugh Tyrold, which Mrs. Crewe suggested FBA
    assume in her editorial capacity.
2   A reference to ADA's constitutionalist politics.

of literally three lines—& you forget them, because they were never received with reproach, nor answered with coldness. By me they were equally valued with the longest, though they gave me not equal entertainment, for I prized them as marks of *affection*, & I required them as *bulletins* of Health. Entertainment, or Information, I never considered as a basis of correspondence, though no one, you may believe, can more delight to meet with them. The basis of Letters, as of Friendship, must be *Kindness*, which does not count lines & words, but expressions & meaning, which is indulgent to brevity, puts a favourable construction upon silence, grants full liberty to inclination, & makes every allowance for convenience. Punctuality with respect to writing is a quality in which I know myself deficient,—but which, also, I have to no one ever promised. To Two persons, only, I have practiced it, my Father & my sister Phillips—there is a third whose claims are still higher; but uninterrupted intercourse has spared all trial to my exactness: my other friends, however near, & however tender, have all accepted my *Letters* like *myself* for better & for worse, &, finding my Heart unalterable, have left my Pen to its own propensities.

Nor am I quite aware what species of "information" you repine at not receiving. An *elaborate composition*, written for admiration, & calculated to be exhibited to strangers, I should not be more the last to write, than you—quick & penetrating to whatever is ridiculous—would be the first to deride & despise: a *gay & amusing rattle* you must be sensible can flow only from the humour of the moment, which an idea of raised expectations represses rather than promotes: a *communication of private affairs*— — — — —no,—the very Letter which produced this complaint contained a statement of personal concerns the most important I have had to write since my marriage:— —[1]

From all this, which reluctantly, though openly, I have written, you will deduct That while you think me unkind (as I apprehend) I think you unjust.

[...]

---

1 Details of Alexander's inoculation for smallpox.

1798

171.   FRANCES BURNEY D'ARBLAY TO
                  CHARLOTTE BURNEY FRANCIS BROOME
                      3 April 1798, West Humble

[...]
[*FBA describes a visit to London.*]
And I went to 6 plays from Chelsea, The Belle's Stratagem—The
Castle Spectre—He's much to blame—Cheap Living—Secrets
worth knowing—& the Heir at Law.[1] The two last by *royal favour*,
in my old place. After my long abstinence from the Theatre, this
was pretty full fare. We are both very fond of Plays & Operas, &
very indifferent to all other public places. [...]

1799

172.   FRANCES BURNEY D'ARBLAY TO
                      SUSAN BURNEY PHILLIPS
                      14 April 1799, West Humble

[...]
I am just now applied to, at last, for my preparations for a 2^d. Edition of Camilla: & I am engaged almost day & night in a revision.
You will believe how entirely, when I tell you it has confined me
from making a visit to Norbury Park, though this is the last week
before the London Journey, which for 6 will separate us. But the
Work is so long, & the people, waiting to the last moment for the
application, are now in such haste, that I am obliged to relinquish
every thing for proceeding with the business. And it would be
unjust not to say I am extremely pleased with the necessity, though
not its urgency; for the times are so changed since the publication,
that the Publishers, who thought they should print the work again
in 5 Months, have been silent about it till these last 10 days: & say
the sale of all books has had a stagnation that has only been forced
by Politicks. And I had really begun to fear a 2^d. Edition would

---

1   By Hannah Cowley (1780), Matthew Lewis (1797), Thomas Holcroft
    (1798), Frederick Reynolds (1797), Thomas Morton (1798), and George
    Colman the younger (1797).

never have been demanded—which was the more alarming, as our account for advertisements, extra—Books, proposals, &c—&c has never been settled, & was to be deducted from the last payment of the Copyright, which is not due till the 2^d. Edition is printed. Besides the *honour & glory*—which I own, poor as we are, goes yet further in our anxiety, mutually, than even the more substantial pen.[1]

[...]

173.   CHARLES BURNEY JR. TO FRANCES BURNEY D'ARBLAY
30 October 1799, London

[CBjr reports the acceptance of FBA's comedy, Love and Fashion, *by Thomas Harris, manager of Covent Garden Theatre.]*
Huzza! Huzza! Huzza

M^r. H.*[arris]* admires the Table[2]—& will bring it into use, in the month of March!—

[...]

But Mr H. must see you—& state his objections to some parts.—[...]

Now, we agreed that Davis, as it stands, w^d. not suit Munden. It must be a Valet of the Old School:—a Quiz:—a sort of Humorist.—At present, He would make little of it.—With Hilaria H. is in love;—& thinks it the first female character on the English Stage:—quite drawn from Nature:—no Book, German, French, nor English, consulted: all from Nature.

He also is delighted with Fineer:—& still more with Lichburn—— Now, I will return the Table, by the Coach tonight f[rom] the Golden Cross, Charing Cross—& hope that it will reach you safely.—— Turn over these Matters in your Mind: settle when you can come to Greenwich; and let me have the Table again, one Week previous to that time; for H. to refresh his Memory.—& when you are at my House, I will contrive the Meeting between you & H. who is surprised, that you never turned your thoughts to this kind of writing before; as you appear to have really a genius for it!—There now!

[...]

---

1   The 2nd edition of *Camilla* did not appear until 1802. Edward and Lillian Bloom's edition of the novel (Oxford UP, 1972) contains a survey of FBA's extensive revisions.
2   FBA's code for *Love and Fashion.*

174.   FRANCES BURNEY D'ARBLAY TO
ESTHER BURNEY BURNEY
19 November 1799, West Humble

[...]

Your extreme contempt, Mrs. Hetty, of my dealings with low tradespeople[1] shall not dishearten me from continuing them; shall I give you a dialogue, which past previous to the delivery of the Goods, & will put you into a little hot water, for a punishment for your haughtiness? Yes, I will; but *read it alone.*—so here turn t'other side in a spare room.

Scene St. James's Street
Enter Agent & Upholsterer,[2] *meeting.*

Ag. I was just going to beat up your quarters.

Up. I am glad to save you the trouble.

Ag. I want to speak to you upon a little business. A Lady—a relation of mine—has written a play—Will you act it?

Up. A Lady?—Is it your sister?—

Ag. Suppose it is—Will you Act it?

Up. If I see nothing that seems positively against its succeeding, certainly. But..—You must let me have it.

Ag. When you please.

Up. Immediately.

Ag. It is at her hermitage. I will send for it.

Up. Do, & directly. But...have you read it?

Ag. I....I don't....know!

Up. pho,—what do you think of it?

Ag. I...don't know.—

Up. Pho,—that's worse still!

Ag. I am no judge.

Up. pshaw—

Ag. Besides—a lady—my sister—how can I speak?

Up. Well, that's true. Let me have it in two days.

Ag. All she urges is secresy. She is bent upon making the attempt unknown.

Up. And why?—A *good* play *will* succeed,—& sometimes a bad one—but if there be a circumstance, as here, that will strongly prepare the public in its favour,—why should we lose that circumstance?

---

1 A reference to the production of *Love and Fashion.*
2 CBjr and Harris.

Ag. I will speak to her about that: but be very secret meanwhile especially if you decline it, as it is then her intention to try the other house,—& it must not be blown upon.

★★★

The result of this dialogue, was sending the Goods forthwith, as soon as fair Copied, to the Upholsterer, but with reiterated charges to secresy, from a firm persuasion the chances are better *without* than *with* expectation.

Therefore, if you meet Agent, be upon your guard, as *he* will make confidents if he knows *I* have, & otherwise is perfectly compliant. [...]

1800

175. FRANCES BURNEY D'ARBLAY TO DR. CHARLES BURNEY
11 February 1800, Greenwich

[*FBA was devastated by the death of SBP on 6 January 1800. She withdrew* Love and Fashion *from production, but not before CB had worked himself into a panic at the prospect of a second theatrical venture. He was especially aggrieved by newspaper gossip columns which had reported that a comedy by FBA was in rehearsal.*]

I hasten to tell you, dearest Sir, M^r. H.[*arris*] has at length, listened to our petitions, & has returned me my poor ill fated[1]—wholly relinquishing all claim to it for this season. He has promised also to do his utmost, as far as his influence extends to keep the news papers totally silent in future. We demand therefore no contradicting paragraph as the report must needs die when the *reality* no more exists. Nobody has believed it from the beginning on account of the premature moment when it was advertised This release gives me present repose which indeed I much wanted—for to combat your—to me—unaccountable but most afflicting displeasure, in the midst of my own panics & disturbance, would have been ample punishment to me, had I been guilty of a crime in doing what I have all my life been urged to, & all my life intended, writing a Comedy. Your goodness, your kindness, your regard

---

1 I.e., FBA's comedy, *Love and Fashion.*

for my fame, I know have caused both your trepidation, which doomed me to *certain* failure, & your displeasure that I ran, what you thought, a wanton risk. But it is *not* wanton, my dearest Father. My imagination is not at my own controll, or I would always have continued in the walk you approved. The combinations for another long work did not occur to me. Incidents & effects for a Dramma did. I thought the field more than open—inviting to me. The chance held out golden dreams. The risk could be only our own for—permit me to say, appear when it will, you will find nothing in the principles, the moral, or the language that will make you blush for me. *A failure*, upon those points only, can bring DIS-GRACE—upon mere control or want of dramatic powers, it can only cause *disappointment*.

I hope, therefore, my dearest Father, in thinking this over, you will cease to nourish such terrors & disgust at an essay so natural, & rather say to yourself with an internal smile, "After all—'tis but *like Father like Child*—for to what walk do I confine myself?—She took my example in writing—She takes it in ranging—Why, then, after all, should I lock her up in one paddock, well as she has fed there, if she says she finds nothing more to nibble—while *I* find all the Earth unequal to my ambition, & mount the skies to content it?[1] Come on then, poor Fan—The World has acknowledged you my offspring—& I will *disencourage* you no more. Leap the pales of your paddock—let us pursue our career—& while you frisk from novel to Comedy, I, quitting Music & Prose, will try a race with Poetry & the Stars.

I am sure, my dear Father, will not infer, from this appeal, I mean to parallel our Works—no one more truly measures their own inferiority, which with respect to yours has always been my pride;—I only mean to shew, that if my Muse loves a little variety—She has an hereditary claim to try it.

176.   FRANCES BURNEY D'ARBLAY TO
        CHARLOTTE BURNEY FRANCIS BROOME
        22 March 1800, West Humble

It seems very long since I have had any communication with my dearest Charlotte—yet would still, I fear, be longer, were I left to the natural bent of my present feelings—which are more than ever

---

1 CB had been writing a poem on the history of astronomy.

averse to writing. The constant Journal—the never omitted memorandums of all that concerned me, which you know to have been kept up ever since I held a pen in my hand, during every absence from my earliest—darling confident—now suddenly broken off, & dissolved, has made the very action of writing laborious—painful—almost anguish to me—

[...]

[*In 1801, the Peace of Amiens was declared between Britain and France, enabling ADA to return to France, in the hopes of securing a pension for his years of military service prior to the Revolution. In order to qualify for the pension, he agreed to accompany Napoleonic forces to San Domingo (Haiti), but his services were rejected by Napoleon when ADA made it clear he would never take up arms against his wife's country. Under the conditions of his passport, ADA found himself unable to return to England for a year, and so FBA and Alexander set out to join him in Paris in April, 1802. The d'Arblays planned to stay for a year, but the outbreak of war between France and Britain in May 1803 trapped them in France for ten years. ADA took a bureaucratic job to support the family, as FBA had no access to her pension or investments in England. With the outbreak of war, correspondence between the two countries became almost impossible.*]

1812

177.   FRANCES BURNEY D'ARBLAY TO
                  ESTHER BURNEY BURNEY
                  March–June 1812, Paris

[...]

[*FBA describes her mastectomy which took place on 30 September 1811.*] About August, in the year 1810, I began to be annoyed by a small pain in my breast, which went on augmenting from week to week, yet, being rather heavy than acute, without causing me any uneasiness with respect to consequences: Alas, "*what was the ignorance!*" The most sympathising of Partners, however, was more disturbed: not a start, not a wry face, not a movement that indicated pain was unobserved, & he early conceived apprehensions to which I was a stranger. He pressed me to see some Surgeon; I revolted from the idea, & hoped, by care & warmth, to make all succour unnecessary. Thus passed some months, during which Madame de Maisonneuve, my particularly intimate friend, joined with M. d'Arblay to press me to consent to an examination. I thought their fears groundless, and could not make so great a conquest over my repugnance. I relate this false confidence, now, as a warning to my dear Esther—my Sisters & Nieces, should any similar sensations excite similar alarm. [...] [*FBA consented to see a celebrated surgeon, M. Dubois.*] It was now I began to perceive my real danger. M. Dubois gave me a prescription to be pursued for a month, during which time he could not undertake to see me again, & pronounced nothing—but uttered so many charges to me to be tranquil, & to suffer no uneasiness, that I could not but suspect there was room for terrible inquietude. My alarm was encreased by the non-appearance of M. d'A. after his departure. They had remained together some time in the Book room, & M. d'A. did not return—till, unable to bear the suspence, I begged him to come back. He, also, sought then to tranquilize me—but in words only; his looks were shocking! his features, his whole face displayed the bitterest woe. I had not, therefore, much difficulty in telling myself what he endeavoured not to tell me—that a small operation would be necessary to avert evil consequences!—Ah, my dearest Esther, for this I felt no courage—my dread & repugnance, from a thousand reasons *besides* the pain, almost shook all my faculties, &, for some time, I was rather confounded & stupified than affrighted.—Direful, however, was the effect of this interview; the pains became quicker & more violent, & the hardness of the spot affected encreased. I took, but vainly, my proscription, & every symtom grew more serious. At this time, M. de Narbonne spoke to M. d'A. of a Surgeon of great eminence, M. Larrey, who had cured a polonoise lady of his acquaintance of a similar malady; &, as my horror of an operation was insuperable, M. de N.[*arbonne*] strongly recommended that I should have recourse to M. Larrey. [...] [*FBA describes the combined efforts of several doctors, whose medicinal treatments produced no effect.*] [...] A formal consultation now was held, of Larrey, Ribe, & Moreau[1]..&, in fine, I was formally condemned to an operation by all Three. I was as much astonished as disappointed—for the poor breast was no where discoloured, & not much larger than its healthy neighbour. Yet I felt the evil to be deep, so deep, that I often thought if it could not be dissolved, it could only with life be extir-

---

1 See *JL* 6: 599n., 600n., 601n., 603n., 608n. for the careers of FBA's doctors.

pated. I called up, however, all the reason I possessed, or could assume, & told them that—if they saw no other alternative, I would not resist their opinion & experience:—the good Dr. Larrey, who, during his long attendance, had conceived for me the warmest friendship, had now tears in his Eyes; from my dread he had expected resistance. [...]

All hope of escaping this evil being now at an end, I could only console or employ my Mind in considering how to render it less dreadful to M. d'A. M. Dubois had pronounced "il faut s'attendre à souffrir, Je ne veux pas vous trompez—Vous souffrirez—vous souffrirez *beaucoup!*—"[1] M. Ribe had *charged* me to cry! to withhold or restrain myself might have seriously bad consequences, he said. M. Moreau, in ecchoing this injunction, enquired whether I had cried or screamed at the birth of Alexander—Alas, I told him, it had not been possible to do otherwise; Oh then, he answered, there is no fear!— —What terrible inferences were here to be drawn! I desired, therefore, that M. d'A. might be kept in ignorance of the day till the operation should be over. To this they agreed, except M. Larrey, with high approbation: M. Larrey looked dissentient, but was silent. M. Dubois protested he would not undertake to act, after what he had seen of the agitated spirits of M. d'A. if he were present: nor would he suffer me to know the time myself over night; I obtained with difficulty a promise of 4 hours warning, which were essential to me for sundry regulations.

From this time, I assumed the best spirits in my power, *to meet the coming blow;*—& support my too sympathising Partner. They would let me make no preparations, refusing to inform me what would be necessary; I have known, since, that Mad^e. de Tessé, an admirable old friend of M. d'A, now mine, equally, & one of the first of her sex, in any country, for uncommon abilities, & nearly universal knowledge, had insisted upon sending all that might be necessary, & of keeping me in ignorance. M. d'A filled a Closet with Charpie,[2] compresses, & bandages—All that to *me* was owned, as wanting, was an arm Chair & some Towels.—Many things, however, joined to the depth of my pains, assured me the business was not without danger. I therefore made my Will— [...]

---

1 "Suffering is to be expected, I don't want to deceive you—you will suffer—you will suffer a great deal!"
2 Unravelled linen used for surgical dressings.

[...] One morning—the last of September, 1811, [...] another Letter was delivered to me—another, indeed!— 'twas from M. Larrey, to acquaint me that at 10 o'clock he should be with me, properly accompanied, & to exhort me to rely as much upon his sensibility & his prudence, as upon his dexterity & his experience; he charged to secure the absence of M. d'A: & told me that the young Physician who would deliver me this *announce*, would prepare for the operation, in which he must lend his aid: & also that it had been the decision of the consultation to allow me but two hours notice.—Judge, my Esther, if I read this unmoved!— [...] sundry necessary works & orders filled up my time entirely till One O'Clock, when all was ready...but Dr. Moreau then arrived, with news that M. Dubois could not attend till three. Dr. Aumont went away—& the Coast was clear. This, indeed, was a dreadful interval. I had no longer any thing to do—I had only to think—Two Hours thus spent seemed never-ending. I would fain have written to my dearest Father—to You, my Esther—to Charlotte James— Charles—Amelia Lock—but my arm prohibited me: I strolled to the Sallon—I saw it filled with preparations, & I recoiled.—But I soon returned; to what effect disguise from myself what I must so soon know?—yet the sight of the immense quantity of bandages, compresses, spunges, Lint— —Made me a little sick:—I walked backwards & forwards till I quieted all emotion, & became, by degrees, nearly stupid—torpid, without sentiment or consciousness;—& thus I remained till the Clock struck three. A sudden spirit of exertion then returned,—I defied my poor arm, no longer worth sparing, & took my long banished pen to write a few words to M. d'A—& a few more for Alex, in case of a fatal result. These short billets I could only deposit safely, when the Cabriolets— one—two—three—four—succeeded rapidly to each other in stopping at the door. Dr. Moreau instantly entered my room, to see if I were alive. He gave me a wine cordial, & went to the Sallon. I rang for my Maid & Nurses,—but before I could speak to them, my room, without previous message, was entered by 7 Men in black, Dr. Larry, M. Dubois, Dr. Moreau, Dr. Aumont, Dr. Ribe, & a pupil of Dr. Larry, & another of M. Dubois. I was now awakened from my stupor—& by a sort of indignation—Why so many? & without leave?—But I could not utter a syllable. M. Dubois acted as Commander in Chief. Dr Larry kept out of sight; M. Dubois ordered a Bed stead into the middle of the room. Astonished, I turned to Dr. Larry, who had promised that an Arm Chair would suffice; but he hung his head, & would not look at me. Two *old mattrasses* M. Dubois then demanded, & an old Sheet. I now began to tremble violently, more with distaste & horrour of the preparations even than of the pain. These arranged to his liking, he desired me to mount the Bed stead. I stood suspended, for a moment, whether I should not abruptly escape—I looked at the door, the windows—I felt desperate—but it was only for a moment, my reason then took the command, & my fears & feelings struggled vainly against it. I called to my maid—she was crying, & the two Nurses stood, trasfixed, at the door. Let those women all go! cried M. Dubois. This order recovered me my Voice—No, I cried, let them stay! *qu'elles restent!* This occasioned a little dispute, that re-animated me—The Maid, however, & one of the nurses ran off—I charged the other to approach, & she obeyed. M. Dubois now tried to issue his commands *en militaire*, but I resisted all that were resistable—I was compelled, however, to submit to taking off my long robe de Chambre, which I had meant to retain—Ah, then, how did I think of my Sisters!—not one, at so dreadful an instant, at hand, to protect—adjust—guard me—I regretted that I had refused M^e. de Maisonneuve—M^e. Chastel—no one upon whom I could rely—my departed Angel![1]—how did I think of her! — how did I long—long for my Esther—my Charlotte!—My distress was, I suppose, apparent, though not my Wishes, for M. Dubois himself now softened, & spoke soothingly. Can *You*, I cried, feel for an operation that, to *You*, must seem so trivial?—Trivial? he repeated—taking up a bit of paper, which he tore, unconsciously, into a million of pieces, *oui—c'est peu de chose—mais—*"[2] he stammered, & could not go on. No one else attempted to speak, but I was softened myself, when I saw even M. Dubois grow agitated, while Dr. Larry kept always aloof, yet a glance shewed me he was pale as ashes. I knew not, positively, then, the immediate danger, but every thing convinced me danger was hovering about me, & that this experiment alone could save me from its jaws. I mounted, therefore, unbidden, the Bedstead—& M. Dubois placed me upon the Mattress, & spread a cambric handkerchief upon my face. It was transparent, however, & I saw, through it, that the Bed stead was instantly surrounded by the 7 men & my nurse. I refused to be held; but when, Bright through the cambric, I saw the glitter of polished Steel—I closed my Eyes. I would not trust to convulsive

---

1 SBP.
2 "Yes—it's no great matter—but—"

fear the sight of the terrible incision. A silence the most profound ensued, which lasted for some minutes, during which, I imagine, they took their orders by signs, & made their examination—Oh what a horrible suspension!—I did not breathe—& M. Dubois tried vainly to find any pulse. This pause, at length, was broken by Dr. Larry, who, in a voice of solemn melancholy, said "Qui me tiendra ce sein?—"[1]

No one answered; at least not verbally; but this aroused me from my passively submissive state, for I feared they imagined the whole breast infected— —feared it too justly,—for, again through the Cambric, I saw the hand of M. Dubois held up, while his fore finger first described a straight line from top to bottom of the breast, secondly a Cross, & thirdly a circle; intimating that the Whole was to be taken off. Excited by this idea, I started up, threw off my veil, &, in answer to the demand "Qui me tiendra ce sein,?" cried "C'est moi, Monsieur!" & I held My hand under it, & explained the nature of my sufferings, which all sprang from one point, though they darted into every part. I was heard attentively, but in utter silence, & M. Dubois then re-placed me as before, &, as before, spread my veil over my face. How vain, alas, my representation! immediately again I saw the fatal finger describe the Cross—& the circle—Hopeless, then, desperate, & self-given up, I closed once more my Eyes, relinquishing all watching, all resistance, all interference, & sadly resolute to be wholly resigned.

My dearest Esther,—& all my dears to whom she communicates this doleful ditty, will rejoice to hear that this resolution once taken, was firmly adhered to, in defiance of a terror that surpasses all description, & the most torturing pain. Yet—when the dreadful steel was plunged into the breast—cutting through veins—arteries—flesh—nerves—I needed no injunctions not to restrain my cries. I began a scream that lasted unintermittingly during the whole time of the incision—& I almost marvel that it rings not in my Ears still! so excruciating was the agony. When the wound was made, & the instrument was withdrawn, the pain seemed undiminished, for the air that suddenly rushed into those delicate parts felt like a mass of minute but sharp & forked poniards, that were tearing the edges of the wound—but when again I felt the instrument—describing a curve—cutting against the grain, if I may so say, while the flesh resisted in a manner so forcible as to oppose &

---

1 "Who will hold the breast for me?"

tire the hand of the operator, who was forced to change from the right to the left—then, indeed, I thought I must have expired. I attempted no more to open my Eyes,—they felt as if hermettically shut, & so firmly closed, that the Eyelids seemed indented into the Cheeks. The instrument this second time withdrawn, I concluded the operation over—Oh no! presently the terrible cutting was renewed—& worse than ever, to separate the bottom, the foundation of this dreadful gland from the parts to which it adhered—Again all description would be baffled—yet again all was not over,—Dr Larry rested but his own hand, &—Oh Heaven! I then felt the Knife rackling against the breast bone—scraping it!—This performed, while I yet remained in utterly speechless torture, I heard the Voice of Mr. Larry,—(all others guarded a dead silence) in a tone nearly tragic, desire every one present to pronounce if any thing more remained to be done; The general voice was Yes,—but the finger of Mr. Dubois—which I literally *felt* elevated over the wound, though I saw nothing, & though he touched nothing, so indescribably sensitive was the spot—pointed to some further requisition—& again began the scraping!—and, after this, Dr Moreau thought he discerned a peccant attom—and still, & still, M. Dubois demanded attom after attom—My dearest Esther, not for days, not for Weeks, but for Months I could not speak of this terrible business without nearly again going through it! I could not *think* of it with impunity! I was sick, I was disordered by a single question—even now, 9 months after it is over, I have a head ache from going on with the account! & this miserable account, which I began 3 Months ago, at least, I dare not revise, nor read, the recollection is still so painful.

To conclude, the evil was so profound, the case so delicate, & the precautions necessary for preventing a return so numerous, that the operation, including the treatment & the dressing, lasted 20 minutes! a time, for sufferings so acute, that was hardly supportable—However, I bore it with all the courage I could exert, & never moved, nor stopt them, nor resisted, nor remonstrated, nor spoke,—except once or twice, during the dressings, to say "Ah Messieurs! que je vous plains!—"[1] for indeed I was sensible to the feeling concern with which they all saw what I endured, though my speech was principally—*very* principally meant for Dr. Larry. Except this, I uttered not a syllable, save, when so often they re-

---

1 "Ah Messieurs! how I pity you!"

commenced, calling out "Avertissez moi, Messieurs! avertissez moi!—"[1] Twice, I believe, I fainted; at least, I have two total chasms in my memory of this transaction, that impede my tying together what passed. When all was done, & they lifted me up that I might be put to bed, my strength was so totally annihilated, that I was obliged to be carried, & could not even sustain my hands & arms, which hung as if I had been lifeless; while my face, as the Nurse has told me, was utterly colourless. This removal made me open my Eyes—& then I saw my good Dr. Larry, pale nearly as myself, his face streaked with blood, & its expression depicting grief, apprehension, & almost horrour.

[...]

God bless my dearest Esther—I fear this is all written—confusedly, but I cannot read it—& I can write it no more, therefore I entreat you to let all my dear Brethren male & female take a perusal—and that you will lend it also to my tender & most beloved Mrs. Angerstein, who will pardon, I well know, my sparing myself—which is sparing her, a separate letter upon such a theme. My dearest Father & my dearest Mrs. Lock live so little in the world, that I flatter myself they will never hear of this adventure. I earnestly desire it may never reach them. My kind Miss Cambridge & Miss Baker, also, may easily escape it. I leave all others, & all else, to your own decision.

[...]

1813

178. Frances Burney d'Arblay to Charles Burney Jr.
22 March 1813, London

[*In the summer of 1812 FBA returned to England with her son Alexander, intending to settle him at Cambridge University, out of reach of Bonaparte's conscription for which he was nearly eligible. Around 1825, FBA wrote a narrative description of their journey, entitled "Dunkirk and Deal" (see JL 6: 702-34). FBA brought the first three volumes of her new novel with her, and spent the winter in London completing* The Wanderer. *She sought the help of her former agent, CBjr, in her negotiations for the sale of her manuscript.*]

---

1 "Warn me, Messieurs! warn me!"

Since we make use—than which nothing can be so right,—of the name of my dear absentee [*ADA*], why not do it according his real idea?—which is, That he would have the offer be put fairly *to Auction*?

If not, in applying from one to another, the work will seem, to all who come second, bandied about, & rejected.!!!

I would wish a short kind of circular Letter, to this effect—

That you shall have shortly *a work* to dispose of for your sister, which, as well as she can judge by the uncopied & yet not quite finished MS. will be about the length of her Cecilia; & which, you frankly make known, you shall commit fairly to the highest bidder—or bidders.

Now this will admit no cavil, for 'tis the honest fact. And no one can be affronted, where all are treated alike.

I would wish it to go to Longman, Murray, Colborn, Robinson—PAYNE, White, Rees, Rivington, Williams, Hurst, Orme, Brown—Richardson, Hookham, Leigh, Mathews, Booker, Hatchard—and as many more as you will; the more the merrier.

If you see this well, Charlotte will copy, & I will send the Billets, *all at the same moment.*

One or two a day, & one after another, will certainly incur an idea that the work is *under examination*, or *has* been, & is offered about *in Succession.*

I would say nothing of *printing* for myself, though if dissatisfied I may *do* it: but I hate all that looks like menace.

I know no other way than this that will really satisfy M. d'A. that *the best has been done:*—

That we may not hear of some man who would have given £100 more than the rest, when it shall be too late.

Colborn has been so civil & respectful, I would not affront him by leaving him out: & he is very obliging to my Father, in lending him Books *Gratis.*

This is a great stake to me! very great indeed, in its consequences!

I have taken these names from only one weeks news papers. I hope you can add some others.

almost every work now, I see, even a play, has 5 or 6 publishers.

The more, for Me, the better, because the pay comes quicker and easier.

To Mr. *Payne*, perhaps, it may be more proper you should *tell* than write this plan.

As I am not ready, I should not be in haste, but for your dont—
& indeed, when I *am* ready, I have no time to lose, since I wish
ardently to superintend the Press.

PRAY call it a work: I am passed the time to endure being supposed to write a Love-tale. I will abide by the consequence.

And also say nothing of its purposes, & all that. It looks like
Puff.

They will take it—or They Will let it alone, from public expectation—be its purpose &c what it may.

If you have not written already to Longman, pray don't till *all
the other* billets are ready for the *same post.*

[*After four months of haggling, FBA, despite her reluctance for a payment
contingent on the sale of successive editions, accepted an offer from Longman and his partners of £1500 down with £500 for the second and
£250 for the third through sixth editions of* The Wanderer, *which she
preferred to their original offer of a fixed sum of £2000. Had the novel
passed through six editions as she hoped, FBA would have gained £3000
from the sale.*]

179. FRANCES BURNEY D'ARBLAY TO DR. CHARLES BURNEY
12 October 1813, Richmond

[...]
I am indiscribably occupied, & have been so ever since my return
from Rams Gate, in giving more & more last touches to my work,
about which I begin to grow very anxious.—I [even feel my honour, now, engaged to finish it to the best of my powers, to "*bring
home*" as my dear Father expects. My Publishers forget they do not
run all the risk themselves in *half* the sum, we *share* the hazard: for
it is only the first fifteen hundred that I am to receive by instalments: the rest is payable merely by succeeding editions, by 250 for
every 2000 Copies that shall successively be sold.

The real win, therefore, is dependent upon success.] I am to
receive merely 500 upon delivery of the MS. The two following
500 by instalments from 9 months to 9 months, that is, in a year &
a half from the day of *publication:*—not of delivery.

If all goes well, the whole will be 3000—but only at the end of
the sale of 8000 copies, [three months after the last set has disappeared.] Oh my dear Padre—if *You* approve the work—I shall have
good hope.
[...]

180.   FRANCES BURNEY D'ARBLAY TO
        MARY PORT WADDINGTON
        24 December 1813, London

[...]

[*FBA discusses Mme. de Staël's most recent work,* De L'Allemagne
(1810). *FBA combined a genuine admiration of Mme. de Staël with a
terror of contamination from her acquaintance. When in Paris, FBA had
gone to farcical lengths to avoid meeting her (see JL, 5: 278-81) but evidently her admiration for the artist remained, despite her avoidance of the
woman.*]

Entre nous, this!—In beginning her Germany,—in which I am
only advanced to about a third of the first Volume, I perpetually
LONGED to write to Her—but imperious obstacles are in the
way—&, next to you, to tell you, as the only person I know likely
to sincerely sympathise with me, the pleasure—the transport,
rather, with I read nearly every phrase. Such acuteness of thought,
such vivacity of ideas, & such brilliancy of expression, I know not
where I have met before. I often lay the book down, to enjoy, for
a considerable time, a single sentence. I have rarely, even in the
course of my whole life, read any thing with so glowing a fullness
of applause [...]

1814

181.   FRANCES BURNEY D'ARBLAY TO
        LONGMAN, HURST, REES, ORME, AND BROWN
        2 February 1814, London

Madame d'Arblay acquaints Mess[rs]. Longman & Co. that a rumour
which has for some time alarmed her; has to day been confirmed
to her for fact—that the first Volume of her work is now reading
in various circles!—![1] How this has been brought to bear she
knows not: she has regularly refused to shew even a page of it: even
her Father, even her Brothers have not read one line: but she is now
in the deepest uneasiness at the offence that must necessarily be

---

1   Longman and Co. had sent advance copies of the first volume of *The
    Wanderer,* without the dedication, to a number of critics, perhaps to
    obtain advance praise for the novel.

given amongst her best friends, by a refusal on her part which seems to exclude those only who ought least to have been excluded. The work must unavoidably risk unfair censures by being seen thus partially; & the Sale will undoubtedly be injured by thus prematurely satisfying curiosity.

She begs leave, also, to observe that the Critics, & very able judges, into whose hands she is informed that the first Volume is fallen, are the LAST who ought to see it in an unfinished state. Their approbation is the most difficult to obtain; & their censure stamps disgrace: She is peculiarly, therefore, vexed that the reading should have been begun under such disadvantages by Sir James Mackintosh,[1] Madame de Staël, & Lord Holland.[2]

Finally, Made. d'Arblay assures Messrs. Longman & Co. that the prefatory pages of which she has spoken, will lose all their purpose in being read After the work which they are written to precede. Her other works she had the uncontested privilege of presenting to her own family & friends, before they were seen by those of her publishers, Messrs. Payne & Cadell.

She solemnly, therefore, entreats That they will call back the Volume, or Volumes, which they have lent out; & not suffer another to go forth, till the Work, in its proper state, shall be delivered to the public at large.

Made. d'A: forbore making this remonstrance to Messrs. Longman till she had made enquiries of the Printer, who has positively protested that from his house not a Copy has ever been sent, or lent, except to Messrs. L:—

If this application should be too late, & the Copy, or Copies, cannot be withdrawn, Me. d'A: must, at least, beg to have some of the 1st. Vols. designed for her own connexions & friends forwarded to her without delay; that she may soften the reproach of what is thought her undue reserve, which, in 5 Letters, from separate quarters, has reached her already.

It would be needless for Made. d'Arblay to add how much she has been flattered, nevertheless, by this eagerness. Her cautions are the mere effect of her solicitude to run less risk of ending it in disappointment & disapprobation: for, if this premature communication be not checked, all the interest of the narration will be broken; all illusion will be abolished;—& the Work will be born old.

---

1 A lawyer, philosopher and author who wrote extensively for the reviews.
2 Henry Vassall-Fox, 3rd Baron Holland.

[The Wanderer *was published on 28 March and reviews began to appear in April 1814.*]

182. [JOHN WILSON CROKER] THE QUARTERLY REVIEW
April 1814

NONE of our female novelists (not even Miss Edgeworth) ever attained so early and so high a reputation as Miss Burney, or, as we must now call her, Madame D'Arblay. Her Evelina, published at the age of seventeen,[1] was a most extraordinary instance of early talent, and excited an expectation of excellence which her Cecilia almost fulfilled, and which her Camilla did not altogether disappoint; but we regret to say, that the Wanderer, which might be expected to finish and crown her literary labours, is not only inferior to its sister-works, but cannot, in our judgment, claim any very decided superiority over the thousand-and-one volumes with which the Minerva Press inundates the shelves of circulating libraries, and increases, instead of diverting, the ennui of the loungers at watering places.

If we had not been assured in the title-page that this work had been produced by the same pen as Cecilia, we should have pronounced Madame D'Arblay to be a feeble imitator of the style and manner of Miss Burney [...]

We are afraid that she is self-convicted of being what the painters technically call a *mannerist*; that is, she has given over painting from the life, and has employed herself in copying from her own copies, till, instead of a power of natural delineation, she has acquired a certain trick and habitual style of portraiture:—but the Wanderer is not only the work of a mannerist, but of a mannerist who is *épuisée*,[2] whose last manner is the worst, and who convinces us that, during the thirty years which have elapsed since the publication of Cecilia, she has been gradually descending from the elevation which the vigour of her youth had attained.

[...]

The characters and incidents of Evelina, Cecilia, and (though somewhat more diversified) of Camilla, have too much resemblance. In each, the plot is a tissue of teasing distresses all of the same class, and in each, are repeated, almost to weariness, portraits

---

1 Croker was mistaken on this point; FB was twenty-five at the publication of *Evelina*.
2 Exhausted.

of the same forms of fashionable frivolity and of vulgar middle life. To bring this more forcibly to our reader's observation we need do no more than recall to their recollection the Willoughbys, and the Branghtons, of Evelina; the Meadowses and Hobsons of Cecilia; the Clarendels and Dubsters of Camilla; and, indeed, almost every personage in each of these dramas, who will invariably be found, "mutato nomine,"[1] in the other two.

[...]

But in the Wanderer there is no splendour, no source of delight to dazzle criticism and beguile attention from a defect which has increased in size and deformity exactly in the same degree that the beauties have vanished. The Wanderer has the identical features of Evelina—but of Evelina grown old; the vivacity, the bloom, the elegance, "the purple light of love"[2] are vanished; the eyes are there, but they are dim; the cheek, but it is furrowed; the lips, but they are withered. And when to this description we add that Madame D'Arblay's endeavours to make up for the want of originality in her characters by the most absurd mysteries, the most extravagant incidents, and the most violent events, we have completed the portrait of an old coquette who endeavours, by the wild tawdriness and laborious gaiety of her attire, to compensate for the loss of the natural charms of freshness, novelty, and youth.

[...]

We have now done with this novel, on which we should not have been justified in saying so much, but that we conceived ourselves in duty bound to attend the lifeless remains of our old and dear friends Evelina and Cecilia to their last abode: but of Madame D'Arblay herself we have a word or two to say.

We learn from the preface, (from which, indeed—so torturous is its construction and so involved its expression—we can gather scarcely anything else,) that these volumes were written between the years 1802 and 1812, in Paris, where she enjoyed, as she informs us, under the mild and beneficent government of Napoleon the Great, "ten unbroken years:"—"neither startled by any species of investigation, nor distressed through any difficulties of conduct, by a precious fire-side, or in select society, a stranger to all personal disturbance."

---

1 Under a different name.
2 Thomas Gray (1716-71), "The Progress of Poesy: A Pindaric Ode" (1757), 1.3.41.

Now really we should have expected, if Madame D'Arblay were restrained by her feelings, whatever they might be, from expressing her detestation of the gigantic despotism, the ferocious cruelty, the restless and desolating tyranny of Buonaparte, that, at least, she should not have sought for opportunities of insinuating her gratitude for the blessings, the tender mercies which France enjoyed under the dominion of that tyger.

Though the whole scene is laid in the time of Robespierre, and though she, in her text, takes very carefully the Buonapartian tone of abuse of the *republican* revolution, yet whenever she has occasion to allude to any of the horrors of that period, she does not fail to subjoin, with a loyal accuracy, a note to testify that she alludes to the tyranny of Robespierre:—she did not see, good lady, that this disclaiming note was the most severe satire against her imperial protector, as it leads the reader to suppose, that without its assistance, it would be doubtful to which of these monsters she alluded. We cannot bear these base condescensions—Madame D'Arblay might have been silent; but she ought not, as an Englishwoman, as a writer, to have debased herself to the little annotatory flatteries of the scourge of the human race.

[...]

183.   Frances Burney d'Arblay to Charles Burney Jr.
2 April 1814, London

[...]
But—put on a Wig! That will warm the dear brains, & keep them clear & vigorous. And you cannot be a Bishop without one: & it will look *de bon augure*—[1]

Besides—

I have news for you that would lift it up! though, now, it must be content to make your own natural ringlets stand on end:—

i.e. viz.—

The Longman's have sent to beg me to prepare my 2^{d}. Edition!—

The orders are so vast, it must soon be wanted!—!

How stands the Hair?

Not quite in elevation?

---

1   Like a good omen.

Well, then,—a bit more

Martin[1] hies to me from Longman's this morning, with the incredible tidings—That the whole edition—of 3000 Copies—is already gone!—by the enormous orders sent from all the Booksellers, joined to their own customers, through out the Kingdom!—

!!!!

What say the Curls?—

Oh put on the Wig!

Here's yet another mounter:—

They entreat me to forbear seeing Revizes, or proofs; not to check the sail: For....not only the whole is gone 2 days before publication—but more-over, They have already orders for 800 more!—

Astonishing! incredible! impossible! I was quite overpowered—Martin shed tears of delight & pride—crying: "If my uncle & I had foreseen this, you should not have had less than £:4000—& ought not!"—Am I really dear Carlos, Awake?

They must print, they say, the two next Editions together!—![2]

[...]

184.   FRANCES BURNEY D'ARBLAY TO
            MARY PORT WADDINGTON
            13-18 October 1814, Richmond

[...]

[*Following the death of her father on 12 April, FBA paid little attention to the largely negative reviews of* The Wanderer.]

I beseech you not to let your too ardent friendship disturb you about the Reviews & critics: & I quite supplicate you to leave their authours to their own severities or indulgence. I have ever steadily refused all interference with public opinion, or private criticism. I am told I have been very harshly mangled—but I attribute it not to what alone would affect me, but which I trust I have not excited, personal enmity; I attribute it to the false expectation universally spread that the Book would be a picture of France—as well as to the astonishing *éclat* of [a] work of 5 Volumes being *all* bespo-

---

1 FBA's nephew, son of JB.
2 In the event only the first edition (of 3000 copies) and half of the second edition (of 1000 copies) were sold. FBA thus realized only £2000 in total for the novel.

ken before it was published. The Booksellers, erroneously & injudiciously concluding the sale would so go on, fixed the rapacious price of 2G^s.—which again damped the sale[1]—but why say *damped*, when it is only *their* unreasonable expectations that are disappointed? for they acknowledge that 3600 Copies are positively sold & paid before the first half year? What must *I* be, if not far more than contented? I have not read, or heard, one of the Criticisms: my mind has been wholly occupied by grief for the loss of my dearest Father, or the inspection of his MSS: & my harrassing situation relative to my own proceedings. Why, then, make myself *black bile* to disturb me further? No; I will not look at a word—till my spirits & time are calmed & quiet & I can set about preparing a corrected Edition. I will then carefully read ALL; & then—the blow to immediate feelings being over, I can examine as well as read, impartially, & with profit, both to my future surveyors & myself.

[...]

185.   FRANCES BURNEY D'ARBLAY TO CHARLES BURNEY JR.
25 October 1814, Richmond

[...]
I do not fret myself, I thank Heaven, about the Reviews. I shall not read any of them, to keep myself from useless vexation—till my spirits & my time are in harmony for preparing a corrected Edition. I shall then read all—&, I expect, coolly & impartially. I think the public has its full right to criticise—& never have had the folly & vanity to set my heart upon escaping its late severity, while reminiscence keeps alive its early indulgence. But if, when all the effect of false expectation is over, in about 5 years, the work has *only* criticism,—then, indeed, I shall be lessened in my own fallen fallen fallen hopes—fed, now, not by any general conceit, but an opinion That—if the others were worthy of good opinion, This, when read fresh, & free from local circumstances of a mischievous tendency, will by no means be found lowest in the scale.

[...]

---

1   FBA's complaint of the novel's high price was probably just. By comparison, *Camilla* had sold for one guinea. In its review of *The Wanderer*, the *Anti-Jacobin Review* 46 (Apr. 1814): 347-54 (353-54) called the price "exorbitant," unprecedented in the sale of novels and detrimental to literature itself.

1815

186.   [WILLIAM HAZLITT] THE EDINBURGH REVIEW
February 1815

[...]

[*Hazlitt presents a history of the novel from Cervantes onwards.*]

It is not to be wondered, if, amidst the tumult of events crowded into this period, our literature has partaken of the disorder of the time; if our prose has run mad, and our poetry grown childish. Among those few persons who "have kept the even tenor of their way,"[1] the author of Evelina, Cecilia, and Camilla, holds a distinguished place. Mrs Radcliffe's "enchantments drear"[2] and mouldering castles, derived a part of their interest, we suppose, from the supposed tottering state of all old structures at the time;[3] and Mrs Inchbald's[4] "Nature and Art" would not have had the same popularity, but that it fell in (in its two main characters) with the prevailing prejudice of the moment, that judges and bishops were not pure abstractions of justice and piety. Miss Edgeworth's tales, again, are a kind of essence of common sense, which seemed to be called for by the prevailing epidemics of audacious paradox and insane philosophy.[5] The author of the present novel is, however, quite of the old school, a mere common observer of manners,—and also a very woman. It is this last circumstance which forms the peculiarity of her writings, and distinguishes them from those masterpieces which we have before mentioned. She is unquestionably a quick, lively, and accurate observer of persons and things; but she always looks at them with a consciousness of her sex, and in that point of view in which it is the particular business and interest of women to observe them. We thus get a kind of supplement and gloss to our original text, which we could not otherwise have obtained. There is little in her works of passion or character, or even manners, in the most extended sense of the word, as implying the sum-total of our habits and pursuits; her *forte* is in describing the absurdities and affectations of external behaviour, or *the manners of people in company*. [...]

---

1   Cf. Gray, "Elegy Written in a Country Churchyard" (1751), l. 76.
2   Milton, "Il Penseroso" (1631), l. 119.
3   Ann Radcliffe's works were the foremost exponents of the Gothic novel.
4   Elizabeth Inchbald (1753-1821) was an actress, dramatist and novelist best known for her sentimental novel *A Simple Story* (1791).
5   Maria Edgeworth (1768-1849) was an Irish novelist and educationalist who also wrote moral tales for children.

Women, in general, have a quicker perception of any oddity or singularity of character than men, and are more alive to every absurdity which arises from a violation of the rules of society, or a deviation from established custom. This partly arises from the restraints on their own behaviour, which turn their attention constantly on the subject, and partly from other causes. The surface of their minds, like that of their bodies, seems of a finer texture than ours; more soft, and susceptible of immediate impression. They have less muscular power,—less power of continued voluntary attention,—of reason—passion and imagination: But they are more easily impressed with whatever appeals to their senses or habitual prejudices. The intuitive perception of their minds is less disturbed by any general reasonings on causes or consequences. They learn the idiom of character and manner, as they acquire that of language, by rote merely, without troubling themselves about the principles. Their observation is not the less accurate on that account, as far as it goes; for it has been well said, that "there is nothing so true as habit."

There is little other power in Miss Burney's novels, than that of immediate observation: her characters, whether of refinement or vulgarity, are equally superficial and confined. The whole is a question of form, whether that form is adhered to, or violated. It is this circumstance which takes away dignity and interest from her story and sentiments, and makes the one so teazing and tedious, and the other so insipid. The difficulties in which she involves her heroines are indeed, "Female Difficulties;"—they are difficulties created out of nothing. The author appears to have no other idea of refinement than that it is the reverse of vulgarity; but the reverse of vulgarity is fastidiousness and affectation. There is a true, and a false delicacy. Because a vulgar country Miss would answer "yes" to a proposal of marriage in the first page, Mad. d'Arblay makes it a proof of an excess of refinement, and an indispensable point of etiquette in her young ladies, to postpone the answer to the end of five volumes, without the smallest reason for their doing so, and with every reason to the contrary. The reader is led every moment to expect a denouement, and is as constantly disappointed on some trifling pretext. The whole artifice of her fable consists in coming to no conclusion. Her ladies stand so upon the order of their going, that they do not go at all. They will not abate an ace of their punctilio in any circumstances, or on any emergency. They would consider it as quite indecorous to run down stairs though the house were in flames, or to move off the pavement though a scaffolding was falling. She has formed to herself an abstract idea of perfection in common behaviour, which is quite as romantic and impracticable as any other idea of the sort: and the consequence has naturally been, that she makes her heroines commit the greatest improprieties and absurdities in order to avoid the smallest. In contradiction to a maxim in philosophy, they constantly act from the weakest motive, or rather from pure affectation.

[...]

We are sorry to be compelled to speak so disadvantageously of the work of an excellent and favourite writer; and the more so, as we perceive no decay of talent, but a perversion of it. There is the same admirable spirit in the dialogues, and particularly in the characters of Mrs Ireton, Sir Jasper Herrington, and Mr Giles Arbe, as in her former novels. But these do not fill a hundred pages of the work; and there is nothing else good in it. In the story, which here occupies the attention of the reader almost exclusively, Madame D'Arblay never excelled.[1]

[*In November 1814, FBA and ADA left their son to commence his studies at Cambridge University, while they returned to Paris. ADA had secured a post in the Royal Bodyguard of the newly restored monarch, Louis XVIII. Following Bonaparte's escape from Elba on 26 February 1815, the d'Arblays left Paris. At her husband's urging, FBA joined the Princesse d'Henin in her flight to the Low Countries on 18 March, while ADA was obliged by his duties as part of the King's Body Guard to follow Louis XVIII to a destination unknown to FBA. FBA arrived safely in Brussels on 26 March, where she was obliged to wait ten days before she received tidings of ADA's safe arrival in Ypres, and his subsequent removal to Ghent where Louis XVIII established his headquarters. The couple had a brief reunion on 2 April, before ADA was ordered to Trèves (Trier) in the Prussian Rhineland, where he was given the perilous task of collecting deserters from Bonaparte's armies and persuading them to fight for Louis XVIII. He departed on 13 May, and FBA settled down for a long wait at Brussels, near many other aristocratic Parisian exiles. Surrounded by acquaintance who provided some social distractions, FBA occupied most of her time writing to ADA. She remained in Brussels throughout the battle of Waterloo, and subsequently wrote a journal of her experiences (see JL 8:339-456).*]

---

1 This review provoked a breach in Hazlitt's longstanding friendship with FBA's brother James.

187.   FRANCES BURNEY D'ARBLAY TO
         ESTHER BURNEY BURNEY
         1–3 July 1815, Brussels

[...]

[*In her haste to escape from Paris, FBA abandoned nearly all her personal belongings, including all the manuscript letters and journals left her by
CB and SBP. She had been working on CB's manuscripts with a view to
publishing his Memoirs. EBB had a particular interest in the project, as
CB had willed the manuscripts jointly to FBA and EBB, who were to
share the profits of any resulting publication. Fortunately, FBA's friends in
Paris had stored her goods safely, and upon her return there in September
she was able to collect them.*]

You may imagine how disturbed I have been about *my & our*, Manuscripts!—I have no news of them, yet; but several of our friends
have given me understand, by various adroit methods, that care has
been taken of *all* that is most essential that we left behind. All the
Mss I possess—all the Works, begun, *middled*, or done, large or
small, that my pen ever scribbled, since the grand Firework of
destruction on my 15th. Birthday, are now There!—unless seized by
the Police. And with them all our joint Mss of my dearest Father—
his Letters—his Memoirs—his memorandums!—And all my
beloved Susan's Journals, & my own that she returned me, with
every Letter I have thought worth keeping, or not had leisure for
burning, from my very infancy to the day of my flight! The variety of uneasy sensations this causes you can readily picture to yourself; though the most serious is involving in my loss my dearest
Esther's share of the result of the meditated publication relative to
our revered Father. Here, at Bruxelles, in the solitude in which I
generally pass my time—without my family—my *maternal* occupa-
tions, or my *conjugal*.—& without my house-keeping, my work, or
a single Book—how usefully & desirably I might have dedicated
my time to the examination & arrangement of those papers! But
when I left Paris, in the carriage of a Friend, & only upon a few
hours warning, I could merely bring a change of linnen, in a nap-
kin, to be packed up by her maid in her own *vache*. [...]

188.   FRANCES BURNEY D'ARBLAY TO JAMES BURNEY
              10–12 July 1815, Brussels

[...]

Alex has given me a *trait* of your truly brotherly feelings upon the
harsh treatment given to my poor Wanderer, in nearly the only
DIFFICULTY in which I had not myself involved her, that came

home to my bosom, which silently, but warmly, even from this distance, embraced you, my dear James.[1] Nevertheless, sincerely as I am sensible to your animation in favour of this my youngest Child, I am myself gifted, happily, with a most impenetrable apathy upon the subject of its Criticisers. I have never read, nor chanced to meet with one word upon the subject. I never expected it would have any immediate favour in the World; & I have not yet shut out from my spying Glass a distant prospect that it may share, in a few years, the partiality shewn to its Elder Sisters. Much was against its chances upon its first coming out. There is no such Foe to public success as high Expectation, though there is no such Friend to personal emolument. And Here, Expectation was founded upon Impossibilities, or Improprieties: half the Public expected, from my long residence in France, Political anecdotes, or opinions; & the other half expected, from the title of the Work, & my own unsettled life, The History of the Author. The first Volume, nevertheless, was received by the reigning Critical Judges, with almost unbounded applause;—Sir James Macintosh, Lord Holland, Me de Stael, Sir S. Romilly,[2] Lord Byron, Mr. Godwin,[3]—& others whose names I do not recollect, sung its panegyric: but Then, the illusion of their own Fancies was not over; one party was not yet quite sure That the Wanderer might not still appear in the Writer: or, rather, the Writer in the Wanderer; & the other, had not yet lost all hope that the scene would change to The Continent, & bring the Reader into the midst of the political bustle. The second volume undeceived both parties: & thence began a Disappointment which,—*I hope*, carried with it a propensity to be displeased through the rest of the Work. Time only can shew the Flattery, or the reality of this idea. If it be true, some future eminent Reader, who, some years hence, shall take it in hand, without any reference, or even knowledge of the circumstances attending its first publication, & who will read, therefore, without prepared prejudice, or partiality, will pronounce "*This is the Genuine*—" Or—"*This is a Spurious* sister of the Young Damsels who were previously honoured with public approbation."

---

1   A reference to JB's repudiation of his friendship with Hazlitt after the latter's negative review of *The Wanderer*.
2   Sir Samuel Romilly, an MP and law reformer.
3   William Godwin (1756-1836), radical author of *Enquiry Concerning Political Justice* (1793).

I ought not, also, to omit another point that has made against any immediate success in Fame—& that is, its immediate success in profit. There can be no doubt that the Bookseller's price did not more widely raise Expectation & Curiosity, than Enmity & Jealousy.

All these concomitant matters, however, will die—& the Book will either Revive, or Expire from the cool & unbiassed judgement of those who may read it, without thinking of its Critics; or even of its Author, hereafter.

If, at the same time, the First vol. had not met with such favour, when seen by *stealth*, & ere the Plan of the Work, or the Premium of the publishers were known, I should not encourage this notion. But I think nobody, impartially, will pronounce The First Volume to be the Best....Ergo.....

But enough; I should not have entered thus largely upon this egoistic subject had not the interest taken in it by my dear James repeatedly reached me. [...]

[*In July 1815 FBA received word that ADA was seriously ill from an infected wound caused by a kick from a horse. She immediately set out on a perilous journey from Brussels to Trèves, arriving safely to find ADA convalescing from his wound, and out of danger. FBA described her journey in a narrative written between September 1824 and July 1825 (see JL 8: 474-541). Once ADA was better, the d'Arblays returned to Paris and thence set out for England, where they rented a house in Bath.*]

1817

189.   Frances Burney d'Arblay's Narrative:
Adventures at Ilfracomb.[1]
1 July—October 1817

[*On his deathbed in 1818, ADA urged FBA to write retrospective narratives of events in her life for the benefit of their son and his descendants. Between 1823 and 1825, FBA composed narratives describing her return to England in 1812, her sojourn in Brussels during the Battle of Waterloo, her journey to Trèves in 1815, and her visit to Ilfracombe in Devonshire in the summer of 1817. Extracts from that narrative are given here.*]

---

1 Composed in 1823. See *JL* 10: 690-714.

The latest desire that was pronounced, with respect to the use of my Pen, by Him whose every expressed desire I now execute as a Law, though with pleasure,—nay delight,—was to enjoin my committing to Paper my extraordinary Adventure at Ilfracomb, with a view to making it known to our invaluable Friend Le Comte Victor de La Tour Maubourg, by my writing it to his dear sister, Madame de Maisonneuve. This I have just done: but, before I part with it, I will run over an English translation of it for my dear Relations & Friends on this side of the Channel: not for my Alexander, who was a party too deeply concerned in it to require the recital.

In the year 1817—the last year of my happiness!—I accompanied my son to Ilfracomb, in Devonshire, whither he went by the kind invitation of his excellent Friend Edward Jacob, to partake of the lessons which that young Tutor, at the Age of Twenty, was giving to 6 or 7 Pupils, preparatory to their taking their degrees at Cambridge on the ensuing January.—[1]

The term for these studies was just finishing, & a few days only remained ere the party was to be dispersed, when I determined upon devoting a whole morning to the search of such curiosities as the Coast & Rocks near my habitation produced. Having deposited a Letter for my Then best beloved on Earth, I marched forth, attended only by his own favourite little Dog, Diane, with an empty large silk Bag, or Ridicule,[2] to see what I could find that I might deem *indigenous*, as a local offering to the collection of my General, who had written me word from Paris, that he was daily increasing his minearological stores, under the skilful direction of his friend, the celebrated Naturalist in that class, M. de Bournon. [...]

My usual walk was to the Sands, to visit the Ocean, & mark its ebb, or flow, & listen to the rustling murmur of the Waves. One Machine only was provided for Bathers, the Limited smoothness of the sands not extending widely enough to admit another. To stand near this spot occupied much of my time from the peculiarity of the objects which it offered to my Eyes. Springs of the purest Water continually presented themselves, & limpid streams every where intersected the passage from my habitation, to the sea, which was not more than a quarter of a mile; & cascades innumerable, bright,

---

1 ADA was absent at the time, spending the summer in France.
2 I.e., reticule.

pelucid & refreshing, danced over the points of Rocks that strewed the Ground all about. This spot of which I speak was the common rendezvous of all of Company that assorted to Ilfracomb, whence, after daily viewing the Sea, & these details, parties were formed for Walks & adjournments or assemblages elsewhere.

We went down to the edge of the Sea, which was clear, smooth, & immoveable as a Lake, the Wind having subsided into a calm so quiet & still, that I could not tell whether the tide were in, or out. Not a Soul was in sight, the time for society being earlier or later. But presently a lady descended, with a Book in her hand, who passed on before us to the right, palpably to read alone. Satisfied by this circumstance that the tide was going out, & all was safe, I began my search, & soon accumulated a collection of beautiful pebbles, each of which seemed to merit being set in a Ring. The pleasure they afforded me, from my prospect of their destination, insensibly drew me on to the entrance of the Wildersmouth,—which is the name given to a series of recesses, formed by the Rocks, & semi-circular, open at the bottom to the Sea, & only to be entered by the Sands at low tide. I coasted two or three of them, augmenting my spoil as I proceeded, & so pleased with its increase, that on per-ceiving the lady I have already mentioned seated on a large flat stone, & composedly engaged with her Book, I hurried past, not to disturb her, & felt urged to profit by this implication of securi-ty that all was safe, to visit the last Recess, whither I had never yet ventured. I found it a sort of Chamber, though with no roof but a clear blue Sky. The top was a portly Mountain, rough, steep, & bar-ren; the left side was equally Mountainous, but consisting of layers of a sort of slate, intermixed with moss; the right side was the ele-vated Capston, which here was perpendicular, & at the bottom were the Sands by which I entered it, terminated by the Ocean. The whole was alltogether strikingly picturesque, wild, & original. There was not one trace of Art, or even of any previous entrance into it of Man. Almost, I could imagine myself its first Human Inmate.

My Eye was presently caught by the appearance, near the top, of a Cavern, at the foot of which I perceived something of so brilliant a whiteness, that, in the hope of a splendid treasure for my Bag, I hastened to the spot. What had attracted me proved a piece of Ivory, consisting of the teeth of some animal in an even row. Vari-ous rudely curious things, at the Mouth of the Cavern, invited investigation; but I durst not penetrate within it, lest some Reptiles should resent my intrusion. Diane, however, brushed forward, &

was soon out of sight; but, while I was busily culling, hoarding, or rejecting whatever struck my fancy, she returned, with an air so piteous, & a whine so unusual, that, concluding she pined to return to a little puppy, of a Week or so old, that she was then rearing, I determined to hasten, but still went on with my search, till the excess of her distress leading her to pull me by the Gown, moved me to take her home; but when I descended—for this Recess was upon a slant,—how was I confounded, to find that the Sands at the bottom, opening to the next Recess, whence I had entered this marine Chamber, were covered by the Waves!—though so gentle had been their motion, & so calm was the Sea, that their approach had not caught my Ear. I hastily remounted, hoping to find some outlet at the top, by which I might escape—but there was none. This was not pleasant; but still I was not frightened, not conceiving, or believing that I could be completely enclosed: the less, as I recollected, in my passage to the Cavern, having had a glympse, as I thought, of the lady who was reading in the neighbouring Recess, through a small aperture. I hastily scrambled to the spot, to look for her, & entreat her assistance...but—how was I then startled, to find that she was gone—and that her Recess, which was on less elevated ground than mine, was fast filling with Water!

I now rushed down to the Sea, determining to risk a wet Jerkin, by wading through a Wave or two, to secure myself from being shut up in this unfrequented place:—but the time was past!—The Weather suddenly changed, the Lake was Gone—& billows mounted one after the other, as if with enraged pursuit of what they could seize & swallow.

I eagerly ran up & down, from side to side, & examined every nook & corner, every projection & hollow, to find any sort of opening through which I could any way pass. But there was none.

Diane looked scared—she whined—she prowled about; her dismay was evident, & filled me with compassion: but I could not interrupt my affrighted search to console her. Soon after, however, she discovered a hole in the Rock, at the upper part, which seemed to lead to the higher sands. She got through it, & then turned round, to Bark, as if triumphing in her success, & calling upon me to share its fruits. But in vain! the hallow was too small for any passage save of my head—& I could only have remained in it as if standing in the Pillory. I still, therefore, continued my own perambulation, but I made a motion to my poor Diane to go, deeming it cruel to detain her from her little one. Yet I heard her howl, as if reduced to despair, that I would not join her.—

Anon, however, she was silent....I looked after her—but she had disappeared.

This was an alarming moment:—alone—without the smallest aid, or any knowledge how high the Sea might mount,—or what was the extent of my danger,—I looked up wistfully at Capstone, & perceived the iron Salmon;[1] but this angle of that Promontory was so steep as to be utterly impracticable for climbing by human feet: & its height was such as nearly to make me giddy in considering it from so close a point of view. I went from it, therefore, to the much less elevated & less perpendicular, Rock opposite; but There, all that was not slate, which crumbled in my hands, was moss, from which they glided. There was no hold whatsoever for the feet, that did not threaten giving way to the first step, & causing a fall on the hard fragments of Rocks spread every where in this chamber, that must almost inevitably have dashed out my brains.

[...]

The rising Storm, however, brought forward the billows with seemingly encreased rapidity, & with certainly augmented noise & violence, &, in turning again towards the sea, I perceived by its approach that my wild Asylum lessened every moment.

Now, indeed, I comprehended the fullness of my danger. If a Wave once reached my feet, while coming upon me with the tumultuous vehemence of this stormy moment, I had nothing I could hold by to sustain me from becoming its prey;—and must inevitably be carried away into the ocean, & sunk to its bottomless Pit:—& while the prospect of this terrific premature Death struck me with dread, the idea of my poor desolate Alexander—of my many, many affectionate Relations & deeply attached Friends— and—Oh more than all! of the piercing agonies of the tenderest of Husbands—& the dearest....

I flew that thought—& darted about in search of some place of safety, rapidly, & all Eye, till, at length, I espied a small tuft of Grass on the pinnacle of the highest of the small Rocks that were scattered about my Prison—for such now appeared my fearful dwelling place.

This happily pointed out to me a spot that the Waves had never yet attained; for all around was sand, stone, or barrenness which

---

1 An iron weather vane in the shape of a salmon was mounted on the top of Capstone Hill on the seafront at Ilfracombe.

bore marks of their visits. To reach that tuft would be safety, & I made the attempt with eagerness; but the obstacles I encountered were terrible. The roughness of the Rock tore my cloaths; its sharp points cut now my feet, & now my Fingers; & the uncooth distances from each other of the holes by which I could gain any footing for my ascent painfully writhed my whole person. I gained, however, nearly a quarter of the height, but I could climb no further; and then found myself on a ledge where it was possible to sit down, & I have rarely found a little repose more seasonable. But it was not more sweet than short, for, in a few minutes a sudden storm of Wind raised the Waves to a frightful height, whence their froth reached the basis of my place of refuge, & menaced to attain soon the spot to which I had risen. I now saw a positive necessity to ascend yet higher, *coûte qui coûte;*[1] &, little as I had thought it possible, the pressing danger gave me both means & fortitude to accomplish it,—but with so much hardship that I have ever since marvelled at my success. My Hands were wounded, my Knees were bruised, & my feet were cut; for I could only scramble up by clinging to the Rock on *all fours.* Nevertheless, my alarm was such for my Life, that the mischief to my limbs I only became conscious of the following day. Presently, however, a new evil cost me the most mortal apprehension. I could only climb by forcing my feet into such nooks or crevices as they could dig for themselves, & by forcing one of them a little too far, I could only draw it back by leaving behind me my Shoe!

Wherever I then tried to place my foot, It was so cut that I was obliged to snatch it away, & my position was so frightful, thus fastened to the Rock by one foot, while the other hung in the air, that I have ever since been astonished how I was able to sustain myself while, with the curved top of my Parasol I gently & cautiously regained my imprisoned shoe, &, placing it one step higher, I had the joy to recover its use.

This relief, however, was followed by a New distress: my other shoe, stuck in yet more deeply by having the whole weight of my poor person to support,—remained, like its Brother, in bondage when I dragged out my other foot. But less frightened now, as I had devized a means of redress, I only most thankfully rejoiced that I had preserved my Parasol, which now repeated its good office: but these efforts broke the Ribbon that had fastened the Shoe to

---

1 At any cost.

my ancle, & every fresh step by which I thus slowly ascended forced me to the same operation, for my shoes were become mere slippers, over which I had no command. Unremittingly, however, I continued my toil, which was equally laborious & dangerous, for had I placed one of my feet where it could not rest, I must have fallen.

When I had reached to about two thirds of the height of my Rock, I could climb no further. All above was so sharp, & so perpendicular, that neither hand nor foot could touch it without being acutely wounded. My head, however, was nearly on a level with the tuft of Grass, & my elevation from the sands was very considerable. I hoped, therefore, I was safe from being washed away by the Waves; but I could only hope; I had no means to ascertain my situation; & hope as I might, it was as painful as it was hazardous. [...]

In this terrible state, painful, affrighting, dangerous, & more than all, solitary—who could paint the transport of my joy, when suddenly, re-entering by the aperture in the Rock through which she had quitted me, I perceived my dear little Diane! For an instant, I felt as if restored to safety—I no longer seemed abandonned, all my terrours were chaced by the most lively hopes, & with a heartfelt gaiety....such as rarely, alas! I have since experienced—I called upon her to join me, in accents the most carressing, & which evidently convinced her of her even exquisite Welcome. Nevertheless, though her tail wagged responsive pleasure, she hesitated, looked amazed, embarrassed, & frightened to see me perched at such a height, & the sea so near me. She stood still, &, barking gently, & in a tone resembling a cry, seemed to supplicate that I would rather join than await her: but I had no choice; far as I am from being a Giantess, the opening through which Diane had passed could only have received my head, & have kept it there, as in a Pillory. I repeated, therefore, my invitation, &, at length, she approached. She soon leapt across the flat stones & the sands which separated us, but how great was the difficulty to make her Climb as I had climbed! Twenty times she advanced only to retreat, from the pain inflicted by the sharp points of the Rock, till, ultimately, she picked herself out a passage by help of the slate, & got upon the enormous Table or Tomb-Stone of which the upper part was my support. But the slant was such, that as fast as she ascended she slipt down, & we were both, I believe, almost hopeless of the desired junction, when, catching at a favourable moment that had advanced her poor paws within my reach, I contrived to bend sufficiently forward to hook her Collar by the curved end of my Parasol, & help her forward. This I did with one hand, and as quick as lightening, dragging her over the slab, & dropping her at my feet, whence she soon nestled herself in a sort of Niche of Slate, in a situation much softer than mine, but in a hollow that for me was impracticable. I hastily recovered my hold,—which I marvel now that I had the temerity to let go: but to have at my side my dear little faithful Diane was a comfort, an enlivening comfort, which no one not planted, & for a term that seemed indefinite, in so unknown a solitude can conceive. What cries of joy the poor little thing uttered when thus safely lodged! & with what carressing tenderness I sought to make her sensible of my gratitude for her return. [...]

I was now, compared to all that had preceded, in Paradise—so enchanted did I feel at no longer considering myself as if Alone in the World. O well I can conceive the interest excited in the french Prisoner by a Spider, even a Spider![1] Total Vacuity of all of Animation in a place of Confinement, where its term is unknown, where Volition is set aside, & where the Captivity is the Work of the Elements, casts the Fancy into a state of solemn awe, of fearful expectation, & of nameless amazement, which I have not words to describe: while the higher Mind, mastering, at times, that Fancy, seeks resignation from the very sublimity of that terrific Vacuity whence all seems exiled—hidden—dead—but Self—seeks,—and finds it in the almost visible security of the omnipresence of God.—

[...]

My next alarm was one that explained that of Diane when she came back so scared from the Cavern; for the Waves, probably from some subterraneous passage, now forced their way through that Cavern, threatening inundation to even the highest part of my Chamber.

This was horrific. I could no longer even speak to Diane—my Eyes seemed transfixt upon this unexpected Gulph, &, in a few short, but dreadful moments, in which the Wind again arose, & drove the sea on with violence, an immense breaker attacked my rock, &, impeded by its height from going strait forward, was dashed in two directions, & foamed onward against each side.—

I did not breathe—I felt faint,—I felt even sea-sick.—on, then, with added violence, came two wide spreading Waves, &, being

---

1 Cf. Byron's "The Prisoner of Chillon" (1816).

parted on their arrival, by my Rock, completely encompassed it, meeting each other on the further & upper Ground. Giddy I now felt—in my fear of losing my strength, or self-command, & falling—yet neither my senses nor my faculties played me false, for I gave up my whole Soul to prayer—for myself & for my Alexanders—& that I might mercifully be spared this Watry Grave, or be endowed with courage & faith for meeting it with firmness.

The next Waves reached to the Uppermost end of my Chamber, which was now All Sea, save the small Rock upon which I was mounted!

What a situation for a Female—Alone—without power to make known her danger—without any resource for escaping its tremendous menace, but by painfully, laboriously, & perillously standing upright, & immoveably on the same spot, till it should be passed—without any human being knowing where to find her, or suspecting where she might be—a Female, & past 60 years of age!—

[...]

[...] A Wave, at length, more stupendous in height, in breadth, in foam, & in roaring noise than any which had preceded it, dashed against my Rock as if enraged at an interception of its progress, & rushed on to the extremity of this savage Chamber, with a foaming impetuosity from which I felt myself splashed. This Moment I believed to be my last of Mortality!—but a moment only it was; for scarcely had I time, with all the rapidity of concentrated thought, to recommend myself—my Husband—the most adored of Husbands—& my poor frantic Alexander, humbly but fervently to the Mercy of the Almighty—when the sudden—the celestial joy broke in upon me of perceiving that this Wave, which had bounded forward with such fury, was the last of the rising tide! for so quick & so over-powering was its re-bound, that it forced back with it, for an instant, the whole body of Water that was lodged on the Ground nearest to the upper extremity of my Recess, & the transporting sight was granted me of an opening to the sands. This sudden recovery of Hope was hailed by a flood of grateful Tears—& Oh! what thanksgiving!—already I felt myself restored to my Husband—my Son—& every dearly loved Friend I possessed in this World.

The violence of this re-bound, nevertheless, produced but a momentary view of the sea-hidden sands; they were covered again the next instant, & as no other Breaker of similar Might made a similar opening, I was still, for a considerable length of time—or what appeared so to me,—exteriorly in the same situation—but internally, Oh how different! I lost Hope no more. The Tide was turned; it could rise, therefore, no higher; the danger was over of so unheard of an end; of vanishing no one knew how or where— of leaving to my kind, deploring Friends an unremitting uncertainty of my Fate—of my re-appearance, or Dissolution. I now wanted nothing but Time, Patience, & Caution, to effect my deliverance: & the requisite Courage for their use no longer demanded Effort,—it was chearful, it was vigourous, it was even gay.

[...]

[*FBA anticipates a long wait for the tide to recede. By now the sun was setting, adding new difficulties to her situation.*]

And when, after all, the Sea should be restored to its Bed, was I sure the sands had not been too deeply & too long immersed to afford me a safe footing? If I sunk into any hole, how could I get out? And if I escaped this transfixture, was I sure I knew my way? I had entered by the broad glare of the Sun, & observed, in the adjoining Recesses, Springs, Rivulets, small ponds or standing Waters, which, with fragments of Rock, intercepted, more or less, the whole passage from hence to my habitation: but as I came without fear, &, unhappily, without Wit, I had by no means remarked their placement, & could not, therefore, by twilight, trust to my short-sightedness for not treading into some swamp, or tottering from some ridge or bank, or stony fragments of which I had mistaken, or could not see the form.

Nor was this all I had to apprehend; many of the Irish Insurgents who had fled from trial, after the last revolt,[1] were said to have crossed the Bristol Channel, & to have landed on the Northern Coast of Devonshire, which was said to be infested with Banditti that occasionally sought refuge in the caverns & subterraneous hiding places of the Wildersmouth;—the horrour of encountering any of these desperate Men, in the Night, alone, & uncertain even of my way, was a yet more appalling perspective than the other. Darkness now came on by large strides, faster & faster, & the gloom of Night threatened to quickly envellop me: I was no longer, however, out at sea, for the Waves had rolled wholly away from my spiral residence: But the more I deliberated upon the various hazards of wandering by myself in so unsequestred a spot, the less I dared make the experiment; &, finally, I formed the

---

1 The rebellion of 1798.

resolution of standing where I was & not venturing to seek my home till the Dawn of the next Day.

[...]

I looked up at Capston; nothing was there, but the now hardly discernable Iron Salmon. I then looked at the opposite side....Ah, gracious Heaven! what were my sensations to perceive two Human Figures! Small they looked, as in a picture, from their distance, the height of the Rock, & the obscurity of the Night; but not less certainly, from their outline Human Figures. I trembled—I could not breathe—Shall I, I thought, be delivered? or are they but Banditti? This frightful doubt made me precipitately bow down my head; I would have amalgamated myself with my Rock to escape observation; but I did not succeed, for in another minute, I was espied, for a voice strong, loud, potent, but unknown to my Ears, called out "Holla!—"

Instantly I felt sure that no Banditti would search thus to proclaim his vicinity, & the exquisite hope as rapidly presented itself that some one saw my deplorable situation with compassion, & might be led to aid me, or to make it known, & therefore I unhesitatingly answered "I am safe!"

"Thank God!" was the eager reply, in a Voice hardly articulate, "Oh thank God!" but not in a Voice unknown—though convulsed with agitation;—it was the Voice of my dear Son!—Oh what a quick transition from every direful apprehension to Joy & delight! yet, knowing his precipitancy & fearing a rash descent to join me, in ignorance of the steepness & dangers of the precipice which parted us, I called out with all the energy in my power to conjure him to wait patiently, as I would myself, the entire going down of the tide.

[...]

[*Alexander wished to reach FBA by means of a boat but she was peremptory in her refusals, insisting on remaining where she was until it should be light enough to cross the sands home. A local inhabitant, an old sailor, descended the cliffs, bringing a lantern. He was soon followed by Alexander and his friend and fellow student, John Le Fevre.*]

[...] my son no sooner perceived that the seaman had found footing, though all was still too Watry & unstable for me to quit my Rock, than he darted forward by the Way thus pointed out, & clambering, or, rather, leaping up to me, he was presently in my arms—Neither of us could think or care about the surrounding Spectators—we seemed restored to each other almost miraculously from Destruction & Death—I pressed him to my Heart—he sobbed upon my shoulder—Neither of us could utter a word—but Both, I doubt not, were equally occupied in returning the most ardent thanks to Heaven.

He could not paint to me—could not try to paint the agonies caused by my disappearance. He concluded I had wandered too far, in my admiration of picturesque Scenery, & that in some lonely spot I had been met by a party of the roving Banditti said to invest the vicinity of Ilfracomb, & had been murdered. This horrific idea nearly deprived him of Reason. [...]

[*FBA relates Alexander's frantic search for her, with the assistance of his friend Le Fevre, who knew the district and suggested that FBA might have been trapped in the Wildersmouth by the rising tide, leading them to walk along the cliffs in the hopes of spotting her.*]

To Mr. Le Fevre, therefore, I probably owe my life! for, had I continued in that lone desolation all Night, it is most likely that a fatal Cold would have fastened upon my lungs, even if had I escaped perishing to death, from my painful & dangerous position, in the Midnight Air, & exposed to the inclemency of the Equinoxial Gales on that bleak Northern Coast.

Impatient to aid, to congratulate, or to see me, visitors of all sorts now scrambled to join me; Miss Mary Ramsay the foremost, followed closely by her youngest Sister, Sarah, who jumped over all obstacles, without heeding that her Hat was blown into the sea. All hands offered to assist my descent from my elevated station—but my heart was too full to accept any but from my Son, though his agitated state made him least able to serve me effectually.
[...]

Every one enquired how I had been able to support such a situation, so alone & without resources; & many asked how I had escaped Fainting away. Others wondered I had not screamed the whole time
[...]

190.   FRANCES BURNEY D'ARBLAY TO
             MESSRS. LONGMAN & COMPANY
             30 August 1817, Ilfracombe

[*FBA annotates the letter "In answer to an account that the Work is at a stand, & utterly hopeless of any renewed sale, all orders for it being withdrawn."*]

Madame d'Arblay begs leave to observe to Messrs. Longman & Co. that when an Edition of 3000 Copies, & half an Edition of one of

1000, are disposed of in 3 years, it seems rather premature to decide that because the sale is then at a stand, it is over forever. Mme. d'Arblay was too far from the presumption of expecting a quicker circulation to regard this estimate as the Funeral of the Work: Messrs. Longman & Co. must not, therefore, be surprised that she puts in her claim to retain for herself, & to bequeath to her family, the right of desiring a half yearly Notice of the future progress, or continued stagnation of this publication.

Mme. d'Arblay will be much obliged to Messrs. Longman & co if they will acquaint her whether the 3^d. Edition is printed, or was stopt? &, also, whether Dr. Charles Burney misunderstood Mr. Straghan that a 5th. Edition had been ordered to Press?—as it is the intention of Mad^e. d'Arblay, should this Book ultimately survive the condemnation of Messrs. Longman, & Co, to prepare a corrected & revised Copy for some future—though perhaps posthumous Impression.

191. FRANCES BURNEY D'ARBLAY'S
MEMORANDUM DIARY ENTRIES FOR 1817
Reading in 1817.

Southey's *Curse of Kehama.*

How a man possessed of the parts, the invention, the morality, & the spirit of poetry evinced in this production, could throw them all wildly away upon a subject without purpose, a Hero without mortality, a scheme of action without possibility, & a string of events not hung together with any meaning, is truly amazing—at least after 15...for till then, any vehicle for indulging the Imagination, which feasts, till then, upon any thing that is staring, excentric, & full of either horrible wonder or visionary bliss, suffices to draw forth Talent, & is amply paid by the mere charm of words. Mais....

[...]

Books read in 1817.
PATRONAGE
by *Miss Edgeworth.*

This Work is replete with solid good sense; shews much real knowledge of the World, & has a large share of wit displayed in sundry acute & sagacious observations. But it is dull & heavy as a whole, wanting interest, void of invention, trite in its Characters, wearisome in its dialogues, & spun out of all animating interest of narrative by shifting attention in almost equal parts to 7 or 8 different Objects. PATRONAGE, too, though shewn with much skill & truth in various points of view, grows tiresome & even nugatory as a Lesson, from the too obvious design of making it one, from personage to personage, so as to mar all effect. *Lord Oldborough*, however, must be excepted from the word *trite*; his Character is delineated with the hand of a master. His sagacity, his self-command, his impenetrable power over his own countenance, manner, air, conduct, & all by which a man may outwardly be judged, are drawn with nicety, discrimination, & *tact*. Even diffusion, here, ceases to be weary, from the justness of the detail. But the idle & unnecessary trite anecdote of finding him a Son & a Father's Heart at the end, seems to me merely inserted to ward off the suspicion that he was painted after Lord Bute, or some other known statesman. The opening of the 4th. volume upon mauvaise honte[1] is admirable: it is the best picture of that distressful feeling that can be made, & offered under a new point of view, in exhibiting its cruel effects on the faculties even in higher life, & with truest merit. But I see no motive, either from story, circumstance, example, moral, or interest, for making the Hero a Foreigner. Niether Virtue, Business, nor Misfortune bring Baron Al[tenberg] to England; he comes from common curiosity, & the Heroine sees him by common accident. He might just as well have been an Englishman &, if *as well*, better: for we should only look Abroad where some peculiarity of contrast, pathos, or Heroism answers some purpose, National or personal, that so only could be exemplified. And this has so often been the case, that the Junction without it is disappointing to awakened expectation.

192.   FRANCES BURNEY D'ARBLAY'S NARRATIVE OF THE
       LAST ILLNESS AND DEATH OF GENERAL D'ARBLAY[2]
       February 1817—3 May 1818

My soul visits ever more my Departed Angel—& I can devize no means to soothe my lonely woe so likely of success, as devoting my Evening solitude to recollections of his excellencies, & of every occurrence of his latter days—till I bring myself up to the radiant serenity of their End!—I will give this expansion to my feelings for a few minutes—a poor half hour—every Evening I pass alone, to

---

1   Bashfulness.
2   Written 17 November 1819-20 March 1820. See *JL* 10: 842-910.

unburthen the loaded heart from the weight of suppression during the long & heavy day.—

I think it will be like passing with Him—with Him Himself—a few poor fleeting—but dearly cherished moments.

It is now 17th of November, 1819—A year & half have passed since I was blessed with his sight!—& though my Grief is divested of its poignancy, my heart has been uniformly & completely a stranger to All Happiness—all peace of Mind—all sensation of Gladness—ever since the dread separation! But I have promised my numerous & kind Friends, & I have promised my Alexander, that I will quit my seclusion, & strive, since still destined to live in this World yet a while, to take, & to Give in it some species of comfort.—

It is not, however, by flying this fatal subject that I shall find consolation: to have my Mind some what disengaged for attempting at any enjoyment in Society, I must indulge & unburthen it when alone.

With my Pen I shall seem still to address Him! at least, to call his loved Image & Idea before me!—

He bid me speak of him—think of him as if he were but gone a Journey before me, to await my arrival & junction!—Oh be such my blessed Fate! Oh God of all Mercy! all pity! all benignity! May my beloved Husband—my darling Sister—now in pure friendship associated in the realms of bliss, Pray for—plead for, await—receive me!—

I will call back the history of his last Illness—ever present as it is to me, it will be a relief to set it down: & its lecture may both solace & aid me in supporting my own final seizure.—It may also do Good to our dear—our unique darling Offspring.

[...]

[*FBA describes how ADA, in Paris during the autumn of 1817, suffered increasing ill health, which was not ameliorated on his return to Bath in October. His illness grew worse, and by the end of December he was unable to leave the house. FBA records long months of ADA's patient suffering from rectal cancer, and her own delusional hopes of his recovery. On 3 May 1818, M. d'Arblay lay dying.*]

I know not the Hour—but about...No, I cannot recollect the hour—but I think about the middle of the Day, he bent forward, as he was supported, nearly upright, by pillows, in his Bed... he bent forward, & taking my hand, & holding it between both his own hands, with a smile celestial, a look composed, serene, benign—even radiant, he impressively said: "Je ne sais si ce sera le dernier mot...mais, ce sera la derniere pensée—Notre Reunion!..."[1]

Oh Words the most heavenly that ever the tenderest of Husbands left for balm to the lacerated heart of a surviving Wife!—I fastened my lips on his loved hands—but spoke not—it was not Then that those Words were my blessing!—they awed—they thrilled—more than, Then, they enchanted & illumined me.

[...]

I sat, watching, in my assigned arm chair; & Alex remained constantly with me. The sleep was so calm, that an hour passed, in which I indulged the softest—though the least tranquil hope, that a favourable crisis was arriving—that a turn would take place, by which his vital powers would be restored, so as to enable him to endure some operation by which his dreadful malady might be overcome.....but...when the hour was succeeded by another hour—when I saw a universal stillness in the whole frame such as seemed to stagnate—if I so can be understood—all around—I began to be strangely moved—"Alex! I whispered, this sleep is critical!—a crisis arrives!—Pray God—Almighty God! that it be t..."

[...]

Mr. Tudor[2] came—he put his hand upon the Heart—the Noblest of Hearts—& pronounced that all was over!

How I bore this is still marvellous to me!—I had always believed such a sentence would at once have killed me—but his Sight!—the Sight of his stillness kept me from Distraction!—Sacred he appeared—& his stillness I thought should be mine—& be inviolable.—

I had certainly a partial derangement—for I cannot to this moment recollect any thing that now succeeded with Truth or Consistency; my Memory paints things that were necessarily real, joined to others that could not possibly have happened, yet amalgamates the whole so together, as to render it impossible for me to separate Truth from indefinable, unaccountable Fiction. Even to this instant, I always see the Room itself changed into an Octagon, with a medley of silent & strange figures grouped against the Wall just opposite to me. Mr. Tudor, methought, was come to drag me

---

1 "I do not know if it will be my last words...but, it will be my last thought—our Reunion!..."
2 ADA's surgeon.

by force away; &, in this persuasion, which was false, I remember supplicating him, with fervent humility, to grant me but one hour, telling him I had solemnly engaged myself to pass it by his side.

By that loved side I stayed two hours—Four times I visited his last remains—his faded—fleeting form.....

But why go back to my Grief?—even yet, at times, it seems as fresh as ever! & at *all* times weighs down my torn bosom with a loaded feeling that seems stagnating the springs of life. But for Alexander—*our* Alexander! I think I had hardly survived! his tender sympathy during the first baneful Fortnight, with his Claims to my fostering care, & the solemn injunctions given me to preserve for him, & devote to him, my remnant life, sustained me at a period which else must have cut off every other.

[...]

1820

193.   FRANCES BURNEY D'ARBLAY TO
            ESTHER BURNEY BURNEY
            28 November 1820, London

[...]

[*After the death of ADA, FBA moved to London to be within reach of her son, who obtained an appointment in the Church after taking holy orders in 1818.*]

But let me now, that I may send a double Letter, perform my promise of detail with respect to the manuscripts of our dear Father.

I am, & have been for some months past, as I told you, elaborately engaged with them: but not in *writing myself*, far from it.—It is in *reading*, in decyfering. The enormous load of Letters, Memoirs, documents, mss: Collections, copies of his own Letters, scraps of authorship, old pocket Bookes filled with personal & business memorandums, & fragments relative to the History of Musick, are countless, fathomless! I shall difficulty come to the conclusion. I entirely think with you that I have lost the time for *pecuniary* publication;—but I lost it from circumstances as unavoidable as they were melancholy. I had scarcely been put in possession of these papers by poor Charles,[1] who had wholly to himself the first over-

---

1   FBA's brother CBjr died on 28 December 1817.

looking & regulating of them all, & through whose hands alone they any of them came into mine, ere my own embarrassments & distresses, & subsequent accidents, Flights, illnesses, or *nursings* in illnesses ten thousand times more terrible to me, absorbed all my faculties—&, with but short intermissions, have nearly continued so to do till within the last few months, that I am—faintly—endeavouring to recover some use of my mind & intellects. Nevertheless, I could not think myself authorized to transfer the business, as I have very long known that my Father *designed & wished & bespoke* me for his Editor. [...]

[*FBA describes how she helped CB to sort, examine, and select his papers, from 1796 until his death in 1814.*]

[...] During my absence on the Continent, he had decided, in case I had not returned, to put Charles into my post, conceiving him, next to myself, most acquainted with his literary habits, intentions, & wishes. Charles, however, gave up *that* with a very good grace, upon my re-appearance, considering the very erroneous ideas he had formed & nourished of the *value* of that post; I mean the *pecuniary* value: for he had concluded the *Memoirs* were such as they would have been if written at the time & in the style of the Italian & German Tours; & had judged of the *Letters* from the high Names of many of the Writers, without knowing their Contents. I, also, at that time, thought the same, & therefore was induced, & with true sisterly satisfaction, to engage to my dear Esther to share with Her, as joint Residuary Legatee, when the expences of Copyists, paper, &c were deducted, the profits of the Publication. I had an affectionate pleasure in this *perspective*, as the labour would be all my own; but I also thought it just, as this trust was not mentioned in the Will—an omission that has often astonished me, considering the unexamined state of his private memorandums, & the various papers that could not have been spread, even in a general Family review, without causing pain, or Confusion, or mischief.—— [...]

At the moment we lost our dear Father, I was in too much affliction for any authorship faculties or calculations; but my internal opinion & expectation were That I had nothing to do but to revise & somewhat abridge his own Memoirs, which I thought would contain 3 Volumes in Octavo; & to select his Correspondence to the amount of 3 more, which would rapidly sell the whole, in chusing them from the Names of Garrick, Diderot, Rousseau, Dr. Warton, Dr. Johnson, Mr. Mason, Horace Walpole. Lord Mornington, Mr. Crisp, Mr. Greville, M^{rs}. Greville Lady Crewe, Mr. Bewley, Mr. Griffith, Mr. Cutler, M^{rs}. Le Noir Lord

Macartney, Lord Lonsdale. Duke of Portland, Mr. Canning Mr. Windham. Mr. Wesley. Mr. La Trobe. Mr. Walker. Mr. Burke. Mr. Malone. Sr J. Reynolds. Mr. Seward. Kit Smart. Mrs Piozzi.[1]

Can anyone read such names, & not conclude that the Press would cover them with Gold?—It was not till I came to Ilfracomb that I was completely undeceived, for it was not till then that I had been able to go seriously to work at my always melancholy task— though Then how *bright* to what any has been since!—Doubts, & strong ones, had, indeed, occurred, from my occasional view of the state of the Repository, in hunting for some secret Letters & papers of Mr. Broome, which Charlotte most earnestly claimed from me, & helped me to seek: but it was at Ilfracomb, in 1817. that my definitive disappointment took place. In reading the Memoirs *de suite*,[2] with a red pencil in my hand, for little erasures & curtailings, I soon unhappily, discovered that they really were so unlike all that their honoured writer had ever produced to the Publick, that not only they would not have kept up his Credit & fair Name in the literary World, if brought to light, but would certainly have left a cloud upon its parting ray—attended by a storm of disapprobation, if not invective, upon the Editor who,—for a fortnight's quick profit from his earlier established Celebrity, had exhibited her faded Father's faded talents.—A fortnight, I say; because, the first curiosity satisfied, the Memoirs would have sunk to Waste, & have been heard of no more.

All the juvenile Voluminous Mss. are filled with *literal* Nurse's tales,—such as, narrated by himself, were truly amusing, as his vivacity & quickness & ready Wit rendered every thing that passed his lips: but on paper, & *read*, not *recited*, they were trivial to poverty, & dull to sleepiness. What respected his family, mean while, was utterly unpleasant—& quite useless to be kept alive. The dissipated facility & negligence of his Witty & accomplished, but careless Father; the niggardly unfeelingness of his nearly unnatural Mother; the parsimonious authority & exactions of his Eldest half Brother; the lordly tyranny of his elder own Brother; the selfish assumingness of his Eldest sister,—& the unaffectionate & Worldly total indifference of every other branch of the numerous race to even

---

1 CB's correspondents included prominent literary figures (Garrick, Diderot, Rousseau, Johnson, Mason, and Smart), statesmen (Burke, Canning, Lord Mornington, and Windham), and musicians (Cutler and Wesley).
2 Consecutively.

the existence of each other,—poor good Aunt Rebecca excepted—all these furnish matter of detail long, tedious, unnecessary,—
& opening to the publick view a species of Family degradation to
which the Name of Burney Now gives no similitude.

In coming to the epoch of Manhood, I had hoped to find some
interesting details, & descriptions, relative to our dear & lovely own
Mother: but—from whatsoever Cause, he is here laconic almost to
silence. 3 or 4 lines include all the history of his admiration and its
effects. Whether these were recollections too melancholy for his
Nerves, or whether the intensity with which he had once felt on
this subject had blunted his remnant sensibility, I cannot determine—but he gives his whole paper at this time to enormous long
paragraphs & endless folio pages, upon the City electioneering for
organs & Concerts, & Stanley's rivalry, & Frasi,[1] & local interests of
the day, now sunk from every memory, & containing nothing that
could either benefit or amuse a single Reader by remaining on
record.

[...]

So much for the Memoirs, which I have now perused throughout, with the most sedulous attention, & have gone over a second
time, in marking & separating every leaf, or passage, that may be
usefully, or ornamentally, Biographical. While all that I thought
utterly irrelevant, or any way mischievous, I have committed to the
Flames. Whatever admits of any doubt, or demands any Enquiry, I
have set apart.

Thus, you see, my dear Esther, I have, at length, made a great
advance—though to produce, I fear, but little purpose. However,
it is not nothing to *me*, in the present state of my health, spirits, &
life, to have dissected this multifarious Work, & to have removed
all that appeared to me peccant parts, that might have bred fevers,
caused infectious ill-will, or have excited morbid criticism or
ridicule.

My Mind has been considerably easier since I have attained thus
far, because, in doing it, I have seen how much evil might have
accrued from its falling into other hands, less aware of various allu-
sions, &c than myself.

---

1 Scholars of the history of music have lamented the destruction of these
   possibly valuable accounts of London musical society. John Stanley was a
   blind organist, and Giulia Frasi, a distinguished singer, was a pupil of
   CB's.

Besides, I am firmly persuaded my dear Father would have made all these omissions himself, had he written these memoirs while still living in the World.—And Then—he would have given to what remained the Zest of observation, Conversation, & Anecdote.

[...]

1821

194.   FRANCES BURNEY D'ARBLAY TO
         ESTHER BURNEY BURNEY
         21 October 1821, London

Your *mind*, my dearest Esther, was always equal to literary pursuits, though your *Time* seems only now to let you enjoy them. I have often thought that had our excellent & extraordinary own Mother been allowed longer life, she would have contrived to make you sensible of this sooner—I do not mean in a common way; for *that* has never failed, but in an UNcommon one; I mean in one striking & distinguished: for she very early indeed began to form your taste for reading, & delighted to find time, amidst all her cares & calls, to guide you, in your most tender years, to the best Authours, & to read them with you, commenting, & pointing out passages Worthy to be got by heart. I perfectly recollect, Child as I was, & never of the party, this part of your education. At that very juvenile period, the difference even of *Months* makes a marked distinction in bestowing and receiving instruction. I, also, was so peculiarly backward that even our Susan stood before me. She could read when I knew not my Letters. But though so sluggish to learn, I was always observant;—do you remember Mr. Seton's denominating me, at 15, *The silent observant Miss Fanny*? Well, I recollect your reading with our dear Mother all Pope's Works, & Pitt's Aeneid.[1] I recollect, also, your spouting passages from Pope, that I learnt from hearing you recite them, before—many *years* before I read them Myself. For it was not till I was 15 a taste of that sort came upon Me. [...]

---

1   Christopher Pitt's translation of the *Aeneid* (1736).

195.   FRANCES BURNEY D'ARBLAY TO
              CHARLOTTE FRANCIS BARRETT
                    25 March 1822, London
[...]
[*FBA discusses William Mason's poem "Elegy on the Death of a Lady"* (1760), *which she had recommended to the "infidel" Miss White in* 1780.]
I had understood you, my dear Girl, to ask me to repeat to you that Elegy as a poem with which you were unacquainted. It was under that persuasion that I had recovered, by studious recollection, in a sleepless Night, the parts of it I had forgotten; & these beautiful verses had again, as many a time before, the power to soothe my restlessness: but it was to you only I had purposed to recite them, though I could not *object* to Julia[1]—how could I? [...] but if, as I afterwards conceived, you had the flattering to *me*, idea that for Julia to listen would be to Julia a lesson, I must explicitly declare that had such been *my* intention, I should have repeated the Elegy in a very different manner, i.e., *simply & plainly*.

I think *Taught* Declamation belongs only to an Actress.

If you ask whether I practiced this rule with Alex,—I answer, No; nor would I, were he within my reach, with Dick. To a *male*, whatever gives courage, & helps Address, encreases his Consequence in Society, & his ease & happiness in himself. I have no time, till we meet, to say what I think upon this part of *education* for a *Female*. For myself, *si je me suis laissée allée*[2] it was not from any *study*—or *design*—or *Imitation*—but from having read the poem with warm admiration till I had it by heart, & then repeating it, in the dead of sleepless Nights, so often, so collectedly, so *all to myself*, that I believe I must have caught every possible meaning of the Poet, not only in every sentiment, but in the appropriation of every word, so as to enable me to pronounce as I conceive him to have thought. This, namely entering into the Poem as if it had been the production of my own brain, gives to me an energy in repeating it that nearly electrifies me from the strong sense with which I enter into every line:—&, in reciting, by accident, all the latter part of it lately to Mrs. Lock, I saw her nearly transfixed by deep attention,

---

1 Julia Barrett, CFBt's eldest daughter and FBA's great-niece.
2 If I let myself go.

joined to surprise & admiration, as this charming Elegy was quite new to her. [...]

1823

196.   FRANCES BURNEY D'ARBLAY TO
              ESTHER BURNEY BURNEY
              5 May 1823, London

[...]

[*FBA thanks EBB for her last two letters.*]

Both your Letters are replete with matters that "come home to my business & feelings"—sometimes very painfully, but always with a true sense of your affection, & a deep regret I cannot avail myself of it as unreservedly as of old—but the times now are such as to make all correspondence in some degree circumspect, or in a great degree dangerous & imprudent. Our hearts would most willingly & mutually open to each other as frankly by pen as by speech—but past is the period & Gone—when we used to scribble with no other thought or care but of one to the other, with that "*abandon*" of confidence that did not merely leave prudence & foresight out the question, but that knew not even of the existence of those horrible logs to free, spontaneous, heart-glowing intercourse. Such was the careless, idle, but dear stuff of our early Letters, both to ourselves & to our Mr. Crisp—O! what striking proofs of this pass now daily before my Eyes in my Letters from our adored Susan! & in mine, all sedulously preserved & restored to me, to herself! They, at present, are what are in review for my solitary hours—& how few dare I keep from the flames! for the very charm of their unbounded their fearless openness, which gave them their principal delight, has cast around them dangers & risks that, should they fall into any hands not immediately our own, might make them parents to mischief, rancour, & ill will incalculable! [...]

197.   FRANCES BURNEY D'ARBLAY TO
              ESTHER BURNEY BURNEY
              c. 19 August 1823, London

What an interesting letter is this last, my truly dear Hetty; 'tis a real sister's letter, and such a one as I am at this time frequently looking over of old times! For the rest of my life I shall take charge and save my own executor the discretionary labours that with myself are almost endless; for I now regularly destroy all letters that either may eventually do mischief, however clever, or that contain nothing of instruction or entertainment, however innocent. This, which I announce to all my correspondents who write confidentially, occasions my receiving letters that are real conversations.... Were I younger I should consent to this condition with great reluctance— or perhaps resist it: but such innumerable papers, letters, documents, and memorandums have now passed through my hands, and, for reasons prudent, or kind, or conscientious, have been committed to the flames, that I should hold it wrong to make over to any other judgement than my own, the danger or the innoxiousness of any and every manuscript that has been cast into my power. To you, therefore, I may now safely copy a charge delivered to me by our dear vehement Mr. Crisp, at the opening of my juvenile correspondence with him.—"Harkee, you little monkey!—dash away whatever comes uppermost; if you stop to consider either what you say, or what may be said of you, I would not give a fig for your letters."—How little, in those days, did either he or I fear, or even dream of the press! What became of letters, *jadis*,[1] I know not; but they were certainly both written and received with as little fear as wit. Now, everybody seems obliged to take as much care of their writing desks as of their trinkets or purses,—for thieves be abroad of more descriptions than belong to the penniless pilferers. [...]

1826

198.   FRANCES BURNEY D'ARBLAY TO
LONGMAN, HURST, REES, ORME, AND BROWN
1 February 1826, London

Memorandum for enquiry.

What numbers[2] have been sold since 1824.?

I have been told that the Word *Waste*—from which I have revolted ever since it was first mentioned to me, in 1817,—does not

---

1 Formerly.
2 Of *The Wanderer*.

mean, as I had at first concluded, either destroying the work, or making it over to Pastry Cooks or Frank Makers:[1] Mr Rees, however, has declined telling me himself *what* he means by it, either by Letter, or upon his Visit.—

If...*sold* the Books have been, as *waste*, or in *any other way*, to whatever disadvantage, it seems to me that I have clearly a Right to the *whole sum* specified in the Agreement. The *Price* of the work was always left to the choice & discretion of the Publishers, but the *Purchase Money* was fixed to be paid by Instalments, without any limitation to time—on the contrary, it is especially left from Generation to Generation as its sale, late or early, becomes due.

My Brother's agency ceased solely from the moment the Agreement was *signed by All Parties*. What he said could never be authority, & must merely have been uttered carelessly, & Vexedly. He had no *Right*, even, to investigate the remaining Copies, but by *my* direction, which might be given either to Him or *any other* I might name.

see Agreement.

Should the Work be *out of Print*, I am entitled to claim the Copy Right, & *every remaining sett*, unless they *re*-print it themselves: for they acknowledge having Printed for the whole 5 Editions; & it is *their* fault alone that can have thrown away *my* property without my Knowledge, or Consent.

It was They, not I, who insisted on printing the whole engagement at once.

Wanderer *second edition*
461 sold before Midsummer 1814
23 . . . . . . do . . 1815
12 . . . . . . do . . 1817 2 Years
19 . . . . . . do . . 1820 3 do
20 . . . . . . do . . 1824 4 do
535
==

---

1 Unsold books would be disposed of to those trades which needed waste paper.

1828

199.   FRANCES BURNEY D'ARBLAY TO
                    ESTHER BURNEY BURNEY
                    6 February 1828, London

[...]

[*FBA describes her progress with her father's* Memoirs.]

You know that, after all the pains I had taken, & time I had employed, in an intended publication of the Letters & Memoirs of our dear Father, we perfectly agreed, on examining the materials, to renounce the plan. And after I had consulted with you viva voce, in putting before you all the packets you had time to look over, we were so completely of the same mind, that I felt lightened of one of the heaviest burthens on my spirits, & from that time, thought no more of the matter, but continued burning the collection as fast as I had leisure to re-read, & consider over what bits & scraps ought to be rescued from the flames, for some *ultimate* short record, preceding such few Letters as could be selected that were promising of any general interest.

Well, thus all remained, till, about 2 years ago, I received an intimation—you will easily guess whence,—That if *I* had given up my design, the Authors of the Literary Biographical works which were constantly printing, would take it up: as they had only forborne to do from respect to intelligence communicated to them from both my Brothers, that I always intended bringing the work to light. This startled me: & I consulted a learned & friendly Divine, who said that if such was the case, it became, in his opinion, a bounden Duty to me to *Take upon myself*, from whom it had been long expected, the preservation of what annals I possessed, or could procure, of the Life of my Father: which otherwise might be mangled in a manner disagreeable to all his Race. This impressed me so deeply, that, upon mature consideration, my very Conscience took part in the counsel, & told me it was certainly MY business, if the Life *must* be printed, to prepare it for the press—because I know it was his intention—& that Charles—who is gone himself!—was to take my place as to all the Manuscriptural possessions & decisions, had I continued in France, because, after me, he thought Charles the most acquainted with the press, & the most *au fait* as to the details of his life, from living most familiarly with him of late years, of any of his family.—All this put together, my dear Etty,—brought me to once again endeavour at the execution of my original intention. But his Memoirs, written in his own honoured hand, or copied by Sarah, Charles himself, little Molly,[1] & some one other, whose writing I know not, I had already, according to our joint decision, *destroyed*, that no future chance might bring to light what we had both decreed could reflect no additional lustre on his so bright literary character, but might diminish its radiance, as has been the case with various posthumous publications. This, however, I could rectify by compiling from my own full sources & retentive Memory, & most confidential repositories, in a Biographical preface—such as dear Mr. Burney[2] suggested 14 years ago, when I mentioned to him the deplorable inferiority of all these Cahiers to the spirited, entertaining, & instructive writings that had made the early, & confirmed the mature Fame of our dearest Father.—Well, *This*, therefore, needed only my own exertions of mingled intellect & memory—& enough, too, God knows! & perhaps beyond Both. However, I resolved *privately* upon the attempt—*Privately*, I say, for raised expectation woud make the poor shattered snail draw back again into her shell.—However, I began closer examination of all that was Epistolary, & even agreed with a Friend of ours to take, properly on Both sides, the *Letters* to Copy for the press—when— lo & behold! what was my consternation on being told 2 Days ago, that I have no right to publish any Letters, without formal consent of the Writers, that were addressed to our Father!—that a Law to that purpose passed while I was abroad, & was—entirely unknown to me![3]—Mean while I have almost *no other*, for our dear Father scarcely ever kept copies!—how very provoking! The writers are almost all Dead—& I know neither of their successors or their existence. [...]

[*FBA finally solved her problem by composing a new full-length Memoir of her father, derived from her own collections of manuscripts and such of his as had survived her previous expurgation.*]

---

1 CB's servant.
2 Charles Rousseau Burney, EBB's husband.
3 After cases in 1813 and 1818, the copyright status of letters had changed. New distinctions were drawn between the physical property of the letter, as paper, which was owned by the receiver; and the abstract, intellectual property of the contents of the letter, which remained the property of its writer. Since the writers retained their incorporeal property rights in the composition, theirs was the sole right to publish.

1832

200.   MEMOIRS OF DOCTOR BURNEY,
      ARRANGED FROM HIS OWN MANUSCRIPTS,
   FROM FAMILY PAPERS, AND FROM PERSONAL RECOLLECTIONS.
      BY HIS DAUGHTER, MADAME D'ARBLAY

[...]

[*Into the* Memoirs *of her father,* FBA *chose to insert an account of her own literary career.*]

A subject now propels itself forward that might better, it is probable, become any pen than that on which it here devolves. It cannot, however, be set aside in the Memoirs of Dr. Burney, to whom, and to the end of his life, it proved a permanent source of deep and bosom interest: and the Editor, with less unwillingness, though with conscious awkwardness, approaches this egotistic history, from some recent information that the obscurity in which its origin was encircled, has left, even yet, a spur to curiosity and conjecture.

[...]

FRANCES, the second daughter of Dr. Burney, was during her childhood the most backward of all his family in the faculty of receiving instruction. At eight years of age she was ignorant of the letters of the alphabet; though at ten, she began scribbling, almost incessantly, little works of invention; but always in private; and in scrawling characters, illegible, save to herself.

One of her most remote remembrances, previously to this writing mania, is that of hearing a neighbouring lady recommend to Mrs. Burney, her mother, to quicken the indolence, or stupidity, whichever it might be, of the little dunce, by the chastening ordinances of Solomon.[1] The alarm, however, of that little dunce, at a suggestion so wide from the maternal measures that had been practised in her childhood, was instantly superseded by a joy of gratitude and surprise that still rests upon her recollection, when she heard gently murmured in reply, "No, no,—I am not uneasy about her!"

But, alas! the soft music of those encouraging accents had already ceased to vibrate on human ears, before these scrambling pot-hooks[2] had begun their operation of converting into Elegies, Odes, Plays, Songs, Stories, Farces,—nay, Tragedies and Epic

---

1 C.f. Prov. 13:24.
2 A hooked stroke made by a child learning to write.

Poems, every scrap of white paper that could be seized upon without question or notice; for she grew up, probably through the vanity-annihilating circumstances of this conscious intellectual disgrace, with so affrighted a persuasion that what she scribbled, if seen, would but expose her to ridicule, that her pen, though her greatest, was only her clandestine delight.

To one confidant, indeed, all was open; but the fond partiality of the juvenile Susanna made her opinion of little weight; though the affection of her praise rendered the stolen moments of their secret readings the happiest of their adolescent lives.

From the time, however, that she attained her fifteenth year, she considered it her duty to combat this writing passion as illaudable, because fruitless. Seizing, therefore, an opportunity, when Dr. Burney was at Chesington, and the then Mrs. Burney, her mother-in-law,[1] was in Norfolk, she made over to a bonfire, in a paved play-court, her whole stock of prose goods and chattels; with the sincere intention to extinguish for ever in their ashes her scribbling propensity. But Hudibras too well says—

> "He who complies against his will,
> Is of his own opinion still."[2]

This grand feat, therefore, which consumed her productions, extirpated neither the invention nor the inclination that had given them birth; and, in defiance of all the projected heroism of the sacrifice, the last of the little works that was immolated, which was the History of Caroline Evelyn, the Mother of Evelina, left, upon the mind of the writer, so animated an impression of the singular situations to which that Caroline's infant daughter,—from the unequal birth by which she hung suspended between the elegant connexions of her mother, and the vulgar ones of her grandmother,— might be exposed; and presented contrasts and mixtures of society so unusual, yet, thus circumstanced, so natural, that irresistibly and almost unconsciously, the whole of A Young Lady's Entrance into the World, was pent up in the inventor's memory, ere a paragraph was committed to paper.

Writing, indeed, was far more difficult to her than composing; for that demanded what she rarely found attainable—secret oppor-

---

1 I.e. step-mother.
2 Samuel Butler, Hudibras (1678), pt. 3, canto 3, 547-48.

tunity: while composition, in that hey-day of imagination, called only for volition.

When the little narrative, however slowly, from the impediments that always annoy what requires secrecy, began to assume a "questionable shape;" a wish—as vague, at first, as it was fantastic—crossed the brain of the writer, to "see her work in print."

She communicated, under promise of inviolable silence, this idea to her sisters; who entered into it with much more amusement than surprise, as they well knew her taste for quaint sports; and were equally aware of the sensitive affright with which she shrunk from all personal remark.

She now copied the manuscript in a feigned hand; for as she was the Doctor's principal amanuensis, she feared her common writing might accidentally be seen by some compositor of the History of Music, and lead to detection.

She grew weary, however, ere long, on an exercise so merely manual; and had no sooner completed a copy of the first and second volumes, than she wrote a letter, without any signature, to offer the unfinished work to a bookseller; with a desire to have the two volumes immediately printed, if approved; and a promise to send the sequel in the following year.

This was forwarded by the London post, with a desire that the answer should be directed to a coffee-house.

Her younger brother—the elder, Captain James, was "over the hills and far away,"[1]—her younger brother, afterwards the celebrated Greek scholar, gaily, and without reading a word of the work, accepted a share in so whimsical a frolic; and joyously undertook to be her agent at the coffee-house with her letters, and to the bookseller with the manuscript.

After some consultation upon the choice of a bookseller, Mr. Dodsley was fixed upon; for Dodsley, from his father's,—or perhaps grand-father's,—well chosen collection of fugitive poetry,[2] stood foremost in the estimation of the juvenile set.

Mr. Dodsley, in answer to the proposition, declined looking at anything that was anonymous.

The party, half-amused, half-provoked, sat in full committee upon this lofty reply; and came to a resolution to forego the *eclat*

---

1 Title of an air from Gay's *Beggar's Opera* (1728).
2 *Fugitive Pieces, on Various Subjects* [...] (1761), published by R. and J. Dodsley.

of the west end of the town, and to try their fortune with the urbanity of the city.[1]

Chance fixed them upon the name of Mr. Lowndes.

The city of London here proved more courtly than that of Westminster; and, to their no small delight, Mr. Lowndes desired to see the manuscript.

And what added a certain pride to the author's satisfaction in this assent, was, that the answer opened by

"Sir,"—

which gave her an elevation to manly consequence, that had not been accorded to her by Mr. Dodsley, whose reply began

"Sir, or Madam."

The young agent was muffled up now by the laughing committee, in an old great coat, and a large old hat, to give him a somewhat antique as well as vulgar disguise; and was sent forth in the dark of the evening with the two first volumes to Fleet-street, where he left them to their fate.

In trances of impatience the party awaited the issue of the examination.

But they were all let down into the very "Slough of Despond," when the next coffee-house letter coolly declared, that Mr. Lowndes could not think of publishing an unfinished book; though he liked the work, and should be "ready to purchase and print it when it should be finished."

There was nothing in this unreasonable; yet the disappointed author, tired of what she deemed such priggish punctilio, gave up, for awhile, and in dudgeon, all thought of the scheme.

Nevertheless, to be thwarted on the score of our inclination acts more frequently as a spur than as a bridle; the third volume, therefore, which finished *The young lady's entrance into the world*, was, ere another year could pass away, almost involuntarily completed and copied.

But while the scribe was yet wavering whether to abandon or to prosecute her enterprise, the chasm caused by this suspense to the workings of her imagination, left an opening from their vagaries to a mental interrogatory, whether it were right to allow

---

1 The West End, comprising the Boroughs of Westminster, Kensington and Chelsea, were the fashionable, aristocratic areas of London. To the east, the City, the oldest part of London, contained the commercial districts.

herself such an amusement, with whatever precautions she might keep it from the world, unknown to her father?

She had never taken any step without the sanction of his permission; and had now refrained from requesting it, only through the confusion of acknowledging her authorship; and the apprehension, or, rather, the horror of his desiring to see her performance.

Nevertheless, reflection no sooner took place of action, than she found, in this case at least, the poet's maxim reversed, and that

"The female who deliberates—is sav'd,"[1]

for she saw in its genuine light what was her duty; and seized, therefore, upon a happy moment of a kind *tête à tête* with her father, to avow, with more blushes than words, her secret little work; and her odd inclination to see it in print; hastily adding, while he looked at her, incredulous of what he heard, that her brother Charles would transact the business with a distant bookseller, who should never know her name. She only, therefore, entreated that he would not himself ask to see the manuscript.

His amazement was without parallel; yet it seemed surpassed by his amusement; and his laugh was so gay, that, revived by its cheering sound, she lost all her fears and embarrassment, and heartily joined in it; though somewhat at the expence of her new author-like dignity.

She was the last person, perhaps, in the world from whom Dr. Burney could have expected a similar scheme. He thought her project, however, as innocent as it was whimsical, and offered not the smallest objection; but kindly, embracing her, and calling himself *le pere confident*, he enjoined her to be watchful that Charles was discreet; and to be invariably strict in guarding her own incognita: and then, having tacitly granted her personal petition, he dropt the subject.

With fresh eagerness, now, and heightened spirits, the incipient author rolled up her packet for the bookseller; which was carried to him by a newly trusted agent,[2] her brother being then in the country.

---

1   Cf. Addison's *Cato* (1713), 4.1, "The woman that deliberates is lost."
2   Edward Francesco Burney.

The suspense was short; in a very few days Mr. Lowndes sent his approbation of the work, with an offer of 20*l*. for the manuscript— an offer which was accepted with alacrity, and boundless surprise at its magnificence!!

[...]

[*FBA describes the publication and success of the novel, and her father's approbation.*]

[...] That a work, voluntarily consigned by its humble author, even from its birth, to oblivion, should rise from her condemnation, and,

"'Unpatronized, unaided, unknown,'[1]

make its way through the metropolis, in passing from the Monthly Review into the hands of the beautiful Mrs. Bunbury; and from her's arriving at those of the Hon. Mrs. Cholmondeley; whence, triumphantly, it should be conveyed to Sir Joshua Reynolds; made known to Mr. Burke; be mounted even to the notice of Dr. Johnson, and reach Streatham;—and that there its name should first be pronounced by the great lexicographer himself; and,—by mere chance,—in the presence of Dr. Burney; seemed more like a romance, even to the Doctor himself, than anything in the book that was the cause of these coincidences.

[...] She had written the little book, like innumerable of its predecessors that she had burnt, simply for her private recreation. She had printed it for a frolic, to see how a production of her own would figure in that author-like form. But that was the whole of her plan. And, in truth, her unlooked for success evidently surprised her father quite as much as herself.

[...]

[*FBA inserts a remnant, somewhat altered, from CB's own Memoirs.*]

Copied from a Memorandum-book of Dr. Burney's,
written in the year 1808, at Bath.

"The literary history of my second daughter, Fanny, now Madame D'Arblay, is singular. She was wholly unnoticed in the nursery for any talents, or quickness of study: indeed, at eight years old she did not know her letters; and her brother, the tar, who in his boyhood had a natural genius for hoaxing, used to pretend to

---

1 Cf. FB's advertisement to *Cecilia* in which she described Evelina as a
   work "unpatronized, unaided, and unowned."

teach her to read; and gave her a book topsy-turvy, which he said she never found out! She had, however, a great deal of invention and humour in her childish sports; and used, after having seen a play in Mrs. Garrick's box, to take the actors off, and compose speeches for their characters; for she could not read them. But in company, or before strangers, she was silent, backward, and timid, even to sheepishness: and, from her shyness, had such profound gravity and composure of features, that those of my friends who came often to my house, and entered into the different humours of the children, never called Fanny by any other name, from the time she had reached her eleventh year, than The Old Lady.

Her first work, Evelina, was written by stealth, in a closet up two pair of stairs, that was appropriated to the younger children as a play room. No one was let into the secret but my third daughter, afterwards Mrs. Phillips; though even to her it was never read till printed, from want of private opportunity. To me, nevertheless, she confidentially owned that she was going, through her brother Charles, to print a little work, but she besought me never to ask to see it. I laughed at her plan, but promised silent acquiescence; and the book had been six months published before I even heard its name; which I learnt at last without her knowledge. But great, indeed, was then my surprise, to find that it was in general reading, and commended in no common manner in the several Reviews of the times. Of this she was unacquainted herself, as she was then ill, and in the country. When I knew its title, I commissioned one of her sisters to procure it for me privately. I opened the first volume with fear and trembling; not having the least idea that, without the use of the press, or any practical knowledge of the world, she could write a book worth reading. The dedication to myself, however, brought tears into my eyes; and before I had read half the first volume I was much surprised, and, I confess, delighted; and most especially with the letters of Mr. Villars. She had always had a great affection for me; had an excellent heart, and a natural simplicity and probity about her that wanted no teaching. In her plays with her sisters, and some neighbour's children, this straightforward morality operated to an uncommon degree in one so young. There lived next door to me, at that time, in Poland street, and in a private house, a capital hair merchant, who furnished peruques to the judges, and gentlemen of the law. The merchant's female children and mine, used to play together in the little garden behind the house; and, unfortunately, one day, the door of the wig magazine being left open, they each of them put on one of those dignified ornaments of the head, and danced and jumped about in a thousand antics, laughing till they screamed at their own ridiculous figures. Unfortunately, in one of their vagaries, one of the flaxen wigs, said by the proprietor to be worth upwards of ten guineas—in those days a price enormous—fell into a tub of water, placed for the shrubs in the little garden, and lost all its gorgon buckle, and was declared by the owner to be totally spoilt. He was extremely angry, and chid very severely his own children; when my little daughter, the old lady, then ten years of age, advancing to him, as I was informed, with great gravity and composure, sedately says; "What signifies talking so much about an accident? The wig is wet, to be sure; and the wig was a good wig, to be sure; but its of no use to speak of it any more; because what's done can't be undone."

"Whether these stoical sentiments appeased the enraged peruquier, I know not, but the younkers were stript of their honours, and my little monkies were obliged to retreat without beat of drum, or colours flying."

[*Reviews of the* Memoirs of Doctor Burney *began to appear in 1833.*]

1833

201.   [JOHN WILSON CROKER] THE QUARTERLY REVIEW
April 1833

WE would willingly have declined the task of reviewing this book. As a literary work we have not a word to say in its favour; and having no hope of improving the style of an author whose most popular production was published nearly sixty years ago, and feeling a great reluctance to give gratuitous pain to a person so respectable as Madame d'Arblay, we wish we could have evaded the subject altogether; but the duty which we owe our readers, our regard for the memory of Dr. Burney, and even our personal estimation of Madame d'Arblay herself, all concur in obliging us to offer some account of these volumes.

Dr. Burney had, as Madame d'Arblay sets out with informing us, not merely intended, but "*directed* that the Memoirs of his life should be published; and his family and friends"—very naturally—"expected them to pass through her hands" (p. v.); but we regret to say, that Madame d'Arblay appears to have disobeyed the "directions" and disappointed the "expectations" which she thus professes to fulfil. Dr. Burney left behind, it seems, "sundry manuscript volumes, containing the history of his life from his cradle almost to his grave:"—*those* were the Memoirs which the Doctor "directed" to be published, and of which "his family and friends expected" Madame d'Arblay to be the editor; but from these voluminous papers Madame d'Arblay has made very scanty extracts, and has become the *writer* of a work essentially her own, and not the *editor* of her father's recollections of his life. Her motives for this course of proceeding are not distinctly stated; but it is hinted that she considered what her father had thus left as unfit for the public eye.

[...]

Madame d'Arblay may have exercised a sound discretion in not giving to the public this mass of materials, *in extenso*; but we do very much doubt whether what she has suppressed could have been more feeble, anile, incoherent, or "*sentant plus l'apoplexie*,"[1] than that which she has substituted for it.

[...]

We must here pause for a moment to complain of a defect in Madame d'Arblay's work even more serious than that of her style—the suppression of dates. We say *suppression*; because we cannot attribute to accidental negligence the silence of the biographer as to the time of her father's first coming to London—of his marriage—of his migration to Lynn—of the birth of his children, and particularly of Madame d'Arblay herself—of the death of his first wife—of his second marriage; and, in short, of all the leading events of the earlier part of his life. It can hardly be personal vanity which produces this silence; yet certainly no spinster of a doubtful age can have a greater aversion to accuracy in matters of date than is exhibited by this lady, who admits that she has been above fifty-five years an author and forty years a wife. But though we readily acquit Madame d'Arblay of being led by *personal* vanity to this studied concealment of dates, yet we shall by and by have occasion to show, that *literary* vanity may have been the motive of this omission, which, in a biographical work, is peculiarly puzzling and provoking [...][2]

---

1 Savouring more of apoplexy.
2 Hemlow's discovery that Esther was born before her parents' marriage suggests that FBA's suppression of all dates in the *Memoirs* may have been intended to conceal that fact (See *HFB* 6).

Madame d'Arblay's book [...] instead of being called "Memoirs of Dr. Burney," might better be described as "Scattered Recollections of Miss Fanny Burney and her Acquaintance." Of her father she tells almost nothing that was not already to be found in the obituary of the *Gentleman's Magazine* and other biographies; and she does not even notice three or four musical works, which we learn from those authorities he composed—a strange omission in the *Memoirs* of a musical professor.

This leads us to a second part of our task—namely, to give some account of what appears to us the *real* object of the work; and if we have covered half-a-dozen pages without touching on that essential subject, it is because Madame d'Arblay, with consummate art— or a confusion of ideas which has the same effect as consummate art,—conceals from her readers, and perhaps from herself, that it is her *own Memoirs*, and *not* those of her father that she has been writing; and we confess that we have a strong suspicion, that it was *because* her father's auto-biography did not fulfil *this* object, that *it* has been suppressed—and this joint-stock history (in which, as in other joint-stock concerns, the managing partner has the larger share) has been substituted for it. Let us not be misunderstood. We do not complain that Madame d'Arblay should write her own Memoirs; on the contrary, we wish she had done so in her own *original* style, instead of perplexing the reader with all those awkward shifts and circumlocutions, by which her modesty labours to conceal that she is writing *her own* life, and making her father's memory, as it were, *carry double*. Very ludicrous indeed are the shifts by which she contrives to pin herself to his skirts, and still more so the awkward diffidence, the assumed *mauvaise honte*, with which, to avoid speaking in the first person, she designates herself by such circumlocutions as "*this memorialist;*" or "*the present editor;*" or "*the Doctor's second daughter;*" or when, after her marriage, she retired to a cottage in Surrey, "*the happy recluse;*" or, finally, by the more compound designation of "*the-then-Bookham-and-afterwards-West-Hamble-female hermit.*" (vol. iii., p. 235.)

We must now revert to the suspicion which we have before expressed, that a little literary vanity has occasioned the remarkable suppression of dates in the earlier portion of these Memoirs; and this leads us to the extraordinary and interesting account of Madame d'Arblay's first appearance in the literary world. At the age of *seventeen*, as we have always seen and heard it stated, Miss Fanny Burney—without the knowledge of her father—without any suspicion on the part of her family and friends that she had any literary turn or capacity whatsoever—published anonymously her celebrated novel of *Evelina, or a Young Lady's Entrance into the World*; which emerged at once into popularity, raised its youthful author, as soon as she avowed it, to a brilliant reputation, and recommended her to the admiration and friendship of some of the most considerable men of the age.

[...]

It was, therefore, not without surprise, that, in the long and circumstantial account given by Madame d'Arblay of the composition of "Evelina," we observed that no allusion was made to what we had always considered the most extraordinary ingredient in the story—the author's age. This induced us to look into the matter a little more closely, when we were additionally surprised to find that every little incident which could have led to any exact calculation of the interval between "burning the manuscripts when the author had attained her fifteenth year," and the publication of "Evelina" in 1778, and, in short, every clue to the date of Madame d'Arblay's birth has been most *curiously* obliterated. To a cursory reader, the interval between "*Caroline Evelyn*" and "*Evelina*," would appear certainly not to exceed two or three years; and the mention of the "disguise of the *young messenger* by the *laughing committee*" would confirm the idea of a boyish and girlish *frolic*. After turning the volumes over again and again, and wasting a good deal of time in pursuit of evidence on this point, we were about to give up the hopes of any new discovery, and to acquiesce in the received opinion, when we discovered a casual hint that she was born at Lynn; and, as her father left that town in 1760, it was clear that she was *somewhat* older than had hitherto been supposed. This induced an inquiry at Lynn, and we have found, in the registry of St. Margaret's parish there, that "Frances, the daughter of Charles and Esther Burney, was baptized in June, 1752;" so that she was *past twenty-five* when "Evelina" was published: and also that her "*disguised young messenger*" (born in 1757) was not only twenty years of age, but had, we believe, already graduated at the university. We need not repeat our observation of the vast difference between a shy, backward, neglected girl of *seventeen*, writing in the *play-room*, and a woman of *five-and-twenty*, who had probably passed seven or eight years in general society; and we are, therefore, not much surprised that Madame d'Arblay, though she may have had no share in propagating the original error, should have shown so little anxiety to correct it. To this feeling, therefore, we are now constrained to attribute that studious omission of dates which had at first appeared quite unaccountable.

[...] As to the style of these Memoirs, there is another cause which may have contributed to give it that strange pomposity which we have had but too much occasion to notice. A novel writer is obliged to make up for the paucity of events by a superabundance of verbal skills. "A potent, pointed, piercing, yet delicious dart"— (vol. i., p. 61); "eyes of finest azure beamed the brightest intelligence" [...] and such hyperboles, may do very well to fill up the space between one event and another, and to give to imaginary beings a certain air of locality and reality; but when all this comes to be applied to *real* matter-of-fact personages, it is absurd. The loss of a friend *in a novel* might be described, without much offence, as Madame d'Arblay notices Dr. Burney's regret for the loss of Mr. Bewley;—but when applied to the effect which the death of a Suffolk apothecary would have on a London music-master, who were, though old acquaintance, no companions, and saw one another but once in two or three years, the fallacy of the pompous expression, thus placed in juxtaposition with the real current of human affairs and human feelings, becomes ridiculous. Fictitious life, of which novels are the history, is made up of words, of epithets, of amplification, of touches—the smaller the better; real history is made up of the larger facts—of what a man *did*, not what he said,—of how a lady acted, not how she looked: fictitious life is described by fancied feelings and imputed motives—which it is given to the omniscient author alone to develope—real life, of those broad interests and plain actions of which all mankind are the witnesses and the judges—and it is, we surmise, by confounding these distinctions, that a charming novelist (for such we shall always consider the authoress of "Cecilia") has become the most ridiculous of historians.

[...]

We have already exceeded our limits, and must conclude with repeating our wish that it were possible to persuade Madame d'Arblay to separate, even now, *her own* from *her father's* Memoirs—to give us *them* as he wrote them, or at least as much of what he wrote as she might judge proper; and to condense and simplify into a couple of interesting (and interesting they would be) volumes, *her own* story and her contemporaneous notes and *bonâ fide* recollections of that brilliant society in which she moved, from 1778 to 1794. We lay some stress on the words *bonâ fide*, not as imputing to Madame d'Arblay the slightest *intention* to deceive, but because we think that we see in almost every page abundant proof, that the habit of *novel-writing* has led her to colour and, as she may suppose, embellish her anecdotes with sonorous epithets and factitious details, which, however, we venture to assure her, not only blunt their effect, but discredit their authority.

[...]

202. FRANCES BURNEY D'ARBLAY TO
CHARLES PARR BURNEY
18 April 1833, London

[...]

As to Hostility to my poor Memoirs[1]—I hope, my dear Charles, you do not suppose I hold Hostility to them & to me one & the same thing? or that I am become so bigotted for obtaining approbation to them, that I am ready—like Bayes in the Rehearsal, to exclaim to the Audience "If you don't like my play—cut off my head!" When I take a turn to thinking or suspecting Hostility to *me*, from my kind Carlos, with the persuasion I have so long entertained of the vivacity as well as verity of his attachment—I must be "*set down*" as—I won't say absolutely a "long-Eared beast" but I will say, & very positively, as non compos.[2]

[...]

[*Nevertheless, FBA was distressed by Croker's review of the* Memoirs. *Her son, together with his cousins Fanny Raper and Charlotte Barrett, composed a manuscript entitled "The Retort Sarcastic" in which they defended FBA against Croker's attack on her supposed literary vanity, in pretending to be 17 when she wrote* Evelina. *The "Retort" claimed that since* Caroline Evelyn *was destroyed when FBA was 15, and* Evelina *commenced immediately afterwards, the claim was a fair one. There was talk of publishing this manuscript but it came to nothing. Hemlow suggests that FBA and her defenders were reluctant to oppose Croker in a public forum. (See HFB 456-60)*]

---

1 Hemlow estimates that FBA received £1000 for the *Memoirs*, while an equal sum was presumably paid to EBB's heirs (See *JL* 12: 785n.).

2 I.e., *non compos mentis*, not in one's right mind.

1838

203. FRANCES BURNEY D'ARBLAY TO CHARLOTTE BURNEY
FRANCIS BROOME AND CHARLOTTE FRANCIS BARRETT
20 April 1838, London

[*After the death of Alexander from influenza on 19 January 1837, FBA
became worried about her hoard of manuscripts, which she could no longer
expect to pass onto his children.*]
[...]—for some time past, I have been in a state of dejection that
heavily weighs me down—& is beyond my conquest.—And it is
all owing to the abundance of business I have to transact that has
all reference, constant reference, to all that is most dear—& most
melancholy!—Were *they* disposed of—those myriads of hoards of
MSS. I might enjoy a more tranquil resignation I might think of
my Alex without that perturbation that makes the *thought* of Him
so tragic! because it is with abrupt recollection, that brings him
with some affecting incident to my sight—And—from his living
with me his whole life, every paper—every Chattel I possess speaks
of him. I would fain make him my theme—yet without this agony.
Make it with a serenity that should only brighten remnant life by
its cheerful prospect—not its inflexible regret—!—

My dear Charlottes both—think for me, with the rest of the
kind thinkers, what I had best do with this killing mass of constant
recurrence to my calamity.—Shall I Burn them?—at once—or
shall I, & Can I, so modify a division as to spare for future times
various Collections that may be amusing & even instructive

Certainly were I younger & could here wait for the examination—but that is not the case. My eyes will work at them no more!
[...]

[*CBFB advised FBA to leave her manuscripts to the discretion of a trust-
worthy friend rather than burn them. FBA accordingly willed all of her
papers to CFBt, entrusting her niece with the task of preparing an edition
of the journals and correspondence for the press. FBA died on 6 January
1840, exactly forty years after the death of her beloved sister Susan. She
was buried in Bath alongside her husband and son. Two years later, in
1842, the first volume of CFBt's edition of* The Diary and Letters of
Madame d'Arblay *was published.*]

References

1. Berg, JJ, vol. 1, pp. 5-6.
2. Berg, JJ, vol. 1, pp. 8-9.
3. Berg, JJ, vol. 1, p. 13.
4. Berg, JJ, vol. 1, pp. 16-18.
5. Berg, JJ, vol. 1, pp. 18-19.
6. Berg, JJ, vol. 1, pp. 19-21.
7. Berg, JJ, vol. 1, pp. 23-24.
8. *ED* 1: 19-21.
9. Berg, JJ, vol. 1, pp. 27, 28-29.
10. Berg, JJ, vol. 1, pp. 43-44.
11. Berg, JJ, vol. 2, pp. 72-73.
12. Berg, JJ, vol. 2, pp. 81-82.
13. Berg, JJ, vol. 2, pp. 89-90.
14. Berg, JJ, vol. 2, pp. 92-94.
15. Berg, JJ, vol. 3, pp. 115-36.
16. Barrett, Egerton ms. 3696, ff. 79r-80r.
17. Berg, JJ, vol. 4, pp. 205-16.
18. Berg, JJ, vol. 4, p. 236.
19. Berg, JJ, vol. 4, pp. 239-41.
20. Berg, JJ, vol. 5, pp. 285-86.
21. Berg, JJ, vol. 6, pp. 350-51.
22. Berg, JJ, vol. 6, fragment numbered in pencil 49.
23. Berg, JJ, vol. 6, p. 399.
24. Berg, JJ, vol. 7, pp. 409, 411-16.
25. Berg, ms. Scrapbook: FBA & Friends (1759-1799), # 7.
26. Berg, JJ, vol. 7, pp. 469-72.
27. Berg, JJ, vol. 7, pp. 479-80.
28. Barrett, Egerton ms. 3694, ff. 20v-23r.
29. Berg, JJ, vol. 8, p. 493.
30. Barrett, Egerton ms. 3694, ff. 25r-25v.
31. Berg, JJ, vol. 8, p. 523.
32. Berg, JJ, vol. 8, ff. 21r-24r.
33. Berg, JJ, vol. 8, pp. 525-28.
34. Berg, JJ, vol. 8, pp. 529-30.
35. Barrett, Egerton ms. 3694, ff. 39r-39v.
36. Berg, JJ, vol. 8, ff. 29r-35v.
37. Barrett, Egerton ms. 3694, f. 67r.
38. Barrett, Egerton ms. 3695, f. 3r.
39. Comyn.

40. Barrett, Egerton ms. 3695, f. 5r.
41. Comyn.
42. Barrett, Egerton ms. 3695, f. 7r.
43. Barrett, Egerton ms. 3695, f. 8r.
44. Barrett, Egerton ms. 3694, ff. 84r–84v.
45. Berg, JJ, vol. 10, pp. 581–82, 584.
46. Berg, JJ, vol. 10, pp. 602–18.
47. Barrett, Egerton ms. 3695, f. 9r.
48. Comyn.
49. Berg, D&L, vol. 1, pt. 1, pp. 635–46, ff. 7r–9v.
50. Berg, D&L, vol. 1, pt. 1, pp. 647–48.
51. *London Review*, 7 (Feb. 1778): 151.
52. *Monthly Review*, 58 (Apr. 1778): 316.
53. Berg, D&L, vol. 1, pt. 1, pp. 651–55.
54. Berg, ms. letter, no pagination.
55. Berg, D&L, vol. 1, pt. 1, p. 658.
56. Comyn.
57. Barrett, Egerton ms. 3695, f. 11r.
58. Berg, ms. letter, no pagination.
59. Berg, D&L, vol. 1, pt. 1, pp. 675–77.
60. Berg, ms. letter, pp. 663–65.
61. Berg, ms. letter, no pagination.
62. Berg, D&L, vol. 1, pt. 1, pp. 667–70.
63. Berg, D&L, vol. 1, pt. 1, pp. 692–704.
64. Berg, D&L, vol. 1, pt. 1, pp. 709–11.
65. Berg, D&L, vol. 1, pt. 1, pp. 725–27, 731–32, 735–36, 745–49.
66. Berg, D&L, vol. 1, pt. 1, pp. 809–10.
67. Berg, D&L, vol. 1, pt. 1, pp. 769–70, 772–83.
68. Berg, D&L, vol. 1, pt. 1, pp. 791–92.
69. *Critical Review*, 46 (Sept. 1778): 202–204 (202–203).
70. Berg, D&L, vol. 1, pt. 1, pp. 795b–96.
71. Berg, D&L, vol. 1, pt. 1, pp. 811–14.
72. Berg, D&L, vol. 1, pt. 1, pp. 828–31.
73. Berg, D&L, vol. 1, pt. 1, pp. 859–60, 871–78.
74. Berg, ms. Scrapbook: FBA & Friends (1759–1799), #11.
75. Berg, D&L, vol. 1, pt. 1, pp. 823–25.
76. Thraliana ms., HM12183, vol. 3, pp. 76–77.
77. Berg, D&L, vol. 1, pt. 1, pp. 896–901.
78. Barrett, Egerton ms. 3694, f. 97 r.
79. Berg, D&L, vol. 1, pt. 1, pp. 911–12.
80. Berg, D&L, vol. 1, pt. 1, pp. 991–92.
81. Barrett, Egerton ms. 3691, ff. 9r–10r.

82. Berg, D&L, vol. 1, pt. 1, pp. 999-1002.
83. Berg, D&L, vol. 1, pt. 1, pp. 1003-1005.
84. Barrett, Egerton ms. 3690, ff. 4r-5r.
85. Berg, D&L, vol. 1, pt. 2, pp. 1100-1104.
86. Berg, D&L, vol. 1, pt. 2, pp. 1111-13.
87. Berg, D&L, vol. 1, pt. 2, pp. 1148-50.
88. Berg, D&L, vol. 1, pt. 2, pp. 1229-35, 1262-64.
89. Berg, D&L, vol. 1, pt. 2, pp. 1096-98 (misnumbered 1798).
90. Berg, ms. letter, no pagination.
91. Berg, ms. letter, no pagination.
92. Berg, ms. letter, no pagination.
93. Berg, D&L, vol. 2, pt. 1, pp. 1426-27.
94. Thraliana ms., HM12183, vol. 4, p. 39.
95. *Burford Papers*, p. 74.
96. Berg, D&L, vol. 2, pt. 1, pp. 1551-53.
97. Berg, D&L, vol. 2, pt. 1, pp. 1556-62.
98. Berg, D&L, vol. 2, pt. 1, p. 1581 (pasted offprint of *Morning Herald*, Tuesday 12 March 1782).
99. Berg, D&L, vol. 2, pt. 1, pp. 1571-73.
100. Berg, D&L, vol. 2, pt. 1, pp. 1585-86.
101. Thraliana ms. HM12183, vol. 4, p. 92.
102. Berg, D&L, vol. 2, pt. 1, pp. 1621-22.
103. Copy in Berg, D&L, vol. 2, pt. 1, pp. 1611-12.
104. Barrett, Egerton ms. 3690, ff. 15r-15v.
105. Berg, ms. letter, no pagination.
106. Berg, ms. letter, no pagination.
107. *DL*, Appendix 1, 2: 481-82.
108. Comyn.
109. Berg, D&L, vol. 2, pt. 1, pp. 1625-26.
110. Berg, ms. letter, no pagination.
111. Berg, D&L, vol. 2, pt. 1, pp. 1647-48, 1660-61.
112. Berg, D&L, vol. 2, pt. 1, pp. 1678-80.
113. *Critical Review*, 54 (Dec. 1782): 414-20 (414, 420).
114. *Monthly Review*, 67 (Dec. 1782): 453-58 (453, 456-57).
115. Barrett, Egerton ms. 3693, ff. 13r-13v.
116. Berg, D&L, vol. 2, pt. 1, pp. 1735-36, 1766-71.
117. Berg, D&L, vol. 2, pt. 1, pp. 1810-11.
118. Draft of a letter, Berg, ms. Scrapbook: FB & Family (1653-1890), # 21.
119. Berg, D&L, vol. 2, pt. 2, pp. 1979-80, 1992-93.
120. Copy in hand of CFBt, Berg, D&L, vol. 2, pt. 2, pp. 2035-38.

121. Barrett, Egerton ms. 3690, ff. 159r–160r.
122. Berg, D&L, vol. 3, pp. 2077, 2080-81, 2083-84.
123. Berg, D&L, vol. 3, p. 2243.
124. Berg, D&L, vol. 3, pp. 2413-18.
125. Berg, D&L, vol. 3, pp. 2431-34, 2443, 2457.
126. Berg, D&L, vol. 3, pp. 2644-45.
127. Berg, D&L, vol. 3, p. 2722.
128. Berg, D&L, vol. 4, pt. 1, pp. 2867-68.
129. Berg, D&L, vol. 4, pt. 1, pp. 2871-73, 2884-85.
130. Berg, D&L, vol. 4, pt. 1, pp. 3062-63.
131. Berg, D&L, vol. 4, pt. 1, pp. 3170-73.
132. Berg, D&L, vol. 4, pt. 1, pp. 3283-84, 3295-96, 3298.
133. Berg, D&L, vol. 4, pt. 3, pp. 3558-60.
134. Berg, D&L, vol. 4, pt. 3, pp. 3657-63.
135. Berg, D&L, vol. 5, pt. 1, box 2, pp. 4063-67.
136. Berg, D&L, vol. 5, pt. 1, box 2, pp. 4192-93.
137. Copy included in FB to SBP, Oct 1790, Berg, D&L, vol. 5, pt. 1, box 2, pp. 4210-12.
138. Berg, D&L, vol. 5, pt. 1, box 2, pp. 4272-73.
139. Berg, D&L, vol. 5, pt. 1, box 2, pp. 4324-29.
140. Berg, D&L, vol. 5, pt. 2, box 3, pp. 4438-41.
141. Berg, D&L, vol. 5, pt. 2, box 4, pp. 4631-32.
142. Berg, D&L, vol. 5, pt. 2, box 5, pp. 4710-14.
143. Berg, D&L, vol. 5, pt. 2, box 5, pp. 4722-23.
144. Berg, D&L, vol. 6, pt. 1, pp. 4804-5.
145. "Apology," *Brief Reflections Relative to the Emigrant French Clergy* [...] (London: Cadell, 1793), iii–v.
146. *Critical Review*, ns, 10 (March, 1794): 318-21 (319-21).
147. Barrett, Egerton ms. 3690, f. 76v.
148. Barrett, Egerton ms. 3690, ff. 80v–81r.
149. Berg, ms. letter, no pagination.
150. PML, ms. MA 35.
151. Burney Collection of Newspapers, BL, Burney Manuscripts 885.
152. Berg, D&L, vol. 6, pt. 1, no pagination; after p. 4837.
153. Berg, ms. letter, no pagination.
154. Berg, D&L, vol. 6, pt. 1, no pagination; after p. 4811.
155. Berg, D&L, vol. 6, pt. 1, no pagination; after p. 4811.
156. Berg, ms. letter, no pagination.
157. Berg, ms. letter, no pagination.
158. Osborn, MSS 3, Box 1, Folder 29.
159. Osborn, MSS 3, Box 1, Folder 29.

160. Berg, D&L, vol. 6, pt. 1, no pagination; after p. 4811.
161. Berg, ms. letter, no pagination.
162. Berg, D&L, vol. 6, pt. 1, pp. 4904-5.
163. Berg, D&L, vol. 6, pt. 1, pp. 4913-14.
164. Bodleian, MS Don. c. 56, ff. 87r-87v.
165. *Analytical Review*, 24 (Aug. 1796): 142-48 (142).
166. *Monthly Review*, ns, 21 (Oct. 1796): 156-63 (156, 161-63).
167. Berg, D&L, vol. 6, pt. 1, pp. 4925-26.
168. Berg, D&L, vol. 6, pt. 1, pp. 4942-44.
169. Berg, D&L, vol. 6, pt. 1, pp. 4976-77.
170. Berg, D&L, vol. 6, pt. 1, pp. 4988-90.
171. Barrett, Egerton ms. 3693, f. 72v.
172. Berg, ms. letter, pp. 5154-55.
173. Berg, ms. Scrapbook: FB & Family (1653-1890), not numbered.
174. Berg, ms. letter, no pagination.
175. Berg, copy, ms. letter, pp. 5228-29, Copies [...] in General d'Arblay's hand of 30 miscellaneous letters, 1794-1814, #7.
176. Berg, ms. letter, p. 5212.
177. Berg, ms. letter, no pagination.
178. Osborn, MSS 3, Box 1, Folder 38.
179. Berg, D&L, vol. 7, pp. 5910-11.
180. Berg, ms. letter, no pagination.
181. Berg, draft ms. letter, no pagination.
182. *Quarterly Review*, 11 (Apr. 1814): 123-30 (123-25, 129-30).
183. Osborn, MSS 3, Box 1, Folder 39.
184. Berg, ms. letter, no pagination.
185. Osborn, MSS 3, Box 1, Folder 39.
186. *Edinburgh Review*, 24 (Feb. 1815): 320-38 (335-38).
187. Berg, ms. letter, p. 6666.
188. PML, ms. MA 35.
189. Berg, [Arblay, F. d'] Holograph Notebook, pp. 6844-6903.
190. Barrett, Egerton ms. 3695, ff. 97r-97v.
191. Berg, ms. Memorandum Book bound in black leather.
192. Berg, [Arblay, F. d'] Holograph Diary, pp. 6956-58, 7095-7102.
193. Barrett, Egerton ms. 3690, ff. 128v-33r.
194. Berg, D&L, vol. 7, unpaginated, after p. 6927.
195. Berg, ms. letter, no pagination.
196. Berg, ms. letter, no pagination.
197. *DL* 6: 407-408.
198. Osborn, MSS 3, Box 1, Folder 55.

199. Berg, ms. letter, no pagination.
200. *Memoirs*, 2: 121-32, 143-45, 168-71.
201. *Quarterly Review*, 49 (Apr. 1833): 97-125 (97-98, 100, 106-107, 110-112, 125).
202. Osborn, MSS 3, Box 1, Folder 45.
203. Berg, ms. letter, no pagination.

Appendix: Contemporary Reviews of The Diary and Letters of Madame d'Arblay

1. *New Monthly Magazine and Humorist* 64 (Feb. 1842): 271-84 (271, 284)

[...] here *is* a portion of the very "Diary" that a month or two ago we could have had no hope of compassing but through the aid of Fortunatus's wishing-cap; and we have no hesitation in declaring that, so far as it proceeds, it greatly surpasses, both in immediate interest and entertainment, and in high literary, historical and social value, whatever our utmost expectations could have assigned to it. [...] In fact this delightful volume proves Miss Burney to have possessed all the qualifications for a social annalist which the most ardent admirers of Johnson's biographer would assign to him, without a single one of those manifold errors, weaknesses, and deficiencies, which compel us to smile at Boswell (not seldom contemptuously), even while we are most amused and obliged by him. That the woman who wrote the greater part of "Evelina" long before she was twenty years of age, must have possessed rare penetration to observe, and rare judgment to estimate, human character—that she must have been gifted with the finest moral tact, and the most delicate sense of humour—that she turned to the most high and pure, yet the wisest and kindest account that "learned spirit of human dealing"[1] with which she was gifted perhaps beyond any other woman of the same age that ever lived;—all this, and much more, those who are acquainted with "Evelina" must be fully aware of [...]

[...] We cannot part from it, however, without recording, as the most comprehensive general criticism we can offer of it, an expression of the affectionate admiration (we can find no other phrase for the feeling) for the entire personal and intellectual character of its writer, with which its perusal has impressed us. For the highest attributes of the heart and intellect, and those which are the most

---

1 *Othello*, 3.3.263-64.

rarely found together;—for the strongest affections coupled with the sweetest and softest temper—for the loftiest and purest principles, giving effect to the gentlest of judgments in regard to the thoughts and actions of others, while they exact the strictest self-scrutiny in regard to her own—for the simplicity of a child, united to the penetration, the understanding, and the moral tact of a philosopher—for an unsurpassed sense of the bad and the ridiculous in human character, without the smallest tendency to satire or sarcasm—for an intense anxiety to *deserve* the applause of the well-judging portion of mankind, without the smallest care about *obtaining* it;—in a word, for the loveliest and most endearing qualities of a feminine heart, united to the most useful and valuable attributes of a masculine mind,—we never remember to have encountered, either in books or in real life, any character claiming such unmingled esteem as that of Dr. Johnson's "Dear little Burney."

2. [John Wilson Croker] *The Quarterly Review* 70 (June 1842): 243-87 (243-45, 251, 259).

WHEN we reviewed, ten years ago, that strange display of egotism which Madame D'Arblay was pleased to call *Memoirs of her Father*, we expressed a wish that she would

> "*condense* and *simplify* into a *couple* of interesting (and interesting they would be) volumes of her *own story* and her contemporaneous notes and *bonâ fide* recollections of that brilliant society in which she moved from 1777 to 1793. [...]"

We were not then in the secret of Madame D'Arblay's having from her earliest youth kept the diary now presented to us; but we *guessed*, from the many passages in the "Memoirs of Dr. Burney," that she was in possession of copious contemporaneous materials for her own, and we candidly forewarned her of the kind of errors into which she was likely to fall in preparing her notes for publication. Our conjectures are now too fully verified: the interest is indeed much less than we anticipated, but in all the rest—the diffuseness—the pomposity—the prolixity—the false colouring—the factitious details—and, above all, the personal affectation and vanity of the author, this book exceeds our worst apprehensions.

At first sight the Diary seems a minute record of all that she saw, did, or heard, and we find the pages crowded with names and teeming with matters of the greatest apparent interest—with details of the social habits and familiar conversation of the most fashionable, most intellectual, and, in every sense, most illustrious personages of the last age. No book that we ever opened, not even Boswell's "Johnson," promised at the first glance more of all that species of entertainment and information which memoir-writing can convey, and the position and respectability of the author, with her supposed power of delineating character, all tended to heighten our expectation; but never, we regret to say, has there been a more vexatious disappointment. We have indeed brought before us not merely the minor notabilities of the day, but a great many persons whose station and talents assure them an historic celebrity—King George III., Queen Charlotte, and their family—Johnson, Burke, Sir Joshua, and their society—Mrs. Montague, Mrs. Thrale, Mrs. Delany, and their circles—in short, the whole court and literary world; and all in their easiest and most familiar moods:—their words—their looks—their manners—and even their movements about the room—pencilled, as it would seem, with the most minute and scrupulous accuracy:—but when we come a little closer, and see and hear what all these eminent and illustrious personages are saying and doing, we are not a little surprised and vexed to find them a wearisome congregation of monotonous and featureless prosers, brought together for one single object, in which they, one and all, seem occupied, as if it were the main business of human life—namely, the *glorification of Miss Fanny Burney*—her talents—her taste—her sagacity—her wit— her manners—her temper—her delicacy—even her beauty—and, above all, her *modesty!*

We really have never met anything more curious, nor, if it were not repeated *ad nauseam*, more comical, than the elaborate ingenuity with which—as the ancients used to say that *all roads led to Rome*—every topic, from whatsoever quarter it may start, is ultimately brought home to Miss Burney. There can be, of course, no autobiography without egotism; and though the best works of this class are those in which *self* is the most successfully disguised, it must always be the main ingredient. We therefore expected, and, indeed, were very willing, that Miss Burney should tell us a great deal about herself; but what we did not expect, and what wearies, and, we must candidly add, disgusts us, is to find that she sees nothing beyond the tips of her own fingers, and considers all the rest of man and womankind as mere satellites of that great luminary of the age, the *author of "Evelina."*

[...]

If all this egotism had been, as it professes, intended for the confidential eye of a sister, it would have been in some degree excusable: but it was not so; and the pretence of its being so intended is but another of the shifts in which her exuberant vanity disguises itself. The journal went the round of her own domestic circle, and was then regularly transmitted to Mr. Crisp and his coterie at Chessington—and afterwards to Mr. and Mrs. Lock of Norbury Park, and to we know not whom else—and it seems, beyond all doubt, to have been prepared and left by her for ultimate publication. Strange blindness to imagine that anything like fame was to be gathered from this deplorable exhibition of mock-modesty, endeavouring to conceal, but only the more flagrantly exposing, the boldest, the most *horse-leech* egotism that literature or Bedlam has yet exhibited.

[...]

The utter inanity and worthlessness of the greater portion of the dialogues, with which Miss Burney expands her volumes, have a tendency to render us, at first sight, indifferent to what is nevertheless a very serious offence,—the unpardonable breach of confidence, in thus stealthily treasuring up for publication every idle word which was uttered in the unsuspicious freedom of private society. [...] The parties are all chatting in private intercourse, sometimes on personal subjects, always in the confidence that there is no tale-bearer by to repeat elsewhere anything that may have been said to the annoyance or disparagement of other parties, still less that there is a deliberate spy, who writes it all down, first for the amusement of her own friends, and eventually for publication to all the world. We can call this by no softer name than *treachery*; and the editor who has thought fit to publish this insipid, yet sometimes, we fear, malicious trash, not only injures the author's character, but, we think, compromises her own.

[...]

3. [Thomas Babington Macaulay] *The Edinburgh Review* 76 (Jan. 1843): 523-70 (523-24, 564-66, 569-70).

THOUGH the world saw and heard little of Madame D'Arblay during the last forty years of her life, and though that little did not add to her fame, there were thousands, we believe, who felt a singular emotion when they learned that she was no longer among us. The news of her death carried the minds of men back at one leap, clear over two generations, to the time when her first literary triumphs were won. All those whom we had been accustomed to revere as intellectual patriarchs, seemed children when compared with her; for Burke had sate up all night to read her writings, and Johnson had pronounced her superior to Fielding, when Rogers was still a schoolboy, and Southey still in petticoats. [...] Since the appearance of her first work, sixty-two years had passed; and this interval had been crowded, not only with political, but also with intellectual revolutions. Thousands of reputations had, during that period, sprung up, bloomed, withered, and disappeared. New kinds of composition had come into fashion, had gone out of fashion, had been derided, had been forgotten. The fooleries of Della Crusca, and the fooleries of Kotzebue, had for a time bewitched the multitude, but had left no trace behind them; nor had misdirected genius been able to save from decay the once flourishing schools of Godwin, of Darwin, and of Radcliffe. Many books, written for temporary effect, had run through six or seven editions, and had then been gathered to the novels of Afra Behn, and the epic poems of Sir Richard Blackmore. Yet the early works of Madame D'Arblay, in spite of the lapse of years, in spite of the change of manners, in spite of the popularity deservedly obtained by some of her rivals, continued to hold a high place in the public esteem. She lived to be a classic. Time set on her fame, before she went hence, that seal which is seldom set except on the fame of the departed. Like Sir Condy Rackrent in the tale,[1] she survived her own wake, and overheard the judgment of posterity.

Having always felt a warm and sincere, though not a blind admiration for her talents, we rejoiced to learn that her Diary was about to be made public. Our hopes, it is true, were not unmixed with fears. We could not forget the fate of the Memoirs of Dr Burney, which were published ten years ago. That unfortunate book contained much that was curious and interesting. Yet it was received with a cry of disgust, and was speedily consigned to oblivion. The truth is, that it deserved its doom. It was written in Madame D'Arblay's later style—the worst style that has ever been known among men. No genius, no information, could save from proscription a book so written. We, therefore, opened the Diary

---

1   Maria Edgeworth's *Castle Rackrent* (1800).

with no small anxiety, trembling lest we should light upon some of that peculiar rhetoric which deforms almost every page of the Memoirs, and which it is impossible to read without a sensation made up of mirth, shame, and loathing. We soon, however, discovered to our great delight that this Diary was kept before Madame D'Arblay became eloquent. It is, for the most part, written in her earliest and best manner; in true woman's English, clear, natural, and lively.

[...]

[*Macaulay makes an estimation of FBA's writings, and concludes that she does not belong to the "highest rank" of artists, but is a superior humorist, after the style of Ben Jonson.*]

It is melancholy to think that the whole fame of Madame D'Arblay rests on what she did during the earlier half of her life, and that every thing which she published during the forty-three years which preceded her death, lowered her reputation. Yet we have no reason to think that at the time when her faculties ought to have been in their maturity, they were smitten with any blight. In the Wanderer, we catch now and then a gleam of her genius. Even in the Memoirs of her Father, there is no trace of dotage. They are very bad; but they are so, as it seems to us, not from a decay of power, but from a total perversion of power.

The truth is, that Madame D'Arblay's style underwent a gradual and most pernicious change,—a change which, in degree at least, we believe to be unexampled in literary history, and of which it may be useful to trace the process.

When she wrote her letters to Mr Crisp, her early journals, and the novel of Evelina, her style was not indeed brilliant or energetic; but it was easy, clear, and free from all offensive faults. When she wrote Cecilia she aimed higher. She had then lived much in a circle of which Johnson was the centre; and she was herself one of his most submissive worshippers. It seems never to have crossed her mind that the style even of his best writings was by no means faultless, and that even had it been faultless, it might not be wise in her to imitate it. Phraseology which is proper in a disquisition on the Unities, or in a preface to a Dictionary, may be quite out of place in a tale of fashionable life. Old gentlemen do not criticize the reigning modes, nor do young gentlemen make love, with the balanced epithets and sonorous cadences which, on occasions of great dignity, a skilful writer may use with happy effect.

In an evil hour the author of Evelina took the Rambler for her model. This would not have been wise even if she could have imitated her pattern as well as Hawkesworth did. But such imitation was beyond her power. She had her own style. It was a tolerably good one; and might, without any violent change, have been improved into a very good one. She determined to throw it away, and to adopt a style in which she could attain excellence only by achieving an almost miraculous victory over nature and over habit. She could cease to be Fanny Burney; it was not so easy to become Samuel Johnson.

In Cecilia the change of manner began to appear. But in Cecilia the imitation of Johnson, though not always in the best taste, is sometimes eminently happy; and the passages which are so verbose as to be positively offensive, are few. There were people who whispered that Johnson had assisted his young friend, and that the novel owed all its finest passages to his hand. This was merely the fabrication of envy. Miss Burney's real excellences were as much beyond the reach of Johnson, as his real excellences were beyond her reach. He could no more have written the Masquerade scene, or the Vauxhall scene, than she could have written the Life of Cowley or the Review of Soame Jenyns. But we have not the smallest doubt that he revised Cecilia, and that he retouched the style of many passages.[1]

[...]

When next Madame D'Arblay appeared before the world as a writer, she was in a very different situation. She would not content herself with the simple English in which Evelina had been written. She had no longer the friend who, we are confident, had polished and strengthened the style of Cecilia. She had to write in Johnson's manner, without Johnson's aid. The consequence was, that in Camilla every passage which she meant to be fine is detestable; and that the book has been saved from condemnation only by the admirable spirit and force of those scenes in which she was content to be familiar.

But there was to be a still deeper descent. After the publication of Camilla, Madame D'Arblay resided ten years at Paris. During those years there was scarcely any intercourse between France and England. It was with difficulty that a short letter could occasionally be transmitted. All Madame D'Arblay's companions were French. She must have written, spoken, thought, in French. [...]

---

1   In fact, Johnson never read *Cecilia* through.

Madame D'Arblay had carried a bad style to France. She brought back a style which we are really at a loss to describe. It is a sort of broken Johnsonese, a barbarous *patois*, bearing the same relation to the language of Rasselas, which the gibberish of the Negroes of Jamaica bears to the English of the House of Lords.

[...]

Yet one word more. It is not only on account of the intrinsic merit of Madame D'Arblay's early works that she is entitled to honourable mention. Her appearance is an important epoch in our literary history. Evelina was the first tale written by a woman, and purporting to be a picture of life and manners, that lived or deserved to live. [...]

Indeed, most of the popular novels which preceded Evelina, were such as no lady would have written; and many of them were such as no lady could without confusion own that she had read. The very name of novel was held in horror among religious people. In decent families which did not profess extraordinary sanctity, there was a strong feeling against all such works. Sir Anthony Absolute,[1] two or three years before Evelina appeared, spoke the sense of the great body of sober fathers and husbands, when he pronounced the circulating library an evergreen tree of diabolical knowledge. This feeling, on the part of the grave and reflecting, increased the evil from which it had sprung. The novelist, having little character to lose, and having few readers among serious people, took without scruple liberties which in our generation seem almost incredible.

Miss Burney did for the English novel what Jeremy Collier did for the English drama; and she did it in a better way. She first showed that a tale might be written in which both the fashionable and the vulgar life of London might be exhibited with great force, and with broad comic humour, and which yet should not contain a single line inconsistent with rigid morality, or even with virgin delicacy. She took away the reproach which lay on a most useful and delightful species of composition. She vindicated the right of her sex to an equal share in a fair and noble province of letters. Several accomplished women have followed in her track. At present, the novels which we owe to English ladies form no small part of the literary glory of our country. No class of works is more hon-

---

1 From Sheridan's *The Rivals* (1775).

ourably distinguished by fine observation, by grace, by delicate wit, by pure moral feeling. Several among the successors of Madame D'Arblay have equalled her; two, we think, have surpassed her. But the fact that she has been surpassed, gives her an additional claim to our respect and gratitude; for in truth we owe to her, not only Evelina, Cecilia, and Camilla, but also Mansfield Park and the Absentee.[1]

4. *Eclectic Review* ns 21 (1847): 57-63 (57, 63).

THE D'Arblay world is dead or dying out. The ideas which satis-fied the generation of Madame D'Arblay as interpretations of the actual and spiritual universe, are already gone by and obsolete. Nei-ther the outward nor the inward world is now regarded as it was fifty years since. [...]

Madame D'Arblay has not been long under the sod, and yet she long outlived the crop of opinions which she cherished as the flowers and fruits of eternal truth. She was a worshipper of feudal aristocracy and hereditary monarchy in the persons of the French and English nobility, and of George the III, and Louis the XVI. For us and our readers, therefore, for all the active minds of this age, all the parts of her books which embody this worship, have only an antiquarian and historical interest and value. Madame D'Arblay had many opportunities of observing the conduct and preserving the conversation of men and woman who have helped to make the world wiser and better. Her prejudices, however, blinded her to their splendours. The companion often of people of genius, she was led to leave their talk comparatively unrecorded, while she devotes tedious pages to the tattle of the princesses, and vapid declamations on the woes of the Bourbons.

[...]

A portrait of the intellectual and voluptuous face of Madame De Stael fronts this [*sixth*] volume. But there is nothing in it respecting her, except an account of the reluctance of Madame D'Arblay to know her in Paris. Poor De Stael lay under suspicions, both in England and France, of being an improper lady. Generous

---

1 Jane Austen's *Mansfield Park* (1814) and Maria Edgeworth's *The Absentee* (1812).

to a marvel, devoted to the service of her friends, returning good for evil to her enemies—exhibiting virtues which would do honour to any character whatever—Madame De Stael could not be honoured with the acquaintance of Madame D'Arblay, because her misfortunes had been distorted, and her conduct maligned by scandalous tongues. Madame D'Arblay saw good and grand qualities in the acts of De Stael, which she knew, yet could not perceive, that in what was unknown, the same qualities must have been at work just because De Stael could not cease to be herself. However much the literary student may regret what deprives him of some views of a nobly gifted woman, it is unquestionable that Madame D'Arblay was right, according to the convention of English propriety. A higher morality, a code of conduct nearer the example of Him who went about doing good, would have regarded, interpreted, and treated the character of De Stael as a whole.

Select Bibliography

Works by Frances Burney

Evelina, or, A Young Lady's Entrance into the World. 3 vols. London: T. Lowndes, 1778.

Cecilia, or Memoirs of an Heiress. By the Author of Evelina. 5 vols. London: T. Payne and Son and T. Cadell, 1782.

Brief Reflections Relative to the Emigrant French Clergy: Earnestly Submitted to the Humane Consideration of the Ladies of Great Britain. By the Author of Evelina and Cecilia. London: Thomas Cadell, 1793.

Camilla: or, A Picture of Youth. By the Author of Evelina and Cecilia. 5 vols. London: T. Payne, T. Cadell Jun. and W. Davies, 1796.

The Wanderer; or, Female Difficulties. By the Author of Evelina; Cecilia; and Camilla. 5 vols. London: Longman, Hurst, Rees, Orme and Brown, 1814.

Memoirs of Doctor Burney, Arranged from his own Manuscripts, from Family Papers, and from Personal Recollections. By his Daughter, Madame d'Arblay. 3 vols. London: Edward Moxon, 1832.

Diary and Letters of Madame d'Arblay (1778-1840). Ed. Charlotte Barrett. 7 vols. London: H. Colburn, 1842-46.

The Early Diary of Frances Burney, 1768-1778. Ed. Annie Raine Ellis. 2 vols. London: George Bell, 1889.

Edwy and Elgiva. Ed. Miriam Benkovitz. Hamden, CT: Editor, 1957.

The Journals and Letters of Fanny Burney (Madame D'Arblay), 1791-1840. Ed. Joyce Hemlow et al. 12 vols. Oxford: Clarendon, 1972-1984.

A Busy Day. Ed. Tara Wallace. New Brunswick: Rutgers UP, 1984.

The Early Journals and Letters of Fanny Burney. Ed. Lars Troide and Stewart Cooke. 3 vols. to date. Oxford: Clarendon, 1988-1994.

The Complete Plays of Frances Burney. Ed. Peter Sabor. 2 vols. London: Pickering, 1995.

Other Primary Sources

Barbauld, Anna Letitia. "Miss Burney." *Evelina: or, The History of a Young Lady's Introduction to the World.* The British Novelists. 2 vols. London: F. C. and J. Rivington, 1810.

Burney, Charles. *The Letters of Dr. Charles Burney: 1751-1784*. Ed. Alvaro Ribeiro. Oxford: Clarendon, 1991.

Burney, Sarah Harriet. *The Letters of Sarah Harriet Burney*. Ed. Lorna Clark. Athens: U of Georgia P, 1997.

Hutton, William Holden. *Burford Papers: Being Letters of Samuel Crisp to his Sister at Burford; and other Studies of a Century (1745-1845)*. London: Constable, 1905.

Lansdowne, 6th Marquis of, ed. *The Queeney Letters, Being Letters Addressed to Hester Maria Thrale by Doctor Johnson Fanny Burney and Mrs. Thrale-Piozzi*. London: Cassell, 1934.

Thrale, Hester Lynch. *Anecdotes of the Late Samuel Johnson, LL. D. During the Last Twenty Years of His Life*. 2 vols. London: T. Cadell, 1786.

—. *The Piozzi Letters: Correspondence of Hester Lynch Piozzi, 1784-1821 (formerly Mrs. Thrale)*. Ed. Edward Bloom and Lillian Bloom. 5 vols. Newark: U of Delaware, 1989-90.

—. *Thraliana: The Diary of Mrs. Hester Lynch Thrale*. Ed. Katharine Balderston. 2nd ed. 2 vols. Oxford: Clarendon, 1951.

Secondary Sources

Armstrong, Nancy. *Desire and Domestic Fiction: A Political History of the Novel*. Oxford: Oxford UP, 1987.

Bloom, Edward and Lillian Bloom. "Fanny Burney's Novels: The Retreat from Wonder." *Novel: A Forum on Fiction* 12 (1978): 215-35.

Bloom, Lillian. "Fanny Burney's *Camilla*: The Author as Editor." *Bulletin of Research into the Humanities* 82 (1979): 367-93.

Campbell, D. Grant. "Fashionable Suicide: Conspicuous Consumption and the Collapse of Credit in Fanny Burney's *Cecilia*." *Studies in Eighteenth-Century Culture* 20 (1990): 131-45.

Campbell, Gina. "How to Read Like a Gentleman: Burney's Instructions to her Critics in *Evelina*." *ELH* 57 (1990): 557-84.

Castle, Terry. *Masquerade and Civilization: The Carnivalesque in Eighteenth-Century English Culture and Fiction*. Stanford: Stanford UP, 1986.

Chapman, R. W. "The Course of the Post in the Eighteenth Century." *Notes and Queries* 183 (1942): 67-69.

Chisholm, Kate. *Fanny Burney: Her Life 1752-1840*. London: Chatto & Windus, 1998.

Cooke, Stewart. "How Much was Frances Burney Paid for *Cecilia?*" *Notes and Queries* 237 (1992): 484-86.

Copeland, Edward. "Money in the Novels of Fanny Burney." *Studies in the Novel* 8 (1976): 24-37.

Cutting, Rose Marie. "Defiant Women: The Growth of Feminism in Fanny Burney's Novels." *Studies in English Literature* 17 (1977): 519-30.

Cutting-Gray, Joanne. *Woman as "Nobody" and the Novels of Fanny Burney*. Gainesville: UP of Florida, 1992.

Darby, Barbara. *Frances Burney Dramatist: Gender, Performance, and the Late Eighteenth-Century Stage*. Lexington: U of Kentuck P, 1997.

Donkin, Ellen. *Getting into the Act: Women Playwrights in London 1776-1829*. London: Routledge, 1995.

Donoghue, Frank. *The Fame Machine: Book Reviewing and Eighteenth-Century Literary Careers*. Stanford: Stanford UP, 1996.

Doody, Margaret. "Beyond *Evelina*: The Individual Novel and the Community of Literature." *Eighteenth-Century Fiction* 3.4 (1991): 359-71

——. *Frances Burney: The Life in the Works*. New Brunswick: Rutgers UP, 1988.

Epstein, Julia. *The Iron Pen: Frances Burney and the Politics of Women's Writing*. Bristol: Bristol Classic Press, 1989.

Favret, Mary. *Romantic Correspondence: Women, Politics and the Fiction of Letters*. Cambridge: Cambridge UP, 1993.

Gallagher, Catherine. *Nobody's Story: The Vanishing Acts of Women Writers in the Marketplace, 1670-1820*. Oxford: Clarendon, 1994.

Grau, Joseph. *Fanny Burney: An Annotated Bibliography*. NY: Garland, 1981.

Harman, Claire. *Fanny Burney: A Biography*. London: Harpercollins, 2000.

Hemlow, Joyce. "Fanny Burney and the Courtesy Books." *PMLA* 45 (1950): 732-61.

——. *The History of Fanny Burney*. Oxford: Clarendon, 1958.

Hemlow, Joyce et al. *A Catalogue of the Burney Family Correspondence 1749-1878*. Montreal: McGill-Queen's UP, 1971.

Kowaleski-Wallace, Beth. "A Night at the Opera: The Body, Class, and Art in *Evelina* and Frances Burney's Early Diaries." *History, Gender and Eighteenth-Century Literature*. Ed. Beth Fowkes Tobin. Athens: U of Georgia P, 1994. 141-58.

Kris, Kathryn. "A 70-Year Follow-up of a Childhood Learning Disability." *The Psychoanalytic Study of the Child* 38 (1983): 637-52.

Lang-Peralta, Linda. "'Clandestine Delight': Frances Burney's Life Writing." *Women's Life-writing: Finding Voice/Building Community.* Ed. Linda S. Coleman. Bowling Green OH: Bowling Green State UP, 1997. 23–41.

Lovell, Terry. *Consuming Fiction.* London: Verso, 1987.

Myers, Sylvia Harcstark. *The Bluestocking Circle: Women, Friendship, and the Life of the Mind in Eighteenth-Century England.* Oxford: Clarendon, 1990.

Nussbaum, Felicity. *The Autobiographical Subject: Gender and Ideology in Eighteenth-Century England.* Baltimore: Johns Hopkins UP, 1995.

van Ostade, Ingrid Tieken-Boon. "Stripping the Layers: Language and Content of Fanny Burney's Early Journals." *English Studies* 72.2 (1991): 146–59.

Pearson, Jacqueline. *Women's Reading in Britain 1750-1835: A Dangerous Recreation.* Cambridge: Cambridge UP, 1999.

Perry, Ruth. *Women, Letters and the Novel.* NY: AMS, 1980.

Roper, Derek. *Reviewing before the "Edinburgh," 1788-1802.* London: Methuen, 1978.

Simons, Judy. *Diaries and Journals of Literary Women from Fanny Burney to Virginia Woolf.* London: Macmillan, 1990.

Spencer, Jane. *The Rise of the Woman Novelist: From Aphra Behn to Jane Austen.* Oxford: Blackwell, 1986.

Straub, Kristina. *Divided Fictions: Fanny Burney & Feminine Strategy.* Lexington: U of Kentucky, 1987.

Thaddeus, Janice Farrar. *Frances Burney: A Literary Life.* London: Macmillan, 2000.

Todd, Janet. *The Sign of Angellica: Women, Writing and Fiction 1660-1800.* New York: Columbia UP, 1989.

Turner, Cheryl. *Living by the Pen: Women Writers in Eighteenth-Century London.* London: Routledge, 1994.